URBAN SOCIAL GEOGRAPHY
an introduction

PAUL KNOX

URBAN SOCIAL GEOGRAPHY
an introduction

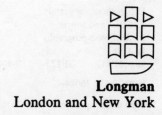

Longman
London and New York

Longman Group Limited
Longman House
Burnt Mill, Harlow, Essex, UK

*Published in the United States of America
by Longman Inc., New York*

© Longman Group Limited 1982

First published 1982

British Library Cataloguing in Publication Data

Knox, Paul
  Urban social geography.
  1. Cities and towns
  2. Anthropo-geography
  I. Title
  909'.09'812   GF125   80-40826

  ISBN 0-582-30044-4

Printed in Singapore by Selector Printing Co (Pte) Ltd

CONTENTS

ACKNOWLEDGEMENTS

This book has emerged from several years of involvement in teaching courses in urban and social geography, mainly at the University of Dundee but also at the University of Oklahoma and the University of Stirling. During this time I have received assistance, advice and encouragement from many sources. Special thanks are due to Martin Cadwallader, Barry Cottam, Joe Cullen and Beverley Wilson for their ideas and constructive criticism at various stages in the preparation of the book itself, and to the students on my courses who have helped me to crystallize my ideas about the subject in general. I have also been fortunate in working with Rose Murray and Nancy Ferrier, who cheerfully produced an excellent typescript at short notice whilst having to cope with the demands of a busy Departmental office. Thanks are also due to Carolyn Bain for assistance and advice in the preparation of draft versions of the illustrations; and to Jimmy Ford for his help with photographic reproduction. I also wish to express my debt to Bryan Coates. He it was who encouraged me in my post-graduate career, supervizing my first uncertain attempts at research, helping me to present my thoughts to others and generally stimulating my interest in human geography and the social sciences. His interest and encouragement have been much appreciated. Finally, my thanks and appreciation to my wife Lynne, who has not only suffered my pre-occupation in writing this book but also provided practical help and encouragement.

Paul Knox,
Dundee,
March 1980

We are grateful to the following for permission to reproduce copyright material:

Associated Book Publishers Ltd for our Fig. 3.7 from Map 2 p. 58 and our Table 3.2 from Table 6 p. 63 *The Urban Criminal* by Dr J. Baldwin, Dr. A.E. Bottoms and Mrs M. Walker published by Tavistock Publications Ltd; Aldine Publishing Company and the authors for our Fig. 4.22 compiled from Fig. 7.2 p. 120, Fig. 7.3 p. 121, Fig. 7.4 p. 122, Fig. 7.5 p. 123 and an extract with permission from Roger M. Downs and David Stea *Image and Environment*. Copyright © 1973 by Aldine Publishing Company, New York; Edward Arnold Publishers Ltd and the author, David Herbert for our Fig. 3.9 from Fig. 2, our Fig. 3.10 from Fig. 3 and extracts from *Progress in Human Geography* Vol. 1, No. 2; Association of American Geographers for our Fig. 5.8 from Fig. 15 p. 33 *Residential Mobility In the City* by Eric G. Moore Washington D.C. AAG Resource Paper for Commission on College Geography No. 13, 1972 reprinted by permission; Ballinger Publishing Company for our Fig. 3.8 compiled from Figs. 7.6a, 7.6b and 7.9 pp. 273–275, our Fig. 6.6 from Fig. 4.15 p. 126 and extract from *Urban Policy Making and Metropolitan Dynamics* edited by Adams. Copyright 1976 Ballinger Publishing Company; Canadian Sociology and Anthropology Association and the authors for our Fig. 7.2 compiled from Figs in 'Residential Segregation and Institutional Completeness: A Comparison of Ethnic Minorities' by Professor Glen Church and Professor Leo Driedger in *Canadian Review of Sociology and Anthropology* Vol. 11:1, 1974; Centre for Environmental Studies for our Fig. 4.20, our Fig. 4.12 from Table 42 p. 111 and an extract from *Liverpool Social Area Analysis* by Webber, Webber, Cullingford and Flynn; Centre for Urban and Regional Studies for our Table 4.1 from Index 7 pp. 60–61 *Measuring Housing Quality* by Duncan Occasional Paper No. 20, 1971; Economic Geography and the author, Peter Salins for our Fig. 4.11 compiled from Fig. 2.5 p. 243 and Fig. 2.10 p. 264 *Economic Geography* Vol. 47, 1971; Faber and Faber Ltd and The MIT Press for our Fig. 2.6 from Fig. 2 p. 52 and Fig. 3 p. 53 *Garden Cities of Tomorrow* by Ebenezer Howard reprinted by permission of Faber and Faber Ltd and The MIT Press; the authors, Forbes and Robertson for our Fig. 5.5 from Fig. 3 and our Fig. 5.6 from Fig. 1 'Intra-Urban Migration in Greater Glasgow' paper given to Population Studies Group of the Institute of British Geographers 1978; Geografiska Annaler for our Fig. 4.4 compiled from Fig. 2 p. 22, Fig. 13 p. 26 and an extract from Johnston *Geografiska Annaler* Vol. 51B 1969; The Trustees of Indiana University for our Fig. 2.5 from p. 662 and an extract from 'The Speculative Builders and Developers of Victorian London' by H.J. Dyos in *Victorian Studies* Vol. 11 1968; The Institute of British Geographers for our Fig. 3.3 adapted from Fig. 2 p. 106 and an extract p. 102 from Smith and Smith *Area* Vol. 10, 1978, our Fig. 4.2 from Fig. 1 p. 110 Smailes *Transactions Institute of British Geographers* No. 21, 1955, our Table 2.1 from Table V p. 180 and an extract p. 181 Clark and Gleave *Social Patterns in Cities* 1973, our Table 5.2 from Table V p. 538 Short *Transactions Institute of British Geographers* Vol. 3 1978 and our Table 5.3 from Table 1 p. 86 Morgan *Transactions Institute of British Geographers* Vol. 1 1976; Katholieke Universiteit for our Fig. 7.1 from Fig. 1 p. 103 Janelle and Millward *Tijdschrift voor Economische en Sociale Geografie* Vol. 67 1976; the author, Professor R. Lawton for our Fig. 2.1 from Fig. 12.7 *An Historical Geography of England and Wales* edited by Dogshon and Butlin; Little Brown and Company for our Fig. 3.5 from a chart p. 202 *The Unheavenly City Revisited* by Edward C. Banfield. Copyright © 1974 by Edward C. Banfield, by permission of Little Brown and Company; McGraw Hill Book Company for our Fig. 3.6 from Fig. 4.6 *The Geography of Crime and Justice* by Harries, our Table 4.10 from Table 6.2, our Table 4.11 from Table 9.1 and an extract from *The Geography of Social Well Being In the United States* by Smith, and our Fig. 7.8 from Fig. 7.2 and an extract from *An Invitation to Geography* by Lanegran and Palm; The MIT Press for our Fig. 4.21 from Figs. 35 and 36 p. 146 and extracts from *The Image of the City* by Kevin Lynch by permission of The MIT Press; New York Magazine for our Fig. 4.23 from Fig. 4 p. 53, our Fig. 4.24 from Fig. 2 p. 53 and our Fig. 4.26 adapted from p. 57 'Mental Maps of New York' by Susana Duncan in *New York* December 19th 1977 Copyright © 1977 by News Group Publications Inc. Reprinted with the permission of New York Magazine; Office of Population, Censuses and Surveys for our Table 5.1 from Table 5.56 *General Household Survey* 1976, reproduced with the permission of Her Majesty's Stationery Office; Oxford University Press for our Fig. 5.7 adapted from Fig. 2.2 p. 33 and an extract from *Urban Social Areas* by Robson, our Fig. 7.3 from Fig. 2.1 p. 24 *Race Relations* by Lee, our Fig. 7.9 adapted from Fig. 11.5 p. 214 and our Table 7.2 adapted from Table 11.4 p. 213, Table 11.5 p. 215 and Table 11.6 p. 218 *Social Problems and the City* by Herbert and Smith and our Fig. 7.10 from Fig. 2(2) p. 10 *Geography and Voting Behaviour* by Busteed, reproduced with the permission of Oxford University Press; Oxford University Press Inc for our Fig. 2.4 adapted from Fig. 5.1 p. 132 *Cities and Immigrants* by Ward. Copyright © 1971 by Oxford University Press, our Table 5.4 from Table 5.6 p. 140 and our Table 5.5 adapted from Table 5.1 p. 115 and Table 5.2 p. 122 *Environmental Choice, Human Behaviour and Residential Satisfaction* by William Michelson. Copyright © 1977 by Oxford University Press Inc. Used by permission; Pergamon Press Inc and the author, Dr David Harvey for our Fig. 6.1 from Fig. 1 and our Table 6.1 from Table 1 *Regional Studies* Vol. 8. Copyright 1974 Pergamon Press Ltd; Pion Ltd and the authors, Clark

and Cadwallader for our Fig. 4.25 from Fig. 3 p. 697 *Environment and Planning* Vol. 5, 1973 by permission of Pion Ltd; Routledge and Kegan Paul Ltd and Humanities Press Inc for our Fig. 3.2 slightly modified from p. 96 *An Approach to Urban Sociology* by P. Mann; Royal Scottish Geographical Society and the author, Professor E. Jones for our Fig. 4.1 slightly adapted from Fig. 2 p. 154 *Scottish Geographical Magazine* Vol. 74, 1958; Royal Scottish Geographical Society for our Fig. 4.6 compiled from Figs. 1 and 2 p. 105 by Knox *Scottish Geographical Magazine* Vol. 92, 1976; Shelter for our Fig. 6.7 from Fig. 2 p. 111 and an extract by Weir in *Roof Shelter's Housing Magazine*, July 1976; Southeastern Geographer for our Fig. 4.18 from Fig. 2 'The Stratification of Quality of Life in the Black Community of Atlanta Georgia' by Sandord H. Bederman *Southeastern Geographer* Vol. 14, No. 1, May 1974; Southwark Borough Developing Department for our Fig. 6.2 from Fig. 7, our Fig. 6.3 from Fig. 8, our Fig. 6.4 from Fig. 9 and our Table 6.2 from Fig. 5 and 6 *London Borough of Southwark Preliminary Research* unpublished report 1974; Stanford University Press for our Table 4.2 from Table II.I p. 4 *Social Area Analysis* by Eshref Shevky and Wendell Bell with the permission of the publishers, Stanford University Press. Copyright © 1955 by the Board of Trustees of the Leland Stanford Junior University; Universitetsforlaget for our Fig. 4.19 from Fig. 3.2 p. 49 Aase and Dale *Levekår i Storby* Norges Offentlige Utredminger November 1978: 52; University of California Press for our Fig. 4.8 from Fig. V.14 and an extract from *The Social Areas of Los Angeles* by Shevky and Bell 1949; University of Chicago and the author, Peter Goheen for our Fig. 2.2 compiled from Fig. 8 p. 123 and Fig. 33 p. 183, our Fig. 2.3 compiled from Fig. 20 p. 142 and Fig. 31 p. 178 *Victorian Toronto 1850–1900* Research Paper No. 127; University of Chicago and the author, Robert Murdie for our Fig. 4.7 from Fig. 4 p. 22, our Fig. 4.12 from Fig. 1 p. 8 and an extract from *Factorial Ecology of Metropolitan Toronto 1951–1961* Research Paper 116, 1969; University of Chicago Press for our Fig. 3.1 from Chart II p. 53 *The City* edited by Park, Burgess and McKenzie, our Fig. 4.13 from Fig. 13 Berry and Rees *American Journal of Sociology* Vol. 74, 1969 and our Table 7.1 compiled from Table 1 p. 227, Table 2 p. 22 and Table 3 p. 231 by Frazier *Contributions to Urban Sociology* edited by Burgess and Bogue 1967; University of Florida for our Fig. 4.17 from *Social Indicators for Tampa, Florida* by Smith and Gray, 1972; University of North Carolina Press for our Table 3.1 from Table 1 p. 223 'Urban Malaise' by Claude S. Fischer *Social Forces* Vol. 52, December 1973. Copyright © 1973 The University of North Carolina Press; John Wiley and Sons Ltd for our Fig. 3.4 from Fig. 6.1 p. 199 and extracts from Hell and Newby *Social Areas In Cities* Vol. 2 by Herbert and Johnston. Copyright © 1976 John Wiley and Sons Ltd, our Fig. 4.9 from Fig. 6.3 p. 204 by Johnston, our Table 5.6 from Table 4.5 p. 139 by Bourne and extracts from *Social Areas In Cities* Vol. I by Herbert and Johnston. Copyright © 1976 John Wiley and Sons Ltd. Reprinted by permission of John Wiley and Sons Ltd.

Chapter 1

INTRODUCTION

At one point in his essay on Boston, Jonathan Raban stops to ask:

'why should the Italians all cram themselves behind the expressway in the North End? Why should Negroes live in Roxbury and Jews in Chelsea? By what law do Boston suburbs turn into rigidly circumscribed ghettoes when they look so much alike, so quaintly attractive, so prim, so dull? For it is as if someone had taken a map of the city and, resolutely blind to its topography, had coloured in irregularly-shaped lumps labelled 'Blacks', 'Jews', 'Irish', 'Academics', 'Gentry', 'Italians', 'Chinese', 'Assorted Others' (Raban 1975: 216).

For the geographer, such questions present themselves in more general terms, so that the major issues become: why do city populations get sifted out according to race and social class to produce distinctive neighbourhoods? And how? In addition, the geographer is interested in a number of supplementary issues. Are there, for example, any other criteria by which individuals and households become physically segregated within the city? To what extent is territory relevant to the operation of local social systems? How does a person's area of residence affect his behaviour? How do people choose where to live, and what are the constraints on their choices? What groups, if any, are able to manipulate the 'geography' of the city, and to whose advantage?

As many writers now acknowledge, the answer to most of these questions is ultimately to be found in the wider context of social, economic and political organization. In short, the city must be seen as a reflection of the society which maintains it. It follows that the study of the city should not be abstracted from its historical, cultural and economic matrix. It also follows that a proper understanding of the city requires an interdisciplinary approach, whatever the ultimate focus of attention. In the city, everything is connected to everything else, and the deficiencies of one academic specialism must be compensated for by the emphases of others. The boundaries of 'urban social geography' are therefore ill-defined, and its subject-matter is shared with history, economics, politics, sociology, demography, anthropology, social psychology, planning and social administration. Moreover, because urban social geography is comparatively recent in its development as an academic specialism, it cannot yet be said to represent a coherent or distinctive approach. Rather, it encompasses an eclectic mixture of ideas, theories and empirical research which collectively can be considered to lead (to borrow Jones and Eyles' definition (1977: 6) of social geography) to: (i) an *understanding* 'of the patterns which arise from the use social groups make of space as they see it, and of the processes involved in making and changing such patterns' and; (ii) an *appreciation* 'of the social patterns and processes arising from the distribution of, and access to, scarce resources' in the city.

This eclecticism is compounded by the coexistence, within geography as a whole, of several different approaches to knowledge and understanding. According to Johnston (1977), three main approaches are identifiable in the current literature of urban geography. The first is a quantitative and descriptive approach, based on a philosophy in which the geographer's role is to document the spatial organization of society. Its explanatory concepts are derived partly from neoclassical economics and partly from the functional sociology of Talcott Parsons. Second is the so-called behavioural approach, which emerged in the mid-1960s as a reaction to the normative assumptions of neoclassical-functional description. The emphasis here is on the study of people's activities and decision-making processes (where to live, for example) within their perceived worlds. Many of the explanatory concepts are derived from social psychology although phenomenological philosophy, with its emphasis on the ways in which people experience the world around them, has also exerted a considerable influence on behavioural research. Finally there is the 'radical' approach, which stresses the constraints on the behaviour of individuals which are imposed by the

1

organization of society as a whole and by the activities of powerful groups and institutions within it. At its broadest level, this approach looks to political science for its explanatory concepts, focusing on the idea of power and conflict as the main determinants of locational behaviour and resource allocation. In this context, the 'managerialist' ideas of Ray Pahl (1969: 1975) have been influential but the chief source of inspiration has been Marxist theory and its modern derivatives.

Although there is some scope for a rapprochement between these different approaches (Gregory 1978; Hay 1979; Johnston 1979a) it seems likely that urban social geography must continue for some time yet as a rather mixed bag, straddling macro and micro concerns with a wide range of methodological and philosophical perspectives but without a commonly agreed theoretical framework. However, as Johnston (1979a) and others have pointed out, this is not necessarily a bad thing, particularly from the educational point of view, where the objective may be the broad one of developing an empathetic understanding of the city. Meanwhile, it should be emphasized that urban social geography is not merely a collection of subject matter and philosophy culled from other disciplines with a common focus provided by a holistic concern for the city. Geography's traditional concern with inter-relationships between people and their physical and social environments provides a basis for study which, while not comprehensive, is broader than most. Moreover, space itself should not simply be regarded as a medium in which social, economic and political processes are expressed. It is of importance in its own right in contributing both to the pattern of urban development and to the nature of the relationships between different social groups within the city. While not necessarily the dominant factor in shaping patterns of social interaction, distance is undeniably important as a determinant of social networks, friendships and marriages. Similarly, territoriality is frequently the basis for the development of distinctive social milieux which, as well as being of interest in themselves, are important because of their capacity to mould the attitudes and shape the behaviour of their inhabitants. Distance also emerges as a significant determinant of the quality of life in different parts of the city because of variations in physical accessibility to opportunities and amenities such as jobs, shops, schools, clinics, parks and sports centres. Because the benefits conferred by proximity to these amenities contribute so much to people's welfare, locational issues also often form the focus of inter-class conflict within the city, thus giving the spatial perspective a key role in the analysis of urban politics. The partitioning of space through the establishment of

de jure territorial boundaries also represents an important spatial attribute which has direct repercussions on several spheres of urban life. The location of local authority boundaries helps to determine their fiscal standing, for example; while the boundaries of school catchment areas have important implications for community status and welfare; and the configuration of electoral districts is crucial to the outcome of formal political contests in the city.

The geographer therefore has a considerable contribution to make to urban social studies. Moreover, the geographer is uniquely placed to provide descriptive analyses of cities. Although it is fashionable to play down the 'mapping' role of geography, the identification of spatial patterns and spatial linkages within the city provides a basic source of material both for educationalists and policy-makers. Similarly, the geographer's traditional concern with the 'distinctiveness of place' and areal differentiation is very relevant to the study of the city, for it is widely accepted that, while cities must be seen as wholes and, ultimately, as part of the wider social and economic system, they comprise a 'mosaic' of different neighbourhoods and districts. Here, the geographer's ability to synthesize a wide variety of environmental, social and economic characteristics and to identify distinctive regions is germane both to theory and practice in urban analysis. Thus, for example, the identification of urban 'problem regions' and their salient characteristics has occupied an increasing number of geographers since the concern for 'relevance' in geographic research emerged as a major issue within the discipline in the early 1970s. More recently, there has been a revival of interest in regionalism as an academic approach, emphasizing the locally unique factors which modify the more general forces which shape urban residential structure. Gregory, for example, in his book on *Ideology, Science and Human Geography*, calls for a general revival of the regional approach (which had been discredited because of the low intellectual level of much work done in its name during the 1950s and 1960s) on the simple grounds that 'spatial structures are implicated in social structures and each has to be theorized with the other' (Gregory 1978: 172).

Certainly it is the distinctiveness of particular neighbourhoods and districts and the 'sense of place' associated with them that gives the city its fascination not only to geographers but also to writers from a wide variety of disciplines. Take, for example, the variety of neighbourhoods one finds in a 'typical' medium-sized British city (Harrison 1974). At one end of the spectrum is the run-down inner-city neighbourhood of old terraces where the dwellings, many of them without an inside lavatory, look out on the blackened remains of dead and dying factories. Children play games in the street amid roaming dogs and old women beating carpets, cleaning windows, or just gossiping. Similar, and yet very different, are the nearby neighbourhoods of terraced housing jammed between railway lines and now occupied by Asian or West Indian immigrants and their families. Even the shops here are immigrant-owned, apart from those run by a few diehard white corner-shopkeepers whose premises betray the poor state of their trade. The houses, having been inherited from the city's indigenous working classes, are now orientalized and caribbeanized by exotic colour schemes: bright pink and dull turquoise, ochre and cobalt blue. Further along the socio-economic spectrum and on the outer edges of the inner city are neighbourhoods of mixed tenure and varied character, where an ageing population struggles to maintain respectability in the midst of a steadily deteriorating environment. Here and there are groups of two or three newer houses, squeezed into gaps in the urban fabric and sporting imitation coach lamps, frosted-glass porches and some young rose bushes in a brave attempt to elevate their status against all the evidence of their surroundings. At about the same distance from the city centre there may be a small neighbourhood of formerly artisan houses which have been 'gentrified' by an influx of prosperous young professionals. The character of such areas is derived more from the life-style of their new inhabitants than from anything else:

Their cars are grimly economic and ecological, as near to bicycles as four wheels and the internal combustion engine will allow – the Deux Cheveaux, the Renault 4L, the baby Fiat and the Volkswagen. Here children play with chunky all-wood Abbatt toys; here girl-wives grill anaemic escalopes of veal; everyone takes the *Guardian* (Raban 1975: 88).

For the most part though, the more prosperous neighbourhoods are suburban. At the top end of the socio-economic scale there is usually a sequestered area of soundly-built, older houses standing in their own plots amid an abundance of trees and shrubbery. With increasing distance from this core of affluence and respectability is a series of neighbourhoods of diminishing status whose individuality is to be found in subtle variations of garage space, garden size and the architectural detail of the houses – all of which are owned, or are at least in the process of being purchased, by their inhabitants. In these neighbourhoods, children definitely do not play in the streets, and the shopping centres are dotted with freezer food centres, fashion shops and boutiques selling cane chairs, paper lamp-shades, herb racks and reproduction tea caddies. Finally, and sharing the fringe of the city with the most recent of the middle-class neighbourhoods, there is a

series of public housing estates, graded into distinctive neighbourhoods through a combination of landscape architecture and the age structure, public comportment and social reputation of their inhabitants. Like the newer privately-built estates, they have few neighbourhood amenities. There are few shops or pubs, probably no doctor's surgery, no playgrounds, and a poor bus service into town.

This picture is by no means exhaustive: a full listing would have to include student bed-sitter neighbourhoods, redeveloped inner-city areas, red light districts, and so on. It is also important to remember that although a similar variety of neighbourhoods exists in cities of other countries, their character and *raison d'être* may be quite different. The present book is concerned with cities in Western countries which have 'post-industrial' societies, particularly those of the English-speaking world, where levels of urbanization are amongst the highest anywhere. References to cities elsewhere are included not to redress this bias but to provide contrasting or complementary examples and to place arguments within a wider setting. The principal focus of attention is upon British and North American cities, reflecting the weight and distribution of published research in urban social geography as well as the origins of much of the relevant social, economic and urban theory. Even within this relatively narrow cultural and geographical realm, however, there are important differences in the nature of the urban environment. These will be elaborated in the body of the text but, as Robson (1975) points out, it is important to guard against 'cultural myopia' from the very beginning of any discussion of urban geography. It is, therefore, worth briefly pointing to the principal differences between British and North American cities. For one thing, British cities are generally much older, with a tangible legacy of earlier modes of economic and social organization embedded within their physical structure and, sometimes, carried over into present-day attitudes and behaviour. Another contrast is in the composition of urban populations, for in Britain the significance of ethnic minority groups is much less than in North America. A third major difference stems from the way in which urban government has evolved. Whereas North American cities tend to be fragmented into a number of quite separate and independent municipalities, British cities are less so and their public services are funded to a significant level by the central government, making for a potentially more even-handed allocation of resources within the city as a whole. This is not unrelated to yet another important source of contrast – the existence of a well-developed welfare state in Britain. This not only affects the size and allocation of the 'social wage' within cities but also has had profound effects on the social geography of the city through the operation of the housing market. Whereas fewer than 5 per cent of US urban families live in public housing, over 30 per cent of the families in most British cities live in dwellings rented from public authorities. Finally, it is worth noting that in Britain, where the general ideology of privatism is less pronounced and where there has for some time been an acute awareness of the pressures of urban sprawl on prime agricultural land, the power and influence of the city planning machine is much more extensive. As a result, the morphology and social structure of British cities owes much to planning codes and philosophies. Thus, for example, the decentralization of jobs and homes and the proliferation of out-of-town hypermarkets and shopping malls has been much less pronounced in Britain than in North America, mainly because of the British planners' policy of urban containment. The corollary of this, of course, is that the central business districts (CBDs) of British cities have tended to retain a greater commercial vitality than many of their North American counterparts.

The format adopted in this book is mainly thematic, with an emphasis on pattern and empirical analysis which directly reflects the nature of much of the work done in urban social geography. Background theory is introduced where relevant but no particular theoretical perspective or academic approach is given special emphasis because the belief which underlies the book is that no single body of theory and no one approach to knowledge can be expected to provide all the answers to the questions currently of concern to urban geographers. It is also worth pointing out at this stage that because the emphasis of the book is on social activities and processes of residential differentiation, there are some aspects of urban structure (such as the nature and location of urban commercial and industrial activity and the spatial characteristics of the CBD) which are only dealt with indirectly, in so far as they affect people's behaviour, their residential opportunities and their general welfare. The chapter which follows is a brief summary of the principal consequences of the evolution of the modern city from its pre-industrial origins through the crucial transformation of the Victorian era to its current form. This not only provides an essential factual foundation upon which to build an understanding of the social geography of the modern city but also serves to introduce a number of important concepts and processes which are elaborated in subsequent chapters.

Chapter 2

HISTORICAL PERSPECTIVES ON THE CITY

An appreciation of urban history is vital to the student of urban social geography. The social relationships, class structures, ideologies and institutions forged during earlier stages of urban development can be directly traced to the modern city, where they continue to shape urban lifestyles and to constrain the behaviour of people businesses and governments. Moreover, the historic city obtrudes as a visible factor in the contemporary landscape of cities throughout Europe and North America, revealing itself in turn as historic artefact, slum district, or, more subtly, as the morphological template upon which successive waves of urban renewal and land-use change have taken place. By examining the historical development of cities it is therefore possible to identify both the physical and the social bases of modern urbanism which are central to the patterns and processes dealt with in subsequent chapters of this book.

This chapter provides an outline to the development of Western cities from the early pre-industrial/ pre-capitalist stages through the transitional stage of the eighteenth and early nineteenth centuries and the crucial Victorian era to the modern capitalist city. The focus of attention is on the changing relationships between people and neighbourhoods in response to changes in economic organization and the consequent effects of changes in technology, social organization, family relationships and people's attitudes towards living in the city. Particular emphasis is given to three themes: the instrumental role of transport technology in the physical development and residential differentiation of cities; the effects of the changing balance of economic power on the ethos and goals of urban government; and the translation of the prevailing spirit and ideology of different groups of people at different times into the bricks and mortar of the built environment. In pursuing this approach it is inevitable that the diversity of individual cities must give way to rather broad generalizations. Yet, as we shall see, cities responded in

different ways and at different times to the common economic and social forces to which they were subject, rendering any generalization vulnerable to the specific experience of an individual town or city. It is important to bear this vulnerability in mind from the outset, therefore, and the reader is encouraged to set the generalizations made here against the greater detail of urban history portrayed in works such as Briggs's *Victorian Cities* (1968) and Warner's *The Urban Wilderness: A History of the American City* (1972).

The transformation of urban structure

The pre-capitalist city

Before the full emergence of capitalistic economies in the eighteenth century and the advent of the Industrial Revolution in the nineteenth century, cities were essentially small-scale settlements based on a mercantile economy and a rigid social order stemming from the tradition of medieval feudalism. The conventional wisdom concerning the social geography of these cities is derived from Sjoberg's (1960) model, in which the spatial expression of the division of pre-industrial society into a small élite and a much larger proletariat was marked by a pleasant and exclusive central core surrounded by a crowded, poorly-built and garbage-strewn periphery. According to Sjoberg, the élite group consisted of those in control of the religious, political, administrative and social functions of the city. Merchants – even wealthy ones – were generally excluded from the élite because a 'pre-occupation with money and other mundane pursuits ran counter to the religious-philosophical value system of the dominant group' (Sjoberg 1960:83). Responding to these values, the élite tended to favour a residential location close to the administrative, political and religious institutions which were typically located in the centre of the city, thus producing an exclusive, high-status core. In time, the élite came to be increasingly segregated from the rest of urban society, partly because of the repulsiveness of the rest of the city and its inhabitants, and partly because of a clustering reinforced by bonds of kinship and inter-marriage amongst the élite.

Beyond this core area lived the lower classes, although not in an undifferentiated mass. Distinct socio-economic clusters developed as a result of the spatial association of craftsmen of different kinds, reinforced by social organizations such as guilds, which fostered the group cohesion and spatial propinquity of their members. Less well-organized groups, including the poor, members of ethnic and religious minority groups, people engaged in particularly malodorous jobs such as tanning, and people who could only find intermittent menial employment carting, sweeping or peddling, found themselves pushed to the outskirts of the city in extensive but densely inhabited tracts of the very worst housing.

This idea of a social geography characterized by an exclusive central core surrounded by a wider area over which status and wealth steadily diminished with distance from the city centre has been questioned by Vance (1971), who attaches much greater significance to the *occupational* clustering arising from the inter-relationships between social and economic organization promoted by the craft guilds. For Vance, the early city was 'many centred' in distinct craft quarters – metalworking, woodworking, weaving, and so on – each with its own shops, workplaces and wide social spectrum of inhabitants. The political, social and economic advantages conferred by guild membership reinforced the external economies derived from spatial association, creating tight clusters of population living under a patriarchal social system headed by the master craftsmen. Within each of the occupational districts, dwellings, workshops and store rooms were arranged with a *vertical* rather than horizontal structuring of space, with workshops on the ground floor, the master's family quarters on the floor above and, higher still, the store rooms and rooms of the journeymen, apprentices and servants. Beyond the specialized craft quarters Vance recognized, like Sjoberg, the existence of a fringe population of the very poorest of the proletariat and a central core area inhabited by the city's élite. Unlike Sjoberg, however, Vance allows these groups only a minor impact on the social geography of the city. The result is a model of the city in which spatial differentiation is dominated by a mosaic of occupational districts, with class and status stratification contributing a secondary dimension which is more important vertically than horizontally.

The urban transformation

As with much social history, we do not yet have enough evidence from comparative studies to judge which of these two models is the more accurate. For present purposes, however, it is probably more helpful to stress the points of common agreement. Both writers portray a city in which everything physical was at a human scale, a 'walking city' in which the distances between home and work were even more tightly constrained by the organization of work into patriarchal and familial groupings. Both portray an immutable social order based on a traditional and essentially non-materialistic value system; and both recognize the existence (though with different emphasis) of a patrician élite residing in the core of the city, a number of occupationally distinctive but socially mixed 'quarters' in intermediate locations, and a residual population of the very poor living on the outskirts of the city.

The modern city has inherited few of these characteristics, social or morphological. Some, like Bologna, Bruges, Norwich and Stirling have been fortunate enough to retain their castles, cathedrals, palaces and other institutional buildings, together, perhaps, with fragments of the pre-industrial residential fabric. Others, like Aigues-Mortes, Bernkastel and Tewkesbury have been by-passed by change and have retained much of the appearance of the pre-industrial city, albeit in a sanitized, renovated and picture-postcard way. For the most part, though, cities have altered radically. Not only has most of the older fabric of the city been replaced (often several times), but the relative location of the city's major components and the relationships between them have greatly altered. The city has been turned inside out, with the rich exchanging their central location for the peripheral location of the poor. Occupational clustering has given way to residential differentiation in terms of status and family structure; power and status in the city are no longer determined by traditional values but by wealth; ownership of land has become divorced from its use; workplace and home have become separated; and family structure has been transformed from an extended, patriarchal system to the small, nuclear family unit.

A social geography has thus evolved which is radically different from Vance's city of socially-mixed occupational districts, and which is the *inverse* of Sjoberg's merchant city: poverty is almost universally concentrated in the inner city, with wealth predominantly on the periphery. The causes of this profound realignment are primarily economic, rooted in the emergence of capitalism as the dominant means of production and exchange and buttressed by the technology which subsequently emerged during the

Industrial Revolution. Not surprisingly, this transformation of economies, societies and cities was complex in its development, with inter-related events often occluding cause and effect. Nevertheless, it is worth sketching out the major components of change – insofar as they affected the social geography of cities – in rough sequence.

Probably the most fundamental change to emerge with the rise of capitalism and its new system of production – the factory – was the creation of two 'new' social groups: the industrial capitalists and the unskilled factory workers. These two groups respectively formed the basis of a new élite and a new proletariat which replaced the old order. As the accumulation of capital by individuals became not only morally acceptable but also the dominant criterion of status and power, the entrepreneurs introduced a new, materialistic value system to urban affairs. Meanwhile, competition for the best and most accessible sites for the new factories and the warehouses, shops and offices which depended on them brought about the first crucial change in land use. Land was given over to uses which could justify the highest rent, rather than being held by a traditional group of users. The factory and commercial sites secured, there sprang up around them large tracts of housing to accommodate the workers and their families. The new urban structure became increasingly differentiated, with homes no longer used as workplaces and residential areas graded according to the rents different sites could command. Social status, newly ascribed in terms of money, became synonymous with rent-paying ability, so that neighbourhoods were, in effect, created along status divisions.

Inevitably, since the size and quality of dwellings was positively linked with price, and price with builders' profits, housing built for the lowest-paid, lowest-status groups was of the lowest quality, crammed in at high densities in order to cover the costs of the ground rent. At the same time, the wealthy moved to new locations on the urban fringe. Edged out from the inner city by factories and warehouses, the wealthy were in any case anxious to add physical distance to the social distance between themsleves and the bleak misery of the growing working-class districts adjacent to the factories. Encouraged by the introduction of new transport services in the early nineteenth century, they were, therefore, easily lured to the fashionable new dwellings being built in the suburbs by speculators with an eye towards this lucrative new market. Later, as the full effects of a dramatic excess of births over deaths (which resulted largely from improvements in medical practice and public health) were reinforced by massive immigration (in response to the cities' increased range and number of opportunities), the rate of urban growth

accelerated. Changes in building technology made it possible for cities to grow upwards as well as outwards, and the cyclical growth of the capitalist economy, with successive improvements in urban transport systems, produced a sequence of growth phases which endowed the modern city with a series of patchy but distinctive suburban zones.

Thus, although the transformation of urban social geography which paralleled the emergence of capitalism was radical and abrupt, it was a complex process, and it is useful to identify several intermediate stages of urban development, each with its own social geography and each contributing to both the morphological and the social inheritance of the capitalist city of today. Although it is dangerous to be pedantic about the timing of historical epochs, several writers have found Mumford's periodization of 1820 to 1870, 1870 to 1920 and 1920 to the present to be effective in dealing with the different stages of American urban development (Mumford 1934, 1940; Borchert 1967; Warner 1972). In Europe, and particularly in Britain, the equivalent periods would approximate to the years 1780 to 1830, 1830 to 1920, and 1920 to the present. Nevertheless, generalizations about phases of urban development anywhere are easily confounded. Mill towns in both Britain and the United States, for example, exhibited many of the features of industrial capitalism at a time when most other cities were still dominated by the petty commodity mode of production which was transitional between the pre-capitalist city and the industrial city of Victorian times (Walker 1978). In this chapter, therefore, nominal periods with overlapping and unwritten chronological boundaries are used to categorize the major stages in the development of the capitalist city: the Transitional City, the Victorian City, and the Modern City.

The transitional city

The last quarter of the eighteenth century and the first half of the nineteenth century were the years of the perfection of machine tools and the development of steam engines. Yet for all the new technology there was little mechanized production, except in textiles and in some aspects of ironworking. More significant for urban development were the new transport networks – canals and railways – which gave impetus to the large regional city and to the consequent organization of the economy around regional marketing and financial centres. Within these cities, business was still very much on a small scale, and in most cases the artisan competed quite successfully with the sweatshop factory. The modest spatial requirements of most business enterprises meant that workshops and factories tended to be dispersed throughout the city, with only a primitive specialization of land use. Even the more fashionable districts of larger cities contained a variety of factories, workshops and other businesses. In New York's Washington Square area, for example, there were nearly fifty factories, turning out pianos, cabinet furniture, chocolate, carriages, trunks, clothing, and even soap and candles (Burrell 1865, reported in Warner 1972:82). Burrell's survey also identified over 500 stores in the area, together with 234 'dram shops', 23 'lager bier saloons', 17 gambling saloons, 7 concert saloons, 76 brothels and 22 'policy shops'.

As Warnes (1973) points out, realistic generalizations about the social geography of the emerging industrial city are difficult to make because of this apparent disorganization and because of the strong local influence of valuable cultivable land and of mineral resources, water power, transport facilities and economic specialization. Nevertheless, the transitional city did have a loose internal structure which could be recognized in both small industrial towns and larger commercial cities. Occupation was still the chief influence on residential location, as Warnes, drawing on the example of Chorley (Lancashire), has shown:

...non-landed gentry, including professional people lived near the centre of towns along with shopkeepers and workers, publicans and small manufacturers of consumer goods, all attracted by the point of most profitable exchange. Small holders, who formed a large proportion of domestic manufacturers, were necessarily more predominant on the less built-up periphery of the town, as would be those groups

working the mineral resources of the area, such as miners and brick-makers. Water-powered factories, and their workers, were also scattered because of the limited number of stream-side sites, but when powered by steam they were attracted to the source of fuel, whether mine or, more often, transport terminal. They were therefore more clustered and often nearer to the centre of the urban area (Warnes 1973: 181).

Johann Kohl, a nineteenth-century observer, summarized this common pattern into the form of an idealized model in which he portrayed the city as being structured both horizontally and vertically, with decreasing desirability of locations above and below the ground floor and first floor of each building and with increasing distance from the city centre (Kohl 1841, reported in Peucker 1968, and Berry and Rees 1969).

Following these observations, the principal features of the social geography of the transitional city are summarized in Table 2.1. In larger cities, these proto-neighbourhoods had a more pronounced atmosphere and character. The central, downtown areas were an unlikely mixture of densely-packed workshops, stores, factories and slaughter-houses side by side with the more genteel firms that dealt in law, banking and insurance. Just beyond this area would be a few streets dominated by the homes of the wealthy merchants, manufacturers and professionals who could afford the increasingly valuable land and who wished to enjoy the prominence and convenience of a central address. Belgravia in London, the Rue du Faubourg St Honoré in Paris, Beacon Hill in Boston, Chestnut Street in Philadelphia and Westmount in Montreal survive as

Table 2.1 Residential structure of the emerging industrial city

	Centre	*Adjacent to centre*	*Intermediate*	*Periphery*
Lower floors	Professional classes Shop and inn keepers	Non-landed gentry Town houses in larger towns and cities	Unskilled and semi-skilled workers in domestic or non-domestic employment.	Landed nobility and gentry Smallholders, domestic manufacturers
	Consumer-goods manufacturers, e.g. bakers, tailors, cordwainers		Mobile population, with recent immigrants. Typical employers: workshops factories, foundries, gasworks, rope works and timber yards	Workers at water-powered factories. Mineral workers, e.g. brickmakers, miners, quarrymen
Upper floors, cellars, yards, back premises	House, shop and office servants	House servants		House servants
Institutions	Religious and educational establishments	Religious and educational establishments	Old and destitute in workhouse and almshouses	

Source: Warnes, 1973: 180.

reminders of the housing preferences of a large section of the élite. These early versions of 'nob hill' and 'millionaires' row' also set the axes of fashion in their respective cities, so that when subsequent growth drove the wealthy further out, their new homes advanced in the same general direction that had been initiated by their inner-city residences (Firey 1947; Hoyt 1939; Johnston 1971).

Near to these prestigious areas were the decaying neighbourhoods in which owners subdivided houses into rooms, garrets and cellars for the poor, who crowded in to be near downtown jobs. These formed the basis for the 'rookeries' which expanded during the Victorian era to overwhelm almost the whole of the inner-city area. In some cases, a local neighbourhood served as a tight-knit industrial quarter of its own, given over to shoemaking or metalworking: a legacy from the occupational districts of the pre-industrial city. Indeed, the largest and most rapidly-growing cities of all, being encircled by a 'shanty-town' housing immigrant labour (Ward 1971), bore a superficial resemblance in their spatial structure to the pattern of Sjoberg's pre-industrial city. For the most part, though, the proletariat of the transitional city mingled with middle-class families, renting small rooms and apartments all over the city, in neighbourhoods which were apparently haphazard and disorganized:

Boardinghouses stood beside prosperous homes, mill workers crowded around a suburban establishment . . . , while the owner's home stood alone across a field from the group. Another row of houses for downtown workers might stand a block away, and back lots were universally crammed with stables and blacksmiths' shops and lumber yards (Warner 1972: 83).

The Victorian city

The Victorian city was at once the product and the agent of almost cataclysmic economic, social and demographic change. It was, as Briggs has observed, 'a characteristic Victorian achievement, impressive in scale but limited in vision, creating new opportunities but also providing massive problems' (Briggs 1968: 16). Central to this whole stage of urban development was the unprecedented *rate* of urban growth, triggered by the movement of immigrants in response to the opportunities and demands of industrialization and reinforced by the growing momentum of the natural increase in population arising from the demographic transition (Lees and Lees 1976; Vance 1977). With London already a sprawling commercial city of 900,000 in 1801, British provincial cities were the first to reflect these demographic changes. Between 1821 and 1831,

Manchester, Leeds, Glasgow, Liverpool, Dundee, Birmingham and Bradford all grew at astonishing rates of between 45 and 65 per cent; and the increase continued in the following two decades, though at a somewhat diminished rate. By 1851, several of these cities had grown to conurbations of a quarter of a million, while London had grown to 2.5 millions and over half the total population of England and Wales lived in settlements classified as 'urban' (Lawton 1972). Later, London's rate of growth gathered momentum, creating an awesome mass of humanity. Between 1881 and 1891 the four communities with the highest rates of population growth in Britain were all in London: Leyton, Tottenham, West Ham and Willesden; and by 1911 London had grown to nearly five millions (Briggs 1968). Elsewhere – in Europe and North America – comparable rates of growth occurred somewhat later, concentrated in the late Victorian period. In the United States, the proportion of the total population living in cities of 25,000 or more increased from 12 per cent in 1860 to 36 per cent in 1920; and in the same period the number of cities of 250,000 or more inhabitants increased from 3 to 25 (Ward 1971). Moreover, whereas Manchester had been the 'shock city' of the early Victorian period, Chicago became the 'shock city' of the 1860s and 1870s, growing from less than 30,000 in 1850 to nearly 300,000 by 1870.

Immigrants and ghettos
The immigrant populations which continually shaped and reshaped the character and composition of Victorian urban society created an urban environment – physical, social and political – which was not only of great contemporary concern but which is also of crucial importance to the understanding of many of the legacies and problems of the modern city. In most of the larger cities and conurbations, the numerically dominant working-class population was derived almost entirely from rural migrants and from immigrants from poorer nations. In the United States, foreign immigrants were especially important. By 1890 New York

contained more foreign born residents than any city in the world. The city had half as many Italians as Naples, as many Germans as Hamburg, twice as many Irish as Dublin, and two and a half times the number of Jews in Warsaw. In 1893 Chicago contained the third largest Bohemian community in the world; by the time of the First World War, Chicago ranked only behind Warsaw and Lodz as a city of Poles. Noticeable also was the fact that four out of five people living in New York in 1890 had either been born abroad or were of foreign parentage (Glaab and Brown 1967: 139).

In Britain, the influx of immigrants was less cosmopolitan, consisting chiefly of poor Irish labourers, many of whom might have preferred to emigrate to

9

North America if they could have saved the extra fare. In the mid-nineteenth century they were the biggest group of immigrants in many British cities – especially Glasgow, Liverpool and Manchester (Lawton 1959) – and to them attached the stigma of the ghetto which was attached successively to Irish, German, Jewish, Italian and Eastern European immigrants in the cities of the United States Upper Midwest and eastern seaboard. These 'internal colonies' and ghettos were in fact the first and most conspicuous consequence of the massive immigration of outsiders on the social geography of the city. Confined to the cheap housing of the deteriorating inner city because their lack of skills and experience could command only the lowest-paid jobs, migrants of different races, language, ethnicity and religion tended to cluster together in response to family ties and the bond of common language and culture in a strange and often hostile environment. While the larger British cities each had their 'Little Ireland' (Briggs 1968), their American counterparts also had their 'Little Deutschland', 'Little Sicily', Chinatown and so on, each with a special character – and notoriety – which often tended to persist for several decades or more (Ward 1971). This spatial differentiation of the inner-city slums was not, however, confined to foreign immigrants. American cities, for example, began to attract large black populations from the rural South soon after 1900 (Hart 1960). And in Paris, migrants from different regions of France tended to cluster in different parts of the city according to contact patterns among friends and relatives; patterns which were strongly influenced by the location of the chief 'port of entry': the various railway stations serving different regions of France (Ogden and Winchester 1975).

These immigrant neighbourhoods had an impact on the social geography of the city far beyond their numerical importance. The high densities and dilapidated housing of the inner city, combined with the inadequate byelaws and a lack of medical knowledge, created problems of public health which spilled over to affect the whole of the city. In early Victorian times, wholesome water was a commodity sold for profit at prices which many could not afford (Gauldie 1974); infectious diseases of all kinds were endemic in large cities, and rates of infant mortality exceeded those of rural areas by a factor of two or three (Weber 1899). So hazardous was the nineteenth-century urban environment that even the gentry of cities like Manchester had a life expectancy considerably shorter than their rural counterparts (Table 2.2). Nevertheless, labourers could expect to live only half as long as the well-to-do, and it was the inner city which contained the filthiest and most hazardous environment (Rosen 1973). Such conditions, together with the high rates of

Table 2.2 Mortality in the Victorian city

Class	Average age at death	
	Manchester	*Rural England*
Professional persons and gentry; and their families	38	52
Tradesmen and their families	20	41*
Mechanics and labourers and their families	17	38

* including farmers and graziers

Source: *Report on the Sanitary Conditions of the Labouring Population of Great Britain* (1842).

unemployment and decreasing real wages among the working class led in turn to the proliferation of crime and social disorganization: each city had its own geography of social pathology which followed closely the pattern of poor housing and disease.

Moreover, these physical and social pathologies have also had an important indirect impact on the social geography of the modern city; for it was an abhorrence of the Victorian slum and an appreciation of its implications for public health and social order which prompted liberal-minded reformers to campaign for the provision of basic services and amenities from the public purse. As a result, the dominance of *laissez-faire* doctrine began to decline, and an era of 'municipal socialism' began to emerge, bringing new public services like sewage and water, new social amenities such as schools and hospitals, and new legislation controlling building standards and housing codes.

Economic specialization and residential segregation
Commercial expansion and, in particular, industrialization, were the driving forces behind these changes. With a more sophisticated technology powered by electricity and with mechanized, in-line production techniques, the Victorians reorganized labour into the factory system of production, seeking the advantages of the division of labour and economies of scale. These advantages not only brought unprecedented opportunities for the mass consumption of all kinds of new products and the collective consumption of new public goods (roads, sewers, parks, schools, and the like), but also brought the opportunity to create and to accumulate personal wealth. In realizing these advantages, however, the organization of the economy, of society, and of cities had to be radically altered.

New social and economic relationships emerged, with a new rhythm of life dictated by the factory clock and disciplined by the needs of machinery (Thompson

1967). As industrial technology became more complex and production larger in scale, bigger financial outlays were required for both machinery and raw materials, fostering the centralization of ownership and control, and allowing a growing economic exploitation of the unskilled workforce. Together with this basic realignment of society into owners and workers, there emerged the need for a secular bureaucracy: an army of clerks and agents to keep accounts, to attend to correspondence and to furnish the news necessary for entrepreneurs to respond to the changing conditions of the market (Mumford 1961). There thus emerged a third class – the middle class – whose purchasing power, residential preferences and attitudes to the city were soon to have a profound effect on its social geography (Friedrichs 1978). Moreover, it is worth noting here that the new social relationships forged in the Victorian city have also made an important contribution to patterns of urban life in the modern city. The kinship ties and extended family system which helped to alleviate the hardships of urban life in working class areas, for example, can still be identified in communities living in the depressed inner areas of modern cities (Coates and Silburn 1970; Young and Willmott 1962). Similarly, the modern suburban ethos of 'minding one's own business' and the culture of privatism centred on the nuclear family unit can be traced to the new social relationships which emerged in Victorian middle-class suburbs.

Urban land, responding to the pressures of changing economic and social organization, became highly specialized. Users of land became spatially separated by their ability to pay for the most attractive sites – whether for industry, businesses or homes – and, as the expanding economy and growing population increased the level of demand for land even more, the extent and intensity of these different urban land-uses also increased, bringing extremely high residential densities to the central area and extending the urban fabric even further into the countryside. Contemporary observers identified two inter-related processes stemming from this new regime of land values: *succession* and *segregation*. With the increased demand for space for non-residential purposes in the downtown areas, there soon emerged a specialized commercial area dominating the whole of the urban core. As commercial activities succeeded the mixed activities of the downtown area, the well-to-do in adjacent inner-city neighbourhoods moved outwards to new homes in the suburbs, creating a second 'specialist' area, quite segregated from other social groups (Woods 1898). At the same time, and as a consequence of the vacation of the inner city by the rich, the older housing left behind was subdivided, downgraded and in some areas altogether replaced by terrace-housing and tenements for the families who moved in to be near the factories, warehouses and shops of the commercial core. New spatial concentrations of the working class were thus collected together near large-scale workplaces, whereas previously they had been spatially dispersed, working in their own homes or in small workshops. The succession of the working classes to the inner city thus created a third element of segregation and completed the basic structure of the social geography of the Victorian city.

Socio-spatial structure

For Victorian observers, one of the most perplexing aspects of their cities was this novel separation of the classes. Nowhere was this more apparent than in Manchester, the first 'shock city' of the age. In 1839 a local clergyman wrote:

There is no town in the world where the distance between the rich and the poor is so great, or the barrier between them so difficult to be crossed . . . The separation between the different classes, and the consequent ignorance of each others' habits and condition, are far more complete in this place than in any other country . . . There is far less personal communication between the master cotton spinner and his workmen . . . than there was between good old George the Third and the meanest errand-boy about his palace (Parkinson 1839, quoted in Briggs 1968: 114).

Probably the best-known and most succinct description of the spatial expression of this segregation is in Engels's work on Manchester in *The Condition of the Working Class in England*, which was written in 1842 and which provided much of the documentation for the theories of his friend Karl Marx. Engels wrote:

Manchester contains, at its heart, a rather extended commercial district, perhaps half a mile long and about as broad, and consisting almost wholly of offices and warehouses. Nearly the whole district is abandoned by dwellers, and is lonely and deserted at night.

This commercial core was surrounded by

unmixed working peoples' quarters, stretching like a girdle, averaging a mile and half in breadth . . . Outside, beyond this girdle, lives the upper and middle bourgeoisie, the middle bourgeoisie in regularly laid out streets in the vicinity of the working quarters . . . the upper bourgeoisie in remoter villas with gardens . . . in free, wholesome country air, in fine comfortable homes, passed once every half or quarter hour by omnibuses going into the city (Engels 1844:80).

This spatial structure of concentric zones, with the working class concentrated near the centre, was to become typical of many Victorian cities (Fig. 2.1). By 1900, London could be seen in terms of four zones round the largely unpopulated commercial core of the city. Charles Booth, in his *Life and Labour of the People*

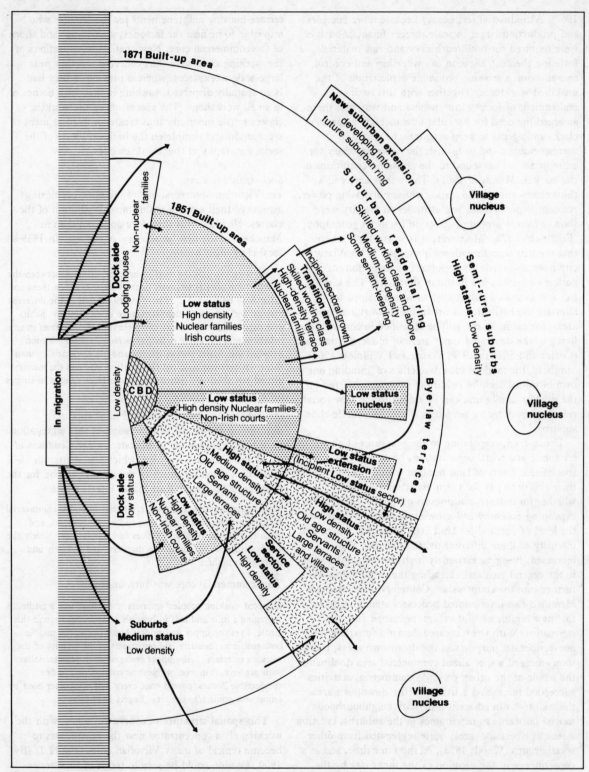

Fig. 2.1 The urban structure of mid-Victorian Liverpool. The arrows represent the main streams of migration and residential mobility. *Source*: Dodgshon and Butlin (1978), p. 352.

of London, provided a series of 'social maps' which showed these zones clearly (Booth 1903). The first zone was characterized by the most severe crowding and extreme poverty, except in the west, where there was a sector of extreme affluence. The second zone was slightly less wealthy in this western sector and rather less crowded and impoverished elsewhere, while the third zone was inhabited by the 'short distance commuter' belonging mainly to the lower middle class. The fourth zone belonged exclusively to the wealthy. This overall pattern of concentric zones was, however, modified by a series of linear features. As competition for central space drove the price of land up and up, industry began to edge outward from the commercial core, following the route of canals, rivers and railways, and so structuring the city into a series of wedges or sectors:

Houses on low-lying land usually, and by rivers, and canals almost invariably, were of poor quality and deteriorated rapidly. In such places the drainage was bad, and the proximity of water, whether as a sewer or as a means of communication, attracted industry. Thus, except in some parts of Westminster, Chelsea and Hammersmith, the Thames was lined with working class and often with slum housing. The valleys of the Wondle, the Lea and the Ravensbourne were disfigured by gasworks, a form of industry that drove away anyone that could afford to live elsewhere, and so attracted building of the cheapest type . . . On the other hand, areas next to parks, as at Clapham or South Hackney, tended to keep their social status longer than those surrounding (McLeod 1974: 5).

North American cities also exhibited a spatial structure with a predominantly zonal pattern but with important sectoral components. In the United States, Chicago was the archetypal example, despite the physical constraints of Lake Michigan. Indeed, the idealized version of the social geography of Chicago in the early decades of the twentieth century has become, for the urban geographer, 'the seed bed of theory, the norm, the source of urban fact and urban fiction' (Robson 1975: 4). In Chicago, both sectors and zones were particularly pronounced because of the effects of the massive inflows of immigrant workers and the radial development of the railroads which fanned outwards from the centre of the city, drawing with them corridors of manufacturing industry (Warner 1972). The residential communities which developed between these radial corridors during successive phases of urban growth were graphically documented by the Chicago 'school' of urban sociology in the 1920s and 1930s (Burgess 1926; Park *et al*. 1925), providing the basis for the ecological ideas which have influenced urban studies ever since (see pp. 35– 40).

This rather orderly image of sectors and zones can be misleading, however. Although these were certainly the dominant patterns to emerge from the cumulative processes of urban development during the nineteenth century, it would be more accurate to think of the Victorian city not in terms of a static model but as an evolving system with rather variable outcomes (Ward 1975). As Goheen has shown in his detailed analysis of Victorian Toronto, the social geography of the early and mid-Victorian era differed from the later Victorian city not so much in the nature of its social cleavages as in the expression of these cleavages on the map (Goheen 1970). Thus, although economic status, family status, housing tenure and religious adherence can all be shown to be important discriminants of both households and neighbourhoods throughout the 'Victorian' stage of Toronto's development, their territorial expression changed quite significantly (Figs. 2.2. and 2.3).

Moreover, as Goheen's maps show, Toronto was at least one large city which clearly did not conform to the general sector-and-zone pattern of other nineteenth century cities. Similarly, recent studies of early- and mid-Victorian Cardiff (Lewis 1979) and late-Victorian Edinburgh (Gordon 1979) have emphasized the transitional nature of their social geography, showing how elements of the pre-industrial urban structure were retained within a spatially reorganized economy and society. Shaw (1979) has pointed to the influence of local physical, environmental and institutional factors in controlling both the general structure of urban development and the detailed pattern of residential differentiation in the Victorian city. In Wolverhampton, for instance, geology exerted a significant influence on the city's social geography through the location of unattractive industrial land uses such as mines, factories and railways (Shaw 1979); and in cities like Leeds, Bradford and Sheffield the preference by the wealthy for better-drained sites with commanding views on higher ground meant that topography was in important determinant of social geography. The pattern of local land-ownership also had an important role in shaping the nature and direction of urban development in many cities, as Ward (1962) has demonstrated tellingly in relation to Leeds. Even when land was released for building, restrictive conditions often influenced the type of property built, thus subverting the idealized sector-and-zone pattern in yet another way. Many of the high-status areas in Edinburgh and Glasgow, for example, resulted from conditions in leasehold covenants which excluded undesirable uses (Gordon 1979). Conversely, the absence of restrictions often led to low-standard development and rapid residential deterioration. Finally, Cowlard (1979) has pointed to the influence of residents' behaviour, both active and passive, in perpetuating the individuality of specific

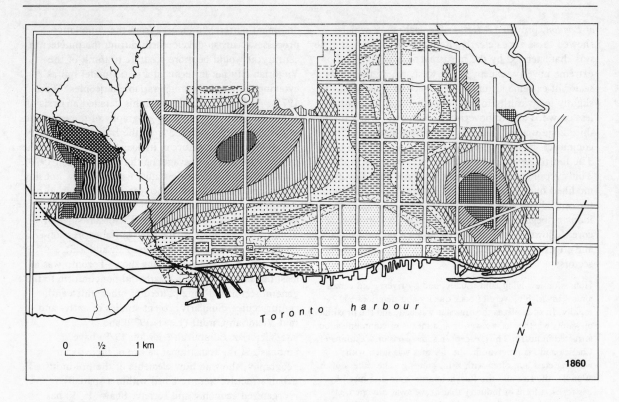

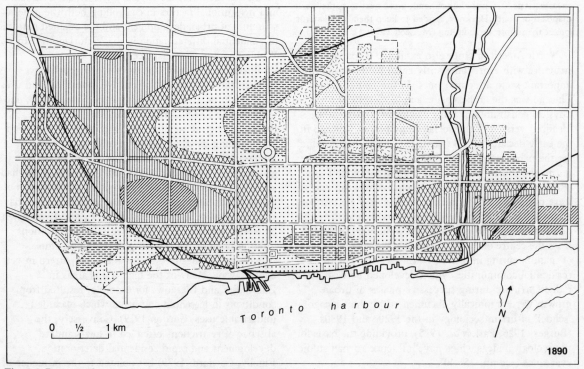

Fig. 2.2 Patterns of economic status in Toronto, 1860 and 1890.
Source: Goheen (1970), pp. 123 and 183 (Key overleaf).

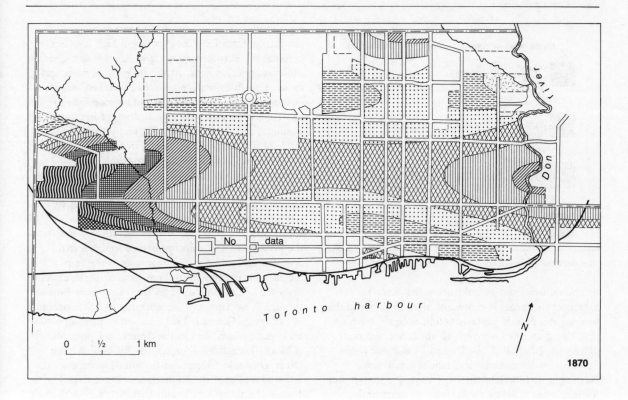

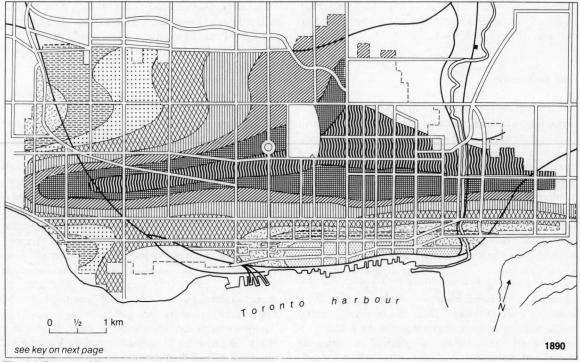

Fig. 2.3 Patterns of family status in Toronto, 1870 and 1890.
Source: Goheen (1970), pp. 142 and 178 (Key overleaf).

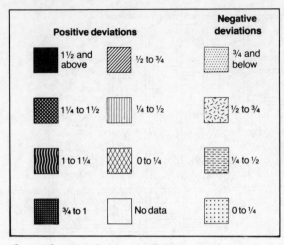

Positive deviations		Negative deviations
1½ and above	½ to ¾	¾ and below
1¼ to 1½	¼ to ½	½ to ¾
1 to 1¼	0 to ¼	¼ to ½
¾ to 1	No data	0 to ¼

(See previous pages).

neighbourhoods and so influencing the character of urban development. It is prudent, therefore, to end this section on a note of caution, noting Briggs's assertion that Victorian cities were not all alike, not 'the same place with different alibis: Dicken's Coketown, alias Smokeover, Mechanicsville, Manchester, Leeds, Birmingham, Elberfeld, Essen, Lyons, Pittsburgh and Youngstown . . . Below the surface, . . . nineteenth century cities not only had different topography [and] different economic . . . structures . . . but they responded differently to the urban problems which they shared in common' (Briggs 1968:33–4).

The modern city

Since the modern city is the central concern of the remaining chapters of this book, it would be pointless to indulge here in a detailed summary of its characteristics and the mechanisms and processes which have produced them. It is, however, instructive to set out the principal aspects of the transformation of urban structure in the modern period alongside those we have noted in relation to pre-capitalist, transitional and Victorian cities.

Like cities of earlier times, the modern city can be seen as the product of changing economic organization, reflecting the social relationships inherent to these changes, moulded by the prevailing means of transport, and continually reshaped by the public policies (or lack of them) and personal life-styles which stem from the dominant spirit of the age. There has, however, been no single shift in economic organization in the modern period equivalent to the rise of industrialism during the nineteenth century. Rather, change has been more complex, with successive 'quantum jumps' in technology bringing a greater range of products for mass

consumption, new means of transport freeing production from fixed locations, and high levels of personal mobility generating large areas of low-density suburban development. At the same time, more and more of the Western economy has switched from farming, mining and heavy manufacturing into the provision of services, the organization of international business, and the administration and provision of all kinds of public goods and social welfare services.

The urban structure arising from this modern economy is epitomized – in its extreme form – by the 'megalopolis', a multi-city, multi-centred urban region characterized by a high proportion of low-density settlement and complex networks of economic specialization – public as well as private – to facilitate the production and consumption of sophisticated products and services. Gottman coined the term megalopolis in relation to the urbanized north-eastern seaboard of the United States stretching from Boston through New York and Philadelphia to Baltimore and Washington (Gottman 1961), but other megalopolitan areas can be identified in the American Upper Midwest (Chicago-Detroit-Pittsburgh), the Rhine-Ruhr axis (Köln-Dusseldorf-Duisburg-Bochum-Dortmund), the Ranstad region of the Netherlands (Rotterdam-The Hague-IJmuiden-Amsterdam-Utrecht), and in the belt of urban development stretching from Liverpool, Manchester, Sheffield and Leeds through Birmingham to London and the Home Counties. Indeed, the whole of England may be compared in size and intensity of urbanization with Gottman's original megalopolis (Hall *et al.* 1973).

Within the modern city and throughout these megalopolitan areas, the pattern of urban life is shaped by the contradictory forces of centralization and decentralization. On the one hand, the concentration of economic and political power in giant corporations and in larger and larger public authorities has made for a centralization of administrative and bureaucratic activity in the central business districts of cities. On the other hand, the new locational freedom of many shops and business enterprises has prompted a decentralization of jobs; and the vast increase in the number of white-collar workers, together with the consequent rise in average incomes and the more widespread availability of automobiles, has decentralized the residential structure of the city, creating enormous tracts of low-density suburban development. As a result, land use in the city has become even more specialized and segregated. 'Shopping strips, one-class suburbs, black ghettos and industrial parks dot the urbanized region. Even the old industrial metropolis's downtown, so formidable a monument fifty years ago, has turned into an office and financial center, while its retailing, wholesaling and manufacturing have been scattered over the whole megalopolis' (Warner 1972:64). This, in turn, has revolutionized people's daily activity patterns. The decentralization of the city, together with the increased personal mobility afforded by the automobile, has increased the range of opportunities available to the affluent urbanite for employment, shopping, recreation and socializing.

In contrast to the advantages which the modern city confers upon the affluent, the poor have neither physical nor economic access to the city's new 'opportunity space'. The unskilled urban worker remains trapped in a localized cycle of poverty (Raynor *et al.* 1974) in which the inter-related effects of poor housing, ill-health, poorly equipped schools, low educational achievement, restricted job opportunities, low wages and unemployment generate an environment of deprivation and social malaise. The persistence of these problems, together with the changing social climate and the increased economic and political powers of urban governments in the twentieth century, have fostered the development of public intervention in order to 'manage' the economic, social and physical environment of the city. Town planning, environmental control and the provision of public housing are three of the more important aspects of this intervention, the origins of which can be traced back to the philanthropic and reformist movements of the nineteenth century (see pp. 29–33). Municipal involvement in urban development is particularly important in European countries, where public housing programmes and compensatory planning (the provision of public goods and services in 'deprived' neighbourhoods) have a very marked effect on the social geography of cities. Indeed, the existence of a large public sector in the housing markets of most European cities is probably the single most important factor in distinguishing European cities from the 'norm' derived from the North American urban experience. This is not to say that municipal involvement in planning and housing policies is unimportant in North America: it is increasingly so; and, encouraged by the federal government, some cities (Los Angeles, for example) have established a reputation for progressive action while many more have assembled large teams of highly qualified planners which would be the envy of many European city planning departments. The chief difference between these planners and their European counterparts is that they do not have the legislative power to implement their plans and strategies, and so must be content with a more advisory role.

These, then, are the principal aspects of urban development in the modern stage. Yet modern cities defy an easy type-casting even more than the Victorian

city and, as we shall see, generalizations about structure, form and social geography are often hedged with numerous qualifications and sometimes seriously disputed. In most circumstances – city, conurbation or metropolis – the characteristics of modern urbanism have been grafted onto a physical and social fabric created in the nineteenth century or before, creating problems of analysis which only an historical perspective can unravel. In a number of cities in the trans-Mississippi West of the United States, however, almost all the urban fabric and urban way of life belongs to the modern period, and if there is an archetypal modern city it must be found in this region. Most people would probably nominate Los Angeles, the automobile city *par excellence*, with a metropolitan population of ten millions spread out at low densities in rather uniform single-family dwellings over the best part of 2,500 square kilometres: an apparent formlessness which contrasts strikingly with the sectors and zones of older cities (Banham 1973; Nelson and Clark 1976).

So much for the general chronology of urban development. The remaining sections of this chapter retrace in detail the development and implications of three of the principal aspects of change which recur throughout the period from the pre-capitalist city onwards: the role of local transport systems in shaping the physical development and residential differentiation of cities, the nature and role of urban government, and the role of new ideas and changing public attitudes in modifying the nature of urban environments.

Transport systems and urban residential differentiation

The fundamental determinants of urban growth and the timing of these major phases of urban development, as noted above, have been economic, stemming from the emergence of capitalism as the dominant mode of production. Generally speaking, the major growth phases of individual cities have been governed by the response of labour and capital to the cycles of national and international prosperity inherent in the capitalist economy, with the production of new residential buildings following effective demand and the availability of capital (Adams 1970; Lewis 1965; Whitehand 1972, 1975). These growth phases have generated successive areas of new housing which are largely responsible for the zonal component of the morphology of many cities. The *nature* of these concentric zones, however, is a result of several factors besides the age and condition of housing built during different growth phases. Whitehand cites innovations in building materials, construction techniques, building standards, architectural styles, methods of house purchase, town planning and intra-urban transport as important morphogenetic factors, and suggests that they also are subject to the periodicity of the overall economy (Whitehand 1977).

Changes in transport systems are considered by many to have been the single most important determinant of urban morphology and residential differentiation within each growth phase (Isard 1942; Ward 1964, 1971; Warner 1962). As these authors point out, the transport technology that prevailed during each boom not only controlled the density and areal extent of urban development but also influenced the suburbanization of the middle classes. Moreover, urban transport systems have also been instrumental in contributing a distinctive sectoral pattern to many cities as the radial routes of successive transport systems have pinned down areas socially and intersected them physically, creating corridors of commercial and industrial land use between which there developed wedges of residential development. The precise effect of transport systems on urban form depends, of course, on the transport technology and growth phase in question. In this section, the effects of each of the major innovations in transport technology are examined in rough chronological order: railways, horse-drawn systems, electric tramways and rapid transit systems, and automobiles.

Railways

Although railways were principally developed for inter-urban transport, they have had a very marked effect on the internal structure of cities. In addition to their general role in stimulating economic expansion (and so accelerating urban growth), railways have affected the development of cities in two main ways. First, the intrusion of railway tracks and termini had the effect of polarizing land use and increasing residential differentiation in inner-city areas. With the start of the railway boom in the 1830s there began a steady realignment of land uses around the central termini and along the railway routes through the built-up area. Retail shopkeepers, transit warehouses and hotels were attracted to the termini, while residential users were repelled. The new rail terminus in Portsmouth, unable to reach the existing city centre because of a ring of barracks and parks encircling the old city, effectively relocated the centre of gravity of the city by drawing the central business district over 1 km from its old site – a phenomenon which was repeated in several other cities (Smailes 1966). Beyond the immediate vicinity of the termini, the criss-crossing of branch lines tended to create shadow areas of middens,

claypits, scrapyards and derelict land. In addition, the huge new viaducts needed to carry the railways into the heart of the city tended to isolate small areas, cutting them off from shops and amenities, depressing land values and encouraging dereliction and marginal uses. Equally significant were the broad swathes created by the mainline tracks and their assorted stockyards, warehouses and factories as they passed through the rest of the city, repelling all but the lowest grade of housing and establishing marked linear features which served as formers for the subsequent development of the city.

These effects were greatest in British cities, where competing railway companies were unwilling to share terminus facilities. Thus, in contrast to the single central station of many large cities in continental Europe and North America, many British cities had two or more termini, together with the extra mileage of approach tracks and sidings. London had as many as 15 termini by the end of the nineteenth century, while Glasgow and Manchester each had four, Belfast, Leeds, Leicester, and Liverpool had three, and Birmingham, Bradford, Dundee, Edinburgh and Sheffield each had two (Simmons 1973). Kellett has shown that in the scuffle for access to British cities the railway companies became the owners of up to 10 per cent of central land and often indirectly influenced the functions of another 20 per cent (Kellett 1969). The exact location of termini and approach routes depended largely on the availability of sufficiently large tracts of land, so that an important controlling factor was the pattern of land ownership. The cost of land was also an important consideration, leading to a preference for the redevelopment of slum areas, where land values were lowest. Fortunately for the railway companies, slum areas and large landholdings often coincided, as in Southwark and Lambeth, where the purchase of parts of the vast slum holdings of the Archbishop of Canterbury and the Lord Bishop of Winchester enabled a railway route to be driven through south London (Kellett 1969). Large numbers of people found themselves displaced in this way, much to the approval of municipal authorities who were glad to be rid of the 'hovels and brothels' which were replaced by the railway infrastructure. Nevertheless, the displaced inhabitants of these areas had to live somewhere, and one of the important secondary effects of railway construction was therefore to increase the congestion of low-income housing areas.

The second main way in which railway development affected the geography of cities was through the growth of commuter traffic. In this respect, American cities experienced a greater impact than European cities, although railway companies everywhere found it difficult to make very large profits from commuter services. Only the most prosperous of the middle classes could afford to commute over the considerable distances between railway stations, and their numbers were relatively small. Nevertheless, both railway travel and out-of-town residences were considered to be genteel, and high status dormitory settlements or 'exurbs', eventually developed around many of the larger cities. According to Kennedy (1962), 20 per cent of Boston's businessmen travelled to work by train in 1848 from exurbs located between 20 and 25 km from central Boston. Similarly, Vance (1964) cites the communities of Burlingame, San Mateo and Belmont as examples of the wealthy exurbs which developed around San Francisco in the 1860s. In addition, railway companies operating from large cities soon began to offer services to intermediate, suburban stations, attracting substantial numbers of commuters of more modest means. The Illinois Central Railroad, for example, carried nearly 14,000 commuters a day from the southern sector of Chicago in 1893 (Yeates and Garner 1976).

In Britain, it was only belatedly that the railways affected suburban development. As in the United States, the railway companies catered mainly for the prosperous middle classes but, in contrast to the development of new exurbs, the suburbanization sustained by the railways in Britain tended to take the form of accretions of low-density villa settlement located at a discreet distance from the railway stations of long-established villages, resorts, market towns and spas which fell within the hinterland of larger cities (Pollins 1964). The railway companies seemed uninterested in exploiting the potential market for passengers from more modest suburban developments adjacent to the cities themselves. Only the Great Eastern Railway actively wooed commuter traffic on the scale of the large American cities of the time, leaving other companies to be accused by contemporary critics of running the railways for the exclusive benefit of the rich (Costelloe 1899). The government, in an attempt to ease the pressure on crowded central areas, sponsored the Cheap Trains Act (1883), which required the railway companies to provide accommodation at fares not exceeding 1d per mile on certain suburban trains, in return for some tax relief. But, although the existence of 'workmen's trains' eventually helped to sustain the growth of new zones of relatively cheap suburban housing – the north London suburbs occupied by large populations of city clerks, for example – the railways did not have their heart in the scheme.

Kellett (1969) has suggested that the reluctance of the companies to exploit the large-scale suburbanization of the lower-middle and working classes was the product of several inter-related factors. First, the railway managers took upon themselves the role of

'gatekeepers', deliberately restricting working-class neighbourhoods to certain parts of the city because they believed that 'throwing open' suburban areas to the working classes would not only 'drive out' the richer and more profitable classes but would also 'spoil' large parts of the city for good. Reinforcing this class prejudice were certain economic factors which made suburban services unattractive to the railway companies. One was that short-haul suburban services always failed to attract goods traffic, which was the staple of the railways; most goods tended to be carted to the suburbs by road. Another factor was connected with the operation of local rates (property taxes). Being large landowners, the railway companies were inevitably liable to high tax bills; but this was aggravated if a rural area became a suburb, for taxes had to be increased on all properties in order to pay for essential public services such as sewage and paving. The most significant point, however, is that if the suburban development was of low quality – and therefore of low taxable value – the overall level of taxation had to be increased much more in order to raise the necessary revenue. Low grade suburban development thus represented a substantial financial burden to companies whose railway lines passed through the area.

Horse-drawn systems

Two of the earliest innovations in intra-urban transport technology were the horse-drawn omnibus (a simple passenger wagon) and the horse-drawn streetcar, or horsecar (a passenger wagon on rails). Together with cable cars and various steam-driven enterprises, these provided the first systems designed especially to cater for the daily ebb and flow of the growing number of people wanting to live in new suburban homes but work in the city centre. The effect of these systems on the fabric of the city was moderated, however, by disadvantages which limited the market for their services. Most serious was the relatively high cost to the passenger. Horses, in the numbers needed to operate a system based on omnibuses or streetcars, were expensive to buy and look after; while cablecars and steam engines also incurred high capital and maintenance costs which were, inevitably, borne by passengers. In addition, all four systems tended to be relatively slow, and the mechanically-propelled systems had the added disadvantage of frightening horses, people, or both. As Yeates and Garner observe, 'One of the chief problems confronting the widespread use of [steam driven systems] seems to have been that the centre of gravity of the engine and carriages was rather high, resulting in unfortunate mishaps on curved and sharp turns. For example, at a later date, the elevated railway curve 73 feet above 110th Street in New York was known as "suicide corner"' (Yeates and Garner 1976:184).

Nevertheless, these were the only mass transit systems available to commuters for most of the nineteenth century, and much of the earliest suburban development was dependent on their existence. The most popular systems were the horse-drawn omnibuses and streetcars, operating on a few routes radiating from the city centre. The example of Boston's early experience of mass transit, drawn from Ward (1964) and Warner (1962) illustrates how these horse-drawn systems began to modify the morphology and social geography of cities during the third quarter of the nineteenth century. In Boston, as in many cities, it was the horsecar which had the greatest spatial impact, for although horse-drawn omnibuses served areas up to ten miles from the city centre their slow speeds and high fares made them unattractive to potential commuters. Horsecars were introduced by several companies during the 1850s, most of them operating, at first, a single route leading from the centre to the edge of town. These installations prompted a crucial change in Boston's social geography, as the wealthier members of the city's middle classes were attracted to large new brownstone terraced dwellings built along the horsecar routes in the outer fringes of the city, reinforcing the idea of suburban living pioneered by the residents of the railway exurbs and endowing previously dull suburban locations with the cachet of social status.

Despite the new attractiveness and feasibility of suburban living, few people seemed willing to spend more than an hour a day travelling to and from work. Given the speed of the horsecar (6 to 8 kph), this restricted its suburbanizing effects to a radius of about 7 km. Moreover, since people were also reluctant to walk very far from their homes to the streetcar stops, much of the suburban expansion took the form of discontinuous ribbon development. Later, crosstown and branch routes were introduced to areas within 4 km of the city centre but in the area between 4 and 7 km from the city the large interstitial areas between the ribbons of upper-middle income residences remained largely untouched by residential development (Fig. 2.4a).

Electric tramways and rapid transit

The electric tram, alias the streetcar or trolley, was the electrically-driven version of the horsecar, powered by way of overhead cables. First introduced in 1887 in Richmond, Virginia, the tram had an immediate and

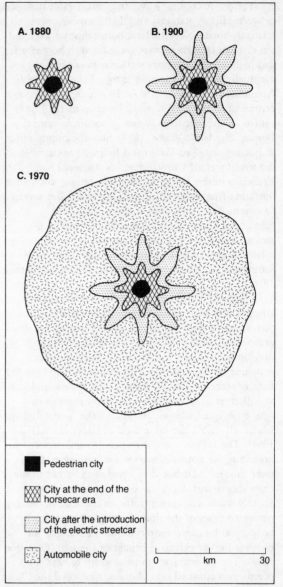

Fig. 2.4 Transport and urban growth. Adapted from Ward (1971), p. 132.

dramatic effect on the fabric of cities, especially in the United States, where more than 200 cities had adopted the system by 1892. The reasons for its popularity were several. Electricity was quieter and more efficient than alternative sources of power, and enabled trams to travel twice as fast as horsecars. Most significant of all though was the fact that the larger carrying capacity of their rolling stock made them cheaper to operate per passenger mile than horsecars, thus allowing a policy of low fares to attract a high volume of passengers. Speculative developers were not slow to realize the potential of the tram in opening up the suburbs to a much wider sector of the middle classes than before, and in most cities there was a flurry of activity as developers and tram operators worked together to promote suburban growth (often as different parts of the same company) during the cyclical boom of the early twentieth century.

The increased speed of the tram doubled the distance that people were able to commute within the critical time of 30 minutes and thus quadrupled the area available for residential development (Adams 1970; Ward 1971). As the suburbs extended and more housing was built the middle classes withdrew almost completely from the inner city, leaving behind a residual population of the poor, together with minority groups of various kinds. As with the horsecar, however, passengers were reluctant to live more than a few minutes walk from the tram stops, and the capital cost of providing branch lines and crosstown routes meant that most suburban expansion continued to be channelled along the major radial routeways (Fig. 2.4b).

In Britain, the impact of electric tramways on suburban development arrived somewhat later than in the United States, and was generally much more modest in scale. Ward (1964) suggests that the less buoyant demographic and economic conditions prevailing in Britain during the late nineteenth century, together with the more stringent building controls of British municipalities, were responsible for limiting the growth of 'streetcar suburbs'. Nevertheless, it would be misleading to suggest that the tram had little effect on the structure of British cities. Tramways in Leeds, for example, carried 94 million passengers a year by 1916, sustaining the development of large but select suburban estates in Potternewton, Lidgett Park, Headingley and Upper Armley (Ward 1964). In Leeds, as elsewhere, the expansion of the tramway system was accomplished by municipal enterprise, motivated by a desire to rationalize intra-urban transport and to ease inner-city congestion by providing a cheap means of transportation for the working classes. As a result, the tramway was able to facilitate the movement of artisans, mechanics, and clerks from the inner city to more salubrious housing further out. This movement was generally constrained, however, by the lack of modestly-priced housing in the outer suburbs; so that the tramways brought the best bargains to the more affluent middle classes who could afford to live in more distant but more expensive suburban housing.

In the larger cities of both Europe and North America the congestion of the core area tended to nullify the efficiency of the tramways, thus prompting the development of elevated tracks and subway systems in structures quite separate from other traffic. These rapid transit systems could travel faster while carrying more passengers, and their effect was to stretch ribbon development even further into the countryside, reinforcing and extending the radial form of the city (Davies 1965). Elevated tracks were introduced in New York City as early as 1878 and in Chicago in 1892, while subway systems were opened in London in 1863, Glasgow in 1897, Boston in 1895, Paris in 1900 and New York City in 1904. The presence of rapid transit stations soon influenced the local pattern of residential construction, land values and population density in the suburbs, with nodes of commercial and residential activity focusing on outlying stations, especially the outer termini. The full effects were delayed until the inter-war period, however, when many of the systems were extended outwards. In London, for example, the subway lines were extended to Edgeware (in 1924), Stanmore (1932) and Cockfosters (1933) at a time when suburban house prices were cheaper than ever before (or since) in relation to personal incomes (Hall 1974). This, combined with a sustained publicity campaign by London Transport about the advantages of life in 'Metroland', triggered one of London's most significant phases of suburban sprawl.

The automobile

The personal mobility conferred by the automobile increased yet again the area within acceptable commuting time of people's workplace. Moreover, by increasing the mobility of goods and raw materials, the internal combustion engine facilitated the decentralization of many jobs, thus increasing even more the potential extent of urban residential development. Car ownership grew rapidly after the introduction of mass production techniques in the 1910s, and the widespread use of cars by commuters had begun by the late 1930s, bringing a low-density sprawl of single-family dwellings to the periphery of the city. This low-density development also rapidly filled the wedge-shaped spaces between the linear development associated with tramways and rapid transit routes, subsequently (since the Second World War) spreading outwards to produce cities 15, 30, or even (in the case of Los Angeles) 80 km across (Fig. 2.4c).

As the incidence of car ownership increased and traffic became more congested, the automobile has also been responsible for reshaping the geography of inner areas. Much of the older fabric of the city has given way to parking lots, and traffic engineering has created 'hot spots' of commercial development while separating residential neighbourhoods from one another with arterial roads. In particular, the parkways, freeways and motorway systems which need gentle curves, 100 metre widths of tarmac and a minimum of intersections in order to cope with contemporary volumes of traffic have imposed a broad, sweeping geometry on the existing fabric of the city, isolating some communities and depressing the environment in much the same way as the railway approaches did 100 years before.

In the United States, where levels of car ownership are significantly higher than in Europe, the automobile has also had a profound effect on the commercial structure of the city. Ribbon developments containing drive-in banks, fast-food outlets, supermarkets and retail stores of all kinds (Berry 1959) have produced characteristic conformations of commercial activity including 'automobile rows' dominated by new- and used-car lots; and 'hamburger rows' containing the ubiquitous McDonald's Hamburger, Dunkin Donut and Kentucky Fried Chicken franchises. The more recent development of out-of-town shopping malls housing air-conditioned avenues of consumer goods shops and department stores has reinforced the trend of retail decentralization, leaving the central business district of many younger cities to offices, hotels and a few specialist shops and department stores.

Parallel developments in the decentralization of industry have made for the emergence of the multi-centred city, with a more complex social geography composed around a series of secondary commercial and industrial foci. The journey to work is therefore no longer dominated by the daily movement of workers from suburb to core, so much as from one suburb to another or from a suburb to a secondary business district or industrial estate. The automobile has also altered patterns of socio-economic segregation, facilitating the settling-out of the middle classes into finely differentiated suburban estates and creating a complex mosaic of neighbourhoods. Within these neighbourhoods though, marriage and friendship patterns have become more diffuse, prompting some writers to announce the end of 'community' and the advent of the 'non-place urban realm' (Webber 1964; see also pp. 41–42). At the same time, poor, car-less families have become increasingly isolated in cheap accommodation near to the low-paid service jobs of the inner city, sustaining the legacy of the Victorian slum within the framework of the modern city.

The changing role of urban government

As cities became larger and more complex in their evolution from the pre-capitalist to the modern stage, so the scope of urban government broadened to include the regulation and provision of all kinds of goods and services, from roads, storm drainage channels, street lighting, water supplies and sewage systems to law enforcement, fire prevention, schools, clinics, transport systems and housing. All these activities have a direct and often fundamental effect on the social geography as well as on the physical morphology of cities, and the contribution of successive generations of urban government can clearly be seen today in the detail of the residential structure and environmental quality of cities. Moreover, the economic and legislative power of modern local authorities makes them a potent factor in moulding and recasting the urban environment. This stands in stark contrast to the situation in the nineteenth century, when local governments had relatively small budgets and played only a minor role in the economic, cultural and social life of cities.

The changing role of urban governments in regulating and subsidizing different aspects of urban life is not only the result of the increased needs and expectations of city dwellers associated with industrialization and urbanization, but also the product of the changing objectives and orientations of the power-holders within local government. As the economic base of cities shifted, the fortunes of different groups changed, cities themselves threw up new problems and challenges, and urban government attracted different types of people with different motivations and objectives. The ethos and orientations of urban government, reflecting these changes, in turn provided the catalyst for further changes in the nature and direction of urban development. The two examples taken here – Britain and the United States – show how the functions of urban government are at once the product of the distribution of economic power and the agent of social and economic change in the city. In addition, both examples show broad parallels in terms of four principal phases in the evolution of urban government.

1. The earliest phase, dating to the first half of the nineteenth century, was a phase of virtual non-government, based on the doctrine of utilitarianism. This *laissez-faire* philosophy rested on the assumption that the maximum public benefit will arise from unfettered market forces. In practice, an oligarchy of merchants and patricians presided over urban affairs but did little to modify the organic growth of cities.

2. The second phase, between 1850 and 1910, saw the introduction of 'municipal socialism' by social leaders in response to the epidemics, urban disorder and congestion of the Victorian city. Urban government in this period developed a strong ethos of public service and paternalism, expressed in a wide range of liberal reforms. At the same time, the increasing power and

responsibility of office-holders facilitated the widespread development of corruption in urban affairs.

3. Between 1910 and 1940 the Depression helped to generate a climate of opinion more favourable to the provision of public goods and social welfare services and, as a result, the legal powers and responsibilities of local government were further widened.

4. In the most recent phase, since 1940, the many roles of urban government have generated large, vertically segregated bureaucracies of professional administrators geared to managing the city and its environment. The professional and the party politician now rule as a duumvirate, the balance of power between the two being variable from function to function and from city to city.

Britain: 'Fit and Proper Persons', shopocracy and bureaucracy

In Britain, the task of exercising municipal government in an increasingly complex urban society arrived at the beginning of the nineteenth century with no precedent to which people could turn. For a long time, the most successful of the urban élite had graduated into the rural gentry and aristocracy, enriching the upper ranks of society with new talent and ideas but leaving the towns with a relatively stagnant leadership (Hennock 1973). During the early nineteenth century, however, an urban aristocracy emerged from the ranks of the rising industrial capitalists: the cotton lords of Manchester, the textile kings of Leeds, the metal magnates of Birmingham, and the jute barons of Dundee, all keen to obtain political power to match and enhance their economic weight. This new urban élite was estranged from the upper echelons of traditional British 'society', however, by its collective struggle against the landed gentry over the Corn Laws, which kept up grain prices to the benefit of Tory landed interests while increasing the costs of food for industrial workers. The city was, in any case, the natural focus of industrialists, who clearly saw that their own fortunes and those of the city were closely inter-related. As it became apparent that municipal government could be the means of promoting local prosperity while increasing the value and productivity of their own capital through civic improvements, businessmen simply could not afford to be left out of civic affairs. So, instead of aspiring towards the squirearchy and a seat on the county bench, the industrialists founded a new local oligarchy with a strong attachment to the town.

As the pace of urban development accelerated and the problems facing municipal government multiplied, more of the successful industrialists, businessmen and

petite bourgeoisie were attracted to office by the same combination of self interest and public service. Meanwhile, revolutionary working-class politics organized under the Chartist movement led to outbreaks of civil disorder which were quickly and heavily repressed with the help of troops (Thompson 1968). For the most part, however, the prevailing climate of opinion continued to endorse the ancient principle that those with the greatest stake in society should have the loudest voice in its affairs; and a large proportion of the people simply expected to be governed by a leadership of educated gentlemen. In this respect, the accelerated elevation of the *nouveaux riches* and *petite bourgeoisie* to municipal office gave rise to widespread complaint about the calibre of councillors and aldermen (Hennock 1973; Newton 1968). Victorians demanded 'station', 'respectability', 'intelligence' and 'education' in their leaders, as well as 'substance' and 'wealth'; and it was widely believed that many of the new recruits to urban government lacked the qualities of 'fit and proper persons'.

Nevertheless, it was the emerging middle classes which increasingly dominated urban affairs, and the politics of city life were characterized more by the contest for power within the middle classes than by a class struggle between the old aristocracy, the bourgeoisie and the proletariat (Fraser 1976). Indeed, the unpropertied working classes were systematically excluded from power by the legal framework of Victorian society. Under the 1835 Municipal Corporations Act, for example, the list of qualified voters was limited to occupiers of taxable property, and candidates for election to the borough council had to own real or personal property worth £1,000 or else occupy a property with a rateable value of at least £30. Even later, when these formal restrictions were relaxed, the vast majority of social groups in the city remained outside the corridors of local power. In Wolverhampton between 1888 and 1890, as many as 33 per cent of council members were owners or controllers of substantial manufacturing enterprises, while manufacturers, professionals and shopkeepers made up 72 per cent of the total. Only 6 per cent were 'workers' (Hennock 1973; Jones 1969). Few workmen, of course, would have had time for council activity (especially with council meetings held during normal working hours) even if they were not alienated from or indifferent to the 'democratic' machinery of local government.

There is, however, some evidence that the proletariat exercised a significant *indirect* effect on the functions of urban government in the nineteenth century. Foster, for instance, has argued that the liberalization of urban politics in the late nineteenth century was the collective response of the ruling classes to a crisis in the social system which was integrally related to the period of working-class consciousness and unrest in the first half of the nineteenth century (Foster 1974; see also Jones 1981). Although the extent of this class consciousness seems to have been rather variable from town to town, the deprivation, inherent unhealthiness and potential violence of 'the mob' undoubtedly had a lot to do with the steady abandonment of the *laissez-faire* doctrine and the corresponding increase in liberal reform during the nineteenth century (see pp. 29–33). Legislation relating to roads, water, sewage and housing all helped to ease the sanitary problems of the Victorian city and to defuse the revolutionary mood of the slums. At the same time, the improved conditions made for economic efficiency and higher productivity, so that what was good for public health and inter-class harmony was also, happily, good for business. For a similar mixture of reasons, civic leaders introduced street lighting, paving, tramways, gas and electricity, transforming urban government itself into a great undertaking on the scale of a large business.

The professional skills and entrepreneurial attitudes developed in the everyday occupations of many councillors now became very appropriate to the job of running the city, and the inspired leadership of a few individuals enabled some cities to become the pace-setters of change. Birmingham, for example, gained a reputation as the 'best-governed city in the world' under the leadership of Joseph Chamberlain, who pursued a municipal doctrine which relied heavily on business principles (Hennock 1973). Nevertheless, the expansion of municipal enterprise did not proceed without check. The demands of 'municipal socialism' on the pockets of ratepayers soon resulted in the election of representatives of small businessmen and the 'shopocracy', who brought a new, prudential disposition to the council chamber; and for the rest of the nineteenth century the debate between 'improvers' and 'economists' over the nature and extent of municipal spending became the central issue of urban politics.

As in the United States, it was the widespread privations of the Depression which finally swung public opinion in favour of a permanent and more fundamental municipal role in providing for many aspects of social well-being. The liberal reforms of the nineteenth century were consolidated, and cities everywhere expanded their activities in health, welfare, housing, education, security and leisure. At the same time, the composition and character of city councils shifted once more. The 75 per cent de-rating of industry by the Local Government Act (1929) and the central government's policy of industrial protection in the 1930s combined to remove from many businessmen the incentive to participate in local affairs (Cox 1976). In

contrast, members of the working and lower-middle classes found a new rationale for being on the council: to speak for the city's growing number of salaried officials and blue-collar employees. These developments led to the replacement of paternalistic businessmen and social leaders by 'public persons' drawn from a wider social spectrum (Lee 1963). In addition, representatives of the working class were installed on city councils through the agency of the Labour party, and party politics soon became an important new facet of urban government. One of the most significant developments to emerge from this was the formulation of coherent policies for urban development by the major parties as part of their respective political platforms, which meant that the subsequent implementation of these policies introduced a new strategic component to the role of urban government and brought even greater demands of judgement, foresight and expertise upon the elected members of the council.

Inevitably, these demands have led to an escalation in the number of professional officers employed to assist councillors in their decision-making. At the same time, however, the effective power of councillors to formulate policy initiatives has decreased. As the technical complexities of municipal finance, public health, educational administration and town planning have increased, councillors have become more and more dependent on the expertise of the professional officers and their staff. Consequently, the activities of urban government are increasingly influenced by the ideologies of the various administrative professions – the conservatism of accountants, the environmental determinism of town planners, and so on – rather than the inclinations of office-bearers or the preferences of the electorate. As is shown in Chapter 8, the behaviour and activities of these 'evangelistic bureaucrats' constitute one of the major influences in the social geography of contemporary British cities.

The United States: city bosses and city managers

The system of local government in most of the United States dates from the nineteenth century, when counties, municipalities and school districts were set up in order to assist state governments in carrying out their responsibilities. Municipalities were established in order to provide essential local services for the inhabitants of urban settlements, whereas counties were given a wider set of administrative functions together with responsibility for basic rural services such as farm roads and policing; school districts were established as independent units because of a strong conviction that public education was of such importance to society as to warrant its economic and political freedom from other local governments (Bollens and Schmandt 1975). The most important exception to this system of local government is the township, which originated during the colonial period and is still prevalent in New England. In addition to the principle of elected representatives guiding urban affairs in the light of their interpretation of the 'public good', an important feature of the New England township system is the element of participatory democracy provided by town meetings, which are held in order to help resolve controversial policy issues.

In the early nineteenth century, neither townships nor municipalities regarded their role as extending beyond the provision of a reasonably sanitary and lawful environment, and city government was quietly dominated by 'natural' leaders drawn from 'established' local families. Later, as in Britain, the intensification of urban problems prompted local authorities to undertake a much greater range of activities, and the creation of a new economic order resulted in a broadened community leadership with a quite different tone. Robert Dahl has documented the best-known model of the political life-cycle of the growing American city. He portrays three successive dynasties in local affairs: the oligarchic 'Patricians' rule first, until they are pushed aside by ambitious 'Entrepreneurs', who are in turn replaced by the rising immigrants and working classes – the 'Ex-Plebes' (Dahl 1961). Nevertheless, it should be borne in mind that this schema often needs considerable modifications in order to match the experience of particular cities, as Frisch (1969), for example, has shown in his research on urban politics in nineteenth-century Springfield, Massachusetts.

Moreover, the governments of different cities developed quite different attitudes towards their responsibilities according to their different social composition and municipal backgrounds. The two principal systems of political ethics to emerge during the nineteenth century have been identified by Hofstadter:

One, founded upon the indigenous Yankee-Protestant political traditions, and upon middle-class life, assumed and demanded the constant, disinterested activity of the citizens in public affairs, argued that political life ought to be run, to a greater degree than it was, in accordance with general principles and abstract laws apart from and superior to personal needs, and expressed a common feeling that government should be in good part an effort to moralize the lives of individuals . . .

The other system was associated with the background of European immigrant populations, and was founded

upon their unfamiliarity with independent political action, their familiarity with hierarchy and authority . . . [It] took for granted that the political life of the individual would arise out of family needs, interpreted political and civic relations chiefly in terms of personal obligations, and placed strong loyalties above allegiance to abstract codes of law or morals. It was chiefly upon this system of values that the political life of the immigrant, the boss and the urban machine was based (Hofstadter 1955:9; see also Banfield and Wilson 1963).

The second of these situations was evident in most of the larger cities, which all contained large immigrant populations; and it was this political environment which propagated the widespread corruption which is held by some to be characteristic of American metropolitan affairs (Gardiner and Olson 1974). While petty corruption associated with the jobbing of contracts for public works was also prevalent in Victorian Britain, the patronage, bribery and organized corruption characteristic of large US cities was never paralleled except, perhaps, in Liverpool (Hennock 1973). The central feature of the system was the political 'machine' whose leaders clearly regarded the conduct of municipal affairs as a personal commercial venture or, more simply, as a source of exploitation and plunder (Callow 1976). The best-known of these machines is probably the Tammany organization in New York, which was set up in the 1790s as a Jeffersonian political club. Initially its power base was derived from the urban poor, whose approval of its stance against imprisonment for debt was consolidated during the depression of 1837–42 by the distribution of food, clothing and fuel by Tammany members. As it became increasingly involved in the local affairs of the Democratic party, the organization acquired patronage and was 'consulted' in the choice of candidates for political office who, when elected, deferred to the wishes of Tammany Hall in the distribution of city jobs. In return, these grateful job-holders donated a portion of their salary to the organization, thus lubricating the wheels of corruption with the vital ingredient of money.

The chief beneficiary of the system, of course, was the mayor, or 'city boss'. In New York, the most notorious of the city bosses was Boss Tweed, but nearly every major city hosted a series of such despots and their collective impact on urban affairs has been fundamental. Besides introducing a diathesis of wholesale corruption to urban government, they also played an important part in bringing immigrant communities into the mainstream of economic and political life by way of the patronage which helped, in turn, to keep the bosses in office. In addition, many of the bosses operating in the late nineteenth and early twentieth centuries were astute enough to appreciate the general economic benefits associated with improvements to the city's infra-structure as well as the personal kudos associated with Great Works. Moreover, the more housing codes, building regulations and municipal ordinances that were passed, the more opportunities there were to solicit graft in return for not enforcing them. As a result, it was often the bosses who were responsible for extending the role of urban government in the provision of public services and amenities. They were also responsible, albeit indirectly, for the introduction of more widespread liberal reform, for, as a consequence of their personal excesses and the connection of the political machines with bootlegging, prostitution and gambling, the climate of public opinion began to swing in favour of progressive candidates sponsored by middle-class reform groups. Only in cities where the majority of the upper-middle classes had moved out to suburban municipalities, taking with them their interest in urban affairs, did the machine system continue to dominate urban politics – as in Chicago, Detroit and Philadelphia (McCarthy 1977).

Elsewhere, reform groups took steps towards eliminating the worst effects of machine politics. In this context, one of the most significant developments was the modification of the mayor/council system of government through the appointment of a 'manager' who would be directly responsible to the city council for the administration of municipal functions of all kinds. First introduced in Staunton, Virginia, in 1908, and widely publicized by its adoption in Dayton, Ohio, in 1914, the city manager/council system is now in operation in a majority of municipalities of between 23,000 and 250,000 population, and in one in four of all larger cities (Bollens and Schmandt 1975). Much of the attractiveness of the system must be attributed to the need for professional assistance in handling the increasing scope and complexity of municipal affairs, especially given the expansion of urban social welfare programmes since the Depression. For the same reason, most cities have become dependent on large bureaucracies staffed by specialist professionals. These include members of research teams and planning departments whose functions are centred on the formulation of strategic policies relevant to the various social and economic problems which afflict the contemporary city. Compared to their counterparts in Britain, however, US city planners have much less weight in influencing the actual outcome of events, with the major exceptions of transport planning and land-use zoning. Warner (1972) believes that the strong American tradition of private property rights and the consequent reluctance to give planners the power to deal with land as a social resource lies at the heart of many urban dilemmas, including environmental degradation, housing problems, and the inefficient and inequitable location of schools, hospitals and other public facilities. Nevertheless, the idea of combating urban problems by

means of coercive, regulatory and redistributive policies has gained considerable momentum since the Second World War and seems certain to have an increasing effect on the social geography of the American city.

Spirit and matter: ideology and the built environment

Just as the functions of urban government can be seen as a reflection of the interaction between the orientation of successive groups of power-holders and the problems and opportunities which confronted them, so can the general layout and townscape of cities be seen as a reflection of the prevailing ideology (in the sense of a political climate, *zeitgeist*, or 'spirit') of a particular period. Of course, the political climate of an age, together with its dominant economic and social formations, its technology, and the functions of contemporary local government, should really be seen as inter-related components of a broader process of urban development, and attempts to link them within a theoretical framework are considered in some detail in subsequent chapters. For the moment, however, it is convenient to focus specifically on the interaction between 'spirit' and 'matter'.

The idea of urban fabric being seen – in part, at least – as the outcome of broad political, socio-economic and cultural forces has been explicit in much writing on urban history (see, for example, Mumford 1961; Curl 1970). As Curl puts it, 'The argument, briefly, is that the political climate is determined by the dominant members of a society, that is, by the ruling classes, and that the political climate thus created in turn influences the design of urban settlements profoundly' (Curl 1970: 1). The best-known examples of the influence of ideology on urban form are non-Western, relating to the influence of religious and cosmological beliefs on town plans. Many Chinese and south-east Asian cities, for example, were laid out as images of the universe (Wheatley 1975; Carter 1975), and there is evidence to suggest that Roman cities were also laid out according to cosmological beliefs (Rykwert 1976). Other examples are not difficult to find, however. Despotism, nationalism, colonialism, and paternalism (i.e. what passes for socialism in most Western cities) have all been shown to have produced distinctive urban environments which can still be identified in the bricks and mortar left over from earlier stages in the development of the Western city.

One of the most striking examples is the symbolization of power in the urban environments created by despotic rulers and nationalistic governments. Renaissance and Baroque cities like Versailles, Richelieu, St Petersburg and Karlsruhe were built in the grand manner – with piazzas, boulevards and monumental architecture – by autocratic rulers, displaying a unity of design which resulted from having been built under the complete control of one hand with the express purpose of reflecting the power and the glory of the secular princes and kings of the emerging nation states of Europe (Lavedan 1941). Similarly, the majestic ground plan and imposing architecture of central Washington can be seen as the result of a deliberate attempt to symbolize the power and self-image of a new nation (Reps 1965).

The centralized power associated with colonialism has also been connected with a characteristic morphology. Here, the *zeitgeist* is concerned with imposing order as quickly and efficiently as possible, with a minimum of embellishment. The result, remarkably often, is a settlement whose layout is dominated by a grid or chequerboard system: easy to survey and thus quickly established (Stanislawski 1946). It was the standard form for new towns established in the aftermath of Alexander's conquest of the Middle East, and was adopted by the Romans for their colonial towns, the grid sometimes surviving in the modern street pattern, as in Chichester, Colchester, Orleans and Zaragoza. With the urban revival of the Middle Ages the grid appeared in Slav towns planted by Germans, in the *bastide* towns of southern France, and in the towns established by the Christian kings of Spain as they reconquered territory from the Moors (Smailes 1966). More recently, the grid appeared with the Jacobean colonization of Ulster and the British colonization of North America. Even after the British had left the United States, the grid spread with the administrative colonization of the West, for the federal survey system was based on a six-mile square subdivided into 36 square sections of 640 acres each. As a result, rectilinear layout has become a prominent feature of the American urban landscape.

The more recent stages of urban development have also been affected by the translation of different ideologies into particular components of the urban environment. As we have seen, two competing ideologies have dominated urban affairs since the early nineteenth century: *laissez-faire* capitalism, and liberalism. The remainder of this section is concerned with the ramification of these two ideologies on the built environment, with particular emphasis on the implications of the development of the increasingly important paternalistic and idealistic value systems associated with the 'liberal' political climate.

The environments of capitalism

There are two ways in which the spirit of capitalism has been clearly imprinted on the fabric of modern cities. The first is connected with the symbolization of wealth and achievement by groups of prosperous merchants and industrialists. Early examples of this include the splendid architecture of Edinburgh's New Town, the elegant Georgian squares and crescents of Bath and London, and the urbane town houses of ante-bellum Boston and New York, built for a 'confident and privileged class' of merchant capitalists (Bell and Bell 1972). The industrial capitalists of Victorian times also felt the compulsion to express their achievements in buildings. The Cross Street area of central Manchester is still dominated by the imposing gothic architecture commissioned by the city's Victorian élite who, preoccupied with the accumulation and display of wealth but with a rather philistine attitude towards aesthetics, left a clear impression of their values on the central area of the city. Manchester, as Kennedy observes, 'was a confident city, and that confidence was expressed in bricks and mortar, in edifices built to last, to show future ages all was well' (Kennedy 1970: 86).

It is possible to infer a parallel rationale in the construction of the edifices of contemporary capitalism. Huge office blocks such as the Prudential Building in Boston and the Pirelli Building in Paris are clearly intended as statements of corporate power and achievement, notwithstanding any administrative or speculative functions. Ford, for example, has described how the 'skyscraper infatuation' that spread through the Midwest in the 1920s and 1930s was a result of 'the desire on the part of many companies to construct monuments to themselves' (Ford 1973: 324). These skyscrapers affected the downtown area of cities both from a functional and a visual standpoint: even single buildings such as the Terminal Tower in Cleveland and the AIU Citadel in Columbus (adorned with statues and lanterns and containing within it a copy of the Hall of Mirrors at Versailes and the Bridge of Sighs in Venice) were able to relocate the focal point of a central business district, blighting adjacent residential areas through the increase in local taxes that their presence brought about while attracting, instead, new commercial and administrative buildings.

The second way in which the spirit of capitalism can be said to have directly affected the fabric of cities is related to the activities of speculative developers, who have been responsible for the design and layout of a large proportion of the housing stock of cities. Their search for profit – surely the essence of the 'spirit' of capitalism – has produced a large amount of working-

Fig. 2.5 A Victorian builder's pattern book.
Source: Dyos (1968), p. 660.

and lower-middle class housing based on a repetitive layout (often gridded) and characterized by uniformity and regimentation. It should be emphasized that this is a generalization which applies only to housing built for families with low or modest incomes, for whom the cost of housing (whether for rent or purchase) was a critical factor: the housing produced by speculative developers for the more affluent middle classes has always reflected their ability to pay for a sounder and more varied environment. In the present context, this could be seen as a reflection of another element of capitalist ideology: that of consumer sovereignty. But it is in the lower end of the market that the most direct expression of capitalism's inherent search for profit is to be found.

Faced with a large but relatively impoverished market, the speculative developers of the nineteenth and early twentieth centuries could only make a satisfactory profit by giving themselves to a high-volume, low-cost product. The latter could only be achieved by producing large tracts of standardized dwellings on rectilinear plots, taking advantage of the division of labour and economies of scale. Thus emerged the brick terraces of English cities, the tall tenements of Glasgow, Edinburgh, Paris, New York, Berlin and Genoa, the wooden 'three-deckers' of New England towns, and the two- and three-storey walk-up apartment buildings of Philadelphia, Chicago and St Louis. (Later these were joined, on the same principle, by the semi-detached and detached single-family dwellings of lower-middle class suburbs in cities everywhere.) Architecture was superseded by pattern books containing plans of known profitability (Fig. 2.5), and houses were built to minimal standards, soon inducing widespread deterioration. The most profitable shape – deep, narrow buildings – allowed only minimum light and air; and the grid pattern which saved so much on survey, construction and administrative costs soon proved a hindrance to traffic as well as being unsuited to the development of centred and bounded neighbourhoods in which 'community' could flourish.

Paternalism and idealism

The paternalistic and idealistic value systems associated with liberalism and the development of 'municipal socialism' are, in part, the product of such shortcomings in housing standards. As a number of writers have shown, these value systems are the result of a complex interaction between social, religious, political and environmental factors, leavened by the originality of a few individuals (Ashworth 1954; Gauldie 1974; Tarn 1973; Philpott 1978). Because of this, the influence of paternalism and idealism on the built environment is

best understood in relation to events in one country, with only occasional sideways glances at what was going on elsewhere. The example taken here is based on events in Britain, where the two ideologies have probably had more influence on urban form than anywhere in the western world.

The context
The general background to the liberal value systems of the nineteenth century has already been outlined in the discussion of urban government. In particular, it has been suggested that the liberalization of urban politics in the late nineteenth century was essentially a pragmatic response by the ruling classes to the dangers associated with the 'condition' of the working classes. The heart of the problem facing adherents to the *laissez-faire* ideology of unrestrained capitalism (and its corollary of non-government) was to be found in the squalor, overcrowding and disease of the inner city slums. For a long time these areas remained *terra incognita* to the great majority of the Victorian middle classes who were, in consequence, unaware of the extent and intensity of the misery to be found there (Wohl 1977). Throughout the second half of the nineteenth century this ignorance was assailed by a series of mordant and alarming commentaries based on the surveys of a few individuals who had become committed to liberal reform. It was not their compassion which dented the spirit of *laissez-faire*, however, so much as the palpable dangers of the slums to the rest of the city's inhabitants (Jones 1971). The regular outbreaks of cholera, typhoid and dysentery were clearly related to conditions in the slums; and in addition there was the constant danger of large-scale fires. Even more important was the Victorian fear of 'the mob', which was greatly reinforced by the revolutionary events throughout Europe in 1848. Even the New World did not escape proletarian unrest: more than twenty major riots occurred in New York City between 1834 and 1871, mostly attributed to 'riffraff' from Europe (Warner 1972). So, with property as well as physical well-being under threat, the middle classes began to accede to the reformist ideas advanced by the liberal pamphleteers.

1840–1870: Private paternalism
The early liberal reformers capitalized on the idea of the 'dangerous classes' in their attempts to promote their cause, but a good deal of careful documentation was also necessary in order to convince Victorians of the need for reform of any kind. One of the most influential figures in this context was Edwin Chadwick who, as First Secretary of the Poor Law Board, was largely responsible for the Board's Report on *The Sanitary*

Conditions of the Labouring Population and the Means of Its Improvement (1842), which drew widespread publicity because of its sheer weight of evidence. This document, together with similar publications, played a significant part in changing the climate of opinion about liberal reform for, reinforced by a particularly widespread outbreak of cholera in 1848, it had the effect of focusing the latent sense of *noblesse oblige* among the aristocracy as well as stimulating the Presbyterian sense of guilt which affected many successful Victorian businessmen. The interested parties formed themselves into associations whose *zeitgeist* is reflected in their titles: the Health of Towns Association, the Association for Promoting Cleanliness Amongst the Poor, the Society for Improving the Conditions of the Labouring Classes, the Metropolitan Association for Improving the Dwellings of the Industrious Classes, and so on. At first they were limited to passing pious resolutions; but they soon began to lead by example, commissioning model housing in order to demonstrate the feasibility of building sound housing for the poor at a profit (Chapman 1971). Although they met with some success, it became evident that decent tenement buildings could not be built as cheaply as had been envisaged, with the result that the rents which had to be charged in order to make even a modest return on capital were beyond the pocket of casual labourers. Meanwhile, the efforts of these paternalistic associations were easily outpaced by the feverish activities of speculative developers who employed 'the builder of walls without footings, the bricklayer who knew how to mix mortar without cement, the carpenter who could lay floors over green joists, the plumber who knew just how to lay drains without traps or how to install cold water systems which had a positive, intimate and lethal acquaintance with the sewage arrangements' (Dyos 1968a: 685).

There followed a period of intellectual debate about housing and public health. Although there was a broad consensus as to the extent and urgency of the problem, observers disagreed both as to its causes and the appropriate remedies. Pons, for example, has shown how contemporary analyses of Manchester ranged from the radical views of Friedrich Engels through the liberal views of Dr James Kay to the eulogistic writings of the Rev. Robert Lamb, who saw the problems of the slums as an unavoidable by-product of the unfolding Destiny of Man (Pons 1978; see also Anderson 1977). Parallel to this debate there emerged a separate, idealistic movement with an underlying anti-urban ideology. The antecedents of this movement had been established earlier in the century with Robert Owen's social experiment at New Lanark (which inspired an ill-fated community at New Harmony in Indiana), and in the 1850s it came to fruition in a series of small communities built by paternalistic factory owners in a spirit of enlightened self-interest (Bell and Bell 1972). These communities, complete with a variety of housing, public baths, wash houses and elevating institutions (like New Lanark's Institute for the Formation of Character) were carefully planted away from towns in the belief that the semi-rural environment would be ideal for the physical and moral welfare of the workers, who would repay the owner not only in grateful loyalty but also in higher productivity. The best-known of these communities is Saltaire, built by Titus Salt in the Aire valley outside Bradford.

During the 1860s the movement lost momentum and was overshadowed by philanthropic housing organizations whose activities were focused on the production of sanitary housing for the poor in large cities. This philanthropy, however, was constrained by the still-dominant ideology of capitalism. Profit still had to be made from such ventures, even if it was only a profit of 5 per cent or so: 'a penance for more fulsome success elsewhere' (Tarn 1973: 43). Like all such movements, the numbers willing to make such a gesture were few; but several wealthy individuals and philanthropic foundations made important contributions to the housing stock of larger cities. In London, for example, the George Peabody Trust completed over 5,000 dwellings for the poor between 1862 and 1895, many of which have survived into the 1970s (Tarn 1973). Like the earlier demonstration projects, however, these philanthropic ventures were only accessible to the 'respectable poor' who could afford the rents which made profit possible; and, despite the efforts of men like Peabody, the housing problem continued to grow faster than philanthropic contributions.

1870–1910: Public paternalism

The political climate of the 1870s was still generally hostile towards any kind of public paternalism, even though most local authorities had acquired powers to undertake essential services such as sewage and water. Indeed, many prominent 'liberal' reformers – such as Octavia Hill – firmly believed in the power of private enterprise and self-help to improve slums without government help. The problems of the poor were widely believed to stem from their 'character' and morals (much blame was attached to the influence of Irish immigrants in this respect), and so the proper solution was seen in terms of amateur social work and educational propaganda. Nevertheless, the failure of model housing, model communities, philanthropic and self-help movements to cope with the potentially dangerous problems of the slums prompted a series of Royal Commissions which led to two Acts of Parliament in 1875. These became landmarks in the history of liberal reform, for they introduced aspects of public intervention with far-reaching effects on the quality of the built environment. The first of these Acts was the Public Health Act, which enabled local authorities to establish model byelaws (i.e. minimum standards for housing development) and to alter or pull down any work which contravened the byelaws. Thus emerged the principle of social control over building activity. The second important Act of 1875 was the Artisans' Dwellings Act which, among other things, allowed local authorities to acquire powers to demolish slum areas if they were considered to be a health hazard. The Act thus took public paternalism an important step towards area planning and urban renewal, although the immediate success of the Act was limited by the high costs of compensation won by slum landlords (Chapman 1971).

Again there followed a period of intellectual debate about the housing question, this time extending to popular newspapers and ladies' tea clubs. One of the most influential publications of this period was Andrew Mearns's *The Bitter Cry of Outcast London* (1883), which drew attention to the continuing moral and sanitary problems caused by overcrowding and called for state and local governments to shoulder more responsibility for housing and environmental problems (Wohl 1977). Almost inevitably, there followed another Royal Commission, this time required to consider the 'Housing of the Working Classes'. It reported in 1885, by which time Parliament was rather distracted by the Irish question. One important outcome of the Commission's report, however, was the Local Government Act of 1888 which reorganized local government into counties and county boroughs, giving them a considerable amount of autonomy. Their creation helped to promote a strong sense of civic pride, and in the more liberal environment that prevailed towards the turn of the century many local authorities began to take full advantage of byelaw and slum clearance legislation. Before long, powers were sought from the Secretary of State to build public housing in areas where neither speculative developers nor philanthropists could profitably build housing for the poor. Some of the first housing schemes were in Scotland, where a long tradition of cultural and economic discipline based on the philosophies of Stewart, Brown, Ferrier and Carlyle had created a *zeitgeist* which made for a firmer and more positive civic government (Best 1968). It was Glasgow, as Allan observes, that first recognized 'that a free market, private philanthropy and public health regulations could not provide an adequate solution . . . and that the City Fathers must at least supervise and plan redevelopment' (Allan 1965: 613); and it was Dundee and Edinburgh,

not London or Birmingham, that quickly followed suit.

The last years of the nineteenth century also saw a resurgence of idealism and the model communities movement, which produced two important developments; Port Sunlight, across the Mersey from Liverpool, and Bournville, outside Birmingham. Both were built by industrialists (W.H. Lever and George Cadbury respectively) seeking room to expand business, but neither were intended to be merely an employer's village. Port Sunlight was intended to demonstrate the viability of profit-sharing at the community level, and Bournville was established as a 'social example', with half of its working population working elsewhere than at the Cadbury Brothers' Factory (Ashworth 1954). Both communities successfully took root, grew and became strong enough to stand by themselves (unlike George Pullman's ill-fated venture south of Chicago, where the townspeople rebelled against the degree of paternalistic control insisted upon by their benefactor), showing that low-density 'garden-suburb' planning was a feasible strategy. Within a few years this idealism was given extra momentum with the publication of Ebenezer Howard's *Garden Cities of Tomorrow* (1902) which codified a great mass of ideas and experience. Howard himself was closely involved in the Garden City Pioneer Co. Ltd, which promoted the development of Letchworth, the first full Garden City. Using Howard's schematic plans (Fig. 2.6), the company laid out roads, parks and factory sites and invited private developers to build carefully regulated housing on prepared sites. The scheme was supported by radicals and liberals because it involved land-use control and centralized planning; and by conservatives because it gave private enterprise the scope to provide housing. More important, it proved to be an economic success. Thus reinforced, Howard's ideas quickly spread, achieving concrete form in several places. New Earswick, near York, had already been commissioned by Joseph Rowntree as a result of Howard's *Garden Cities*, and it was quickly followed by Hampstead Garden Suburb (1907–14) and numerous smaller garden suburbs such as Woodlands in Doncaster, Fallings Park in Wolverhampton and Altrincham in Manchester (Tarn 1973).

1910–1945: Professionalized paternalism

The combination of this movement with the framework of housing legislation and the increasingly liberal political climate provided the background for the emergence of the town planning movement (Cherry 1979), which has become one of the most important single factors in shaping the morphology and social geography of the British city. After seeing the undernourished and undersized recruits for the Boer War, even the most rigid of conservatives were ready to

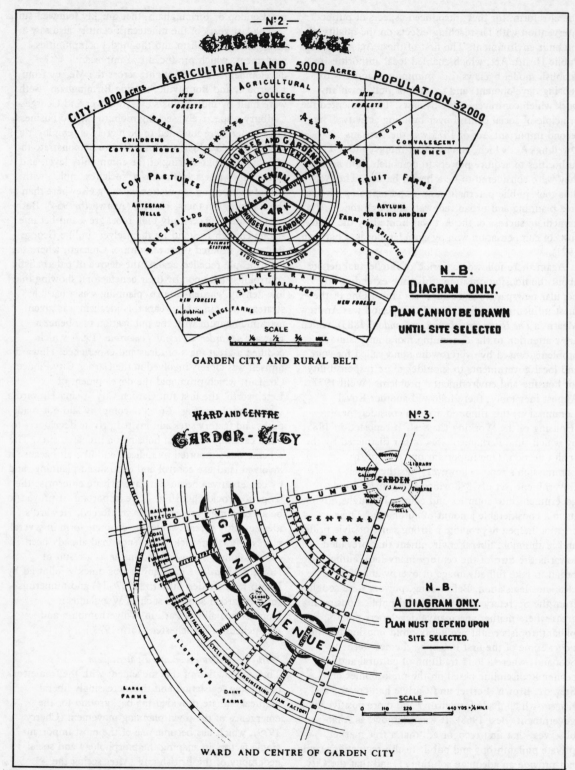

Fig. 2.6 Ebenzer Howard's ideas for a garden city.
Source: Howard (1965), pp. 52 and 53.

shelve some of their most prized social theories in favour of a more widespread, formalized system of paternalism. An important catalyst in the emergence of such a system was Patrick Geddes, a professor of botany at Dundee, an amateur urban social geographer and an active campaigner for social and housing reform. Geddes had formal or informal affiliations with all of the relevant societies and was in touch with most of the prominent planners and architects of the day, and so came to be one of the leading figures behind the formulation of the first Town Planning Act (1909). This Act encapsulated all of the paternalistic and idealistic value systems which had developed during the nineteenth century, and clearly subscribed to the environmental determinism which has underlain the ideology of the planning profession ever since. In the words of the Bill introducing the Act:

The object of the Bill is to provide a domestic condition for the people in which their physical health, their morals, their character and their whole social condition can be improved . . . The Bill aims in broad outline at, and hopes to secure, the home healthy, the house beautiful, the town pleasant, the city dignified, and the suburb salubrious. It seeks, and hopes to secure, more and better homes, better houses, prettier streets, so that the character of a great people, in towns and cities and villages, can be still further improved and strengthened by the conditions under which they live . . .

It was not until the interwar period, however, that town planning received the impetus which has made it such an important factor in contemporary urban geography. The impetus came from an unlikely alliance between three different movements, each concerned, for

their own reasons, about urban sprawl. Rural conservationists were worried about the loss of prime agricultural land (about 25,000 hectares per annum in the 1930s), and their case was given some urgency by the impending threat of war. Urban idealists were also concerned about the degeneration of the garden city idea into the semi-detached ribbon development which characterized much of the sprawl; and the lobby for the depressed regions of the country had a keen interest in curbing the energy of the big cities in order to promote growth elsewhere. There thus developed a strong anti-urban alliance, epitomized in a collection of essays entitled *Britain and the Beast* (Williams-Ellis 1938): the 'beast' in question being urbanization. This anti-urban school of thought had a profound influence on subsequent planning strategy, largely as a result of the inspired efforts of Patrick Abercrombie, who had interests in each of the allied anti-urban movements and who was responsible for introducing the influential concepts of green belts and overspill policies to town planning in his plan for London in 1944 (Hall 1974). These ideas, together with the garden city idealism, the paternalism and evangelical zeal inherited from the nineteenth century, and the new ideas of men like Clarence Perry (on planned neighbourhoods) and Le Corbusier (on high-rise living) have dominated the ideology of the planning profession ever since. Their impact on the postwar British city has been substantial, and a detailed consideration of the spatial outcomes associated with their application is presented in Chapter 8.

Chapter 3

THE SOCIAL DIMENSIONS OF MODERN URBANISM

An important part of the geographer's task of illuminating the nature and causes of spatial differentiation is to lay bare the inter-relationships between man and environment. In urban social geography, this involves a consideration of the complex interaction between individuals, social groups and the diverse physical and socio-economic environments of the city. The objective in this chapter is to provide some commentary on the theories and ideas relevant to this task. Many of the ideas described are derived from other disciplines – chiefly urban sociology and environmental psychology – although the focus throughout is on their spatial implications. This chapter is thus based on the contention that the spatial order of the city can only be properly understood against the background of the underlying dimensions of social organization and human behaviour in the city. The suggestion is not, however, that the spatial order of the city is completely subordinate to social factors; the influence of space and distance on individual behaviour and social organization will be a recurring theme in this chapter.

Urban life in western culture

In general, the overall relationship between man and the physical and social environments afforded by cities has traditionally been viewed as bad. Cultural expressions, public opinion and social theories about city life have all erred towards negative impressions and have tended to be highly deterministic, blaming the ills of city life on the inherent attributes of urban environments (an important exception here is the strand of social thought represented by Marxist social theory, which is considered in detail in subsequent chapters).

Evidence from a sizeable number of attitudinal surveys suggests that most people believe city environments to be unsatisfactory. One Gallup Poll showed that even among Americans currently living in cities, only 20 per cent preferred cities to non-metropolitan environments. When the question was posed: 'If you could live anywhere you wanted to, would you prefer a city, suburban area, small town or farm?', the answers were: City 13%; Suburb 31%; Small town 32%; Farm 23%. (American Institute of Public Opinion, 1973). Data from British and Scandinavian surveys show a similar anti-urban leaning (Abrams 1973; Mann 1965). Moreover, these attitudes show up not only in hypothetical residential preferences but also in evaluations of actual communities. Satisfaction with the overall 'quality of life' and with several major components of well-being tends to decline steadily with the transition from rural to metropolian environments (Table 3.1). Such data, however, are notoriously difficult to interpret. A case in point is the apparent ambiguity of results which show people professing to prefer rural or small-town living but whose behaviour has brought them to the city, presumably in pursuit of a higher material level of living. The city thus emerges as neither good nor bad, but as a 'necessary evil'.

This lop-sided ambivalence towards the city – a grudging functional attraction accompanied by an intellectual dislike – has long been reflected in the literature and art of western society (including the idiom of popular songs: e.g. the work of Bob Dylan, Joni Mitchell, Paul Simon and Pete Townshend). Raymond Williams, for example, has clearly shown that while British literature has occasionally celebrated the positive attributes of city life, there has been a much greater emphasis on its defects, paralleled by the persistence of a romanticist portrayal of country life: for every urban thrill and sophistication there are several urban laments and rural yearnings (Williams 1973). Surveys of American literature and intellectual thought have also emphasized the image of the city as an arena of conflict and desolation (Gelfant 1954; Strauss 1961; Tuan 1978; White and White 1962), though Paterson is able to demonstrate how the city has in addition been variously regarded as a catalyst, a challenge and a 'stage' for the

Table 3.1 Perceived quality of life by community size, USA c1970

Question	Community size				
	<2,500	*2,500–50,000*	*50,000–500,000*	*500,000–1 million*	*>1 million*
	Per cent satisfied				
'Would you say that you are satisfied or dissatisfied with the quality of life in your community?'	84	81	69	77	61
'On the whole would you say that you are satisfied or dissatisfied with . . .?'					
Your income :	67	68	65	63	64
Your work :	90	89	86	84	83
Children's education :	68	66	65	58	55
Your housing :	84	80	76	71	70

Source: Fischer 1973: (Table 1) 223.

enactment of human drama and personal lifestyle by certain schools of thought (Paterson 1976; see also Hurst 1975). The idea of the city in Western culture is thus 'a montage of mixed and clashing elements: . . . of senseless, brutal crime; of personal freedom and boundless hopes; of variety, choice, excitement; of callous and uncaring people; of social groups diverse enough to satisfy each individual's unique needs; of crass and crushing materialism; of experiment, innovation and creativity; of anxious days and frightful nights' (Fischer 1976: 17).

New York, to most people, is probably the best exemplar of this diversity. On the one hand it is able to prompt the horrific stereotype of urban life portrayed in Feiffer's play *Little Murders*, in which the principal character asks:

You know how I get through the day? . . . in planned segments. I get up in the morning and think, O.K. a sniper didn't get me for breakfast, let's see if I can go for a walk without being mugged.

O.K., I finished my walk, let's see if I can make it back home without having a brick dropped on my head from the top of a building. O.K., I'm safe in the lobby, let's see if I can go up in the elevator without getting a knife in my ribs.

O.K., I made it to the front door, let's see if I can open it without finding burglars in the hall. O.K. I made it to the hall, let's see if I can walk into the living room and not find the rest of my family dead (Feiffer 1968: 88).

On the other hand, the advantages of life in a city like New York include accessibility to a tremendous variety of opportunites. Fischer cites the reaction of a 'refugee' New Yorker living in Vermont:

I kept hearing this tempting ad for a Czechoslovakian restaurant . . . When the ad went on to say that this particular place had been chosen by the critic of the *Times* out of all the Czech restaurants in New York as the very best, I could have broken down and cried. We hardly get a choice of doughnut

stands in Vermont; New Yorkers idly pick and choose among Czech restaurants (Fischer 1976:59).

Fischer suggests that it is possible to recognize four basic themes within this ambivalent imagery of cities, each expressed as polarities:

Rural		Urban
Nature	versus	Art
Familiarity	versus	Strangeness
Community	versus	Individualism
Tradition	versus	Change

Fischer points out that there is a 'tension' in these pairings which derives from the fact that neither half is universally 'better' or 'worse' than the other. Instead, they pose dilemmas of personal choice. Depending on which horn of the dilemma they have grasped, philosophers and poets have become either pro-urbanists or (as is usually the case) anti-urbanists (Fischer 1976).

Urbanism and social theory

These polarities are also present in the stock of social theories concerning city life. The strangeness, artificiality, individualism and diversity of urban environments have been seen by many social scientists as fundamental influences on human behaviour and social organization. The deterministic and environmentalist perspective has had a profound effect on urban social geography as well as on sociology and all the cognate disciplines. It stems from the writings of European social philosophers such as Durkheim, Weber, Simmel and Tönnies, who were seeking to understand the social and psychological implications of the urbanism and urbanization associated with the Industrial Revolution of the nineteenth century.

The kernel of this classic sociological analysis is the association between the scale of society and its 'moral order'. Basically, the argument runs as follows. In pre-industrial society small, fairly homogenous populations contain people who know each other, perform the same kind of work and have the same kind of interests: they thus tend to look, think and behave alike, reflecting a consensus of values and norms of behaviour. In contrast, the inhabitants of large cities constitute part of what Durkheim called a 'dynamic density' of population subject to new forms of economic and social organization as a result of economic specialization and innovations in transport and communications technology. In this urbanized, industrial society there is contact with more people but close 'primary' relationships with family and friends are less easily sustained. At the same time, social differentiation brings about a divergence of life styles, values and aspirations, thus weakening social consensus and cohesion and threatening to disrupt social order. This, in turn, leads to attempts to adopt 'rational' approaches to social organization, a proliferation of formal controls and, where these are unsuccessful, to an increase in social disorganization and deviant behaviour.

The impact of these ideas on urban geography came chiefly by way of their adoption and modification by the various research orientations which sprang from the Department of Sociology in the University of Chicago under the leadership of R.E. Park, a former student of Georg Simmel. Park gave a timely impetus to the study of urban communities in the rapidly changing urban scene of Chicago in the early decades of the twentieth century. Like earlier theorists, he believed that urbanization produced new environments, new types of people and new ways of life which were manifested in 'a mosaic of little worlds which touch but do not interpenetrate' (Park 1916: 608). He encouraged the 'exploration' and empirical documentation of these social worlds by his colleagues and, as a result, there developed an influential series of 'natural histories' of the distinctive groups and areas of Chicago in the 1920s: juvenile gangs, hobos, the rooming house area, prostitutes, taxi-hall dancers, the Jewish ghetto, and so on (Short 1971; Theodorson 1961). These studies represented part of an approach to urban sociology which became known as *human ecology*, the nature of which is discussed below.

A closely related and equally influential approach to urban sociology also sprang from Chicago a few years later: the so-called Wirthian theory of urbanism as a way of life. Wirth's ideas, although they contained much of the thinking inherent to human ecology, synthesized a wide range of deterministic principles relevant to individual as well as group behaviour. Wirth, like Park, had studied under Georg Simmel and was heavily influenced by Simmel's work on 'The Metropolis and Mental Life' (1905). Putting Simmel's ideas together with subsequent work from the human ecologists, Wirth produced his classic essay, 'Urbanism as a way of life' (1938), which became one of the most often quoted and reprinted articles in the literature of the city. Wirth attributed the social and psychological consequences of city life (i.e. urbanism) to the combined effects of three factors which he saw as the products of increasing urbanization: (1) the increased size of populations; (2) the increased density of populations; and (3) the increased heterogeneity, or differentiation, of populations. At the *personal* level the effect of these factors, Wirth suggested, is as follows: faced with the abundant and varied physical and social stimuli experienced in the large, dense and highly diverse city environment, the individual has to adapt 'normal' behaviour in order to cope. City dwellers thus become, for example, aloof, brusque and impersonal in their dealings with others: emotionally buffered in their relationships. Nevertheless, the intense stimuli of city environments will sometimes generate what has subsequently been dubbed a 'psychic overload' (Milgram 1970), leading to anxiety and nervous strain. Furthermore, the loosening of personal bonds through this adaptive behaviour tends to leave people both *unsupported* in times of crisis and *unrestrained* in pursuing ego-centred behaviour. The net result, Wirth argues, is an increase in the incidence, on the one hand, of social incompetence, loneliness and mental illness and, on the other, of deviant behaviour of all kinds: from the charmingly eccentric to the dangerously criminal.

At the same time, Wirth draws a parallel picture of *social* change associated with the increased size, density and heterogeneity of urban populations. The specialized neighbourhoods and social groupings resulting from economic competition and the division of labour result in a fragmentation of social life between home, school, workplace, friends and relatives; and so people's time and attention are divided among unconnected people and places. This weakens the social support and control of primary social groups such as family, friends and neighbours, leading to a lack of social order and an increase in 'social disorganization'. Moreover, these trends are reinforced by the weakening of social norms (the rules and conventions of proper and permissible behaviour) resulting from the divergent interests and life-styles of the various specialized groups in the city. The overall societal response is to replace the support and controls formerly provided by primary social groups with 'rational' and impersonal procedures and institutions (welfare agencies, criminal codes supported by police forces, etc.). According to Wirth, however, such an order can never replace a communal order based on consensus and the moral strength of small primary groups. As a result, situations develop in which social norms are so muddled and weak that a social condition known as *anomie* develops: people, unclear or unhappy about norms, tend to challenge or ignore them, thus generating a further source of deviant behaviour. The influence of these ideas in urban sociology, environmental psychology and urban geography has been very great, even to the point of straitjacketing subsequent research orientations. Wirthian theory and its derivations recur throughout this chapter in discussions of social interaction, community studies, territoriality and the geography of deviant behaviour but, as will be shown, his determinism has by no means remained unchallenged.

Human ecology

Thanks largely to the impetus of the deterministic urban sociologists based in Chicago there is now a considerable literature relating specific geographical phenomena to their environmental context and which could collectively be classified under the general banner of ecological studies. In this section, however, attention is limited to the ecological studies associated with the early writings of the Chicago school: studies of 'human ecology'. This work is associated in particular with Park, together with E.W. Burgess and R.D. McKenzie, and is concerned, at the most general level, with the study of 'the spatial and sustenance relationships in which human beings are organized . . . in response to the operation of a complex of environmental and cultural forces' (McKenzie 1968: 19). The distinctive feature of the approach adopted by the human ecologists, however, is the conception of the city as a kind of social organism, with individual behaviour and social organization governed by a 'struggle for existence'. The biological analogy provided Park and his colleagues with an attractive general framework in which to place their studies of the 'natural histories' and 'social worlds' of different groups in Chicago. Just as in plant and animal communities, Park concluded, order in human communities must emerge through the operation of 'natural' processes such as dominance, segregation, impersonal competition and succession. If the analogy now seems somewhat naïve, it should be remembered that it was conceived at a time when the appeal of Social Darwinism and classical economic theory was strong. Moreover, ecological studies of plants and animals

provided a rich source of concepts and a graphic terminology with which to portray the sociology of the city.

One of the central concepts was that of *impersonal competition* between individuals for favourable locations within the city. This struggle was acted out primarily through market mechanisms, resulting in a characteristic pattern of land rents and the consequent *segregation* of different types of people according to their ability to meet the rents associated with different sites and situations. Economic differentiation was thus seen as the basic mechanism of residential segregation, and the local *dominance* of a particular group was ascribed to its relative competitive power. Functional relationships between different individuals and social groups were seen as *symbiotic* and, where such relationships could be identified as being focused within a particular geographical area, the human ecologists identified *communities*, or *natural areas*: 'territorial units whose distinctive characteristics – physical, economic and cultural – are the result of the unplanned operation of ecological and social processes' (Burgess 1964: 458). As the competitive power of different groups altered and the relative attractiveness of different locations changed in the course of time, these territories were seen to shift. Once more, ecological concepts were invoked to describe the process, this time using the ideas of *invasion* and *succession* derived from the study of plant communities.

These concepts were all brought together by Burgess in his model of residential differentiation and neighbourhood change in Chicago (Burgess 1925). Observations on the location and extent of specific communities formed the basis for the identification of an urban spatial structure consisting of a series of concentric zones (Fig. 3.1). These zones were seen by Burgess as reflections of the differential economic competitive power of broad groups within society, whereas the further segregation of smaller areas within each zone – such as the ghetto, Chinatown and Little Sicily within the zone of transition – were seen as reflections of symbiotic relationships forged on the basis of language, culture and race. The model was set out in terms of dynamic change as well as the spatial disposition of different groups. Zones I to V represent, in Burgess's words, 'both the successive zones of urban extension and the types of areas differentiated in the process of expansion' (Burgess 1924: 88). As the city grew, the changing occupancy of each zone was related to the process of invasion and succession, and Burgess was able to point to many examples of this in Chicago in the early 1900s as successive waves of immigrants worked their way from their initial quarters in the zone of transition (Zone II) to more salubrious

37

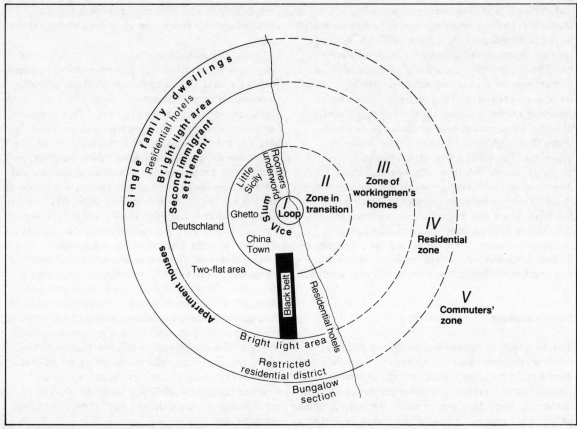

Fig. 3.1 Burgess's zonal model applied to Chicago.
Source: Park, Burgess and McKenzie (1925), p. 53.

neighbourhoods elsewhere. In his diagrammatic model, some of the early immigrant groups – the Germans are explicitly noted – have already 'made it' to the area of superior accommodation in Zone III and become the dominant group, replacing second-generation American families who had moved out to colonize the outer residential zone (Zone IV).

Within this broad framework a wide range of studies was produced by the 'school' of human ecologists. Berry and Kasarda (1977) suggest that their work can be classified into three types:

1. Studies focusing on the process of competition, dominance and succession and their consequences for the spatial distribution of populations and land use. Such work is best represented by the early writings of Park, Burgess and McKenzie described above.
2. Detailed descriptions of the physical features of 'natural' areas along with the social, economic and demographic characteristics of their inhabitants. Well-known examples of this type of work include Wirth's study of *The Ghetto* (1928) and Zorbaugh's

portrayal of Chicago's 'near' North Side in *The Gold Coast and the Slum* (Zorbaugh 1929). Zorbaugh's work provides a good example of the intimate portrayal of individual social worlds set in the framework of the broader ecological theory. The near North Side area was part of the zone in transition and contained four distinctive natural areas: the Gold Coast, a wealthy neighbourhood adjacent to the lakeshore; a rooming house area with a top-heavy demographic structure and a high population turnover; a bright-lights district – Towertown – with brothels, dance-halls and a 'bohemian' population; and a slum area containing clusters of immigrant groups. Zorbaugh showed how the personality of these different quarters related to their physical attributes – the 'habitat' they offered – as well as to the attributes and ways of life of their inhabitants. Moreover, he was also able to illustrate the dynamism of the area, charting the territorial shifts of different groups resulting from the process of invasion and succession.

3. Studies of the ecological context of specific social phenomena such as delinquency, prostitution, and

mental disorders. A central concern was the investigation of ecologies which seemed to generate high levels of deviant behaviour, and typical examples include the work by Shaw *et al.* on *Delinquency Areas* (1929) and Faris and Dunham's work on *Mental Disorders in Urban Areas* (1939). Much of this work had a clear 'geographical' flavour since it often involved mapping exercises. It also provided the stimulus for a number of the more recent studies discussed below in the section on 'Urban environments and deviant behaviour' (pp. 48–61).

Despite its far-reaching effects on the orientation of a great deal of subsequent work in urban sociology and urban geography, traditional human ecology has been abandoned in favour of a much-modified ecological approach based on the idea of identifying key social variables and examining their relationships within an 'ecosystem' or 'ecological complex'. This resurgence of ecological research took place after a long period of neglect during the 1940s and 1950s following a series of theoretical and empirical critiques, including those of Alihan (1938), Davie (1937), Gettys (1940) and Firey (1945). The most general criticism was directed towards the biological analogies. As Timms observes: 'At times the Chicago school seems to have been unduly dazzled by the brilliance of their biological analogies and to have ignored the substance with which they worked' (Timms 1976: 27). Moreover, such analogies had been brought into great disrepute by parallel concepts such as *Lebensraum*, which were given great emphasis by the *geopolitics* used to justify some of the territorial claims of Germany's Third Reich. Other criticims were more specific, centring on the excessive reliance on competition as the basis of social organization, the failure of its general structural concepts (such as the natural area and concentric zonation) to hold up under comparative examination, and its almost complete exclusion of cultural and motivational factors in explaining residential behaviour.

This last criticism was perhaps the most damaging of all. The first (and therefore best-known) critic of the Chicago school on the grounds that they overlooked the role of 'sentiment' and 'symbolism' in people's behaviour was Walter Firey, who pointed to the evidence of social patterns in Boston where, although there were 'vague concentric patterns', it was clear that the persistence of the status and social characteristics of distinctive neighbourhoods such as Beacon Hill, The Common and the Italian North End could be attributed in large part to the 'irrational' and 'sentimental' values attached to them by different sections of the population (Firey 1947). In short, social values could – and often did – over-ride impersonal, economic competition as the basis for socio-spatial organization. It is also worth noting here that Firey's work is of further significance in that it directed the attention of geographers and sociologists to the importance of the subjective world in the understanding of social patterns in cities: a theme which has only recently begun to be fully explored (see pp. 100–111).

In fairness to the Chicago school, it should be acknowledged that they themselves did not regard their ideas on human ecology as either comprehensive or universally applicable. Park, for instance, clearly distinguished two levels of social organization: the *biotic* and the *cultural* (Park 1936). The former, he argued, was governed by impersonal competition whereas the latter was shaped by the consensus of social values. These cultural aspects of social organization clearly encompass Firey's notions of sentiment and symbolism, and Park and his colleagues were well aware of their influence. Park believed, however, that it was possible to study the biotic level of social organization separately, treating social values and communications as a kind of superstructure of the more basic level of the community (Robson 1969). It is thus not so much the denial of non-biotic factors as the inadequacy of their treatment which led to the unpopularity of traditional human ecology.

Since the demise of traditional human ecology in the 1940s there have been several reformulations of the original ideas and concepts and, with the consequent excision of the crude mechanistic and biotic analogies, there has been a considerable revival of interest in ecological approaches. Wirth's synthesis of the effects of urban life on individual and social behaviour represented the first significant shift away from the biotic approach. Later, the concept of natural areas was reformulated by Hatt (1946), who emphasized that natural areas, defined as discrete territories containing a homogeneous population with distinctive social characteristics, could offer a useful framework for further social analysis. This is a strategy which has been adopted subsequently by social geographers in many avenues of investigation, even though the term 'natural area' has been abandoned in favour of less deterministic terminology such as 'social areas' or 'neighbourhood types'. Further important contributions to the refinement of the ecological approach were made by Hawley (1950) and Schnore (1965). Hawley presented the ecological approach as the study of the form and development of community structure, emphasizing the functional inter-dependence within communities that results from the collective adaptation competition. Schnore, building on Quinn's work (1939), was able to place human ecology in perspective by elaborating in detail

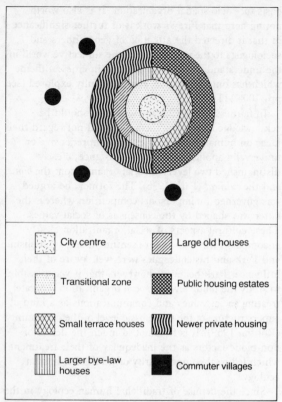

City centre

Transitional zone

Small terrace houses

Larger bye-law houses

Large old houses

Public housing estates

Newer private housing

Commuter villages

Fig. 3.2 Mann's model of a British industrial city.
Source: Mann (1965), p. 96.

the pre-conditions and assumptions implicit in the work of Burgess and others. Schnore's own preference, like Hawley and Duncan (Duncan and Schnore 1959) is for an approach in which the notion of ecology is used as a conceptual or statistical framework within which to analyse the internal structure of the city. Theodorson (1961) has classified these writers as 'neo-orthodox' ecologists and their work, modified sufficiently to avoid the worst shortcomings of traditional human ecology, has been an important link with much of the work on social patterns in cities carried out during the 1960s and 1970s. The re-emergence of ecological approaches during the 1960s is illustrated by Mann's (1965) adaption of Burgess's concentric zone model to the conditions prevailing in the industrial towns of northern England (Fig. 3.2); and Suttles's work (1968) on the Addams area of Chicago provides a good example of contemporary work which parallels the 'natural histories' of the human ecologists. Further examples of such work will be referred to throughout the remainder of this chapter; for a general review of the role of contemporary ecological studies in research on social and spatial organization, see Berry and Kasarda (1977).

Social interaction in urban environments

A quite different approach to the study of social organization in urban environments has developed from the pursuit of another of Georg Simmel's suggestions: that the essentials of social organization are to be found in the forms of interaction among individuals (Simmel 1905). As Irving has shown in a lengthy review of the subject (Irving 1978), empirical studies of social interaction really stem from the work of Arensberg, Chapple and Warner some decades later (Arensberg 1937; Chapple 1942; Warner and Lunt 1941; Warner and Srole 1945). This work has provided inspiration for a continuing stream of empirical social research of considerable interest to geographers, and provides a logical preface to the consideration of the more complex and elusive properties of neighbourhoods and communities.

At the most fundamental level, interactionist research seeks to establish the nature of non-random interaction patterns at the 'dyadic' or 'triadic' level: that is, between two or three individuals. A good deal of this research has involved the temporal and sequential characteristics of personal relationships, focusing on considerations of initiative, role and status (Irving 1978), but it is the qualities of the *nature* and *intensity* of interaction which hold most interest for geographers. It is common for the nature of interaction to be classified according to whether it takes place in the context of primary or secondary settings. *Primary* relationships include those between kinfolk – based on ties of blood and duty – and those between friends – based on ties of attraction and mutual interest. Beyond this distinction, the nature of primary relationships may be further qualified. For example, family relationships may be differentiated according to whether the setting is a 'nuclear' unit – husband, wife and offspring – or an 'extended' unit which includes members of more than two generations. Interaction between friends may be differentiated according to whether the friendship is based on age, culture, locality, and so on.

Secondary relationships are more purposive, involving individuals who group together to achieve particular ends. Such relationships are conveniently subdivided into those in which there is some intrinsic satisfaction in the interaction involved – known as 'expressive' interaction – and those in which the interaction is merely a means of achieving some common goal – 'instrumental' interaction. Both kinds are normally set within a broad group framework. Expressive interaction, for example, is typically facilitated by voluntary associations of various kinds: sports, hobby and social clubs, and 'do-gooding' associations. Instrumental interaction, on the other hand, normally takes place within the framework of business associations, political parties, trades unions and pressure groups. In addition, some writers would include interaction between members of ethnic, religious, and even cultural groups under the label of purposive secondary relationships. Jones and Eyles (1977), for example, argue that such relationships exist essentially to protect or advance the interests of individuals who are similarly placed on cultural, economic or political spectra.

Social distance and physical distance

This perspective illustrates the complexity of reality and the difficulty of pigeon-holing human behaviour. Moreover, the difficulties of conceptual and empirical classifications of different types of interaction are compounded by the fact that the propensity for, and intensity of, interaction of all kinds is strongly conditioned by the effects of distance: both *social distance* and *physical distance*. There is, however, some overlap in practice between these two concepts of distance; and a further level of complexity is introduced by the fact that patterns of interaction are not only affected by the physical and social structure of cities but that they themselves also have an effect on city structure. Unravelling the processes involved in this apparently indivisible chain of events is a central concern of urban social geography. Before proceeding to a consideration of more complex situations, however, some initial clarification of the role of social and physical distance is in order.

The idea of *social distance* has a long history, and is graphically illustrated by Bogardus's attempt (1926) to measure the perceived social distance between native-born white Americans and other racial, ethnic and linguistic groups. He suggested that social distance could be reflected by a ranked scale of social relationships which people would be willing to sanction: the further up the scale, the closer the perceived distance between people:

1. to admit to close kinship by marriage;
2. to have as a friend;
3. to have as a neighbour on the same street;
4. to admit as a member of one's occupation within one's country;
5. to admit as a citizen of one's country;
6. to admit only as a visitor to one's country;
7. to exclude entirely from one's country.

It is now generally accepted that the less social distance there is between individuals, the greater the probability of interaction of some kind. Similarly, the greater the physical proximity between people – their 'residential propinquity' – the more likelihood of interaction of some kind. The exact influence of social and physical distance depends to some extent on the nature of the interaction concerned, however. Instrumental interaction related to trades unions or political parties, for instance, will clearly be less dependent on physical distance than instrumental interaction which is focused on a local action group concerned with the closure of a school, the construction of a power station, or the organization of a Coronation or Jubilee party. In most cases, of course, the influences of social and physical distance are closely interwoven and difficult to isolate. Research has shown, for example, that voluntary associations tend to reflect class and lifestyle, with membership depending largely on social distance. Middle-class groups, in particular, have been shown to have a propensity to use voluntary associations as a means of establishing and sustaining social relationships. But, because of the close correspondence between social and residential segregation, membership of such associations is also strongly correlated with locational factors (Bottomore 1954; Stacey 1960; Willmott and Young 1960).

Geographers, of course, have a special interest in the role of distance, space and location. There is, however, no real consensus on the role of propinquity in stimulating or retarding social interaction. One well-known study which is often quoted in support of the importance of distance at the micro-scale is that conducted by Festinger, Schacter and Back on the friendship patterns within two housing projects, in which it was found that friendship patterns appeared to be governed by 'the mere physical arrangement of the houses' (Festinger, Schacter and Back 1950: 10). Their results, however, were based on a sample drawn from a very special case – the interaction between married engineering students studying at the Massachussetts Institute of Technology – and so the generality of their findings must remain in doubt. Indeed, subsequent studies have shown that the more diverse the inhabitants of housing projects, the less dominant the role of propinquity seems to be (Kuper 1953; Priest and Sawyer 1967). Some writers have suggested that propinquity is only of importance during the settling-down phase of a new housing development (Mowrer 1958; Simey 1954). Others, like Gans (1961; 1967) stress that social distance and a communality of values are always the major determinants of friendship patterns. This view has been reinforced by the writings of Melvin Webber and his followers who, while acknowledging the effects of propinquity, suggest that the constraints of distance are rapidly diminishing in the 'shrinking world' of modern technology and mass communications (Webber 1963; 1964). They argue that improvements in personal mobility, combined with the spatial separation of home, workplace and recreational opportunities, have released people from neighbourhood ties. Not everyone, of course, benefits from mobility to the same extent: some people are 'localites', with restricted 'urban realms'; others are 'cosmopolites', for whom distance is elastic and who inhabit a social world without finite geographical borders. This tendency towards an aspatial basis for social interaction has been seen by others as a result not so much of increased personal mobility as a product of modern city planning and social values. Ward, for example, in his book on *The Child in the City* (1978), argues that modern housing estates have 'annihilated' community spirit and replaced it with a parental authoritarianism which restricts the outdoor activities of children and so retards the development of locality-based friendships from the earliest years of a person's life.

Against such arguments must be set the work of writers such as Carey and Mapes (1972), Homans (1950; 1961), Mogey (1956) and Warren (1963), who point out that the residential neighbourhood must continue to provide much raw material for social life, especially for relatively immobile groups such as the poor, the aged, and mothers with young children. Even the more mobile must be susceptible to chance local encounters and the subsequent interaction which may follow; and most householders will establish some contact with neighbours from the purely functional point of view of mutual security. Moreover, the most telling argument in support of the role of propinquity, as Irving (1978) observes, is the way in which residential patterns – whether defined in terms of class, race, ethnicity, life-style, kinship, family status or age – have persistently exhibited a strong tendency towards spatial differentiation. In a pioneering study, Duncan and Duncan (1955b) showed that the residential segregation of occupational groups in Chicago closely paralleled their social distance and that the most segregated categories were those possessing the clearest rank, i.e. those at the top and the bottom of the socio-economic scale. Subsequent studies of socio-economic groups elsewhere (Fine, Glenn and Monts 1971; Laumann 1966; Tilly 1961) and of ethnic groups (Kantrowitz 1973; Tauber 1965; Timms 1969) and religious groups (Poole and Boal 1973) in a number of different cities have all reported a similar degree of residential segregation. Moreover, the indications are that residential differentiation is increasing, not decreasing as implied by Webber's argument.

There are several good reasons why segregation should persist within urban society. As Suttles (1968;

1972) has emphasized, the spatial segregation of different 'communities' helps to minimize conflict between social groups while facilitating a greater degree of social control and endowing specific social groups with a more cohesive political voice. Moreover, as Beshers (1962) noted, an important reason for the residential clustering of such groups is the desire of its members to preserve their own group identity or life-style. One of the basic mechanisms by which this segregation can be achieved is through group norms which support marriage within the group and oppose marriage between members of different social, religious, ethnic or racial groups. The organization of groups into different territories facilitates the operation of this mechanism by restricting the number of 'outside' contacts. Thus 'people marry their equals in social status; neighbours tend to be social equals; they marry their neighbours' (Ramsøy 1966: 783). But while Ramsøy was able, in her study of Oslo, to substantiate the correlation between distance and mate selection first observed in Philadelphia and New Haven by Abrams (1943) and Kennedy (1943), she was not able to tease out the causal relationships between distance, segregation and endogamy. She poses the question:

Is it the *workplace* which brings together men and women doing the same kind of work, is it the *family*, urging manipulating or encouraging its offspring to find a 'suitable', *i.e.* socially equal, mate, or is it the *neighbourhood*, putting into daily contact persons belonging to the same economic stratum (Ramsøy 1966: 779).

While this question has still not been answered satisfactorily, it should by now be clear that the debate as to whether physical or social distance is the more decisive factor in influencing patterns of social interaction is rather academic. As Irving observes, 'the two have become mutually reinforcing in a modern urban context' (Irving 1978: 268). In order to make further progress in understanding patterns of social interaction in cities we must now turn to a closer examination of their *structure* and go on to grasp the rather thorny issue of 'community'.

Social networks, neighbourhoods and communities

It will be clear by now that interpersonal relations extend well beyond a series of dyadic or triadic interactions of different kinds. Most people are involved in several different relationships which may be inter-connected to a greater or lesser extent. We not only have friends, but know friends-of-friends; and kinfolk do not exist in isolation: we may get to know a complete stranger because he or she is a member of the same club or organization as an uncle, an aunt, or a cousin. The way in which these social linkages are structured is often very complex and, *in toto*, they represent the foundations of social organization. Not surprisingly, therefore, the analysis of these linkages has attracted a good deal of attention. Most of the research associated with this approach – known as *social network analysis* – can be traced back to the work of Elizabeth Bott, which was in turn influenced by Barnes's (1954) study of social networks on a Norwegian island. Basically, social network analysis attempts to illustrate the structure of social interaction by treating persons as points and relationships as connecting lines (Granovetter 1976). The analysis of social networks thus allows the researcher to 'map out the complex reality of the interpersonal worlds surrounding specific individuals' (Smith 1978: 108), and has the advantage of not being confined, *a priori*, to any specific level of analysis such as the family or the neighbourhood. As with the analysis of other kinds of network – in transport geography (Taffe and Gauthier 1973) and physical geography (Haggett and Chorley 1969) – this approach facilitates not only the 'mapping' of the 'morphology' of networks (Fig. 3.3), but also the quantification of certain key characteristics such as their 'connectedness', 'centrality', 'proximity' and 'range' (Boissevain 1974; Roistacher 1974).

Any one person may belong to several different and non-overlapping social networks at the same time, and each of these networks may well have different properties: some may be spatially bounded while others are not; some may have dendritic structures while others are web-like, with interlocking ties, clusters, knots or sub-graphs. Bott's original formulation of types of social network was based on the notion of a continuum of networks ranging from *looseknit* (where

few members of the network know each other independently) to *closeknit* (where most members of the network know each other); but this, like the more sophisticated typologies developed by Mitchell and others (Mitchell 1969) presents practical difficulties in operationalizing a definition of linkage. Should it extend beyond kinship and friendship to acquaintance or 'knowledge of' another person, or what? And how is friendship, for instance, to be measured? In an attempt to minimize such confusion, Bell and Newby (1976) have proposed a typology of social situations which incorporate the notion of the complexity as well as the structure of social networks (Fig. 3.4). They illustrate the typology by way of the extreme and limiting cases: 'A' and 'B' in the diagram:

A is the traditional community as normally understood: social relationships are multiplex in that, for example, neighbours are workmates are kinsmen are leisure-time companions, and the social network has a dense structure in that everyone knows everyone else. B is the situation of idealized urban anonymous anomie: social relationships are uniplex (the taxidriver and his fare), fleeting, impersonal and anonymous, and the social network structure is single-stranded in that only one person knows the others (Bell and Newby 1976: 198–9).

This incorporation of the overlap and complexity of different networks brings us away from abstraction and a step nearer to reality. One person who has illustrated the practical relevance of network analysis is Christopher Smith, who has investigated the 'pro-social' behaviour of informal self-help networks which exist in modern cities (Smith 1978; Smith and Smith 1978). Smith suggests – in contrast to the postulates of Wirthian theory – that self-help networks emerge in cities in order to provide help in many different contexts, and that their existence prevents formal welfare agencies from being swamped.

In the mental health area, for example, help is being provided every hour of the day by people from all walks of life, including neighbours, relatives, ministers and shop-keepers. Dozens of helping hands and sympathetic ears are called on each day . . . Instead of going to an agency for help, many people prefer to search out someone in their own social network. It is quicker and cheaper; it is often more successful;

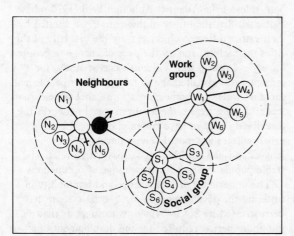

Fig. 3.3 The morphology of a husband's social network. *Source*: Smith and Smith (1978), p. 106.

Structure

Plexity	Dense	Looseknit	Single
Multiplex	A		
Simplex			
Uniplex			B

Fig. 3.4 A typology of social situations. *Source*: Bell and Newby (1976), p. 199.

and it is certainly less humiliating than going to a mental health centre (Smith and Smith 1978: 102).

The focus of these self-help networks is often the 'natural neighbour' (Collins and Pancoast 1976): a person with a propensity to become involved or make himself available in resolving the problems of other people, whether for self-aggrandizement, altruism, or some other motive. They are usually untrained amateurs who may not consciously recognize their own role in helping others. Indeed, they may not actually provide any direct help themselves but act as 'brokers', putting people in touch with someone who can help.

A major problem in illuminating the structure of these networks, like any others, is the difficulty of empirical social research which necessarily involves a great deal of fieldwork. Moreover, the study of social networks, although a step in the right direction, does not provide the geographer with a sufficiently holistic approach: there remain the fundamental questions of the extent to which social networks of various kinds are spatially defined, and at what scales: questions which have as yet received little attention (Wellman and Crump 1978; Wellman 1979). This brings us to a consideration of the ideas of 'neighbourhood' and 'community'. The concept of community is elusive. It has a long history in all of the disciplines concerned with individual or group behaviour and has generated a huge literature, much of which is plagued by circular argument and semantic ambiguities. These difficulties are more acute for the geographer, who must also pursue the question of whether 'community' can be synonymous with 'neighbourhood' or 'locality', and in what circumstances.

According to classic sociological theory, communities should not exist at all in cities; or, at best, only in a weakened form. This idea first entered sociological theory by way of the writings of Ferdinand Tonnies (1887), who argued that two basic forms of human association could be recognized in all cultural systems. The first of these, *Gemeinschaft*, he related to an earlier period in which the basic unit of organization was the family or kin-group, with social relationships characterized by depth, continuity, cohesion and fulfilment. The second, *Gesellschaft*, was seen as the product of urbanization and industrialization which resulted in social and economic relationships based on rationality, efficiency and contractual obligations amongst individuals whose roles had become specialized. This perspective was reinforced by the writings of sociologists such as Durkheim (1893), Simmel (1902), Sumner (1906) and, as we have seen, Wirth (1938), and has become part of the conventional wisdom about city life: it is not conducive to 'community', however it might be defined.

Urban villages and the mutuality of the oppressed

There is, however, a good deal of evidence to support the idea of socially cohesive communities in cities. Writers such as Jane Jacobs (1961) have portrayed the city as an inherently human place, where sociability and friendliness are a natural consequence of social organization at the neighbourhood level. Moreover, this view is sustained by empirical research in sociology and anthropology. Studies such as those by Liebow (1967) and Suttles (1968) have demonstrated the existence of distinctive social worlds which are territorially bounded and have a vitality which is focused on local 'institutions' such as taverns, pool halls and laundromats. Herbert Gans, following his study of the West End of Boston, suggested that we need not mourn the passing of the cohesive social networks and sense of self-identity associated with village life (Gans 1962), for he found that these properties existed within the inner city in a series of 'urban villages'. The focus of Gans's study was an ethnic village (the Italian quarter), but studies in other cities have described urban villages based on class rather than ethnicity. The most frequently cited example of an urban village of any kind is Young and Willmott's description of life in Bethnal Green, the residents of which have become something of a sociological stereotype. Young and Willmott found 'a *sense* of community . . . a feeling of solidarity between people who occupy the common territory' (Young and Willmott 1957: 89, emphasis added) which was based on a strong local network of kinship, reinforced by the localized patterns of employment, shopping and leisure activities.

A similar situation was described in Leeds by Hoggart (1958), in Swansea by Rosser and Harris (1965) and in a series of subsequent studies of inner city life on both sides of the Atlantic. Although Pahl (1970b) has cautioned that the utility of these studies is limited by their rather different objectives, by the diversity of the cities themselves, and by the pace of change in people's life styles (Young and Willmott's classic study, for example, was executed at a time when fewer people had cars and when the homogenizing influence of television was still quite weak), the localized social networks they describe do tend to have common origins. In short, urban villages are most likely to develop in long-established working-class areas with a relatively stable population and a narrow range of occupations.

The importance of permanence and immobility in fostering the development of local social systems has been stressed by Stacey (1969), who suggests that the minimum period required for the development of a distinctive locally-based social system is between 50 and 80 years, assuming the majority of the population to have been born and bred in the area; and most writers agree that the relative immobility of the working classes (in every sense: personal mobility, occupational mobility and residential mobility) is an important factor. Immobility results in a strengthening of *vertical* bonds of kinship and *horizontal* bonds of friendship. The high degree of residential propinquity between family members in working-class areas not only makes for a greater intensity of interaction between kinfolk but also facilitates the important role of the matriarch in reinforcing kinship bonds. As sociologists such as Young and Willmott (1957) and Klein (1965) stress, the matriarch plays a key role by providing practical support (e.g. looking after grandchildren, thus enabling a daughter or daughter-in-law to take a job) and by passing on attitudes, information, beliefs and norms of behaviour. Primary social interaction between friends is also reinforced by the residential propinquity which results from immobility. Relationships formed among a cohort of children at school are carried over into street life, courtship and, later on, the pursuit of social activities in pubs, clubs and bingo halls.

Another important factor in fostering the development of close-knit and overlapping social networks in working class areas is the economic division of society which leaves many people vulnerable to the cycle of poverty, as Jackson (1968) suggests in his *Working Class Community*. He argues that the shared and repeated experience of hard times, together with the cohesion and functional interdependence resulting from the tight criss-crossing of kinship and friendship networks, generates a mutuality of feeling and purpose in working-class areas: a mutuality which is the mainspring of the social institutions, ways of life and 'community spirit' associated with the urban village.

The fragility of communality

The cohesiveness and communality arising from immobility and economic deprivation is a fragile phenomenon, however. The mutuality of the urban village is underlain by stresses and tensions which follow from social intimacy and economic insecurity, and several studies of working-class neighbourhoods have described as much conflict and disorder as cohesion and communality. The one factor which has received most attention in this respect is the stress resulting from the simple shortage of space in working-class areas. High densities lead to noise problems, inadequate play space and inadequate drying facilities and are associated with personal stress and fatigue. Children, in particular, are likely to suffer from the psychological effects of the lack of privacy, as

Walter Greenwood observed so acutely in his *Love on the Dole*. Jackson notes that 'The only place which is private in the way that a professional worker's "study" might be, is the lavatory . . . The lavatory is the place where the man studies his wage chit, or the woman a new and daring purchase' (Jackson 1968: 157). Where even the lavatory must be shared with other households privacy is still further eroded, and stress or conflict is even more likely. As Coates and Silburn drily observe: 'In St. Ann's, sharing an outdoor lavatory, as did many of our respondents, may be conducive to heightened social contact, but not always in an entirely happy way' (Coates and Silburn 1970: 94). The fragility of working-class communality also stems from other sources. Coates and Silburn, for example, identified three other stressors in the St Ann's area of Nottingham. The first was the conflict of values which arose from the juxtaposition of people from a variety of ethnic and cultural backgrounds, notwithstanding their common economic experiences. The second was the disruption of social relationships arising as one cohort of inhabitants aged, died and was replaced by younger families, who, even though they were essentially of the same class and life-style, represented an unwitting intrusion on the quieter lives of older folk. Finally, they noted the disruption associated with the presence of undesirable elements – 'problem families', transients and prostitutes – in the midst of an area of respectable families. It seems likely that the relative strength of these stressors may be the crucial factor in tipping the balance between an inner-city neighbourhood of the 'urban village' type and one characterized by the anomie and social disorganization postulated by Wirthian theory.

Suburban neighbourhoods

In contrast to the close-knit social networks of the urban village, suburban life is seen by many observers as the antithesis of 'community'. Lewis Mumford, for example, wrote that the suburbs represent 'a collective attempt to lead a private life' (Mumford 1940: 215), and this view was generally endorsed by a number of early studies of suburban life, including the Lynds' (1956) study of Muncie, Indiana, and Warner's study of 'Yankee City' (New Haven) (Warner and Lunt 1941, 1942; Warner and Srole 1945). Further sociological work such as Whyte's *The Organization Man* (1956) and Stein's *The Eclipse of Community* (1960) reinforced the image of the suburbs as an area of loose-knit, secondary ties where lifestyles were focused squarely on the nuclear family's pursuit of money, status and consumer durables and the privacy in which to enjoy them.

Subsequent investigation, however, has shown the need to revise the 'suburban myth' of 'non-community' (Berger 1960; Donaldson 1969). Although there is little evidence for the existence of suburban villages comparable to the urban villages of inner-city areas (Connell 1973), it is evident that many suburban neighbourhoods do contain localized social networks with a considerable degree of cohesion as Gans showed, for example, in his study of Levittown (Gans 1967). Indeed, it is now suggested by some that the social networks of suburban residents are in fact more localized and cohesive than those of inner-city residents, even if they lack something in *feelings* of mutuality (Fischer 1976).

Fischer, like others, points to the high levels of 'neighbouring' in American suburbs and suggests that this may be due to one or more of a number of factors:

1. that the detached house is conducive to local social life;
2. that the suburbs tend to be more homogeneous, socially and demographically, than other areas;
3. that there is a 'pioneer eagerness' to make friends in new suburban developments;
4. that suburban residents are a self-selected group having the same preferences for social and leisure activities;
5. that physical distance from other social contacts forces people to settle for local contacts.

The cohesiveness of suburban communities is further reinforced by social networks related to voluntary associations of various kinds. Americans, as de Tocqueville (1946) observed, have a pronounced habit of joining, of organizing social contacts around some cause or activity, and this is especially true of middle-class suburbanites. Furthermore, it appears from the evidence at hand that suburban relationships are neither more nor less superficial than those found in central city areas (Baldassare and Fischer 1975; Fischer and Jackson 1976).

Nevertheless, there are some groups for whom suburban living does result in an attenuation of social contact. Members of minority groups of all kinds and people with slightly atypical values or life-styles will not easily be able to find friends or to pursue their own interests in the suburbs (Gans 1967; Tomeh 1964). This often results in such people having to travel long distances to maintain social relationships. Those who cannot or will not travel must suffer a degree of social isolation as part of the price of suburban residence. The elderly provide a case in point; a study of the elderly in San Antonio, Texas, found that the further out they lived, the fewer friends they reported, the less active they were socially, and the lonelier they were (Carp

1975). Moreover, it should also be acknowledged that the nature and intensity of social interaction in suburban neighbourhoods tends to vary according to the *type* of suburb concerned. Muller (1976a) argues that American suburbs have become differentiated as a result of two complementary trends. The first of these is the general reorganization of 'cultural space' around different lifestyles related variously to careerist orientations, family orientations, 'ecological' orientations, etc., and constrained by income and life cycle characteristics (see, for example, Feldman and Thielbar 1975). The second is the increasing tendency for people to want to withdraw into a 'territorially defended enclave' inhabited by like-minded people, in an attempt to find refuge from potentially antagonistic rival groups. The net result of the two trends is the emergence of distinctive 'voluntary regions' in the suburbs (see also Zelinsky 1975), a process which has been reinforced by the proliferation of suburban housing types which now extend from the 'normal' detached single-family dwelling to include specialist condominium apartments, 'townhouse' developments and exclusive retirement communities. Following Berry (1973) and Suttles (1975), Muller recognizes four major types of suburban neighbourhood, each with a rather different pattern of social interaction.

1. *Exclusive upper income suburbs*: These neighbourhoods are typically situated in the outermost parts of the city and consist of large detached houses built in extensive grounds, screened off by trees and shrubbery. This makes casual neighbouring rather difficult, and so local social networks tend to be based more on voluntary associations such as churches and country clubs.

2. *Middle-class family suburbs*: The dominant form of the middle-class American suburb is the detached single-family dwelling, and the dominant pattern of social interaction is based on the nuclear family. As in the more exclusive suburbs, socializing with relatives is infrequent, and emphasis on family privacy tends to inhibit neighbouring. Since the care of children is a central concern, much social contact occurs through family-orientated organizations such as the PTA, the Scouts, and organized sports; and the social cohesion of the neighbourhood derives to a large extent from the overlap of the social networks resulting from these organizations. However, with the tendency for young people to defer marriage, for young couples to defer child rearing, and for land and building costs to escalate, there has recently emerged a quite different type of middle-class suburb based on apartment living. Social interaction in these neighbourhoods tends to be less influenced by local ties, conforming more to Webber's (1963) idea of an aspatial community of interest.

3. *Suburban cosmopolitan centres*: This apparently contradictory label is given to the small but rapidly increasing number of suburban neighbourhoods which serve as voluntary residential enclaves for 'professionals, intellectuals, students, artists, writers and mutually tolerated misfits' (Muller

1976a: 17): people with broad rather than local horizons, but whose special interests and lifestyle nevertheless generate a cohesive community through a series of overlapping social networks based on cultural activities and voluntary organizations such as bridge clubs, theatre groups and meditation classes. These neighbourhoods are very much a contemporary phenomenon, and are chiefly associated with suburbs adjacent to large universities and colleges.

4. *Working-class suburbs*: Blue-collar suburban neighbourhoods have multiplied greatly in number since the 1940s to the point where they are almost as common as middle-class family suburbs in many American cities. But although these neighbourhoods are also dominated by single-family dwellings, patterns of social interaction are quite different. An intensive use of communal outdoor space makes for a high level of primary local social interaction, and community cohesion is reinforced by a 'person-orientated' rather than a material- or status-orientated lifestyle. Moreover, the tendency for blue-collar workers to be geographically less mobile means that people's homes are more often seen as a place of permanent settlement, with the result that people are more willing to establish local ties (Berger 1971).

European suburban neighbourhoods do not conform particularly well to this typology, largely because of the greater economic constraints on the elaboration of different lifestyles. Exclusive upper income suburbs are sustained by fewer cities; and there are very few examples to be found of the 'suburban cosmopolitan centre'. Moreover, the magnitude of the public housing sector in many European countries means that a large proportion of the suburbs are publicly-owned working-class neighbourhoods: altogether different to the North American suburban working-class neighbourhood. In Britain, suburban council estates have been the focus of a great deal of sociological research, much of which was originally motivated by a concern for the effects on the extended family system and old locality-based social networks which were expected to result from the suburbanization of working-class families. This approach dovetailed nicely with the idea of *embourgeoisment* (Merton 1957; Parsons 1951), which held that increased affluence among the working classes results in conformity with the traditional norms and patterns of social interaction of the middle classes. It was thus expected that the suburbanization of relatively affluent working-class families would result in a loosening of social networks of all kinds. The credibility of the *embourgeoisment* thesis has been much weakened, however, by a series of studies of the 'affluent worker' and working-class suburbs which have shown that, despite a greater relative affluence than before and despite suburban living, there is little evidence that working-class households are adopting middle-class ways of life (Goldthorpe *et al*. 1967, 1968). On the other hand, it is

clear that resettling working-class families in suburban estates does result in some disruption of primary social ties with the result that, for a time at least, social cohesion is reduced (Goldthorpe *et al*. 1967, 1968; Willmott and Young 1960). An important contributory factor is this respect is the aloofness generated by status uncertainty as the result of movement to a new and socially unknown environment (see, for example, Willmott and Young 1960). This, together with the reduction in the frequency of contact with kinfolk, leads to the development of a more home-centred way of life, so that many suburban public housing estates are characterized by low levels of neighbouring and a lack of social participation in organized activities in clubs and societies. Not every household is equally affected by status uncertainty and home-centredness, however; and not every household is of the same socio-economic status. There often emerges, therefore, a social polarization within council estates between the 'roughs' and the 'respectables'; and it is often the relationship between these two groups which determines the nature of social networks within the community. In a study of a Liverpool estate, for example, the 'rough' group dominated the area's organized social activities while the 'respectable' group withdrew from this kind of interaction (Lupton and Mitchell 1954). In a study of Watling, the position was reversed (Durant 1959).

Status panic and crisis communality

One thing which suburban neighbourhoods everywhere seem to have in common is a lack of the mutuality, the permanent but intangible 'community spirit' that is characteristic of the urban village. An obvious explanation for this is the newness of most suburban communities: they have not had time to fully develop a locality-based social system (Stacey 1969). An equally likely explanation, however, is that the residents of suburban neighbourhoods are simply not likely to develop a sense of mutuality in the same way as urban villagers because they are not exposed to the same levels of deprivation or stress. This reasoning is borne out to a certain extent by the 'crisis communality' exhibited in suburban neighbourhoods at times when there is an unusually strong threat to territorial exclusivity, amenities, or property values. Examples of the communality generated in the wake of status panic are well documented, and the best-known is probably the case of the Cutteslowe walls (Collinson 1963). In 1932 Oxford City Council set up a housing estate on a suburban site to the north of the city and direc[tly] adjacent to a private middle-class estate. Th[e] owners, united by their fear of a drop bot[h] of their neighbourhood and in the value of their property and drawn together by their mutual desire to maintain the social distance between themselves and their new proletarian neighbours, went to the length of building an unscaleable wall as a barrier between the two estates. More recent examples have tended to be related to the threat posed by urban motorways, airports, or the zoning of land for business use (Molotch 1972; Wolf and Lebeaux 1969), although in North America public housing is still sufficiently controversial to generate crisis communality among middle-class suburbanites.

Communities and neighbourhoods: definitions and classifications

Whatever the stimulus, however, suburban communality rarely seems to survive the resolution – one way or another – of the central issue. This raises once more the problem of defining communities. As we have seen, the nature and cohesiveness of social networks vary a lot from one set of socio-spatial circumstances to another, and it is not easy to say which situations, if any, reflect the existence of 'community', let alone which of these are also congruent with a discrete geographical territory. Twenty-five years ago Hillery (1955) unearthed over 90 definitions of 'community' in the social sciences, but found that the nearest he could get to common agreement was the presence, in most definitions, of some reference to: (1) area; (2) common ties; and (3) social interaction.

Since Hillery's survey there have been numerous attempts to resolve the problem (see, for example, Bell and Newby 1971; Scherer 1973) and, although there is still no real consensus, it is increasingly clear that both 'community' and 'neighbourhood' should be regarded simply as general terms for a cluster of inter-related situations relating to specific aspects of social organization. Blowers (1973) has offered a typology of neighbourhoods which reflects this approach. He postulates a continuum of neighbourhoods, the extremes of which are determined by the extent of social interaction and common ties. At one end of the ....ourhoods: general localities ......cise limits; *physical* ......environments with clear ......bourhoods are distinctive ......terms of both environ- ......stics; *functional neighbour-* ......cular activity patterns – ......ple; and, finally, ...hose which contain ......rimary social interaction.

Bell and Newby (1976) also recognize the multidimensional nature of local social organization. They suggest that it is useful to think in terms of a loose hierarchial relationship between neighbourhood, community and communality. Thus *neighbourhoods* are territories containing people of broadly similar demographic, economic and social characteristics, but are not necessarily significant as a basis for social interaction. *Communities* exist where a degree of social coherence develops on the basis of interdependence, which in turn produces a uniformity of custom, taste and modes of thought and speech. Communities are 'taken-for-granted' worlds defined by reference groups which may be locality-based, school-based, work-based or media-based. *Communality*, or 'communion', exists as a form of human association based on affective bonds. It is 'community experience at the level of consciousness' (Bell and Newby 1976: 197), but it requires an intense mutual involvement that is difficult to sustain and so only appears under conditions of stress.

Urban environments and deviant behaviour

In addition to the variations in social organization which occur among different social groups in different parts of the city, geographers have for a long time been interested in variations in the occurrence of unconventional or deviant behaviour within cities. The notion of deviance covers a multitude of social sins, but geographers have been most interested in behaviour with a distinctive pattern of intra-urban variation, such as prostitution, suicide, truancy, delinquency and drug addiction. In fact, most aspects of deviant behaviour seem to exhibit a definite spatial pattern of some sort, rather than being randomly distributed across the city. But, whereas there is little disagreement about the nature of the patterns themselves, theory and research in geography, sociology and environmental psychology are less conclusive about explanations of the patterns. Some writers, for instance, see deviant behaviour as a pathological response to a particular social and/or physical environment. Others argue that certain physical or social attributes act as environmental cues for certain kinds of behaviour; others still that certain environments simply attract certain kinds of people. Until very recently, almost all the theorizing about spatial variations in deviant behaviour shared a common element of environmental determinism, usually traceable to the determinists of the Chicago school. In this section the more influential aspects of this theory are outlined before going on to examine briefly the intra-urban geography of one kind of deviant behaviour – crime and delinquency – as an illustration of the

47

complexity of the actual relationships between urban environments and human behaviour.

Determinist theory

There is no need to reiterate at length the relationships between urban environments and deviant behaviour postulated by adherents to Wirthian theory (see pp. 36–37). The general position is that deviant behaviour is a product either of adaptive behaviour or maladjustment to city life, or to life in certain parts of the city. Thus the aloofness and impersonality which are developed in response to the competing stimuli and conflicting demands of different social situations are felt to lead to a breakdown of interpersonal relationships and social order and to an increase in social isolation, which in turn facilitates the emergence of ego-centred unconventional behaviour and precipitates various kinds of deviant behaviour.

Evidence to support these tenets of determinist theory has been assembled on several fronts. The idea of psychological overload resulting from complex or unfamiliar environments has been investigated by environmental psychologists and popularized by Toffler (1970), who suggests that the need to 'scoop up and process' additional information in such situations can lead to 'future-shock': the human response to overstimulation. The nature of this response has been shown by psychologists to take several forms: 'Dernier's strategy', for example, involves the elimination from perception of unwelcome reality, and in an extreme form can result in the construction of a mythological world which becomes a substitute for the real world (Smith 1977) and in which deviant behaviour may be seen by the person concerned as 'normal'. Another response is for people to 'manage' several distinct roles or identities at once (Goffman 1959, 1971). According to determinist theory, this is characteristic of urban environments because of the physical and functional separation of the 'audiences' to which different roles are addressed: family, neighbours, co-workers, club members, and so on. Thus, people tend to be able to present very different 'selves' in different social contexts. Again, the extreme form of this behaviour may lead to deviancy. The city, with its wide choice of different roles and identities becomes a 'magic theatre', and 'emporium of styles' (Raban 1975), and the anonymity afforded by the ease of slipping from one role to another clearly facilitates the emergence of unconventional and deviant behaviour. Moreover, as Berger *et al.* (1973) and Goffman (1971) have pointed out, further deviancy or pathology may result from the strain of having to sustain different

and perhaps conflicting identities over a prolonged period.

Most interest, however, has centred on the impersonality and aloofness which apparently results from the psychological overload associated with certain urban environments. Milgram (1970) has illustrated various manifestations of this impersonality, the most striking of which is the collective paralysis of social responsibility which seems to occur in central city areas in crisis situations. Milgram cites the well-known example of the murder of Catherine Genovese in illustrating this phenomenon. Ms Genovese was stabbed to death in a respectable district of Queens in New York, and her murder was evidently witnessed by nearly 40 people, none of whom attempted even to call the police. Other evidence of the lack of 'bystander intervention' and of an unwillingness to assist strangers comes from experiments contrived by psychologists (see, for example, Berkowitz and McCauly 1972; Korte and Kerr 1975; Latane and Darley 1969). Such asocial behaviour is itself deviant to some extent, of course; but its significance to determinist theory lies in the way in which it fosters the spread of more serious forms of deviancy by eroding social responsibility and social control.

The net result of these various forms of adaptive behaviour is thus a weakening of personal supports and social constraints and a confusion of behavioural norms. This, in turn, gives a further general impetus to deviant behaviour. Feelings of isolation among the 'lonely crowd' are associated with neurosis, alcoholism and suicide (Riesman 1950); and the anomic state induced by the weakening of behavioural norms is associated with various forms of crime and delinquency. Academic opinion, however, is by no means unanimous as to the utility of determinist theory in explaining patterns of deviant behaviour. It is difficult to establish either proof or refutation of the connections between stress, adaptive behaviour, social isolation, social disorganization, anomie and deviancy because of the difficulty of controlling for the many intervening variables such as age, class, education and personality. Nevertheless, many investigations of intra-urban variations in deviant behaviour have found it useful to invoke determinist theory in at least partial explanation of the patterns encountered (see, for example, Mintz and Schwartz (1964) on mental illness, Maris (1969) on suicide, and Castle and Gittus (1957) on 'social defects'). To the extent that determinist theory is founded on the effects of urbanism on human behaviour, the inference must be that some parts of the city are more 'urban' (in the Wirthian sense) than others, with more social disorganization, a greater incidence of anomie and, consequently, a higher incidence of deviant behaviour.

Crowding theory

There is now a considerable literature linking high residential densities, irrespective of other characteristics or urbanism, with a wide range of deviant behaviour. High densities and a sense of crowding, it is argued, create strains and tensions which modify behaviour, inducing aggression, withdrawal or, if these strategies are unsuccessful, mental or physical illness. The initial link between crowding and stress is attributed by many to an innate sense of *territoriality*. This idea has been popularized by ethologists such as Ardrey (1966, 1970) and Morris (1967) who believe that humans, like many other animals, are subject to a genetic trait which is produced by the species' need for territory as a source of safety, security and privacy. According to Ardrey (1966), territoriality also satisfies the need for stimulation (provided by 'border disputes') and for a physical expression of personal identity. These needs are believed to add up to a strong 'territorial imperative': a natural component of behaviour which will clearly be disrupted by crowding.

The whole approach draws heavily on behavioural research with animals, where the links between crowding, stress and abnormal behaviour can be clearly established under laboratory conditions (Esser 1971). Calhoun, for example, in his celebrated studies of rat behaviour, showed that crowding led to aggression, listlessness, promiscuity, homosexuality, and the rodent equivalent of juvenile delinquency (Calhoun 1962). Projecting these ideas directly to human behaviour leads to the idea of crowded urbanites as 'killer apes'. One sociologist, for example, writes that 'We have caged ourselves in zoos of our own creation; and like caged animals we have developed pathological forms of behaviour' (van den Berghe 1974: 787.) Critics of crowding theory have emphasized the obvious dangers involved in extending animal behaviour to humans: people are not rats; it is by no means certain that humans possess any innate sense of territoriality; and in any case even the most crowded slums do not approach the levels of crowding to which experimental animals have been subjected (Freedman 1975; Reiser 1973). It is difficult, however, to establish conclusively whether or not there is any connection among humans between territoriality, crowding and deviant behaviour. Territoriality may exist in humans through cultural acquisition even if it is not an innate instinct for, as Edney (1976) has pointed out, territoriality in the form of property rights does provide society with a means of distinguishing social rank and of regulating social interaction. Moreover, there is a considerable body of evidence to support the idea of territorial behaviour in urban man, whatever the source of this behaviour may

be. Lee Rainwater, for example, has illustrated the function of individuals' home territory as a haven (Rainwater 1966), while Clare Cooper has speculated on the role of the home as an expression of identity (Cooper 1976). Others have demonstrated the existence of what seems to amount to a territorial imperative at the societal level. The simplest example of this is the existence of gang 'turfs' which are rigorously and ceremonially defended by gang members (Patrick 1973; Yablonsky 1970). More complex and sophisticated social groups also seem to exhibit territorial behaviour. Suttles, for example, has documented the 'foreign relations' of different social groups occupying 'defended neighbourhoods' in American inner-city areas (Suttles 1968, 1972); and Boal has illustrated the extreme territoriality that exists in the area around the Shankhill/Falls divide in Belfast, where aggression between members of rival Catholic and Protestant communities has resulted in complete segregation (Boal 1978).

Accepting that humans do acquire some form of territoriality, it does seem plausible that crowding could induce stress and so precipitate a certain amount of deviant behaviour. The evidence, however, is ambiguous. Some studies report a clear association between crowding and social and physical pathology (Carstairs 1969; Sharrod and Downs 1974); others report contradictory findings (Baldassare and Fischer 1976; Cassel 1972), and the whole debate continues to attract controversy in all of the social and environmental disciplines (see, for example, Baum and Epstein 1979; Booth 1976; Boots 1979; Choldin 1978; Gad 1973; Kirmeyer 1978; McCarthy and Saegert 1978; Schmitt *et al*. 1978).

Design determinism

In addition to the general debate on crowding theory, a growing amount of attention has been directed towards the negative effects of architecture and urban design on people's behaviour (Kaplan and Kaplan 1978; Mercer 1975; Rapoport 1977). In broad terms the suggestion is that the design and configuration of buildings and spaces sometimes creates micro-environments which discourage 'normal' patterns of social interaction and encourage deviant behaviour of various kinds. A considerable amount of evidence has been accumulated in support of this idea. The inhibiting effects of high-rise and deck-access apartment dwellings on social interaction and child development, for example, have been documented in a number of different studies (Jephcott 1971; Newson and Newson 1965; Rainwater 1966; Yancey 1971); and from these it is a short step to studies which point to the correlation between certain aspects of urban design and the incidence of particular aspects of deviancy such as mental illness and suicide (Wing 1974).

The nature of these relationships is not entirely clear. One interesting proposition has recently been put forward by Peter Smith (1977), who suggests that the configuration of buildings and spaces creates a 'syntax' of images and symbolism to which people respond through a synthesis of 'gut reactions' and intellectual reactions. Environments which are dominated by an unfamiliar or illogical visual language are thus likely to appear threatening or confusing: qualities which may well precipitate certain aspects of malaise or deviant behaviour. This, however, is a comparatively new notion, and requires more empirical investigation before its utility can be confirmed. A better-known and more thoroughly examined link between urban design and deviant behaviour is Oscar Newman's concept of 'defensible space'. Newman (1972) suggested that much of the petty crime, vandalism, mugging and burglary in moden housing developments is related to an attenuation of community life and a withdrawal of local social controls caused by the inability of residents to identify with, or exert any control over, the space beyond their own front door. This, he argued, was a result of the 'designing out' of territorial definition and delineation in new housing developments, in accordance with popular taste among architects. Once the space immediately outside the dwelling becomes public, Newman suggested, nobody will feel obliged to 'supervise' it or 'defend' it against intruders. Newman's ideas have been confirmed by empirical work (see, for example, Mawby 1977; Tata *et al*. 1975) and enthusiastically received in the professions concerned with urban design, where they have created a new conventional wisdom of their own: defensible space is now an essential component in the praxis of urban design. Useful as the idea of defensible space is, however, its relevance is clearly restricted to a fairly narrow range of deviant behaviour.

Alienation

The concept of alienation is a central construct of Marxian theory, where it is seen as a mechanism of social change contributing towards the antithesis of the dominant mode of production. It also has wider socio-political connotations, however, with some relevance to the explanation of deviant behaviour (Fischer 1973; Schacht 1971; Seeman 1971). In its wider sense, alienation is characterized by feelings of powerlessness, dissatisfaction, distrust, and a rejection

of the prevailing distribution of wealth and power. These feelings usually stem from people's experience of some aspect of the social, political or economic system. Some people may be alienated because they feel the structure of these systems prevents their effective participation; others may be alienated because they disagree with the very nature of the systems – perhaps because of their ineffectiveness in satisfying human needs (Olsen 1968). Whatever the source, such feelings are clearly experience-based and therefore spatially focused, to a certain extent, on people's area of residence. This makes alienation an attractive explanatory factor when considering spatial variations in people's behaviour, as the early deterministic theorists were quick to note (Park 1916; Wirth 1938). The major interest in this respect has been the relationship between alienation and political behaviour, but it has also been suggested that certain aspects of deviant behaviour may be related to feelings of alienation (Philliber 1977; Schacht 1971). Such behaviour may be manifested in apathy: mildly unconventional in itself but more significant if it is prevalent enough to erode social order. Alternatively, alienation may precipitate deviance directly through some form of activism – which can range from eccentric forms of protest to violence and terrorism.

Compositional theory

Compositional theory is the product of another school of thought which has developed out of the writings of the Chicago determinists. Compositionalists emphasize the cohesion and intimacy of distinctive social worlds based on ethnicity, kinship, neighbourhood, occupation, or lifestyle, rejecting the idea that these social networks are in any way diminished by urban life (Gans 1962, 1967; Lewis 1952; Reiss 1955). They also minimize the psychological effects of city life on people's behaviour, suggesting, instead, that behaviour is determined largely by economic status, cultural characteristics, family status, and so on: the same attributes that determine which social worlds they live in.

Compositional theory is not framed explicitly to analyse deviant behaviour, but it does offer a distinctive perspective on the question. Deviancy, like other forms of behaviour, is seen as a product of the composition of local populations, with the social mores, political attitudes and cultural traits of certain groups being more productive of unconventional or deviant behaviour than others. The pattern of sexually transmitted disease in London serves to illustrate this compositionalist perspective. The incidence of this particular manifestation of deviant behaviour has a very marked peak in the bed-sitter land of West-Central London, especially around Earls Court. The explanation, in compositionalist terms, is the high proportion of young transients in the area – mostly young single people living in furnished rooms – whose sexual mores are different from those of the rest of the population and whose vulnerability to VD and other sexually transmitted diseases is increased by the presence of a significant proportion of young males who have themselves been infected before arriving in London. According to London's urban folklore, much of the blame in this respect is attached to Australians who arrive in London having visited Bangkok (Phillips 1977).

Subcultural theory

Subcultural theory is closely related to compositional theory. Like the latter, subcultural theory subscribes to the idea of social worlds with distinctive socio-demographic characteristics and distinctive lifestyles which propagate certain forms of behaviour. In addition, however, subcultural theory holds that these social worlds, or subcultures, will be *intensified* by the conflict and competition of urban life; and that *new* subcultures will be spawned as specialized groups generated by the arrival of immigrants and by the structural differentiation resulting from industrialization and urbanization reach the 'critical mass' required to sustain cohesive social networks (Fischer 1975). Fischer suggests that 'Among the subcultures spawned or intensified by urbanism are those which are considered to be either downright deviant by the larger society – such as delinquents, professional criminals, and homosexuals; or to be at least 'odd' – such as artists, missionaries of new religious sects, and intellectuals; or to be breakers of tradition – such as life-style experimenters, radicals and scientists' (Fischer 1976: 38). What is seen as deviancy by the larger society, however, is seen by the members of these subcultural groups as a normal form of activity and part of the group's internal social system.

Subcultural theory does not in itself carry any explicitly spatial connotations but, as Karp *et al*. point out, the continued existence of subcultural groups depends to a large extent on avoiding conflict with other groups. Conflict may be avoided, they suggest, by implicit *behavioural* boundaries beyond which groups 'promise' not to trespass: a kind of social contract; but the most effective means of maintaining inter-group tolerance is through *spatial* segregation (Karp, Stone and Yoels 1977). This idea makes subcultural theory attractive in explaining spatial variations in deviant

behaviour. It has proved useful, for example, in studies of delinquent behaviour (Cohen 1955; Herbert 1976b; Mays 1963; Phillipson 1971).

Subcultural theory also fits in conveniently with the idea of *cultural transmission*, whereby deviant norms are passed from one generation to another within a local environment. This process was identified over 100 years ago by Mayhew (1862) in the 'rookeries' of London, where children were 'born and bred' to the business of crime; and it was given prominence by Shaw and McKay (1942) in their study of delinquency in Chicago. Another concept relevant to the understanding of deviant behaviour within a localized subculture is the so-called *neighbourhood effect*, whereby people tend to conform to what they perceive as local norms in order to gain the respect of their local peer group. Empirical evidence for this phenomenon has been presented in a number of studies. One well-known example comes from Brian Robson's study of attitudes towards education in different parts of Sunderland, where 'No matter what the area, the attitudes of individual families were more familiar to those prevailing around them to those of their objective social class' (Robson 1969: 244). People's behaviour also seems directly susceptible to a neighbourhood effect: Hoivik, for example, suggests that the paradoxical syndrome of 'suburban poverty' in new owner-occupier estates is largely a product of neighbourhood effects which serve to impose middle-class consumption patterns on incoming families, many of whom have incomes which are really insufficient to 'keep up with the Jones's' but who nevertheless feel obliged to conform with their neighbours' habits (Hoivik 1973; see also Tallman and Morgner 1970). A similar process has been observed in relation to voting behaviour by Johnston (1974), and it seems likely that many deviant attitudes and deviant forms of behaviour will also be subject to a neighbourhood effect, although few studies have investigated the idea in this context. Important exceptions include the investigations of crime and delinquency in British cities by Baldwin, Bottoms and Walker (1976) and Herbert (1976b) which are discussed in more detail below.

Multi-factor explanations: the example of crime and delinquency

The difficulty of reconciling the apparently conflicting evidence relating to these different theories has, inevitably, led to a more flexible approach in which multi-factor explanations of deviant behaviour are admitted without being attached to a specific theoretical perspective. This, as Herbert (1976a) observes, is common to all branches of social deviance research, although it is probably best illustrated in relation to crime and delinquency. Empirical studies of spatial variations in crime and delinquency have lent support, variously, to theories of crowding, social disorganization, anomie, design determinism and deviant subcultures; but, as West (1967) points out, it is difficult to assemble evidence in support of any one theory in preference to the rest. In the absence of any alternative all-embracing theoretical perspective, an eclectic multi-factor approach thus becomes an attractive framework of explanation.

The evidence which can be drawn from studies of spatial variations in crime and delinquency is, like much social geographical research, subject to important qualifications relating to the nature of the data and methods of research which have been employed. It is, therefore, worth noting the more important difficulties and pitfalls involved in such research before going on to illustrate the complexity of inter-relationships between environment and behaviour which is suggested by the results of empirical research. One of the most fundamental problems concerns the quality of data. David Smith (1974b) has emphasized the fragility of data relating to crime and delinquency, pointing to several sources of error and confusion. Most research has to rely on official data derived from law enforcement agencies, and these data are usually far from comprehensive in their coverage. Many offences do not enter official records because they are not notified to the police; and data on offenders are further diluted by the relatively low detection rate for most offences (Fig. 3.5). More disconcerting is the possibility that the data which are recorded do not provide a representative sample. Many researchers have argued that official data are biased against working-class offenders (Mays 1963), suggesting that the police are more likely to allow parental sanctions to replace legal sanctions in middle-class areas, that working-class areas are more intensively policed, and that crime reporting by adults is similarly biased. Conversely, 'white-collar' crimes – fraud, tax evasion, expense account 'fiddles', and so on – tend to be under-reported and are more difficult to detect, even where large amounts of money are involved. Some critics have suggested that this bias has been compounded by the predilection in empirical research for data relating to blue-collar crimes. This may be attributable in part to the differential availability of data on different kinds of offence, but it also seems likely that data on white-collar crimes have been neglected because they are, simply, less amenable to deterministic hypotheses.

In any event, the net result may well be that empirical studies present only a partial picture of

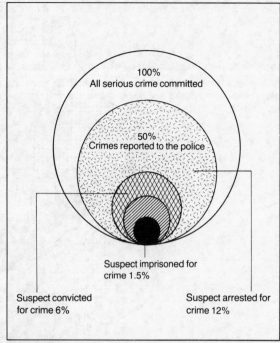

Fig. 3.5 Crime and law enforcement in the United States. *Source*: Banfield (1974), p. 202.

intra-urban patterns of crime and delinquency. As Smith observes, the geography of crime in Washington, D.C., changes dramatically according to whether or not the definition of 'crime' includes the white-collar 'suite crimes' of the business district and middle-class suburbs, the political crimes associated with the Watergate Centre, and the war crimes which may be associated with the Pentagon (Smith 1974b). Because data for many important crime and crime-related variables are only available for groups of people rather than individuals, many studies have pursued an ecological approach, examining variations in crime between territorial groups. Such an approach is inherently attractive to geographers but it does involve certain limitations and pitfalls. The chief limitation of ecological studies is that they cannot provide conclusive evidence of causal links. Thus, although certain categories of offenders may be found in crowded and/or socially disorganized areas, their criminal behaviour may actually be related to other causes – alienation or personality factors, for example – and the ecological correlation may simply result from their gravitation to a certain kind of neighbourhood. The chief pitfall associated with ecological studies is the so-called 'ecological fallacy': the mistake of drawing inferences about *individuals* on the basis of correlations calculated for areas. One pertinent example is the frequently-encountered association within British cities

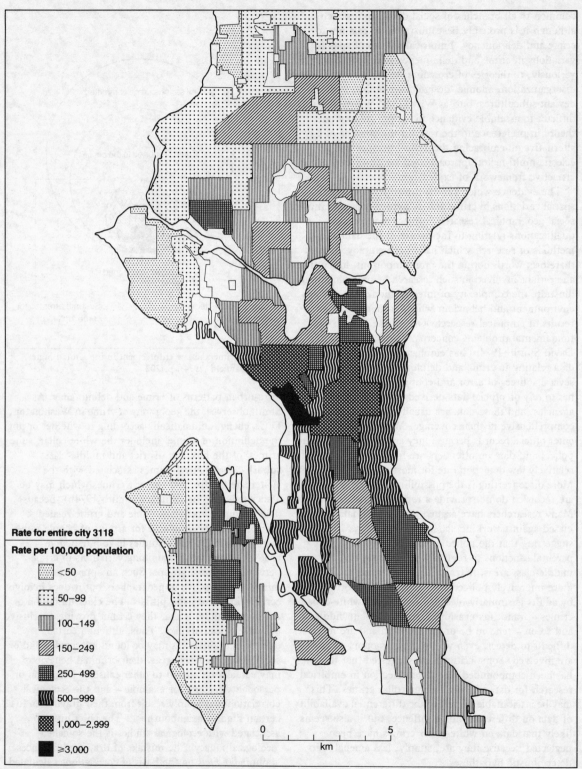

Rate for entire city 3118

Rate per 100,000 population

	<50
	50–99
	100–149
	150–249
	250–499
	500–999
	1,000–2,999
	≥3,000

0   5

km

Fig. 3.6 Violent crime in Seattle: total offences reported 1960–1970.
Source: Harries (1974), p. 76.

between crime rates and neighbourhoods containing large numbers of coloured immigrants. The inference drawn by many is that coloured immigrants and their subcultures are particularly disposed towards crime and delinquency; but research at the level of the individual has in fact shown that 'coloured immigrants are very much less involved in the crime and disorder that surround them in the areas where they live than their white neighbours' (Lambert 1970: 124).

Bearing these limitations in mind, what conclusions can be drawn from empirical studies about the factors which precipitate crime and delinquency? It is not possible to do justice to the extensive literature on criminology and the geography of crime in a text such as this: the serious student should consult the specialist work of Baldwin, Bottoms and Walker (1976), Harries (1974), or Pyle (1974). Nevertheless, it is possible to give some indication of the current state of the art. Following Herbert (1976a, 1977; 1979), it is useful to distinguish between factors influencing the pattern of *occurrence* of crime and delinquency and those influencing the pattern of *residence* of offenders.

Most cities exhibit very distinctive areas where the occurrence of crime and delinquency is well above average. Many, in fact, conform to the archetypal pattern identified in Chicago in the 1920s (Shaw *et al.* 1929), with low rates in the suburbs increasing steadily to a peak in the inner city and CBD. The very different cities of Seattle (Fig. 3.6) and Sheffield (Fig. 3.7), for example, both experience very marked concentrations of crime in the inner city/CBD area. Patterns of occurrence vary considerably, however, by the type of offence. In Cleveland, for example, the geography of murder differs considerably from the geography of assault, while the geography of larceny is different from both (Fig. 3.8). Ecological analyses of occurrence patterns for different offences provide some clues as to the relationships between crime and urban environments, and there are several studies which are useful in this context. In his pioneering study of crime in Seattle, Schmid (1960) demonstrated the concentration of shoplifting and cheque fraud offences in the CBD, of larceny and burglary in suburban areas, and of robbery and female drunkeness in the 'skid row' area of the city. In a later study of the same city, the dominant pattern of crime occurrence was found to be associated with inner-city areas of low social cohesion, where there was a concentration of burglary, car theft and handbag snatching (Schmid and Schmid 1972). In Akron, Ohio, Pyle (1974) found a similar general association between the occurrence of crime and poverty; and the nature of this relationship has been further elaborated in recent studies of Akron (Pyle 1976) and Cleveland (Corsi and

Harvey 1975; Pyle 1976), where detailed ecological analysis revealed a distinct association in both cities between low-income neighbourhoods and crimes of violence, including murder, rape and assault. Pyle (1976) also found evidence to suggest that transitional areas – with a high proportion of land devoted to manufacturing and wholesaling, a decaying physical environment, and an ageing population – are associated with a separate and equally distinctive concentration of offences which includes larceny, robbery and car theft as well as assault and murder. Another important relationship to emerge from these studies of Akron and Cleveland is the correlation between property crimes – burglary, larceny and car theft – and stable, mid- and upper-income suburban neighbourhoods.

These findings lend some support to the emphasis given to spatial variations in *opportunities* for crime by Boggs (1965) in her study of St. Louis and by Baldwin, Bottoms and Walker (1976) in their study of Sheffield. Both studies were able to demonstrate the importance of the 'opportunity factor' in explaining occurrence patterns of several offences. In the Sheffield study, for example, a marked relationship between property values and house-breaking offences was revealed (Table 3.2). The ecology of other offences also seemed to confirm the general importance of opportunity factors, although the evidence was not always conclusive. As Herbert (1977a) observes, this uncertainty derives in part from the scale of analysis: ecological studies are simply not able to reflect the environmental nuances which influence the exact location of offences. The importance of the micro-environment has been emphasized by the US National Commission on the Causes and Prevention of Violence (1969), which concluded that accessibility, visibility, control of property, residential density and state of physical repair are the most significant aspects of the micro-environment of violent crime. Other studies have illustrated the importance of micro-environmental features in explaining other kinds offence. Brantingham and Brantingham (1975) for example, showed that the incidence of burglary in Tallahassee was higher in peripheral blocks of housing estates, where burglars could benefit from the weaker social control of 'anonymous' boundary areas; and Ley and Cybriwsky (1974) found that the occurrence of abandoned and stripped cars in Philadelphia, which appeared to have a random spatial distribution at the 'micro' scale, was closely related to vacant land, doorless sides of buildings, and institutional land use. Also relevant at this scale, of course, is Newman's concept of defensible space. David Herbert has provided a useful summary of the general relationship between environmental features and the location of criminal offences in his review of urban crime and delinquency

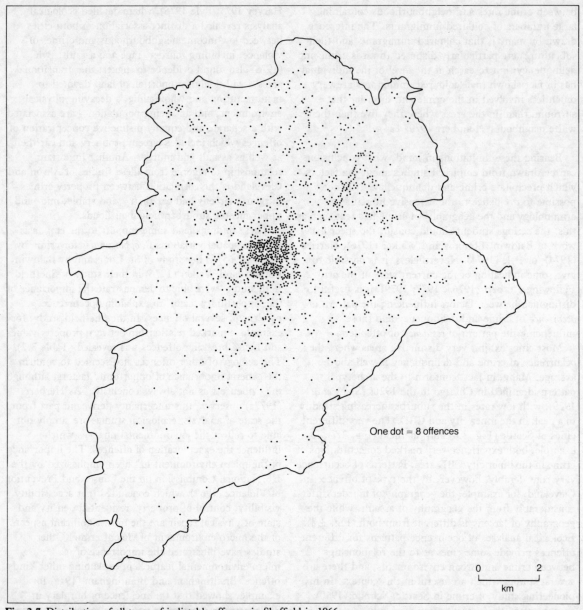

One dot = 8 offences

0   2
km

Fig. 3.7 Distribution of all types of indictable offences in Sheffield in 1966.
Source: Baldwin, Bottoms and Walker (1976), p. 58.

(Fig. 3.9). As he observes, 'there are qualities attached to the offence location which relate to the *built* environment – its design, detailed land use – and to the *social* environment – status, local activity patterns, local control systems' (Herbert 1977a: 224, emphasis added). To these might be added certain features of the *perceived* environment: the offender's image of the attractiveness or vulnerability of particular neighbourhoods, streets and buildings (see, for example, Carter and Hill 1976).

Patterns of *residence* of offenders are subject to a much wider range of explanatory factors although, like patterns of occurrence, they display a consistent social order and clustering which makes them suitable for ecological analysis. Although there are variations by type of offence and age of offender, the classic pattern is the one described by Shaw and McKay (1942) for Chicago and other American cities: a regular gradient, with low rates in the suburbs and a peak in the inner city. In his review of intra-urban variations in crime and

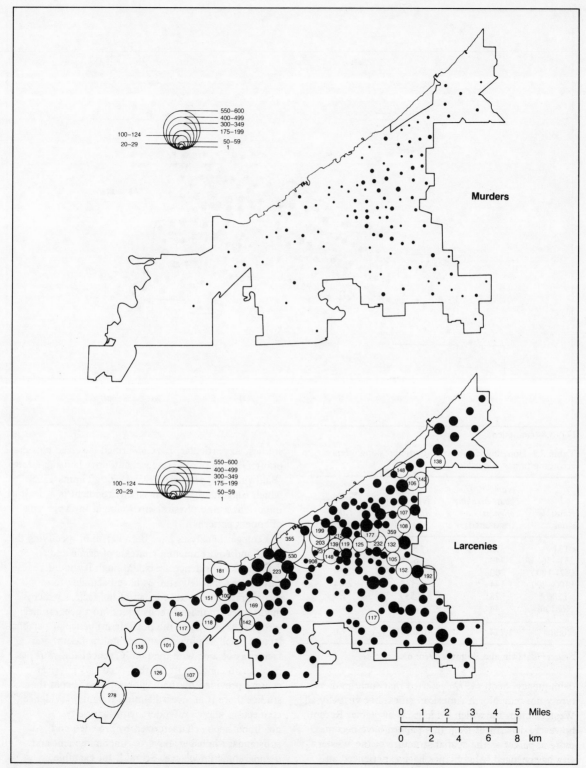

Fig. 3.8 The distribution of murders, larcenies and assaults in Cleveland, Ohio (continued overleaf).
Source: Payle (1976), pp. 273 and 275.

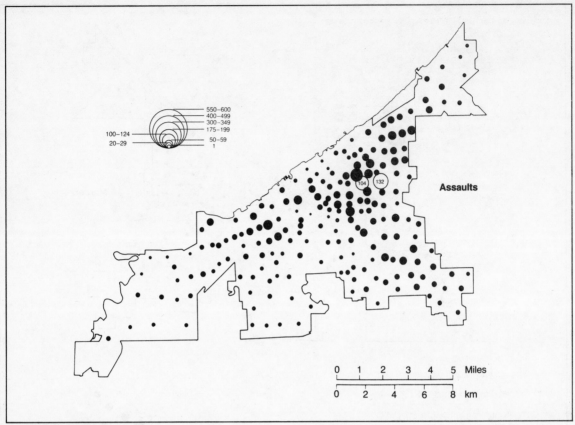

Fig. 3.8 (continued)

Table 3.2 Households subject to house-breaking offences according to rateable value

Rateable value	Number of house-breaking offences (estimated)	Number of dwellings in Sheffield	Rate per 1,000 dwellings
<£31	350	58,342	6.0
£31–56	440	66,357	6.6
£57–100	200	35,372	5.9
£100–200	144	6,165	23.4
>£200	28	539	51.9
Not known	44	—	—
Total	1,214	166,775	7.0

Source: Baldwin and Bottoms 1976: 63.

delinquency, Scott (1972) asserted that such gradients typify not only North American cities, but virtually all Western cities for which evidence is available. Recently, however, departures from this pattern have become more apparent as the spatial structure of the Western city has changed. Many cities have experienced an outward shift of offenders' residences with changes in residential mobility and housing policies. British

studies, in particular, have identified localized clusters of offenders in peripheral local authority housing estates (Baldwin 1975; Herbert 1975; 1976b; Timms 1965), which suggests that the social environment is at least as important as the physical environment in explaining offenders patterns.

Ecological analyses have been useful in specifying the social and environmental contexts of crime and delinquency residence areas, although it should be emphasized that few studies have been able to incorporate, or control for, all of the factors which might affect individual behaviour. Most geographical research has set aside the possible influence of personal factors (such as physical and mental make-up) and factors associated with the family, school and workplace in order to concentrate on the social and physical context provided by the neighbourhood. From these studies there is an overwhelming weight of evidence connecting known offenders with inner-city neighbourhoods characterized by crowded and substandard housing, poverty, unemployment and demographic imbalance. Schmid, for example, concluded that crime areas in Seattle 'are generally characterized by all or most of the following factors: low

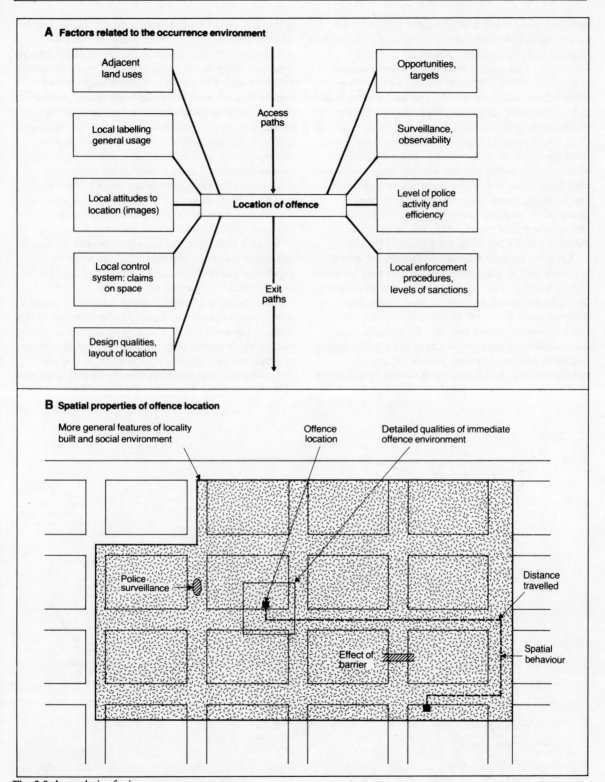

Fig. 3.9 An analysis of crime occurrence patterns.
Source: Herbert (1977), p. 223.

social cohesion, weak family life, low socio-economic status, physical deterioration, high rates of population mobility and personal disorganization' (Schmid 1960: 678). This general finding has been confirmed in subsequent studies of the city (Gittus and Stephens 1973; Schmid and Schmid 1972) and has been replicated in studies of other cities (see, for example, Herbert 1977b; Scott 1972; and Wallis and Maliphant 1967). In cities where peripheral clusters of offenders are found, there appears to be an additional syndrome linking offenders with public housing developments containing high proportions of families of particularly low social and economic status, many of whom have been 'dumped' in 'problem estates' through the housing allocation mechanisms of public authorities (Baldwin, Bottoms and Walker 1976; see also pp. 149– 153).

A few studies have followed up this general ecological approach with an examination of the less tangible local factors which may be related to crime and delinquency: the dominant values and attitudes associated with different areas. Herbert's study of delinquency in Cardiff provides a good example. By administering a questionnaire survey to residents of several 'delinquent' neighbourhoods and several 'non-delinquent' neighbourhoods, he was able to show that 'spatial order in the incidence of delinquency is underlain by

systematic variations in related attitudes and behaviour' (Herbert 1976b: 490). Herbert found significant differences in the way in which people 'labelled' areas in their own mind as either delinquent or non-delinquent. He also found differences between delinquent and non-delinquent areas in people's conception of what amounts to delinquent behaviour: residents of the former were much less disposed towards reporting petty theft and damage to public property than were residents of non-delinquent areas. Similarly, parents in non-delinquent areas were much more inclined to administer sanctions in the home when it came to dealing with misbehaviour. Parents in delinquent areas tended to refer truancy to school authorities, for example, rather than deal with the issue themselves.

While it is tempting to cite evidence such as this in support of particular theories and concepts, past experience shows that it is possible to find support for quite different theories within the same pool of evidence. In this situation it seems sensible to accept a multi-factor explanation. Again, Herbert has provided a useful framework within which to subsume the various factors which appear to be involved (Fig. 3.10). Areas of crime and delinquency are linked to several local environmental contexts and generally related to a nexus of social problems. Poverty is the central focus of the

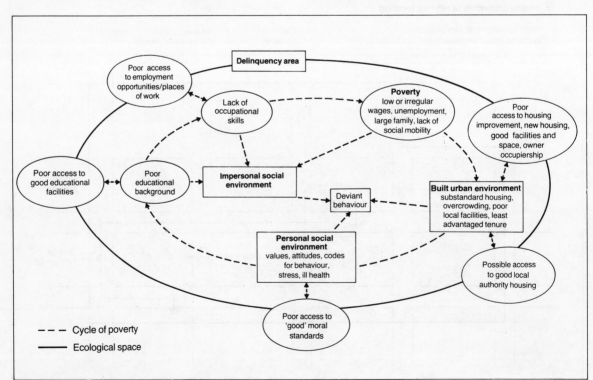

Fig. 3.10 Delinquency residence: the cycle of disadvantage and its spatial connotations.
Source: Herbert (1977), p. 227.

model, and is seen as the product of structural factors which, through differential access to educational facilities and employment opportunities, produce an 'impersonal social environment' (i.e. local population) consisting of 'losers' – the aged, the unemployed, misfits and members of minority groups:

. . . poverty limits individuals to particular types of built environment; at worst to the most disadvantaged housing classes, at best to local authority tenure; both may mean inadequate spatial access to facilities. Disadvantages of the impersonal *social* environment may be compounded by a poor *personal* social environment in which the prevalence of

'unfavourable' values and attitudes may have deleterious effects (Herbert 1977b: 226–7).

While it does not directly further social or geographical theory, Herbert's model does illustrate the complexity of man-environment relationships in the city. Moreover, it also has the advatage of being able to accommodate not only the more deterministic ideas which have been outlined in this section but also the structural explanations of spatial order which are outlined in subsequent chapters and which are favoured by critics of environmental explanations of deviancy (Peet 1975, 1976; Taylor, Walton and Young 1973).

Chapter 4

OVERVIEWS OF SPATIAL DIFFERENTIATION

Areal differentiation has for many years been one of the dominant paradigms of urban social geography. Following the tradition of regionalization within the discipline as a whole, urban geographers have sought to regionalize towns and cities in attempts to produce high-level generalizations about urban form and structure. These generalizations provide useful models with which to generate and test hypotheses and theories concerning urban growth processes and patterns of social interaction in cities. Moreover, many geographers regard the 'regionalization' of cities, like regionalizations of countries or continents, as a basic task of geographical analysis, providing an overall descriptive synthesis which is of fundamental utility in its own right. Whatever the perspective, the initial objective is to identify areas within cities which exhibit distinctive characteristics and which can be shown to be relatively homogeneous. Such areas may be termed neighbourhoods, neighbourhood types, residential areas, urban sub-areas, urban social areas, or urban regions, according to the semantic tastes of the researcher and the type of analysis employed. As in other fields of geographical enquiry, a wide range of techniques and methodologies is available to the researcher concerned with areal differentiation and there is an increasing tendency to adopt more quantitative forms of analysis. There are, however, several distinctive approaches to the identification of urban sub-areas, each with a rather different criterion of areal differentiation. In this chapter three of the most important approaches are examined. These are concerned, respectively, with aspects of the built environment, the socio-economic environment, and the perceived environment. It should be emphasized, however, that these different approaches are significant only because they represent, for the purposes of analysis, a convenient simplification of reality. A comprehensive 'regionalization' of the city would encompass aspects of all three approaches in a more holistic approach. Moreover, the separation of the

morphological, socio-economic and perceived environments is seldom complete: many studies of social areas include the physical condition of housing as a variable, for example, while studies of urban morphology frequently rely on class-based categorizations of housing type.

The built environment

The study of the physical qualities of the urban environment is one of the longest-established components of urban geography, especially in Britain, where the study of 'townscapes' and 'morphological regions' has occupied a prominent place in urban studies. Morphological studies are concerned, by convention, with variations in the style, layout and function of buildings; and they are most logically related to historical aspects of urban growth. As demonstrated in Chapter 2, the built environment is to a large extent a product of the social, economic and technological conditions prevailing at the time of its construction. It has also been noted (p. 17) that most cities experience distinct cycles of building activity which tend to be governed by general economic trends. It therefore makes sense to analyse urban morphology in an historical context, relating the various characteristics of style, layout and function to specific growth phases. This, in fact, is the traditional approach to the analysis of morphological regions in the city. But, although several writers have made major contributions to the description of the general characteristics of morphologies associated with major historical periods (see, for example, Burke 1976; Hiorns 1956; Lavedan 1926–52; Morris 1972; Reps 1965), the use of growth phases as a tool for illustrating the internal structure of cities has been of limited value, largely because simple age categorizations tend to obscure important deviations from the dominant morphological expression of a particular period but also because of the difficulty of accurately establishing the timing of past economic booms and the associated urban growth phases.

More successful have been studies which have incorporated aspects of style, function and layout as explicit criteria in identifying morphological regions. Thurston (1953) and Stedman (1958), for example, were able to produce detailed vignettes of the townscapes of St. Albans and Birmingham in this way. Thurston, in his study of St. Albans, classified each street according to land use, age, building height and building materials, and then aggregated contiguous streets (using the subjective 'eyeball' method) to produce sub-regions with a morphological unity distinguishing them from adjoining areas. Stedman's analysis of townscapes in Birmingham contained an even stronger element of subjectivity, the whole exercise being based on 'careful inspection on the ground' (Stedman 1958: 129) and an (unspecified) 'analysis' of 1:2500 plans. He was, nevertheless, able to present an exhaustive description of townscapes based on the age, function and density of the built environment. Equally effective but less well-known is Emrys Jones's (1958) study of townscapes

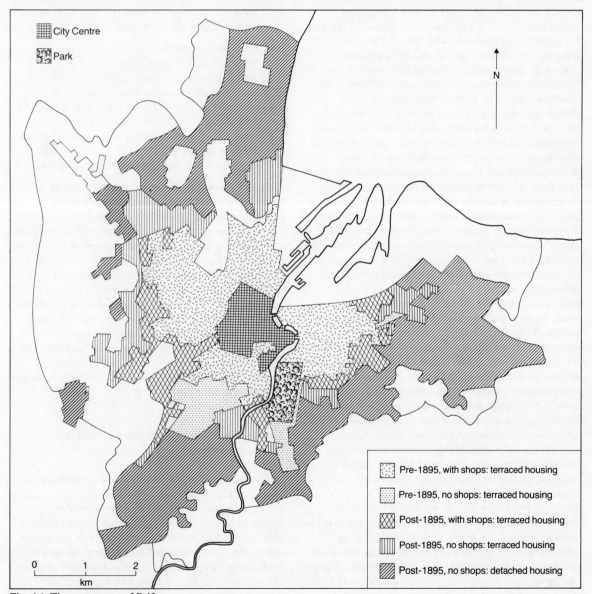

Fig. 4.1 The townscapes of Belfast.
Source: Jones (1958), p. 154.

Legend:
- City Centre
- Park
- Pre-1895, with shops: terraced housing
- Pre-1895, no shops: terraced housing
- Post-1895, with shops: terraced housing
- Post-1895, no shops: terraced housing
- Post-1895, no shops: detached housing

in Belfast, in which the principal features of the built environment were mapped using a simple classification based on age (before and after 1896), function (residential areas with and without local shops) and style (detached and terrace housing) which effectively discriminated between five kinds of townscape in addition to the CBD area (Fig. 4.1).

The whole approach was taken a step further by Smailes who, in a series of publications, stressed the need for rigorous field surveys and for generalizations about townscape patterns. Smailes himself produced a generalized morphological diagram of a 'typical British county town' (Smailes 1955) using a typology of townscapes based on a distinction between the 'kernel' (or historic core) and later additions to the urban fabric consisting of 'terrace-ribbing' and 'villa studding' (Fig. 4.2). Subsequently, Smailes elaborated this typology to incorporate the townscapes of larger cities (Smailes 1966). The core, he argued, provided a distinctive townscape unit in towns and cities of all sizes, although its features – the internal specialization of commercial land uses and the dominance of display frontage on most streets – are much more fully developed in larger cities. Smailes recognized that the surrounding tracts of residential development – the 'integuments' of the city – are the product of successive phases of urban growth, each subject to the influence of different social, economic and cultural forces; and he also allowed for processes of change *within* the city. The growth of every town, he suggests, 'is a *twin process* of outward *extension* and internal reorganization. Each phase adds new fabric – outside in the form of accretions, within in the form of replacements. At any time, many of the existing structures are obsolescent and in their deterioration are subject to functional changes; they are converted for new uses' (Smailes 1966: 87, emphasis added). The older, innermost zones of the city are especially subject to this internal reorganization, with the result that a distinctive townscape element is created, containing a mixture of residential, commercial and industrial functions within physically deteriorating structures. Small factories and workshops make an important contribution to the ambience of such areas. Some of these factories may be residual, having resisted the centrifugal tendency to move out to new sites, but a majority are 'invaders' that have colonized sites vacated by earlier industries or residents. Typically, they occupy old property that has become available in side streets off the shopping thoroughfares in the crowded but decaying residential zone surrounding the CBD. They are thus able to enjoy the advantages of proximity to a relatively cheap labour force as well as to the retail outlets and transport termini of the CBD.

Beyond this inner zone, Smailes suggests, industrial, commercial and residential townscape elements are clearly differentiated. Terrace and villa-type development, associated in different sectors of the city with different social and economic groups, are contiguous with radial prongs and suburban enclaves of industry, but do not intermingle with them. Similarly, shopping and central services present localized townscapes in outlying clusters amid tracts of housing. The 'outer integuments' of the city thus contain several distinctive townscapes, not least of which are several kinds of residential townscape. Again, Smailes (1964) has proposed a general typology relevant to British cities, consisting of the following:

1. residential hotels and boarding houses;
2. blocks of flats or apartments;
3. terrace houses with front gardens;
4. terrace houses without front gardens;
5. detached or semi-detached villas and bungalows with garage or adequate garage space;
6. detached or semi-detached villas and bungalows without garage space;
7. large detached houses in extensive grounds.

Smailes is, however, cautious about attributing any spatial symmetry to these townscapes. Rather, he suggests, townscapes will be arranged in an imperfect zonation, interrupted by radial arteries of commercial and industrial development, by major roads and railway tracks, and distorted by the peculiarities of site and situation. In addition, he points out that most urban development is characterized by the persistence of *enclaves* of relict townscapes which tend to impair the symmetrical pattern which may otherwise emerge: palaces, castles, cathedrals, university precincts, boulevards, public parks and common lands all tend to resist the logic of market forces and so survive as vestigial features amid newly developed or redeveloped neighbourhoods.

Fixation lines, fringe belts and the diffusion of townscape elements

These early attempts to establish the distribution and characteristics of morphological regions in cities, though providing a useful starting point for further study, were not particularly incisive. By the early 1960s, urban geographers had become acutely aware of the lack of theoretical, conceptual and methodological devices available in morphological analysis (Norborg 1962) and these shortcomings, together with a general shift in interest towards economic and social phenomena, relegated morphological studies to an unfashionable

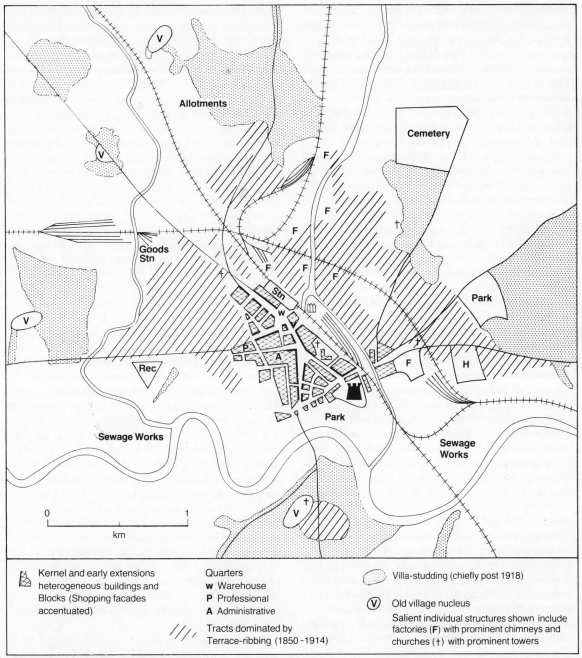

Fig. 4.2 Smailes' model of urban structure.
Source: Smailes (1955), p. 110.

status from which they have still not fully recovered.

There have, however, been several significant contributions to the study of intra-urban variations in the built environment. One person who is credited with advancing the status of morphological studies is Conzen, who was able to illustrate the process of townscape

development from the evidence of an examination of the growth of Alnwick, in Northumberland (Conzen 1960). Conzen's work was very detailed, involving 49 categories of morphological elements in a town of only 7500 inhabitants; but from his detailed observations he was able to extract some useful generalizations which had been, at best, only implicit in previous studies. He also emphasized the marked difference in stability of the three major elements of townscape – building style, layout and function – showing that while the function of buildings is relatively volatile, the street plan of a town tends to persist over long periods. Thus, despite the constant reorganization and renewal of the built environment, the plan (and, often, parts of the fabric) of earlier townscapes tends to remain, forming a template upon which new townscapes must emerge.

In describing the process of townscape development, Conzen introduced the concepts of *fringe belts* and *fixation lines* to the vocabulary of morphological study. Conzen argued that the growth phases used in traditional analyses of urban morphology were often selected arbitrarily and so tended to give a false impression of the pattern of townscape development. A more sensitive approach, he suggested, must involve the identification of structural features which act as physical barriers to construction – 'fixation lines' which govern the pattern of urban development. These fixation lines may take the form of physical features such as rivers; they may be man-made features such as railways and fortifications; or even intangible features such as the pattern of land ownership. Eventually, it is argued, pressure for urban development will overcome these fixation lines and building will spill over to create a fringe belt. Such features, according to Conzen, exhibit an inner zone characterized by higher density development and an outer zone where development is more piecemeal and varied in character. With successive phases of urban growth, these fringe belts will either be *preserved*, with undeveloped ground being retained as open spaces; or they will be *translated* into a different townscape element as succeeding land uses invade the area.

Although Conzen's observations do not by any means amount to a theory or even a model of urban morphology, they do help to explain the broad pattern of urban development. The control exerted over urban morphology by the inertia of ground plan and the influence of fixation lines is clearly reflected in the morphology of Köln, for example (Fig. 4.3). The old town, or *Altstadt*, consisting of a Roman grid nucleus with irregular mediaeval extensions, was enclosed by fortifications erected by the Prussians in the early nineteenth century, when the city was developed as a fortress against the French. These fortifications created a marked fixation line which was only breached later in the century with the construction of a new residential zone some 500 metres wide known as the *Neustadt*. This area, in turn, was surrounded by new fortifications in the 1880s, creating a new fixation line which was reinforced by the route of the railway. Subsequent fringe belt

development was displaced by a military regulation proscribing building of any kind in the area immediately outside the city walls, so that late-nineteenth-century growth tended to take the form either of high density internal redevelopment or new building in the daughter settlements of Deutz, Weidenpesch, Dickendorf, Klettenberg, and Zollstock, which have now become engulfed by Köln itself, but with further outward growth currently constrained by a new fixation line in the form of the autobahn. Although the fortifications were demolished between 1907 and 1911, their influence on Köln's morphology is still apparent, for their site is now occupied by a sinuous green belt (Fig. 4.3). After the demilitarization of the city in 1918 there followed a rapid sprawl of residential and industrial development, with the classic radial-concentric plan of the city being accentuated by the focusing of major routeways on the bridges near the centre of the city. During the Second World War over 75 per cent of the city's fabric was destroyed by allied bombing, and so most of the pre-war townscapes have disappeared. The basic morphological pattern embodied in the city's layout has been retained, however, partly because of a lack of initiative in the city's planning office in the immediate post-war period, but mainly because of the intrinsic stability of the street pattern: even badly damaged roads, tramlines and the associated subterranean services (sewage and electricity lines, etc.) represent an enormous capital asset, and such assets are not lightly set aside by urban governments at any time.

One of the most significant outcomes of Conzen's work is that it has prompted further research by others. Whitehand, for instance, has pursued the idea of fringe belts in some detail and has been able to add to Conzen's ideas on morphogenesis (Whitehand 1967, 1972, 1974). In particular, he has amplified the relationship between residential and non-residential development within fringe areas, showing how 'institutional' land uses (public parks, gardens and playing fields, cemeteries, schools, hospitals, sewage plant, etc.) dominate fringe areas until an economic boom period, when housebuilders outbid institutional users for land:

. . . we must envisage a situation in which, by the end of a boom period, a zone of housing will have been added to the built-up area, but, scattered beyond it and sometimes lying within it, will be the sites of institutions. During a housing slump, while the house builder is largely inactive, institutions will develop the majority of the most accessible sites which, added to what were outlying institutional sites created during the previous housing boom period, will form a zone with a strongly institutional character. Repeated cycles of booms and slumps are likely to result in a series of alternating zones characterized by different proportions of institutions and housing (Whitehand 1974: 110).

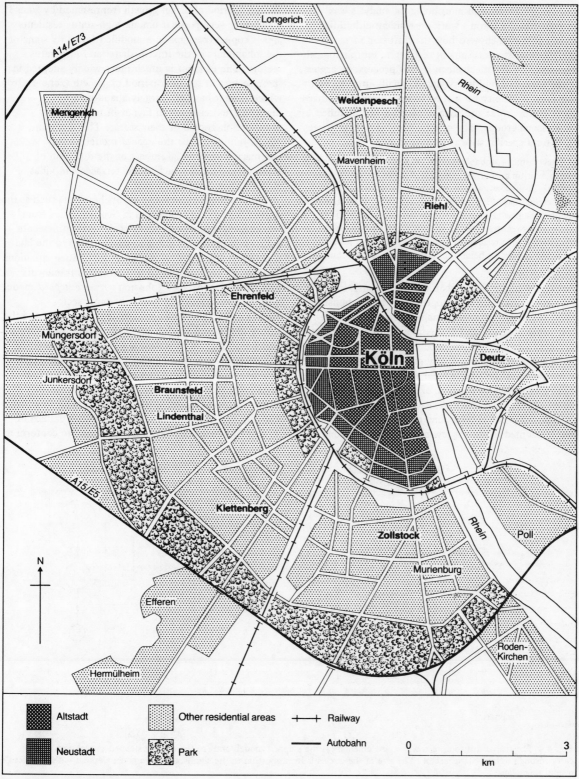

Fig. 4.3 The morphology of Köln.

Another advance in morphological analysis was provided by Johnston's work on residential building styles. Johnston showed how the diffusion of architectural styles results in distinctive morphological regions. The key mechanism in this process, he argues, is the spread of building styles originally introduced to one area of the city for a specific social group to other parts of the city as the style is adopted and modified by other social groups. The general case, as Johnston sees it, is for a specific style to be introduced

as a new fashion (probably architect-designed) on the periphery of the built-up area in the high-status sector, at which time building in the low-status sector would be in styles developed at an earlier date. By the time the lower status inhabitants had adopted the new fashion the city would have extended further and even newer styles would be under development in the more fashionable residential areas. The low status residential areas will always lag behind the more fashionable (Johnston 1969a: 22).

Assuming an idealized urban structure consisting of four concentric zones of progressively newer housing subdivided into three sections inhabited respectively by low-, intermediate- and high-status families, Johnston presents a model of townscape development which reflects the significance of any given building style within each of the twelve areal subdivisions of the city. Fig. 4.4a illustrates the type of situation described above. In this example a townscape element is introduced in the second zone of the high-status sector but is adopted by only a few residents of that zone. In

the next period of urban growth (represented by zone 3) it becomes very popular among high-status residents and is copied (perhaps in a modified form) by some of the inhabitants of the intermediate- and low-status sectors. The element is much more widely adopted in these sectors in the next period of growth (zone 4), by which time it has been largely abandoned by higher-status residents in favour of newer styles pioneered in zone 3 of their sector. This situation, which Johnston calls the *stepped* model, clearly summarizes the spatial impact of the diffusion of townscape elements such as the terraces and villas of British cities described above.

Other situations may also occur, however, such as the outward spread of tenements in Scottish cities from working-class inner-city areas of the early nineteenth century to middle- and higher-status areas of the late nineteenth and early twentieth century. Such situations can also be accommodated in Johnston's framework: in this particular instance Johnston's *reverse stepped* model with a carry-through in the high-status sector (Fig. 4.4b) seems most appropriate. Johnston tested the utility of his own models using data from Melbourne, and found that 74 of a total of 114 different building characteristics (including measures of building height, building materials, building plan, and architectural style) appeared to fit either the stepped model or the reverse stepped model, with a carry-through in either the high- or low-status sector. The spatial pattern of L-shaped houses, for example, was found to conform to

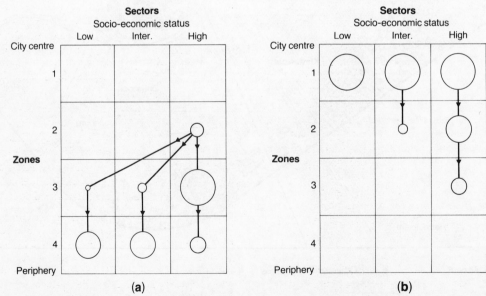

Fig. 4.4 The spatial diffusion of townscape elements: (a) the stepped model, and (b) the reverse stepped model with carry-through to high-status sector. The size of the circles is in proportion to the significance of a given element within an area's overall townscape.
Source: Johnston (1969), p. 26.

the stepped model, while the pattern of semi-detached houses and flats matched the reverse stepped model with a carry-through in low- and high-status sectors respectively. But, as Johnston points out, it is the more complex pattern of townscapes resulting from the *inter-relationships* of the variables which is of most significance in delimiting morphological regions. When architectural styles are classified according to their building materials, for instance, the complexity of the real townscape becomes apparent. Thus, although the general pattern of L-shaped houses exhibits the characteristics of the stepped model, L-shaped houses in weatherboard and tile are found in all sectors of the outer zones (indicating a general middle-class usage) while L-shaped houses in weatherboard and corrugated iron are mainly characteristic of the outer zones of the low-status sector.

Subjective descriptions

Identifying the underlying morphological regions produced by the inter-relationships among *all* the relevant characteristics of building style, layout and usage represents a massive task which, many would argue, can only be tackled with sophisticated multivariate statistical techniques. Yet, although such techniques have been widely available since the late 1960s, their application in morphological studies has been limited – in marked contrast to studies of the socio-economic structure of the city. This reticence is attributable in part to the difficulty of adequately quantifying all the components of townscape. As Burke observes, townscapes are not simply the sum of the attributes of style, layout and function: it is the form in which these morphological elements are set in relation to each other and to unbuilt spaces that creates the *genius loci* which lends distinctiveness to one morphological region in comparison with another. Indeed, a good case can be made for an entirely subjective approach, with morphological regions being articulated by written descriptions rather than statistical analysis. The strength of written description in conveying the flavour and character of particular parts of the city is illustrated in these brief extracts from Jonathan Raban's *Soft City*. Of Kentish Town, in London, he writes:

Most of the houses are survivals of the most notorious period of Victorian speculative jerry-building. They were erected in short terraces of what were accurately described by their builders as 'fourth-rate residences' . . . Their doors and windows are cheaply gabled and scalloped, and in line on the terrace they look like brick railway carriages, their decorations skimped, their narrow front strips of garden a long balding

patch of tarry grass with motor scooters parked under flapping tarpaulins with holes in them (Raban 1975: 109).

And of Roxbury, in Boston:

Roxbury was the first and the sweetest of the nineteenth century 'streetcar suburbs' of Boston . . . The churches, the houses, the tall trees on the streets, are there still. The paint is pocky, much of the wood is rotten, and slats of shingling have fallen away exposing the skeletal frames, but the basic lineaments of the old dream are clear enough even now. It takes a few minutes before you notice that the windows are mostly gone and only a few shutters are left. Each house stares blindly through eyes of cardboard and torn newspaper. Burn marks run in tongues up their sides, and on most blocks there is a gutted shell, sinking onto its knees in a flapping ruin of blackened lath and tar-paper. Our own century has added rows of single-storey brick shacks, where bail-bondsmen and pawnbrokers do their business. What were once front lawns are now oily patches of bare earth. The carcases of wrecked Buicks, Chevrolets and Fords are jacked up on bricks, their hoods open like mouths, their guts looted. No-one is white (Raban 1975: 215).

Reyner Banham is another writer who is able to capture the 'feel' of a townscape in this way. He provides an evocative description of the principal townscapes of a whole city in his exposition of the architecture of Los Angeles (Banham 1973). Unconstrained by the jargon and conventions of urban geography, Banham divides Los Angeles into three major morphological regions, or 'architectural ecologies' (Fig. 4.5).

    1. *Surfurbia* – the coastal strip of Los Angeles stretching from Malibu to Balboa, and typified by the Beach Cities of Playa del Rey, El Segundo, Manhattan Beach, Redondo Beach and, further south, Huntingdon Beach. The townscape here consists of a narrow strip of four or five streets deep and draws its distinctive character from beach houses, fantasy architecture, surfboard art and beautified oil rigs.

    2. *The Foothills* – stretching along the lower slopes of the Hollywood Hills and the Santa Monica Mountains between Pacific Palisades and Highland Park, with an exclave on the slopes of Palos Verdes, the morphology of the Foothills reflects the marked correlation in Los Angeles between altitude and socio-economic status. It is characterized by:

narrow, tortuous residential roads serving precipitous house plots that often back up directly on unimproved wilderness . . . The fat life of the delectable mountains is well known around the world, wherever television re-runs old movies . . . it is the life, factual and fictional, of Hollywood's classic years . . . Where would the private eyes of the forties have been without laurel shrubberies to lurk in, sweeping front drives to turn the car in, terraces from which to observe the garden below, massive Spanish Colonial Revival doors at which to knock, . . . or rambling split-level ranch house plans in which to

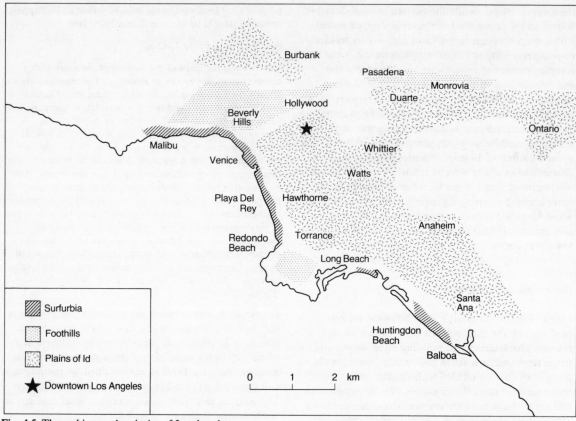

Fig. 4.5 The architectural ecologies of Los Angeles.

lose the opposition, . . . and the essential swimming pool for the bodies? (Banham 1973: 101).

3. *The Plains of Id* – the greater part of the Los Angeles metropolitan area, also familiar to television viewers and part of the popular image of the city:

an endless plain endlessly gridded with endless streets, peppered endlessly with ticky-tacky houses clustered in indistinguishable neighbourhoods, slashed across by endless freeways that have destroyed any community spirit that may once have existed, and so on . . . endlessly (Banham 1973: 161).

Although encompassing a wide variety of socio-economic neighbourhoods, the whole area, Banham suggests, is characterized by the 'dingbat' – a two-storey walk-up apartment block built of wood and stuccoed over, with simple rectangular forms and flush smooth surfaces to the sides and rear but with an eclectic facade containing all kinds of architectural styles and fantasies:

a statement about the culture of individualism . . . the true symptom of Los Angeles' urban Id trying to cope with . . . residential densities too high to be subsumed within the illusions of homestead living (Banham 1973: 175–7).

Superimposed on these three major morphological regions is a fourth 'ecology', *Autopia*: the built environment of the freeway system which, says Banham, is physically large enough and functionally important enough to amount to 'a single comprehensible place, a coherent state of mind, a complete way of life, the fourth ecology of the Angeleno' (Banham 1973: 213). Other distinctive morphological elements in the city include the downtown area – distinctive because of its relative lack of high density commercial development and historic 'centrality' – and various enclaves of West Coast architecture scattered around the city, from the pioneer architecture of Frank Lloyd Wright and Irving Gill to the fantasy architecture of restaurants, fast food outlets and shopping centres and residential indulgences like Venice – built complete with lagoon and canal bridges and now a hippy haven.

Multivariate analysis

In contrast to Banham's individualistic treatment of urban morphology are the attempts of a few analysts to apply multivariate statistical techniques to townscape analysis. These studies are designed to discover the actual association of physical features which distinguish morphological regions. As with all statistical analysis, of course, their utility is governed by the quality and selection of the data used; and it can be a particularly burdensome task to collect house-by-house (or even block-by-block) data for all the relevant characteristics of buildings for the whole of an urban area. Not surprisingly, some analysts have preferred to concentrate on samples or case studies. Corey (1966), for example, focused on one neighbourhood – Corryville – in his pioneer multivariate analysis of urban morphology in Cincinnati. Using a combination of principal components analysis and discriminant analysis, he analysed the relationship between 40 variables selected to represent different aspects of building age, type and size, building materials, roof type and porch type; and was able to produce an 'objective' classification of morphological regions within the study area.

One particularly useful application of such techniques is Openshaw's (1969) study of South Shields, in Durham, which goes on to relate statistically-derived morphological regions to the socio-economic characteristics of their inhabitants. A close relationship between socio-economic status and morphological regions is implicit in much socio-geographical writing but, as Herbert has observed, 'the assumption that certain social and demographic characteristics are associated with . . . various types of housing . . . [are known] to be broadly accurate but they have not in fact been proved' (Herbert 1967: 6). Openshaw, using canonical correlation techniques, was able to prove the association, at least as far as the evidence from a 10 per cent sample of households and houses in South Shields enumeration districts would allow. Although not all of the variation in his data could be explained, he found strong relationships between:

1. morphological elements associated with late Victorian byelaw terracing and low-status tenants renting unfurnished accommodation;
2. inter-war housing and high-status, car-owning owner-occupiers;
3. post-1963 public housing and population with a young age structure and a high fertility rate; and
4. high-status Edwardian housing and families in social class III (intermediate), indicating a subdivision of dwellings as they have 'filtered down' the social scale (see p. 132).

A similar analysis of Edmonton, Canada, concluded that the major constructs of residential morphology showed meaningful spatial relationships with the social dimensions of the city (McCann and Smith 1972), while Morgan (1971, 1973) has also demonstrated a broad fit between morphological regions and social areas in Exeter. Such relationships, however, are subject to considerable qualification. Important social and demographic variations, for example, often exist within morphologically homogeneous regions. Moreover, the *nature* of the link between morphological and social areas in a city – the particular socio-economic groups associated with particular morphological regions – does not appear to be very consistent from one city to another; although there is considerable scope for further research in this direction.

Environmental quality

One other approach to the geography of the built environment which should be mentioned here is the analysis of spatial variations in environmental quality. This is a topic which extends beyond the immediate characteristics of urban morphology to include aspects of amenity provision and factors such as noise and air pollution which are not necessarily a function of the local built environment. The focus, however, is on the condition of streets and buildings, an aspect of the built environment which has been of increasing interest to town planners and community groups as well as to geographers. Indeed, much of the methodology appropriate to such studies has been developed by planning agencies in Europe and North America in preparing strategic plans and delimiting environmental 'action areas' of various sorts. In a majority of cases, the 'quality' of residential environments is evaluated by field survey and involves the allocation of points to buildings or groups of buildings according to the presence or absence of environmental *defects* of various sorts, and these points are subsequently summed to give an overall index score for the location (Duncan 1971). A good example of the technique is represented in Table 4.1, which shows an extract from an environmental quality assessment schedule developed for the Tees-side Survey and Plan (1969).

Although such schedules are employed most frequently in detailed surveys of perhaps just a few city blocks, it is possible to employ sampling procedures in order to cover a much larger area, either to provide a background for more detailed investigations or simply to obtain a generalized picture of intra-urban patterns of environmental quality. Such an approach was employed by the author in a study of environmental quality in Sheffield, using a schedule designed to award up to 100 penalty points according to the relative degree of deficiency in a number of specific aspects of the

Table 4.1 Extract from an environmental quality assessment schedule

	Penalty points	Maximum
Traffic:		
normal residential traffic	0	
above normal residential traffic	3	6
large amount ind. and through traffic	6	
Visual quality:		
higher standard than environment	0	
same standard as environment	1	3
lower standard than environment	3	
Access to Public Open Space:		
park/POS within 5 mins walk	0	3
no park/POS within 5 mins walk	3	
Access to shops and primary schools:		
primary school and shops within 5 mins walk	0	
primary school but no shops in 5 mins walk	2	
shops but no primary school in 5 mins walk	5	7
no primary school or shops in 5 mins walk	7	
Access to public transportation to major centre:		
less than 3 mins walk	0	3
more than 3 mins walk	3	
Landscape quality:		
mature, good quality abundant landscape	0	
immature, insufficient amounts	2	5
total or almost total lack of landscape	5	
Air pollution:		
negligible	0	
light	3	9
heavy	9	
Privacy:		
no overlooking on either side	0	
overlooking on one side	2	5
overlooking on both sides	5	
Noise:		
normal residential standard	0	
above residential but not ind./comm. std.	2	5
ind./comm. e.g. main street standard	5	

Source: Duncan 1971: 60–1.

environment, including the visual quality of houses, streets and gardens, the separation of pedestrians and traffic, access to public open space, and the presence of 'street furniture' such as bus shelters, post boxes, street lighting and telephone kiosks (Knox 1976). The resulting map and transects reveal a large variation in the quality of the environment (from less than 10 to nearly 90 defect points), with a clear spatial patterning (Fig. 4.6). Environmental quality is positively associated with distance from the city centre and with owner-occupied and local authority housing; and negatively associated with the occurrence of industrial land use and the age of the built environment. In terms of its spatial configuration, the index exhibits a markedly zonal pattern, with a steady improvement from the highly defective inner areas to the high quality suburban environments: a pattern which, it is worth noting, bears only a loose resemblance to the pattern of socio-economic status in the city. Deviations from the zonal pattern were found to be related principally to the effects of topography, local authority redevelopment schemes, and industrial location. To the west of the city centre, for example, the high quality environment of the suburbs intrudes markedly inwards, following the high-status housing associated with the Hallam Ridge. Conversely, the 'islands' of better environmental quality to the south-east and north-west of the city centre are associated with recent local authority developments. The areas which show up most clearly on the map are those in the Norfolk Park and Netherthorpe districts, although it is likely that a finer mesh of sampling points (only 100 were used in the survey) would have highlighted more such areas. Finally, the greatest distortion of the concentric pattern is represented by the extensive area of low-quality environment stretching north-eastwards from the cutlery quarter near the CBD, along the floor of the Don valley to Attercliffe and Carbrook. Here, the inhabitants of the terrace houses that were contemporary with and adjacent to the older cutlery factories and steelworks must live with the dereliction, noise, fumes and congestion associated with present concentrations of traffic and industry.

Again, it is difficult to generalize about intra-urban patterns because of the paucity of empirical research. Moreover, it should be acknowledged that the available measurement techniques are far from perfect. In particular, it would be fallacious to assume that assessment techniques carry any real degree of objectivity, since the choice of the aspects of 'quality' to be measured and the weightings assigned to different degrees of quality (or defectiveness) are always dependent on the subjectivity of those who design the schedule. We therefore have to rely to a great extent on the experience and expertise of those 'who know best' (or who think they do) about measuring environmental quality, and their decisions will always be debatable. Weightings, for example, can only be justified by assuming the researcher's awareness of the consensus of values amongst the people whose environment is being measured. As Southworth and Southworth (1973) have

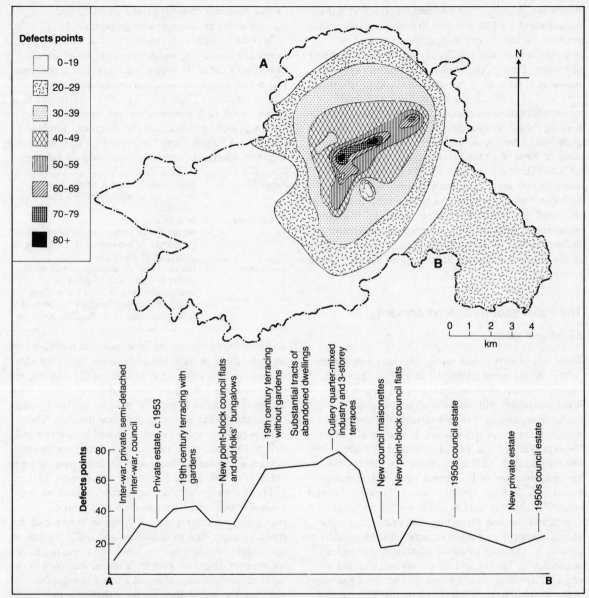

Fig. 4.6 Environmental quality in Sheffield.
Source: Knox (1976), p. 105.

shown, however, there seems to be a considerable dissonance in the operational definitions of environmental quality used by planners – in the United States, at least. Because of this uncertainty, and because of the implications of basing important practical decisions (such as whether to schedule an area for demolition or to designate an area as eligible for home improvement grants) on the basis of index scores, there has been some opposition to the idea of quantifying environmental quality, at least as a planning tool (see for example, Dennis 1978). What is really needed, of

course, is some comprehensive attitudinal survey of what components of environmental quality people think are important, and how important they feel they are in relation to one another. In reality, however, people's opinions will differ widely, for environmental quality is highly income-elastic. The less well-off, with more urgent needs to satisfy, may well be relatively unconcerned about many aspects of environmental quality; whilst the rich, having satisfied their own material needs, may be particularly sensitive to environmental factors such as the appearance of houses, streets and gardens. This problem, together with the magnitude of the task involved in evaluating community preferences, must mean that such surveys will be regarded as impracticable for all but the most intensive of studies. Perhaps the solution is simply to ask the residents of each street or neighbourhood to rate their own level of satisfaction with the quality of their environment on some numerical or semantic scale. But here we should necessarily become involved in awkward questions of definition. Thus if two people each give a score of 9 out of 10 for environmental quality, how do we know that they are both evaluating the same concept? One may be thinking more of noise and pollution whilst the other sees the question in terms of the visual qualities of the built environment. If we try to standardize the response by offering a comprehensive definition of what environmental quality is, we are back to the problem subjective definitions on the part of the researcher.

The socio-economic environment

Social area analysis

Social area analysis, *sensu strictu*, provides a means of portraying the social geography of a city as part of a deductive model of social change based largely on Wirthian theory. Although the object of heated academic argument, it is undoubtedly the source of most modern social area studies. It was developed by Shevky, Williams and Bell (Shevky and Williams 1949; Shevky and Bell 1955) in an attempt to identify the 'community areas' of Los Angeles and San Francisco. Faced with the wide variety of social, demographic and economic data that were available for census tracts in American cities and suspecting that single 'diagnostic' variables such as income or occupation were unlikely to provide an adequate means of portraying a complex phenomenon, Shevky and his co-workers decided to employ classifying criteria based on a series of postulates about social differentiation in the industrial society of postwar North America. Drawing heavily on Wirth's ideas, it was argued that urban social areas were the product of three major trends deriving from the *increasing scale* of society: (i) changes in the range and intensity of relations, (ii) an increasing functional differentiation, and (iii) an increasing complexity of social organization. These trends, it was suggested, were manifested respectively in terms of changes in the division of labour (with a shift towards clerical, supervisory and management functions), in the role of the household (with a movement of women into urban occupations and a spread of 'alternative' family patterns), and in the composition of local populations

(with a tendency towards greater mobility and, consequently, greater spatial segregation).

In order to encompass these trends in a methodology capable of classifying social areas in terms of census data, Shevky *et al*. translated each one into a construct which could be measured by a composite index of census variables (Table 4.2). The three constructs were termed *social rank*, *urbanization* and *segregation* (although Bell preferred 'economic status', 'family status', and 'ethnic status' respectively), and the variables selected to represent them were as follows:

Social Rank	: 1. percentage of manual workers 2. percentage of adults with less than 9 years schooling
Urbanization	: 1. fertility rate 2. percentage of women in the labour force 3. percentage of housing stock consisting of single-family dwellings
Segregation	: 1. the combined proportions of minority ethnic groups : blacks, other races, foreign-born whites from Eastern and Southern Europe, foreign-born persons from continents other than Europe.

The index used to measure each construct was based on an unweighted average of standardized scores for each of these variables (for a full account of the method, see the reviews by Johnston (1976) and Rees (1972)). With the resultant index scores it is possible to classify each census tract using a process of logical division. The most popular strategy is that proposed by Shevky and Bell in 1955, in which the social rank and urbanization indexes are plotted orthogonally, with the range of each index (0 to 100) divided into four equal parts. This yields 16 types, which can be further divided on the basis of above- or below-average scores on the segregation index. Figure 4.7 shows an example of the typology using data from Shevky and Bell's analysis of San Francisco. Such figures, sometimes referred to as social space diagrams, provide a useful summary of the socio-economic composition of a city's population. Locating the information on these diagrams in geographical space provides a map of the city's social areas which can then be used as the basis for further study. Shevky and Bell claimed that these social areas 'generally contain persons having the same level of living, the same way of life, and the same ethnic background; and we hypothesize that persons living in a particular type of social area would systematically differ with respect to characteristic attitudes and behaviours from persons living in another type of social area' (Shevky and Bell 1955: 20).

Such properties make social area analysis an attractive basis for sample surveys in urban areas, since it can be used to inform researchers about the likely

Table 4.2 Social area analysis: steps in construct formation and index construction

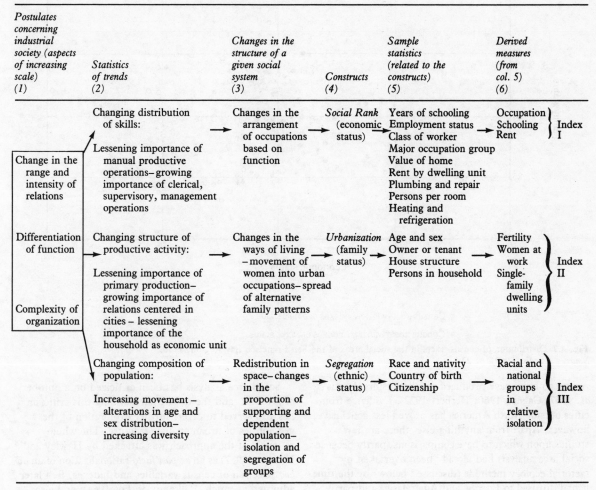

Postulates concerning industrial society (aspects of increasing scale) (1)	Statistics of trends (2)	Changes in the structure of a given social system (3)	Constructs (4)	Sample statistics (related to the constructs) (5)	Derived measures (from col. 5) (6)
Change in the range and intensity of relations	Changing distribution of skills: Lessening importance of manual productive operations– growing importance of clerical, supervisory, management operations	Changes in the arrangement of occupations based on function	*Social Rank* (economic status)	Years of schooling, Employment status, Class of worker, Major occupation group, Value of home, Rent by dwelling unit, Plumbing and repair, Persons per room, Heating and refrigeration	Occupation Schooling Rent } Index I
Differentiation of function / Complexity of organization	Changing structure of productive activity: Lessening importance of primary production– growing importance of relations centered in cities – lessening importance of the household as economic unit	Changes in the ways of living – movement of women into urban occupations– spread of alternative family patterns	*Urbanization* (family status)	Age and sex, Owner or tenant, House structure, Persons in household	Fertility Women at work Single-family dwelling units } Index II
	Changing composition of population: Increasing movement – alterations in age and sex distribution– increasing diversity	Redistribution in space– changes in the proportion of supporting and dependent population– isolation and segregation of groups	*Segregation* (ethnic) status)	Race and nativity, Country of birth, Citizenship	Racial and national groups in relative isolation } Index III

Source: Shevky and Bell 1955: 4.

location of certain social groups and to show where a particular social environment will be found. Since they are purported to be sensitive measures of social differentiation, social area scores have also been employed in behavioural research as independent variables in attempts to explain the incidence of particular phenomena (see, for example, Polk's work (1957) on juvenile delinquency). In addition, of course, maps of social area scores provide a means of identifying the spatial relationships between social areas. Shevky and Bell's analysis of San Francisco (Fig. 4.8) revealed a marked area of low social rank and low urbanization characteristics (i.e. high family status) in the south-east of the city around the industrial and commercial district facing the Bay, a large area characterized by high social rank and low urbanization in the south-west of the city, a small area of low social rank and high urbanization in the transitional zone between the CBD and the docks

area; and a larger area of low social rank and low urbanization in the north of the city, with a particularly marked concentration of minority group members around the CBD in the north-east. This pattern, however, owes much to San Francisco's unique site and topography and it is therefore difficult to include in any generalizations about the spatial relationships of urban sub-areas. This question was pursued by Anderson and Egeland (1961), who selected four almost circular and topographically uniform US cities (Akron, Dayton, Indianapolis and Syracuse) with populations ranging from 200,000 to 500,000 and used analysis of variance techniques to establish whether the cities' social area scores exhibited zonal or sectoral patterns, or neither. They found a consistent pattern, with social rank scores in each city exhibiting a significant sectoral pattern while the urbanization scores conformed to a pattern of concentric zones. Similar analyses of other North

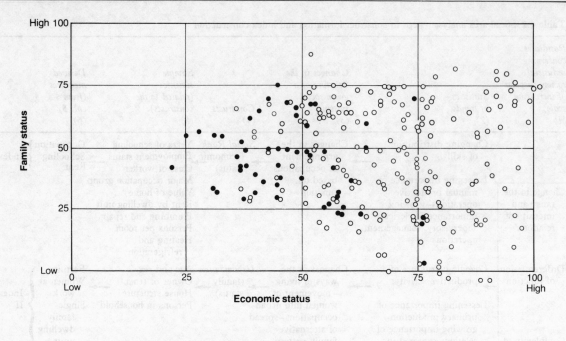

○ Census tracts with low indexes of ethnic status

● Census tracts with high indexes of ethnic status

Fig. 4.7 Distribution of census tracts in the social areas of the San Francisco Bay Region, 1950. *Source*: Murdie (1969), p. 22.

American cities have produced parallel results (Curtis *et al*. 1967; Gagnon 1960; Herbert 1972). Evidence from cities outside North America has proved less conclusive, however. Apart from anything else, there are few studies upon which to base comparisons, partly because social area analysis had already been overtaken by factorial ecology methods (discussed below) by the time it had diffused to Europe and Australasia, and partly because of variations between countries in the composition and availability of the census data required for social area analysis. Thus McElrath (1962) had to substitute a literacy ratio for the education variable in his study of Rome, and could calculate neither the proportion of single-family dwellings nor the segregation construct. The spatial pattern revealed by his analysis did exhibit a sectoral-zonal configuration, although he also found a marked zone on the periphery of the city occupied by large families of low economic status. In Britain, Herbert (1967a) applied a similarly-modified social area analysis to Newcastle-under-Lyme, Staffordshire; but the small size and atypical economic structure of the town, together with doubts about the validity of the census data Herbert used (they were based on a 10 per cent sample of enumeration districts with very small populations) tend to weaken the value of the study as a basis for comparison.

Social area analysis has been criticized on a number of grounds, and the debate surrounding this criticism has also served to divert further exploration of the generalities of urban spatial structure. The whole rationale of the approach was attacked by Hawley and Duncan (1957) as an *ex post facto* rationalization of an *ad hoc* selection of census variables and indexes. Bell later admitted as much (Bell and Moskos 1964); and also accepted the suggestion by Anderson and Bean (1961) that the urbanization construct might in fact mask two quite separate social trends – 'familism' and 'urbanism'. Moreover, to the extent that Wirthian theory itself remains controversial, the whole conceptual basis of social area analysis must be open to doubt. This position was reinforced by the results of empirical tests by Udry (1964), who showed that the trends Shevky and Bell postulated were not typical of the United States over previous decades. Udry also went on to point out that there is in any case no basis for translating a theory of societal change into a typology of social areas: nowhere do the advocates of social area analysis suggest the mechanisms or processes by which homogeneous social groups end up in different territories. Other criticisms noted by Timms (1971) in his extensive review of the schema include the charge that social change is represented in overly economic terms and that little attention is given to differences in people's value

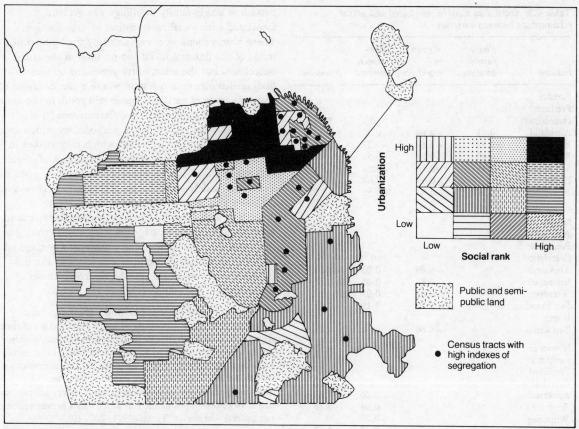

Fig. 4.8 The social areas of San Francisco, 1950.
Source: Shevky and Bell (1949), Fig. V.14.

orientations or to the distribution of power. McElrath's reformulation of the schema (1968) represents an attempt to overcome these shortcomings. Greater attention is given to the relationships between structural change and social differentiation, with *industrialization* leading to differentiation in terms of occupational structure, educational achievement, family structure and female activity rates; and *urbanization* leading to differentiation in terms of geographical mobility, life-cycle characteristics and ethnic status. Little attempt, however, is made to spell out the key process of residential clustering.

These criticisms of social area analysis also prompted a good deal of empirical testing. Surprisingly, perhaps, the methodology stands up rather well to these tests, although certain shortcomings are revealed. One aspect of the methodology which has been widely tested is the relationship between the constructs postulated by Shevky and Bell. The indexes measuring each construct should be statistically independent of one another according to the logic of the procedure, and it also follows that the variables selected to represent each

construct should be closely related to one another while having no significant association with variables representing other constructs. The predicted relationships between the variables is set out in Table 4.3, together with the correlation coefficients computed from the data used in social area analysis of several different cities. These results demonstrate a broad consistency, with the observed relationships matching the predicted relationships quite closely. The one significant exception is the unspecified correlation between occupation and fertility, thus lending some substance to the doubts expressed by Anderson and Bean about the soundness of the urbanization construct.

A more rigorous test of the inter-relationships between the variables (not just the pairwise relationships) is provided by factor analysis, a technique which enables the analyst to ascertain the major independent patterns of variation in a data matrix (see p. 79). Bell himself used this technique on data for San Francisco and found that the six constituent variables of the three constructs did in fact collapse to three independent dimensions representing, as hypothesized,

Table 4.3: Social area analysis: predicted and actual relationships between variables.

Indicant	Single family dwellings	Women in workforce	Non-manual workers	Ethnicity
Fertility				
Predicted correlation*	+	−	0	0
Auckland	0.61	−0.60	−0.37	0.22
Brisbane	0.53	−0.69	−0.27	−0.18
Winnipeg	0.45	−0.53	−0.53	
San Francisco	0.48	−0.76	−0.68	0.21
Rome		−0.69	−0.68	
Ten Cities †	0.31	−0.64	−0.55	−0.12
Single family dwellings				
Predicted Correlation		−	0	0
Auckland		−0.89	−0.03	−0.24
Brisbane		−0.81	−0.05	−0.58
Winnipeg		−0.68	0.07	
San Francisco		−0.75	0.19	−0.25
Rome				
Ten Cities		−0.66	0.11	−0.26
Women in workforce				
Predicted Correlation			0	0
Auckland			0.20	0.43
Brisbane			0.04	0.16
Winnipeg			−0.03	
San Francisco			0.48	0.07
Rome			0.64	
Ten Cities			0.16	0.11
Non-manual workers				
Predicted Correlation				0
Auckland				−0.66
Brisbane				−0.13
Winnipeg				
San Francisco				−0.14
Rome				
Ten Cities				−0.23

* + denotes high positive correlation
 − denotes high negative correlation
 0 denotes insignificant correlation
† The ten cities analysed by Van Arsdol *et al.* (1958): Akron, Atlanta, Birmingham, Kansas City, Louisville, Minneapolis, Portland, Providence, Rochester, Seattle.

Source: Timms 1971: 164; Herbert 1972: 144.

social rank, urbanization and segregation. Van Arsdol *et al.* (1958) replicated this analysis in their ten-city study, with broadly similar conclusions; although in four Southern cities (Atlanta, Birmingham, Kansas City and Louisville) patterns of fertility were associated with social rank as well as urbanization and in Providence the

pattern of single-family dwellings was evidently associated with social rank instead of urbanization. These observations were explained by the authors in terms of the unusual social composition of the cities concerned, but the uncertainty generated by their findings led others to question whether the inclusion of a wider variety of variables would still result in the same three principal dimensions of differentiation. This initiated an inductive research methodology which soon eclipsed social area analysis and which is discussed in detail below. One of the major contributions of social area analysis *sensu strictu*, therefore, has been to generate a new and widely-accepted research strategy. However, it should also be acknowledged as a classifying procedure with intrinsic empirical value. Furthermore, notwithstanding the details of the argument relating to the underlying theory of social change, the conceptual basis of the schema is useful in emphasizing the link between urban structure and the macro-processes of social change. As Timms concludes:

The most important contribution which Shevky and his colleagues have made . . . lies not so much in the details of their arguments as in the emphasis they place on the relationship between the city and the wider society of which it is a part. In sensitizing the student of the city to the reciprocal relations which exist between the characteristics of the urban community and those of the encompassing society Shevky and Bell have helped to bridge the gap which exists between urban and general sociologies (Timms 1971: 209–10).

These 'reciprocal relations' were to become somewhat obscured by the statistical sophistry associated with studies of factorial ecology and it is only recently that urban geographers have redirected their attention towards them.

Studies of factorial ecology

Factor analysis, together with the associated family of multivariate statistical techniques which includes principal components analysis, has become one of the most widely used techniques in social research of all kinds; and it is now generally the preferred approach for identifying the major dimensions of social differentiation in cities and for portraying their spatial expression. In this context, factor analysis is used primarily as an inductive device with which to analyse the relationships between a wide range of social, economic, demographic and housing characteristics, with the objective of establishing what common patterns, if any, exist in the data. This, of course, is in direct contrast to social area analysis, where these relationships are pre-determined by deductive 'theory'. As noted above, the approach stems directly from attempts to validate the hypotheses implicit in social area analysis. Following the factor analyses by Bell (1955) and van Arsdol *et al.* (1958) of the six standard social area analysis variables, Anderson and Bean (1961) extended the approach, seeking to establish whether the inclusion of other variables would still result in the three dimensions postulated by Shevky and Bell. Using data for 13 variables for census tracts in Toledo, Ohio, they in fact discovered four major independent patterns of association – 'dimensions' – in the data: one representing social rank, one representing segregation, and two representing separate parts of the urbanization construct. Their work prompted other studies, notably by sociologists such as Gittus (1964), Sweetser (1965a; 1965b) and Schmid and Tagashira (1965), and within a short time the techniques diffused to geographers and planners, helped by an increasing general interest in quantitative techniques. In addition, innovations in computer technology and programming encouraged the use of a larger selection of input variables and so led to a more explicitly inductive approach. Subsequently, the bandwagon effect generated by the 'quantitative revolution' in geography led to factorial ecology studies of a wide range of cities, thus forming the basis for reliable high-level generalizations about urban socio-spatial structure.

The method

It is not within the scope of this book to discuss details of the methodology of factor analysis and related techniques. Useful outlines are provided by Johnston (1978) and Rummel (1967), while both Johnston (1971; 1976a) and Rees (1971; 1972) provide extended critiques of the methodology in the context of factorial ecology studies. Essentially, they can be regarded as summarizing or synthesizing techniques which are able to identify groups of variables with similar patterns of variation. These are expressed in terms of new, hybrid variables called factors or components which account for measurable amounts of the variance in the input data and which, like 'ordinary' variables, can be mapped or used as input data for other statistical analysis. The relationships and spatial pattern which they describe are known collectively as a *factorial ecology*. The basic procedures involved in factorial ecology studies are shown in Fig. 4.9, together with an indication of the output associated with each stage of the analysis. It should be noted at the outset that the term factor analysis has come to represent a family of statistical techniques which includes principal components analysis and principal axes factor analysis, the two techniques which have found widest application in geographical studies. Similarly, it is important to note that both techniques can be executed in a number of

different ways, depending on the nature of the data and the context of the analysis. The initial stage in any analysis, however, is the assembly of the data matrix. Where necessary, the data are transformed in order to meet the requirements of linearity which arise because of the next stage – the preparation of a product – moment correlation matrix. This matrix is then factored, using a variant either of principal components analysis or of factor analysis *sensu strictu*. The former is a statistically 'closed' model which assumes that all the variance in the data can be accounted for by inter-relationships between the variables being analysed. Factor analyses, on the other hand, assume that there are other variables not included in the analysis which will have contributed something to the patterns in the data. Operationally, the distinguishing feature between the two is that principal components analyses operate on a correlation matrix in which the values in the main diagonal are entered as 1.0, while in factor analyses these are replaced by estimates of the common variance (usually the squared multiple correlation between the

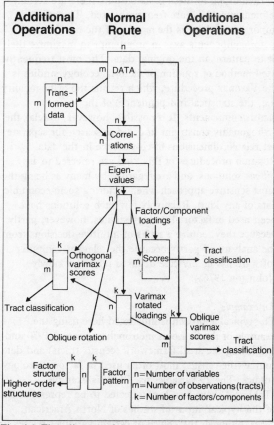

Fig. 4.9 Flow diagram of the procedures involved in the factorial ecology method.
Source: Johnston (1976), p. 204.

relevant variable and all the others). The usual factoring procedure produces a series of hybrid variables, each statistically independent of one another and each successively accounting for a smaller proportion of the total variance in the input data. Since the objective of the technique is to identify only the major dimensions of co-variance in the data, it is usual to retain only those factors/components which account for a greater proportion of the total variance than could any one of the original variables. These are identifiable through the relevant *eigenvalues*, which should have a minimum value of 1.0 and whose magnitude is in direct proportion to the explanatory power of the factor/component to which it relates. The composition of the factors/components is reflected in another part of the output: the *loadings*, which are simply correlation coefficients computed between the new hybrid variables and each of the original input variables. The spatial expression of the factors/components is derived from the respective vectors of *scores*, computed as the sum of the products of the original (standardized) variables and the relevant loadings.

In addition to these basic outputs there are certain refinements which are frequently used. The most important of these is the *rotation* of the factor/components axes in an attempt to maximize their fit to patterns in the original data. The most frequently used method of rotation in factorial ecology studies is the Varimax procedure, which retains the orthogonality (i.e. the statistical independence) of the factors/components. It is possible, however, to relax the orthogonality constraint in order to search for separate yet related dimensions of co-variance in the data. Rotation procedures of this kind are referred to as *oblique* solutions, and are regarded by many as being the most sensitive approach when factoring socio-economic data of any kind. Relatively few such solutions have been used in factorial ecology studies, however; partly because they require a series of intuitive decisions from the analyst and partly because the relevant computer software has in any case diffused relatively slowly (Johnston 1976a).

An example
The typical approach is illustrated here using the example of the St Louis metropolitan area in 1970 and employing the areal framework (census tracts) and data source (the census) most often used in factorial ecology studies. The 29 variables used in this example (Table 4.4) have also been selected to be representative of the 'typical' input of studies of North American cities, although the choice of certain variables relates to a preliminary inspection of census data. Thus the proportion of persons of Italian origin is included

Table 4.4 Input variables for factorial ecology of St Louis, 1970

1. Female activity rate
2. % aged less than 5
3. % aged 65 or over
4. % males never married
5. % high school graduates
6. Median school years completed
7. Sex ratio
8. % black
9. % German origin
10. % Italian origin
11. % Spanish speaking
12. Persons per household
13. % living in same house as 1965
14. % males economically active
15. % males unemployed
16. % Managers and Administrators
17. % operatives
18. Median family income
19. % families below poverty level
20. % dwellings owner-occupied
21. % dwellings vacant
22. % dwellings lacking plumbing
23. Median number of rooms
24. % roomers
25. % households living at a density of >1 person per room
26. Median value of houses
27. Median contract rent
28. % dwellings with more than one bath room
29. % dwellings privately rented.

because such persons constitute a sizeable minority of the city's population; Mexican Americans, on the other hand, are numerically unimportant in St Louis and so are excluded from the analysis. Using a Varimax rotation of a principal axes solution, the input variables collapse to five major dimensions which together account for 74 per cent of the variance in the initial data set (Table 4.5). By far the most important of these is factor I, which alone accounts for over 40 per cent of the variance. An examination of the highest loadings on this factor (Table 4.5) suggests that it is strongly and positively associated with variables reflecting socio-economic status: income, education, occupation and material possessions. Factor II represents a combination of variables associated with ethnicity and poverty – high-lighting the association between the distribution of the city's black population, single males, families living below the poverty line, and areas with a high proportion of rooming houses – and explains just over 12 per cent of the total variance. Factor III (which explains nearly 9 per cent of the variance) is equally distinctive, representing a life-cycle dimension which contrasts the distribution of older persons with those of large households, young children and economically active males. Factor IV isolates three variables relating to what amounts to a syndrome of housing instability,

Table 4.5 St Louis: factor structure

(A) *Explanatory power of each factor*:

Factor	% Variance explained	Cumulative %	Eigenvalue
I	41.3	41.3	11.5
II	12.3	53.6	3.4
III	8.8	62.5	2.5
IV	6.3	68.7	1.7
V	5.3	74.0	1.5

(B) *The nature of the factors*

Factor	Loadings	
I. 'Socio-economic status'	% high school graduates	0.909
	Median value of houses	0.882
	Median school years completed	0.866
	Median family income	0.850
	% managers and admin.	0.833
	% dwellings with >1 bathroom	0.818
II. 'Ethnicity/poverty'	% black	0.840
	% males never married	0.656
	% families below poverty level	0.641
	% German	−0.626
	% roomers	0.624
III. 'Life-cycle'	% aged > 65 years	−0.796
	Persons per household	0.759
	% aged < 5 years	0.759
	% males economically active	0.520
IV. Housing instability	% living in same house as 1965	−0.598
	% dwellings vacant	0.595
	% dwellings owner–occupied	−0.593
V	Female activity rate	0.630
	% dwellings lacking plumbing	−0.566

emphasizing the relationship between population turnover, vacancy rates and rented housing. The highest loadings on the fifth and least important factor, on the other hand, are rather ambiguous, showing a positive association with female activity rates and a negative association with substandard dwellings.

Figure 4.10 shows the spatial expression of the three leading dimensions of residential differentiation in St Louis. While a detailed examination of the social geography of St Louis need not detain us here, it is worth noting the principal features of these maps. The pattern of socio-economic status described by factor I consists of a large sector of high-status neighbourhoods extending west and south from the western margin of the central city, together with smaller areas of high status in the outer suburban zones of the metropolitan area. Low-status neighbourhoods, on the other hand, are more fragmentary, and are located around the downtown area of the city, with small sectoral extensions towards the south-east and north-east. In contrast, extreme scores on the second factor are mostly found in St Louis city, with a basic contrast between the high incidence of blacks, single males and poor families in the northern part of the central city area and the low incidence of such families and individuals in the southern part of the city where, the factor loadings suggest, there is also a high incidence of persons of German origin. Factor III – the life-cycle factor – exhibits yet another distinctive pattern, differentiating between 'youthful' neighbourhoods on the suburban fringe of the metropolitan area and 'aged' neighbourhoods within and adjacent to the central city. The basic spatial expression of this dimension is thus zonal, although the geometry of the zones is by no means regular.

The generality of factorial ecologies
The most striking feature of these results is the similarity between the three leading dimensions of the factorial ecology and the social area analysis constructs of social rank, segregation and urbanization. What is even more significant, however, is that the results of the St Louis example are fairly typical of those found in the great majority of studies of other North American cities and, indeed, of cities in Australia, New Zealand, and some other parts of the world. Not only does this lend empirical support to the constructs postulated by Shevky *et al.* (although this does not suggest any support for the associated theory of increasing scale); it also raises the possibility of building a more sensitive model of urban residential differentiation from comparative analyses of factorial ecologies. Several attempts have been made to review the relevant literature in search of generalizations about urban structure (Rees 1971, 1972, 1979; Timms 1971). By far the major finding is that residential differentiation in the great majority of cities is dominated by a socio-economic status dimension, with a second dimension characterized by family status/life-cycle characteristics and a third dimension relating to segregation along ethnic divisions. Moreover, these dimensions appear to be consistent even in the face of variations in input variables and in the statistical solution employed; and evidence from the limited number of studies of factorial ecology *change* which have been undertaken shows that

Status

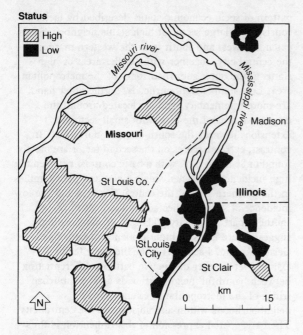

Ethnicity/Poverty

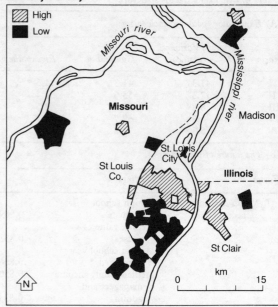

＊ **Central Business District**

Age Structure

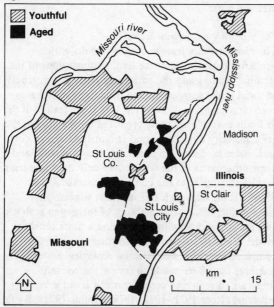

Fig. 4.10 Factorial ecology of St Louis: spatial patterns of three leading dimensions of residential differentiation. Shaded areas represent highest and lowest deciles of the factor scores.

these major dimensions tend to persist over periods of two or three decades at least (Greer-Wootten 1972; Hunter 1974; Johnston 1973a; Murdie 1969). There also appears to be a consistent pattern in the spatial expression of these dimensions, both from city to city and from one census year to the next. Salins, for

example, has shown how the socio-economic status dimension of four US cities – Buffalo, Indianapolis, Kansas City and Spokane – was reflected in an essentially sectoral pattern in 1940, 1950 and 1960, while the family status dimension exhibited a zonal gradient over the same period (Fig. 4.11); patterns of ethnicity were subject to greater change, although they were consistent in exhibiting a clustered pattern with a tendency to extend in a sectoral fashion (Salins 1971). Cross-reference with other studies confirms the generality of these findings, and the significance of sectoral and zonal configuration of the two leading dimensions has been further substantiated by analysis of variance tests conducted on the relevant sets of factor scores (Murdie 1969, 1976; Rees 1970).

Murdie has suggested that socio-economic status, family status and ethnicity should be regarded as representing major dimensions of social space which, when superimposed on the physical space of the city, serve to isolate areas of social homogeneity 'in cells defined by the spider's web of the sectoral-zonal lattice' (Murdie 1969: 168). The resultant idealized model of urban ecological structure is shown in Figure 4.12. Yet, as Murdie acknowledges, these sectors and zones are not simply superimposed on the city's morphology: they result from detailed interactions with it. Radial transport routes, for example, are likely to govern the positioning of sectors and to distort zonal patterns, as indicated in Chapter 2. Similarly, the configuration of

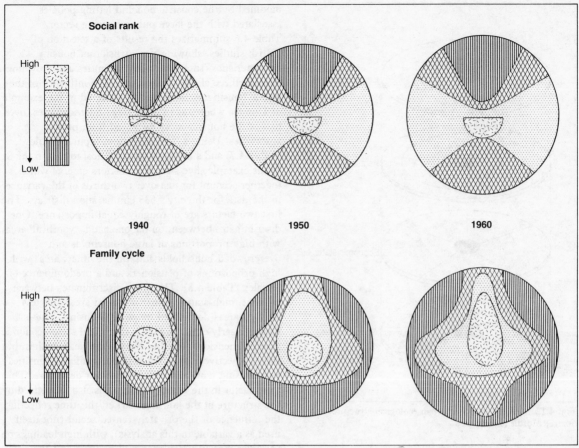

Fig. 4.11 Changing patterns of social rank and family status in American cities, 1940–1946.
Source: Salins (1971), pp. 243 and 245.

both sectors and zones is likely to be influenced by specific patterns of land use and by patterns of urban growth. By introducing such features to the idealized model it should be possible to provide a closer approximation to the real world. One attempt to do this is represented in Figure 4.13, which is based on the example of Chicago (Berry and Rees 1969). In this model, the major dimensions of residential differentiation – socio-economic status (A), family status (B) and ethnicity (C) – are superimposed on each other to form a series of relatively homogeneous communities (D). These attributes are then integrated with a number of other factors which tend to modify or distort the basic 'sectoral-zonal lattice'. First, it is suggested that the segregated ethnic areas will contain the entire range of life-cycle characteristics, but in a compressed form, so that zonal variation in family status will differ by direction about the city centre (E). A second distortion results from variations in the growth of the city (F), the effect of which is to create a star-shaped city, with 'tear faults' developing as zones cross sectoral boundaries,

displacing zones outward in the early-growth sectors (G). Thirdly, the decentralization of industry is introduced (H), resulting in the formation of areas of relatively low socio-economic status around some of the peripheral industrial centres (I).

It is important to emphasize that such models represent a high level of generalization and that the results of many studies are ambiguous or even contradictory. In Montreal, for example, the socio-economic status dimension is not 'pure', for it contains some 'ethnic' elements (Foggin and Polese 1977; Greer-Wootten 1972). Nevertheless, many geographers have suggested that the idealized model has substantial generality throughout the Western culture area. This is certainly borne out by factorial ecologies of cities in Canada (Davies and Barrow 1973), Australia (Jones 1969) and New Zealand (Johnston 1973b, 1973c), but evidence from studies of European cities tends to be less conclusive. Scandinavian cities tend to conform, in general, to the 'Western' model, although the absence of substantial ethnic minorities in

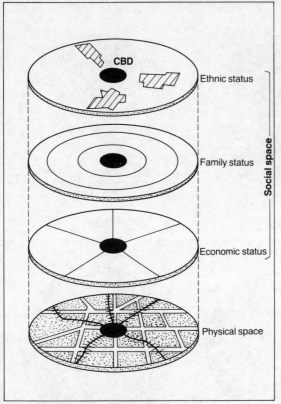

Fig. 4.12 Idealized model of urban ecological structure. *Source*: Murdie (1969), p. 8.

Scandinavian society precludes the emergence of the ethnicity dimension. Thus Janson found, in his study of Swedish cities, a socio-economic status dimension distributed sectorally and three family status dimensions corresponding to different stages in the family life-cycle: 'young familism' associated with newer suburbs, 'established familism' in zones developed in the 1940s, and 'post-familism' in older inner-city districts (Janson 1971). Similarly, the principal dimension of residential differentiation in Helsinki has been shown to be related to social rank, with the second and third most important dimensions being related to family status: 'progeniture' (associated with fertility and new housing) and 'urbanism' (associated with female activity rates) (Sweetser 1965a, 1965b). In Copenhagen, the three leading dimensions have been interpreted as family status, socio-economic status and population change respectively (Pedersen 1967).

British cities, however, do not conform so closely to the general Western model. Indeed, it has been suggested (Herbert 1968; D. Evans 1973) that British cities exhibit a distinctive ecological structure, with the principal dimensions of the classical model being

modified by the construction and letting policies associated with the large public housing sector. Table 4.6 summarizes the results of a selection of British studies, showing the intrusion of housing characteristics (such as tenure, amenities and crowding) into the three classic dimensions. The influence of the public housing sector is clearly reflected in the example of Dundee where, as in other large Scottish cities, over half of the housing stock is rented from public authorities. Using a 'typical' mix of input variables (Table 4.7) and a methodology identical to that in the St Louis example, five significant factors emerge which together account for just over two-thirds of the variance in the data for the city's 533 enumeration districts. The first two factors are of roughly equal importance. One discriminates between, on the one hand, 'youthful' areas with high proportions of large households and overcrowded households and, on the other, areas with high proportions of pensioners and a predominance of females (Table 4.8). The other discriminates between affluent, high-status, owner-occupied areas and less affluent areas dominated by public housing. These factors clearly echo the family status and socio-economic status dimensions found in North American studies, but their respective association with occupational densities and housing tenure mark an important departure. The third factor in the Dundee example is also influenced by the structure of the housing market, this time reflecting the influence of the privately-rented sector (not itself used as a variable in this analysis), with high loadings on variables measuring substandard housing and the incidence of New Commonwealth immigrants and the unemployed. The fourth factor isolates a specialist part of the housing market – bed-sitter accommodation – while the final factor highlights neighbourhoods with a particularly high turnover of population.

The overall spatial expression of these factors is indicated in Figure 4.14. Although Dundee, like Chicago, is restricted by its site, there is a clear sectoral-zonal structure to the city's generalized ecology. The distinctive feature of the diagram, however, is the extensive low-status peripheral zone (C) which, together with the adjacent zone of intermediate status, older residents (D), coincides with the city's vast public housing stock. In contrast, the two sectors of high-status neighbourhoods, each differentiated in terms of age structure and occupational density (A and B) are approximately coincident with the city's owner-occupied housing stock; while the inner-city core of substandard bedsitter accommodation coincides with much of the privately-rented housing. The city's factorial ecology thus appears to be determined principally by the three major housing sub-markets, with their associated characteristics contributing

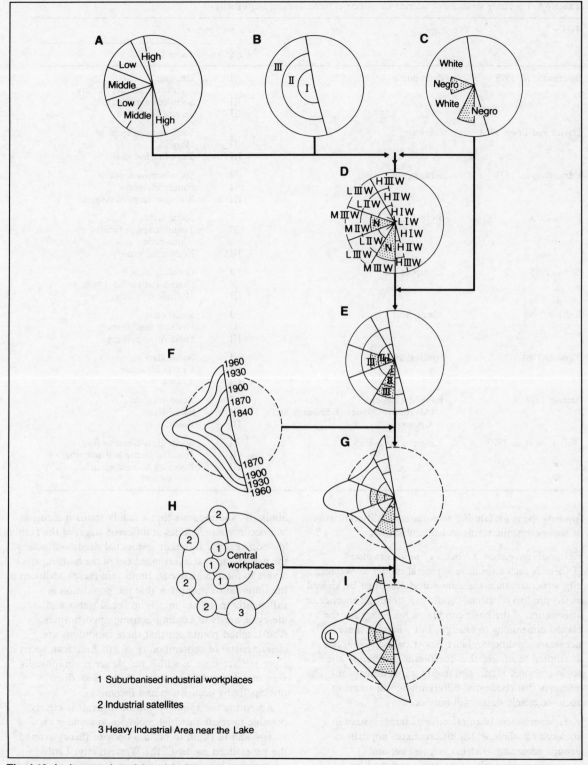

Fig. 4.13 An integrated spatial model of the metropolis.
Source: Berry and Rees (1969), Fig. 13.

Table 4.6 The factor structure of selected British cities (three leading factors only)

Author	City	Factor Structure	
		Factor	Label
Bateman *et al*. 1975	Portsmouth	I	Housing tenure/amenities/fertility
		II	Socio-economic status
		III	Service families
Davies and Lewis 1973	Leicester	I	Socio-economic status
		II	Mobility
		III	Stage in life-cycle
Edwards *et al*. 1971	Birmingham	I	Socio-economic status
		II	Family life-cycle
		III	Rooming house/transients
Evans 1973	Swansea	I	Social status
		II	Tenure/stage in family life-cycle
		III	Residential quality
Gittus 1965	Liverpool	I	Dwelling density
		II	Shared and rented dwellings
		III	Multiple dwellings
Robson 1969	Sunderland	I	Social class
		II	Housing conditions
		III	Subdivided housing
Thomas 1968	Nottingham	I	Social class
		II	Family life-cycle
		III	Tenure
Timms 1977	Four Scottish cities (Aberdeen, Dundee, Edinburgh and Glasgow)	I	Residentialism
		II	Social Rank
		III	Post-family
Wilkinson *et al*. 1970	Kingston-upon-Hull	I	Social class/overcrowding
		II	Housing tenure and amenities
		III	Rooming house/zone in transition

towards the more familiar sectoral-zonal differentiation of socio-economic status and family status.

Factorial ecologies as a product of social structure
If there is such a thing as a general model of Western city structure, then these modifications must be viewed as the product of special conditions, or of the absence or attenuation of the basic conditions necessary for the classic dimensions to emerge. But what are these necessary conditions? Janet Abu-Lughod (1969) has attempted to answer this question in relation to the socio-economic status and family status dimensions. She suggests that residential differentiation in terms of socio-economic status will only occur:

1. where there is an effective ranking system in society as a whole which differentiates population groups according to status or prestige; and
2. where this ranking system is matched by corresponding subdivisions of the housing market.

Similarly, she suggests that a family status dimension will occur where families at different stages of the family life-cycle exhibit different residential needs *and* where the nature and spatial arrangement of the housing stock is able to fulfil these needs. Implicit in these conditions is the important assumption that the population is sufficiently mobile to match up social status and life-cycle needs to existing housing opportunities. Abu-Lughod points out that these conditions are characteristic of contemporary North American society: a pre-welfare state in which people are geographically very mobile, and where social status is ascribed principally by occupation and income.

Accepting the validity of these ideas, it is clearly possible to relate factorial ecologies to a wider view of society and to begin to build a body of theory around the generalized model of the Western city. Little attempt has been made to do this, however; researchers have been pre-occupied more with the technical pros

Table 4.7 Input variables for factorial ecology of Dundee, 1971

1. Female activity rate
2. % aged 0–14
3. % pensioners
4. % students
5. Marriage rate
6. Fertility rate
7. % born in New Commonwealth
8. % Irish
9. % dwellings owner-occupied
10. % dwellings rented from public authority
11. % households sharing accommodation.
12. % households with exclusive use of all basic amenities
13. % households overcrowded
14. % dwellings with only 1–3 rooms
15. % large households
16. % households without a car
17. % households who had moved in last 5 years
18. % professionals
19. % unemployed
20. % who had changed occupation
21. Sex ratio

Table 4.8 Dundee: factor structure

(A). Explanatory power of each factor

Factor	% variance explained	Cumulative %	Eigenvalue
I	25.1	25.1	5.3
II	20.1	45.2	4.2
III	10.0	55.2	2.1
IV	6.0	61.2	1.3
V	5.8	67.0	1.2

(B). Nature of the factors

Factor	Loadings	
I. 'Familism/crowding'	% pensioners	−0.931
	% aged 0–14	0.925
	% large households	0.889
	% overcrowded	0.703
	sex ratio	−0.612
II. 'Social class/housing class'	% owner-occupied	−0.916
	% without a car	0.884
	% professionals	−0.844
	% small dwellings	0.654
	% public housing	0.555
III. 'Substandardness/ethnicity'	% with all basic amenities	−0.816
	% public housing	−0.669
	% New Commonwealth born	0.569
	Marriage rate	0.523
	% unemployed	0.474
IV. 'Bedsitters'	% students	0.677
	% sharing accommodation	0.594
	Marriage rate	−0.549
V. 'Transients'	% 5-year movers	0.836
	Sex ratio	−0.446
	% changed occupation	0.398

and cons of different aspects of factor analysis. But, as Herbert (1972) shows, Abu-Lughod's work provides a useful framework against which deviations from the general model can be explained. Herbert gives the example of the frequently-encountered association between the socio-economic status dimensions and measures of fertility which 'spoil' the clarity of the two leading dimensions, as in the factorial ecologies of Atlanta, Birmingham, Kansas City and Louisville reported by van Arsdol *et al.* (1958). In such cases, it is suggested, socio-economic status exists as a system for ranking people in social space and is matched geographically by residential segregations. Family size, however, is not independent of social status; and the housing market is not geared to a sufficient range of life-cycle stages. In the specific cases represented by the four cities in the study by van Arsdol *et al.* the reason for this aberration is found in the unusually high proportion of blacks: 'The presence of the Negro population, with its distinctive characteristics of low status and high fertility, together with imposed constraints upon mobility and a limited housing market, diminishes the likelihood of family status emerging as a separate and independent dimension for the city as a whole' (Herbert 1972: 176). In short, deviations from the 'norm' of North American society produce distortions of the 'typical' ecological structure of cities.

Similar reasoning can be used to explain other atypical results. In Montreal, where the socio-economic status dimension overlaps with ethnicity, the explanation can be found in the unusually large minority population of French-speakers which occupies most of the lower part of the social ladder with the result that ethnicity and social status are not independent phenomena (Foggin and Polese 1977). In Swedish cities, the existence of three separate family status dimensions can be attributed to the relative immobility of Swedes, compared to American norms (Janson 1971). The tendency for the ecology of English cities to be dominated by housing market characteristics can be seen as a reflection of the country's more highly developed public sector. The association between the family status dimension and measures of crowding found in most British studies, for example, can be related to the letting policies of local authority housing departments, many of which allocate public housing on the basis of family size, among other things, as an indicant of housing need (see also pages 149–151). Similarly, the use of economic criteria of housing need in determining people's eligibility for council houses

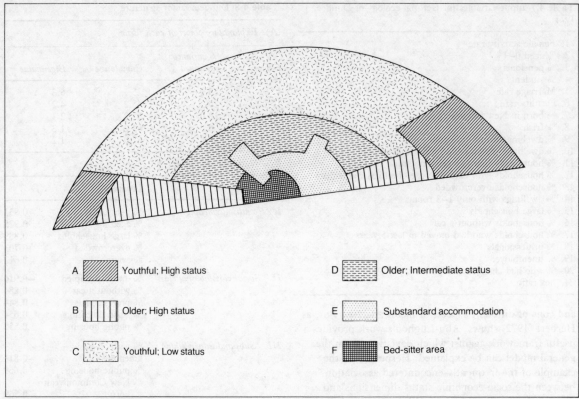

A   Youthful; High status

B   Older; High status

C   Youthful; Low status

D   Older; Intermediate status

E   Substandard accommodation

F   Bed-sitter area

Fig. 4.14 Generalized residential structure of Dundee.

ensures that there is a close association between socio-economic status and housing tenure.

Some unresolved difficulties

Notwithstanding the considerable potential of factorial ecologies, several important methodological issues remain as stumbling blocks in the pursuit of a more sophisticated theory of residential differentiation. These issues have been the subject of extensive debate, the details of which are summarized by Johnston (1976a). Among the chief limitations identified by Johnston is the fact that most analyses rely almost exclusively on decennial or quinquennial censuses for their data. This means that research is often constrained by a lack of data covering a full range of socio-economic characteristics, since many census authorities have been chary of demanding information on sensitive subjects such as religion and have been unwilling to expend limited resources collecting information on complex phenomena such as people's lifestyle or activity patterns.

This may help to explain Palm's interesting finding that the geography of 'communities of interest' in Minneapolis-St Paul, as reflected by patterns of newspaper and magazine readership, was quite different

from the factorial ecology of the city (Palm 1973). Indeed, the generality of factorial ecology results may be partly attributable to similarities in the input variables used in different studies. The territorial units for which aggregate census data are published may also have a considerable effect upon the analysis. Despite the probability that the boundaries of census sub-areas will not match actual patterns of residential variation on the ground, the implicit assumption in the methodology is that these territories are homogeneous. Research by Newton and Johnston, however, has shown that not only do census sub-areas tend to be relatively heterogeneous, but that the incorporation of measures of homogeneity in the data matrix can suggest important qualifications to 'classical' factorial ecologies. In their analysis of Christchurch, New Zealand, they found that areas ranked highest on the socio-economic status dimension were also the least homogeneous in their population characteristics; while the suburban areas ranked highest on a 'life-style' dimension (associated with family status and housing quality variables) exhibited a fairly high level of homogeneity in their population characteristics (Newton and Johnston 1976). Another, more intractable problem arising from the boundary locations of census sub-areas is that of spatial autocorrelation, although the *extent* to which this distorts the results of factorial ecologies is a matter of debate (Cliff and Ord 1973). It should also be recognized that census sub-areas represent only one of the very large number of ways that a city can be sub-divided, thus raising the question as to whether the same factorial ecology would result from different spatial frameworks; and, if not, whether the difference is a product of scale-specific processes or merely an artefact of the data set.

Another important stumbling block concerns the interpretation of the results of factorial ecologies. In addition to the hazards of the ecological fallacy (see p. 53) which are by now well known to geographers, there are certain less well-known dangers involved in the substantive interpretation of the output of factor analyses. In particular Johnston (1976a) cites the danger of 'overinterpretation' in situations where, despite low inter-correlations between variables (suggesting that their distributions are more different than similar), high loadings may still be generated. Overinterpretation may also arise where the input includes several variables which between them define a 'closed system' of a particular phenomenon. Thus the inclusion of variables measuring the percentage of the population in each of an exhaustive series of occupational categories would almost certainly produce an 'occupation' dimension which, because of correlations with other variables, is likely to lead to a spurious result. Another problem of overinterpretation has been identified by Palm and Caruso (1972), who suggest that the tendency to interpret factors using only a few major loadings leads to a coarse labelling of factors which obscures important variations in variables with lower loadings.

In an attempt to sidestep some of these problems, analysts whose main interest is in the *overall* spatial pattern defined by the input variables rather than in the underlying dimensions of differentiation and their associated spatial expression have sometimes used grouping procedures such as cluster analysis and multiple discriminant analysis in order to achieve a multivariate classification of census sub-areas. Such techniques generally group sub-areas according to their proximity in n-dimensional space (where n = the number of input variables), so that the result is a typology of sub-areas in which within-group variation is minimized and between-group variation is maximized. The number of groups or clusters of sub-areas produced depends, in part, upon subjective decisions by the analyst, although there is a clear relationship between the number of groups and the sensitivity of the classification: the fewer the groups the greater the loss of detail (for a full discussion of such techniques see Everitt (1974) and Johnston (1976b)). Figure 4.15 shows the results of a cluster analysis of Dundee enumeration districts using the same input variables as in the factorial ecology example; and a summary of the distinctive characteristics of each cluster of enumeration districts is given in Table 4.9. These clusters may be thought of as representing 'neighbourhood types'. As Figure 4.15 shows, enumeration districts of the same type are not always contiguous; but there is a fairly high degree of spatial coherence, reflecting the distinctive socio-economic 'regions' which exist within the city. As with the factorial ecology, it is possible to identify a central 'bed-sitter' zone surrounded by low-status neighbourhoods, with major high-status sectors to the east and west and a broad zone of public sector neighbourhoods to the north. The cluster analysis, however, clearly reflects the finer differentiation which exists within these areas. The low-status inner-city areas are differentiated in terms of both ethnicity and family status variables, for example; while there are evidently wide differences in the demographic composition of neighbourhoods in the public sector to the north of the city. Such differences are demonstrated very effectively by bar graphs (Fig. 4.16). This simplicity of presentation, together with the comprehensiveness of the approach, has made multivariate grouping procedures increasingly popular among analysts concerned with identifying urban regions, whether as a geographical synthesis or as a sampling framework for further research. Planners, in particular, have been attracted to these techniques because of the relative ease with which the output can be understood by non-professionals. In detail, however, the methodology involved is not without pitfalls. Indeed, some cluster

Table 4.9 Dundee: cluster characteristics (cluster numbers refer to those in Fig. 4.15)

Cluster	Dominant characteristics*
1	Owner-occupiers, car-owners, professionals
2	Migrants, professionals
3	Public housing, high fertility
4	Public housing, youthful population, high marriage rate, low car ownership
5	Public housing, overcrowding, high fertility, high female activity rates, high proportions of children
6	Students, shared accommodation, Irish, migrants
7	Public housing, pensioners, small households,
8	Lack of basic housing amenities, small dwellings, Irish, pensioners
9	New Commonwealth born, lack of basic housing amenities, high fertility
10	Unemployment, lack of basic housing amenities, small dwellings, young population, high marriage rate

* Variables for which the cluster average is greater than one standard deviation from the mean of the city's 533 enumeration districts.

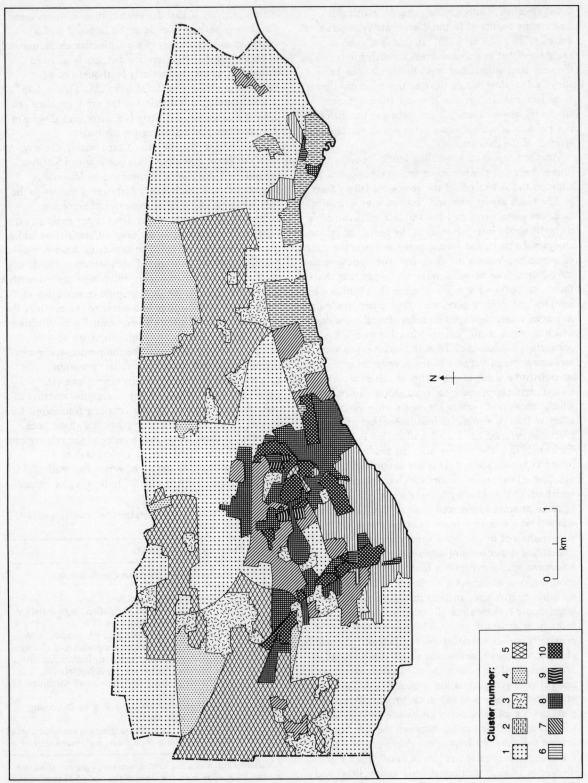

Fig. 4.15 A typology of neighbourhood types in Dundee

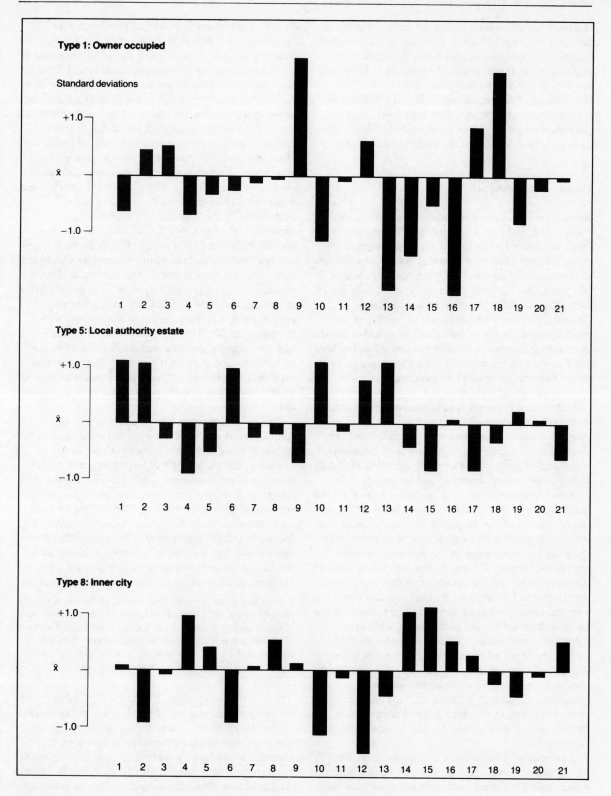

Fig. 4.16 Socio-economic characteristics of selected neighbourhood types in Dundee.

analysis procedures are based on an initial factoring of the data; and all multivariate grouping procedures, like factorial ecologies, are subject to the constraints imposed by the shortcomings of census data. Moreover, the nature of the technique makes inter-city comparisons of residential typologies very difficult so that, in relation to the search for high-level generalizations about urban residential structure, factor analysis is likely to remain the preferred technique.

Urban social indicators

As we have seen, one of the major shortcomings of traditional factorial ecology studies is that the mix of input variables overlooks many important aspects of urban life, including environmental quality, accessibility to facilities like hospitals, shopping centres, libraries and parks, and the local incidence of social pathologies such as crime, delinquency and drug addiction. Recently, however, the emergence of 'quality of life' and 'territorial justice' as central concerns within human geography has meant that much more attention has been given to such issues, allowing the presentation of a rather different perspective on patterns of socio-economic differentiation.

It should be acknowledged at the outset that interest in patterns of social well-being and the quality of life (the two terms are used here synonymously) and the distribution of social *malaise* in cities is by no means new. Charles Booth used a set of six variables, including measures of poverty, crowding and mortality, to construct a composite index of 'social conditions' for the neighbourhoods of Victorian London (Booth 1893), and the description of the geography of personal and social pathologies has received a great deal of attention over the years in connection with the ecological theories outlined in Chapter 3. Nevertheless, it is fair to say that it is only within the last decade or so that patterns of deprivation and variation in the quality of life have been a central concern within geography. The reasons for the rather sudden awakening of interest in what have collectively been called 'welfare' issues (Smith 1977, 1979a) can be traced to the events of the 1960s: the rioting and disorder in American cities associated with the blacks' struggle for civil rights, and the 'revolutionary' alliance between students and factory workers in parts of Europe associated with popular protest against the hegemony of Big Business and Big Government.

The scale of these events was impressive: in the Watts riots in Los Angeles in 1965, 34 people were killed, over 1,000 were badly injured, more than 500 buildings were looted and burnt down, and $100 m. of

damage was sustained; in Berlin, Hamburg, Munich, Frankfurt and Hanover, five days of rioting followed the police shooting of student leader Rudi Dutschke; and at the height of the revolutionary movement in France in May 1968, over 800,000 people turned out to march in Paris, while over two-thirds of the country's workforce joined in a general strike. But the long term effects of these events were more significant, if less dramatic. Society in general became sensitized to a wide range of social and environmental issues; and geographers and other social scientists, in parallel with politicians and the media, began to examine these issues more closely. One major focus of interest was the question of the distribution of the 'bads' or 'ills' which were, apparently, the inevitable handmaidens of economic growth. Reinforced by a welter of mass media features, concern for those sections of the community who found themselves the victims rather than the beneficiaries of national economic growth helped to shift the objectives of national and local governments away from the promotion of economic growth to the improvment of the quality of life. This inevitably raised the question of how to recognize improvements to the quality of life when they did occur, for it was clear that traditional yardsticks of national and local performance were wholly insensitive to many of the qualitative aspects of life.

Part of the collective response of academics, administrators and policy-makers was manifested in the so-called 'social indicators movement'. Rather ironically, the initial impetus for the movement came from the North American Space Administration, which sought to develop quantitative measures of the 'social spin-off' of its activities (Bauer 1966). Within a short time, however, social indicators had established a firm footing in federal administrative thinking. Official interest was first declared in a document produced by the United States Department of Health, Education and Welfare, which went on to define a social indicator as:

a statistic of direct normative interest which facilitates concise, comprehensive and balanced judgements about the conditions of major aspects of a society. It is in all cases a direct measure of welfare and it is subject to the interpretation that, if it changes in the 'right' direction, while other things remain equal, things have got better, or people are 'better off' (USDHEW 1969: 97).

The task of developing such indicators has subsequently occupied a large number of scholars and policy-makers in the United States, Europe, Australasia and Japan, and there now exists an extensive literature on the construction and use of social indicators in a variety of contexts (see, for example, OECD 1977; Smith 1973b). As David Smith has shown, *territorial* social indicators provide a very useful descriptive device in the context of geographical analysis. Smith has made a strong case for a 'welfare approach' to human geography, with the central concern being 'who gets what, where, and how?'. Following this approach, territorial social indicators are seen as fundamental to 'the major and immediate research task' of describing the geography of social well-being at different spatial scales. This, it is argued, will not only provide the context for empirical research concerned with *explaining* the mechanisms and processes which create and sustain territorial disparities in well-being but will also facilitate the *evaluation* of these disparities in the light of prevailing societal values and, if necessary, the *prescription* of remedial policies (Smith 1973b, 1974a, 1977). Since the early 1970s, something of a start has been made on the application of territorial social indicators at the intra-urban level. Two kinds of study are of particular interest here: those which attempt to describe variations in the overall level of local social well-being – 'quality of life' studies – and those which attempt to identify particular sub-areas whose residents are relatively disadvantaged – studies of 'deprivation'.

The quality of urban life

Quality of life studies are of interest here because they offer the possibility of portraying the essential socio-geographical expression of urban communities on a conceptual scale which ranges along a continuum from 'good' to 'bad', thus providing a potent index with which to regionalize the city. The construction of such an index presents a number of difficulties, however. The first task is to set out a defition of social well-being which can be translated into a composite statistical measure: something which has taxed social scientists a great deal. The range of factors which potentially influence people's well-being for better or worse is enormous. Moreover, opinions about the importance of different contributory factors often vary between socio-geographical groups; and factors which might be important at one geographic scale can be completely irrelevant at another. Smith (1973b: 46) concludes that 'we are apparently faced with the problem of trying to measure something which is not directly observable, for which there is no generally accepted *numeraire*, and which theory tells us is some function of things which ultimately rest on societal values'. Any search for conclusive or universal definitions of social well-being is therefore futile. Nevertheless, as Smith himself argues, 'the imperative of empirical analysis in welfare geography means that we must be prepared to move in where the angels fear to tread' (Smith 1973b: 47). In this spirit, it is possible to set out those components of social well-being about which there is likely to be at least a broad consensus. At the most general level, the United Nations Organization has identified the areas of agreement between member nations as to the main components of national 'levels of living': nutrition, clothing, shelter, health care, educational opportunities, leisure, security, the social environment, and the physical environment (Drewnowski 1974). At a more detailed level, Smith has proposed seven 'general criteria' of social well-being relevant to the United States (Tables 4.10). These criteria were established by conducting a content analysis of a sample of the literature on social indicators and contemporary social problems and they formed the basis of Smith's own empirical research on the geography of social well-being in the United States (Smith 1973b). His analysis of Tampa, Florida, provides a good case study of intra-urban variations in the quality of life. Table 4.11 shows the 47 variables used to operationalize the seven criteria of social well-being and illustrates vividly the

Table 4.10 Smith's criteria of social well-being

I. Income, wealth and employment
 (i) Income and wealth
 (ii) Employment status
 (iii) Income supplements

II. The living environment
 (i) Housing
 (ii) Neighbourhood
 (iii) Physical environment

III. Health
 (i) Physical health
 (ii) Mental health

IV. Education
 (i) Achievement
 (ii) Duration and quality

V. Social order (or disorganization)
 (i) Personal pathologies
 (ii) Family breakdown
 (iii) Crime and delinquency
 (iv) Public order and safety

VI. Social belonging (alienation and participation)
 (i) Democratic participation
 (ii) Criminal justice
 (iii) Segregation

VII. Recreation and leisure
 (i) Recreation facilities
 (ii) Culture and the arts
 (iii) Leisure available

Source: Smith 1973: 70.

Table 4.11 Criteria of social well-being and variables used in Smith's Tampa study

Criteria and variables

I. *Economic status*
  (i) Income
    1. Income per capita ($) of persons 14 and over, 1970
    2. Families with income less than $3000 (%) 1970
    3. Families with income over $10,000 (%) 1970
    4. Persons in families below poverty level (%) 1970
  (ii) Employment
    5. Unemployed persons (% total workforce) 1970
    6. Persons aged 16–24 working less than 40 weeks (%) 1969
    7. White-collar workers (%) 1970
    8. Blue-collar workers (%) 1970
  (iii) Welfare
    9. Families on AFDC program (%) October 1971
    10. Persons aged 65 and over on Old Age Assistance (%) Oct. 1971

II. *Environment*
  (i) Housing
    11. Average value of owner-occupied units ($) 1970
    12. Owner-occupied units valued less than $10,000 (%) 1970
    13. Average monthly rental of rented units ($) 1970
    14. Rented units with monthly rentals less than $60 (%) 1970
    15. Units with complete plumbing facilities (%) 1970
    16. Deteriorating and dilapidated houses (%) 1971
  (ii) Streets and sewers
    17. Streets needing reconstruction (% of total length) 1971
    18. Streets needing scarification and resurfacing (% of total length) 1971
    19. Sanitary sewer deficiencies (% of total area) 1971
    20. Storm sewer deficiencies (% of total area) 1971
  (iii) Air pollution
    21. Maximum monthly dustfall (tons/sq. mile) 1969
    22. Average suspended particulates 1969 (μgm/m^3/day) 1969
    23. Maximum monthly sulfation 1969 (mg SO_3/100 cm^2/day) 1969
  (vi) Open space
    24. Area lacking park and recreation facilities (%) 1971

III. *Health*
  (i) General mortality
    25. Infant deaths (per 1,000 live births) 1970
    26. Death rate (per 10,000 persons 65 or over) 1970
  (ii) Chronic diseases
    27. Cancer deaths (per 100,000 population) 1970
    28. Stroke deaths (per 100,000 population) 1970
    29. Heart disease deaths (per 100,000 population) 1970
    30. New active tuberculosis cases (per 10,000 population) 1970

IV. *Education*
  (i) Duration
    31. Persons aged 18–24 with 4 or more years high school or college (%) 1970
    32. Persons over 25 with 8 years or less school (%) 1970
    33. Persons over 25 with 4 years high school (%) 1970
    34. Persons over 25 with 4 years college (%) 1970

Criteria and variables

V. *Social disorganization*
  (i) Personal pathologies
    35. Narcotic violations arrests (per 10,000 residents) 1971
    36. Venereal disease cases (per 10,000 population) 1970
  (ii) Family breakdown
    37. Families with children, having husband and wife present (%) 1970.
    38. Persons separated or divorced (% never married) 1970
  (iii) Overcrowding
    39. Dwellings with more than 1.0 persons per room (%) 1970
  (iv) Public order and safety
    40. Criminal violation arrests (per 1,000 residents) 1971
    41. Juvenile delinquency arrests (per 10,000 residents) 1971
    42. Accidental deaths (per 1000,000 population) 1970
  (v) Delinquency
    43. Juvenile delinquency arrests by residency (per 10,000 population, 1971)

VI. *Participation and equality*
  (i) Democratic participation
    44. Registered voters (% population 18 and over) 1971
    45. Eligible voters voting in mayoral election (%) 1971
  (ii) Equality
    46. Racial distribution index 1970
    47. Income distribution index 1970

Source: Smith 1973: 123–4.

scope of quality of life studies: measures of welfare dependency, air pollution, recreational facilities, drug offences, family stability and public participation in local affairs are all included, in marked contrast to the urban geographer's conventional view of the city. Smith acknowledges that his selection of variables 'is a compromise between the ideal and what was possible given the constraints of time and resources', but maintains that 'the data assembled provide a satisfactory reflection of the general concept of social well-being and embody many important conditions which have a bearing on the quality of individual life' (Smith 1973b: 125). An overall measure of social well-being was derived from these data using the relatively simple procedure of aggregating, for each census tract, the standardized scores on all the variables. The resultant index is mapped in Figure 14.17. Despite the rather peculiar shape of the city, with its CBD close to the bay and its southern suburbs surrounded on three sides by water, there is a clear pattern to the geography of well-being: a sink of ill-being occupies the inner city area, with relatively poor areas extending towards the city limits in a north-easterly direction. The best areas occupy the opposite sector of the city, although most suburban neighbourhoods enjoy a quality of life which is well above the average.

Similar results have emerged from quality of life

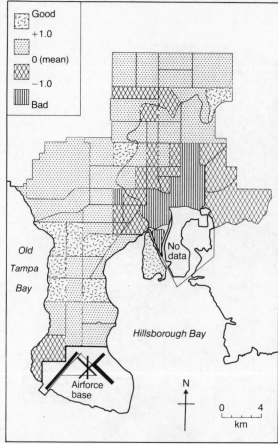

Fig. 4.17 Standard scores on a general indicator of social well-being for Tampa, Florida.
Source: Smith (1973), p. 126.

the city's black sector enjoy an above-average quality of life; and scores of the very highest level are achieved by black census tracts in the high-status Cascade area.

One of the major potential weaknesses of this kind of approach is the implicit assumption that the aggregation of a series of measures of different aspects of social well-being will produce a meaningful statistic. Although this procedure may be an acceptable expedient in many circumstances, it is clear that social well-being should in fact be regarded as the product of a series of contributory factors which are *weighted* according to their relative importance to the people whose well-being is under consideration. It is evident, for example, that British and American people do not regard housing conditions as being as important to their well-being as their health, whereas both factors are felt to be much more important than accessibility to recreational facilities (Abrams 1973; Campbell, Converse and Rodgers 1976). Moreover, these values tend to vary significantly between socio-geographical groups: Lovrich, for example, has described the very different priorities of Anglo, Black and Mexican-American voters in Denver (Lovrich 1974); and in Britain, intra-urban variations in attitudes to education have become part of the conventional wisdom of a whole generation of educationalists (Douglas 1964; Robson 1969). There are plenty of reasons for such variations. To begin with, some aspects of social well-being (leisure and material consumption, for example) are highly income-elastic, so that successive increases in expendable income will bring about marked increases in the intensity with which they are valued. This conforms conveniently with Maslow's (1970) suggestion that human motivation is related to a hierarchy of human needs, so that as people's basic needs – for nutrition, shelter and personal safety – are satisfied, motivation turns towards higher goals such as the attainment of social status, prestige, and self-expression. Accepting this model of behaviour, it follows that people with low levels of material well-being will attach more importance to materialistic than to aesthetic, spiritual or cultural aspects of life. People's values also vary according to their stage in the family life cycle, and to their membership of particular religious or cultural groups. Moreover, the social geography of the city is itself likely to generate or reinforce differences in values from one neighbourhood to another, for the socio-demographic composition of different neighbourhoods creates distinctive local reference groups which contribute significantly to people's attitudes to life (Eyles 1973).

The crucial issue for quality of life studies is whether these variations in people's values are great enough to blunt the effectiveness of unweighted bundles of statistics such as those used by Smith and

studies in Gainesville, Florida (Dickinson *et al*. 1972) and Atlanta, Georgia (Bederman 1974). Both studies describe a sharply bi-polar society, in which the geography of social well-being exhibits both sectoral and zonal elements. In addition, both studies have demonstrated the close association between race and the quality of life. Bederman's study shows this relationship particularly well. Using a methodology similar to Smith's (but with a somewhat narrower definition of the quality of life), Bederman demonstrates that the area with the lowest quality of life – a sector extending north-westwards from the inner slums just south of the CBD – also had a predominantly black population (Fig. 4.18); as did 39 of the city's 54 worse-than-average census tracts. Closer inspection of the relationship between the quality of life and racial composition, however, shows a marked stratification in the quality of life of black communities. Thus, while black inner-city neighbourhoods were found to be at the very bottom of the ladder, neighbourhoods further south-west within

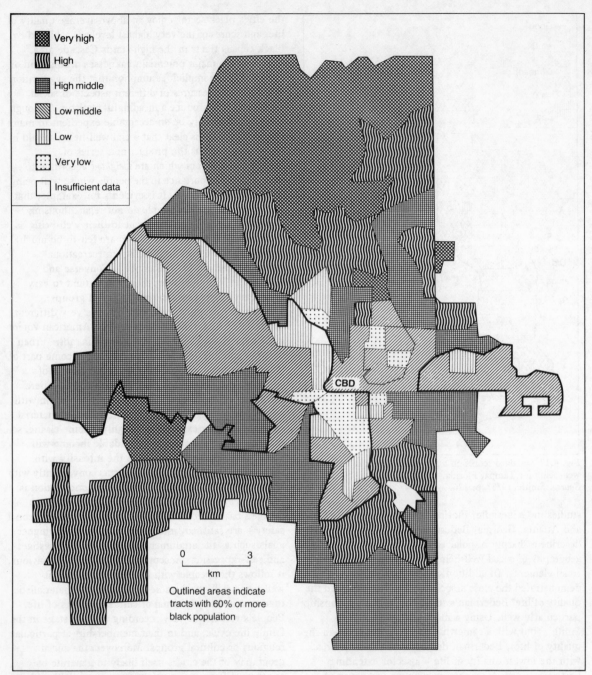

Fig. 4.18 The quality of life in Atlanta, Georgia.
Source: Bederman (1974), p. 32.

Bederman. Unfortunately, few studies have pursued this question in any detail, largely because of the difficulties involved in obtaining reliable data on people's values: the cost of properly-conducted surveys is simply too great for most research projects. Nevertheless, the available evidence suggests that

weighting indicators of local well-being according to prevailing local values does not make a significant difference to overall patterns of the quality of life. The chief source of evidence for this conclusion is a study of the geography of social well-being in Dundee reported by Knox and MacLaran (1978). In this study, an overall index of 'level of living' was computed for each of 14 neighbourhood types using survey data on 50 variables relating to eleven 'domains' of life: health, housing, employment opportunities, education, personal security, income and consumption, leisure, social and political participation, access to amenities, environmental quality, and social stability. According to this unweighted index, the owner-occupied neighbourhoods to the east and west of the city were by far the best-off, followed by more central neighbourhoods containing the most stable and sought-after of the city's older public housing estates. At the other end of the spectrum were most of the inner-city neighbourhoods, together with a few of the outlying suburbs of more recent public housing. Data on people's values collected in the same survey showed that there were statistically significant differences between the fourteen neighbourhood types in the importance attached to all but two of the domains (income/finance and leisure); but when these data were used to weight the level of living index it was found that 'The results of these calculations show that weighted description, although it is arguably more sensitive to variations in well-being . . . produces much the same picture, ecologically, as the conventional unweighted approach' (Knox and MacLaran 1978: 224). Interestingly, the survey results also showed that people tended to attach most value to the things they found themselves to be best at, or had most of – thus helping to explain the close relationship between the weighted and unweighted index values.

Patterns of deprivation

Interest in welfare issues quickly spread from the pursuit of overall yardsticks of well-being to the construction of territorial indicators designed explicitly to identify 'problem areas' and areas of 'social stress' or 'social malaise', where urban deprivation was at its worst (Smith 1979b). Much of the impetus for this work came from professional planners and administrators wanting quantitative measures of the intensity of deprivation in order to be able to formulate spatial policies with which to rectify or ameloriate the problem. Many of the resultant policies have taken the form of *positive discrimination*, directing resources into areas which have been identified as the locus of deprivation. It should be noted at once that the utility of such policies is open to some doubt: their effect on the social geography of the city is discussed in Chapter 8. In this chapter, however, interest is in the indicators themselves and the spatial patterns which they describe.

The main reason for this interest is simply that patterns of deprivation represent an important facet of the geography of the city (Herbert 1975). In this context, it is useful to regard deprivation as multi-dimensional, directing attention to the spatial configuration and inter-relationships of different aspects of deprivation. The Norwegian geographer Asbjorn Aase (1978) has suggested that these patterns may be of three different kinds:

1. *random*, with no observable co-variance between different aspects of deprivation;

2. *compensatory*, where the local occurrence of particular aspects of deprivation is accompanied by above-average conditions in relation to other aspects of life;

3. *accumulative*, where there is a high degree of spatial overlap in the distribution of deprivations, resulting in areas of 'multiple deprivation'.

To these we must add a fourth possibility: that the distribution of deprivations may form distinctive constellations of problems, thus reflecting different *kinds* of deprived areas containing different combinations of deprivation. At this point it is necessary to emphasize that we are concerned here with *area* deprivations, expressed in terms of the average characteristics of spatially-defined groups of people. Once again, therefore, it is necessary to guard against the dangers of ecological fallacy: not everyone in a deprived area is necessarily deprived; and not every deprived person in an area of 'multiple deprivation' is necessarily multiply deprived.

Aase's own empirical research (with Britt Dale) suggested that the tendency within Norwegian cities is for the accumulative distribution of deprivations. In Trondheim, for example, low-status neighbourhoods tended to fare badly on most of the 19 indicators used to measure relative levels of deprivation and prosperity (Fig. 4.19). The same tendency for the accumulative distribution of deprivations is evident in Fig. 4.20, which shows the distribution of fourteen different aspects of deprivation in Liverpool, by wards. In every case, the worst levels of deprivation are to be found in the inner city, with certain suburban neighbourhoods consistently falling within the two next-worst categories. This tendency has encouraged the development of overall measures of deprivation: if the distribution of deprivations is accumulative, it seems fair to aggregate indicators to produce a single index of 'multiple deprivation'. A good example of this approach is provided by the work of Scottish Development Department researchers on areas of multiple deprivation in Glasgow (SDD 1973). This work was brought about by the need to identify priority areas for a £7 m. urban aid programme announced in 1971. Working at enumeration district level, six census indicators of deprivation – covering aspects of unemployment,

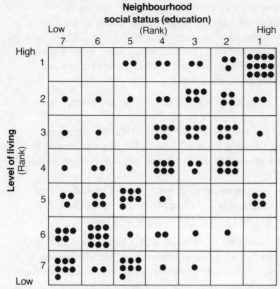

Fig. 4.19 The localization of deprivations in Trondheim, Norway: rankings for 19 level-of-living indicators among 7 areas.
Source: Aase and Dale (1978), p. 49.

occupation, household structure, housing amenities and overcrowding – were derived from the census and used to compute an overall index based on rank scores. Non-census data were also mapped, and the visual coincidence of these aspects of deprivation was used to verify the results of the census-based index. The final definition of problem areas covered more than a third of the city (by area), and included several areas of public housing as well as much of the older tenemental housing stock of the inner city.

This kind of approach has been criticized on several grounds, however, including the desirability of aggregating indicators of several different aspects of deprivation and the validity of assigning them equal weight in the overall index (Craig and Driver 1972; Hatch and Sherrot 1973). Most significant of all though is the danger that aggregate measures in fact mask distinctive combinations of deprivations in one part of the city or another. Although the examples outlined above suggest that the general trend is for an accumulative distribution of deprivations in inner city areas and (in Britain) in some peripheral public housing estates, detailed statistical analysis sometimes reveals significant localized constellations of particular aspects of deprivation. In Belfast, for example, Boal *et al*. (1978) found that a factor analysis of seven social malaise variables produced two major dimensions of deprivation : one characterized by unemployment, illegitimacy, high proportions of children in public care and high rates of mortality from bronchitis and

associated with inner-city neighbourhoods, and the other characterized by high levels of unemployment, overcrowding and delinquency and associated with a sectoral distribution westwards from the city centre.

Another study which demonstrates the existence of deprived areas of different kinds within cities is Coulter's (1978) analysis of 1 km-square census data for the seven largest British conurbations: Birmingham, Glasgow, Leeds, Liverpool, London, Manchester and Newcastle upon Tyne. According to Coulter, the most common syndrome of deprivation in these conurbations involves overcrowding, unemployment, low wages (reflected by high proportions of unskilled workers), low levels of car ownership and high levels of ill-health, and is typically located centrally within the core of the conurbation. This, however, is by no means the only deprivation syndrome in evidence. Leeds, Liverpool, Glasgow and (to a lesser extent) Manchester all exhibit an additional syndrome of deprivation involving poor housing – mostly privately-rented, furnished accommodation – associated with inner-city areas containing high proportions of New Commonwealth immigrants. In addition, some conurbations have distinctive syndromes of deprivation which are associated with outer suburban areas. Some council estates within the outer zone of the Birmingham, Glasgow and Manchester conurbations, for example, suffer particularly from a syndrome involving low educational achievement, low wages and lack of a car.

Perhaps the most illuminating research of this kind is the analysis of deprivation and social pathology in Liverpool undertaken by the Planning Research Applications Group as a follow-up to their pioneering Social Malaise Study (Webber 1975). Table 4.12 summarizes the distribution of a wide range of symptoms of deprivation, revealing a marked variation in the nature and intensity of deprivation between the five principal types of neighbourhood in the city. By far the worst off are the inner council estates, with four times the city-wide level of delinquency, three times the average levels of job instability among youths and of school absenteeism, and over twice the average levels of disinfestation, children in long-term care, low reading ability, educational subnormality, unemployment and family poverty (as reflected by childrens' eligibility for free school meals). Rooming-house areas also score badly across a wide range of indicators, but are particularly characterized by high proportions of children in care, by large numbers of housing repair notices, and by a high incidence of infectious diseases. Finally, the nature of the symptoms of deprivation in the city's peripheral council estates is different again, centring on family poverty, youth unemployment and the incidence of possession orders.

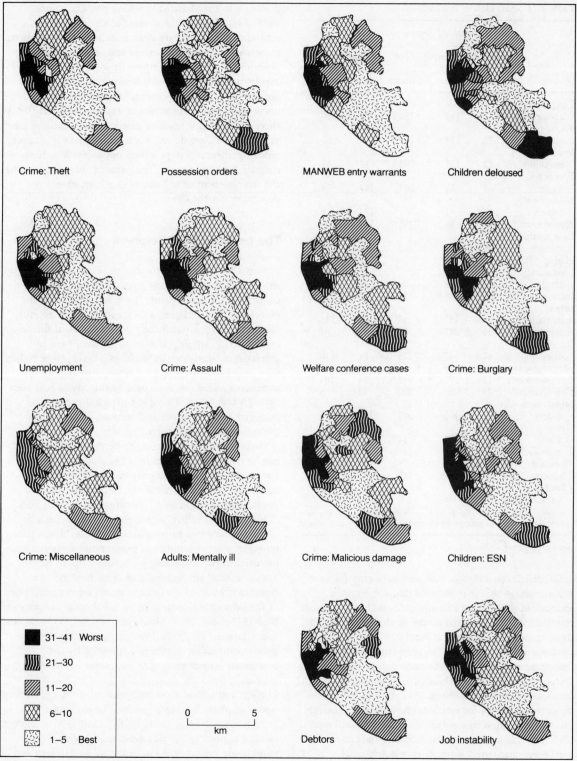

Fig. 4.20 Patterns of deprivation in Liverpool.
Source: Brooks (1977), p. 26.

Table 4.12 Social malaise in Liverpool

	Neighbourhood performance*				
	High status areas	Rooming house areas	Inner council estates	Outer council estates	Older terraced housing
Long term unemployment	32	136	250	102	89
Youth unemployment	33	110	199	145	63
Youth job instability	17	151	302	112	68
Free school meals	29	81	201	147	74
Educationally sub-normal	42	91	212	127	79
Absenteeism	18	98	295	121	76
Low reading ability	30	91	210	131	86
Higher education grants	225	123	32	67	54
Immunization	96	89	37	77	156
Infant mortality	75	157	158	69	118
Illegitimacy	35	247	185	83	96
Infectious diseases	68	167	143	82	110
Short-term care	22	199	154	113	95
Long-term care	15	272	212	74	104
Delinquency	21	91	397	93	75
Supervision orders	22	108	313	111	75
Repair notices	52	191	58	22	215
Disinfestation	58	82	265	84	104
Possession orders	27	124	189	136	77
Children born	78	146	108	78	125

* calculated as a percentage of the mean for the city as a whole.

Source: Webber 1975: 111

Webber's research was designed explicitly for ease of replication, so that it is possible that comparable analyses of deprivation in other cities will soon provide the basis for a generalized model of the geography of deprivation. Nevertheless, it would be wise to be cautious about the findings of such studies. Several important conceptual and methodological issues remain unresolved, not least of which is the question of defining 'deprivation' more rigorously. As Edwards has observed, the rush for empirical results has effectively put the cart before the horse, with deprivation being 'defined' only in terms of the available indicators. 'To put it less charitably, it has been a hotch-potch approach in which any variable deemed by the researcher to be even vaguely relevant ... has been

thrown into the statistical melting pot' (Edwards 1975: 281). This partly a result of the difficulty of obtaining data which are *direct* indicators of deprivation: the use of surrogate indicators and indicators of phenomena which are supposedly symptomatic of deprivation inevitably leads to ambiguity and obfuscation. More important, however, is the uncertainty about the nature of deprivation itself. While there are several schools of thought on the matter (see pp. 207–208), we do not yet have a generally accepted model or theory of deprivation upon which to base empirical measurement. The paradox, of course, is that the development of the one is to a large extent dependent on the other.

The perceived environment

Whereas traditional approaches to the analysis of urban spatial differentiation have been almost exclusively concerned with measuring, mapping and classifying objective characteristics, a new approach has recently emerged which is not merely different but in direct contrast. It is wholeheartedly subjective, with an emphasis on studying the world as it seems to be rather than as it is : not as physical reality but as perceived experience. The aim is to portray the city as it is seen through the prism of people's personal experience, coloured by their hopes and fears and distorted by prejudice and predilection.

Although this interest in the perceived environment can be traced back to Lewin (1938) – a psychologist, de Lauwe (1952) – a sociologist, and Boulding (1956) – an economist, it was not until the early 1960s and the publication of papers by Lowenthal (1961) and Kirk (1963) that the utility of perception studies became known widely to a geographical audience. Since then, however, a large number of geographers have become involved in the increasingly interdisciplinary field of environmental perception, and there now exists a significant body of scientific research on the perception of the urban environment by its inhabitants (Downs and Stea 1973; Gold 1979; Moore and Gollege 1976; Pocock and Hudson 1978). Furthermore, general interest in perception studies has been reinforced by the emergence within geography of a school of thought stemming from the phenomenological tradition of Husserl and giving a central position to the experiential 'sense of place' associated with different urban environments (Tuan 1974, 1978; Relph 1976). The net effect has been to provide geographers with a stimulating new dimension of study. As Herbert and Johnston observe (1976b : 13), 'It has been the arrival of this new dimension, perhaps more than any other, which has pulled up social geographers with a jolt.' Not only does it provide a powerful antidote to the impression that cities are populated by land uses and pathologies rather than people; it also provides an enlightening background to the behavioural patterns which contribute so much to the 'objective' geography of the city.

Central to the whole approach are the images, inner representations, mental maps and schemata derived from people's perception of the environment. These are the result of a process in which personal experience and values are used to filter the barrage of environmental stimuli to which the brain is subjected, thus producing a partial, simplifield (and often distorted) version of reality. The same environmental stimuli may thus evoke different responses from different individuals, with each person effectively living in his or her 'own world'. Nevertheless, it is logical to assume that certain aspects of imagery will be held in common over quite large groups of people because of similarities in their socialization, past experience and present urban environment.

What are these images like? What urban geographies exist within the minds of urbanites, and how do they relate to the objective world? As yet it is possible to give only tentative answers to these questions, for the study of the perceived environment is still in its infancy, and most existing work has been produced in an *ad hoc*, atheoretical way. What is clear is that people do not have a single image or mental map which can be consulted or recalled at will. Rather, we appear to possess a series of latent images which are unconsciously operationalized in response to specific behavioural tasks. In this context, a useful distinction can be made between :

1. the *designative* aspects of people's imagery which relate to the mental or cognitive organization of space necessary to their orientation within the urban environment; and
2. the *appraisive* aspects of imagery which reflect people's feelings about the environment and which are related to decision-making within the urban environment.

Designative aspects of urban imagery

The seminal work in this field was Kevin Lynch's book *The Image of the City*, published in 1960 and based on the results of lengthy interviews with (very) small samples of middle- and upper-class residents in three cities : Boston, Jersey City, and Los Angeles. In the course of these interviews, respondents were asked to describe the city, to indicate the location of features which were important to them, and to make outline sketches, the intention being to gently tease out a mental map from the subject's consciousness. From an examination of the resultant data, Lynch found that people apparently structure their mental image of the city in terms of five different kinds of *elements*. These are :

1. *Paths* : the channels along which the observer customarily, occasionally, or potentially moves. They may be streets, walkways, transit lines, canals, railroads. For many people, these are the predominant elements in their image. People observe the city while moving through it, and along these paths the other environmental elements are arranged and related.

2. *Edges* : Edges are the linear elements not used or considered as paths by the observer. They are the boundaries between two phases, linear breaks in continuity : shores, railroad cuts, edges of developments, walls. They may be barriers more or less penetrable, which close one region off from another; or they may be seams, lines along which two regions are related and joined together.

3. *Districts* : Districts are the medium-to-large sections of the city, conceived of as having two-dimensional extent, which the observer mentally enters . . . and which are recognizable as having some common, identifying character.

4. *Nodes* : are the strategic spots in a city into which an observer can enter, and which are the intensive foci to and from which he is travelling. They may be primarily junctions, places of a break in transportation, a crossing or convergence of paths . . . Or the nodes may simply be concentrations which gain their importance from being the condensation of some use or physical character, as a street-corner hangout or an enclosed square. Some of these concentration nodes are the focus and epitome of a district, over which their influence radiates and of which they stand as a symbol.

5. *Landmarks* : Landmarks are another type of point-reference, but in this case the observer does not enter them . . . They are usually a rather simply defined physical object : building, sign, store, or mountain. (Lynch 1960 : 47–8).

As Lynch points out, none of these elements exist in isolation in people's minds. Districts are structured with nodes, defined by edges, penetrated by paths and sprinkled with landmarks. Elements thus overlap and pierce one another, and some may be psychologically more dominant than others.

Lynch also found that the residents of a given city tend to structure their mental map of the city with the same elements as one another, and he produced ingenious maps with which to demonstrate the collective image of Boston (Fig. 4.21), using symbols of different boldness to indicate the proportion of respondents who had mentioned each element. Another important finding was that, whereas the collective image of Boston was structured by a fairly dense combination of elements, those of Los Angeles and Jersey City were much less

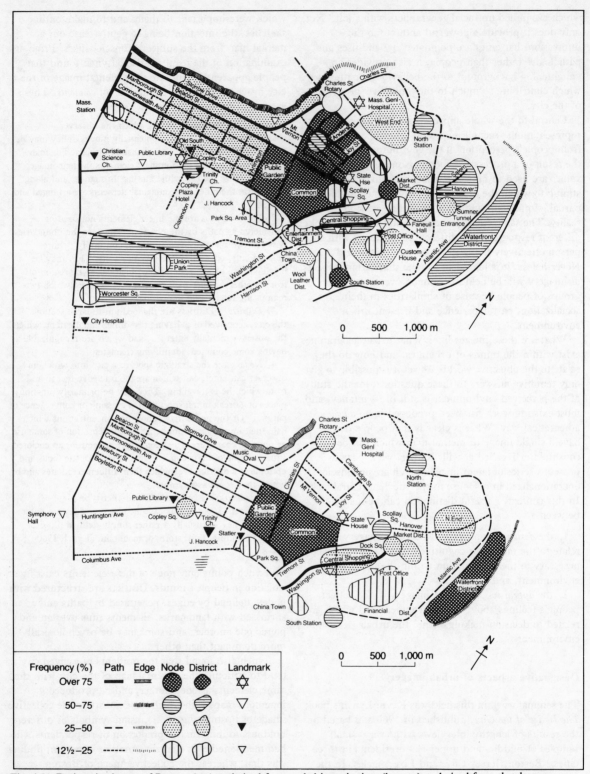

Fig. 4.21 Designative images of Boston: (top) as derived from verbal interviewing; (bottom) as derived from sketch maps. *Source*: Lynch (1960), p. 146.

complex. Lynch suggested that this reflected a difference in the *legibility* or imageability of the cities resulting from differences in the 'form qualities' of the built environment. These, he argued, include the clarity and simplicity of visible form, the continuity and 'rhythm' of edges and surfaces, the dominance (whether in terms of size, intensity of interest) of one morphological unit over others, and the presence or absence of directional differentiation in terms of asymetries, gradients and radial features.

Although Lynch's work has been criticized for its intuitive approach to the identification of image elements and the validity of attempting to aggregate the imagery of people with quite different backgrounds and experience has been questioned (Lee 1976), his techniques have found wide application elsewhere (Harrison and Howard 1972; Milgram and Jodelet 1976; De Jonge 1962; Orleans 1973; Francescato and Mebane 1973; Goodey *et al*. 1971), and these studies provide an intriguing pool of information about the way different groups of people in different places structure their image of the city. Amsterdam, for example, was found to be much more legible to its inhabitants than were Rotterdam or The Hague to theirs, apparently because of its striking spider-web pattern of concentric canals and its strong linear core incorporating the Mint Square, the Central Station and The Dam – a great square containing the Royal Palace. The same study, however, found evidence to suggest that although environments with salient paths and nodes tend to be most legible, people also like *illegible* environments, possible because of abstract qualities such as 'quaintness' (De Jonge 1962). A comparison of Milan and Rome found that both cities are highly legible, but in different ways : the mental maps of Milanese are structured by a clearly-connected set of paths relating to their city's radial street pattern, whereas Romans' mental maps exhibit a greater diversity of content and tend to be structured around the landmarks and edges associated with their city's historic buildings, its hills, and the course of the Tiber (Francescato and Mebane 1973).

The same study was also able to demonstrate the differences which exist between the social classes in their image of the city. Basically, middle-class residents held a more comprehensive image than lower-class residents, covering a much wider territory and including a larger number and greater variety of elements. A similar conclusion can be drawn from the maps compiled from respondents living in different neighbourhoods in Los Angeles, where ethnicity is closely associated with socio-economic status. The high-status, white residents of Westwood, (a 'foothills' neighbourhood situated between Beverly Hills and Santa Monica) have a well-formed, detailed and generalized image of the entire Los Angeles Basin (Fig. 4.22a), whereas the middle-class residents of Northridge (a suburb in the San Fernando Valley) have a less comprehensive image which is oriented away from the city proper (Fig. 4.22b):

As a sign on the Ventura Freeway proclaims : 'Topanga Plaza (in the [San Fernando] Valley) is downtown for over a million people'. Thus, although they have a reasonably detailed image of the San Fernando Valley extension of the city, the Santa Monica mountain chain effectively segregates Northridge residents from the rest of this sprawling metropolis (Orleans 1973 : 118– 19).

At the other end of the socio-economic ladder, residents of the black ghetto neighbourhood of Avalon, near Watts, have a vaguer image of the city which, in contrast to the white images which are structured around the major east-west boulevards and freeways, is dominated by the grid-iron layout of streets between Watts and the city centre (Fig. 4.22c). Reasons for these differences are not hard to find. The greater wealth and extended education of higher-status whites confers a greater mobility, a greater propensity to visit other parts of the city, and a tendency to utilize a wider range of information sources. In contrast, the less mobile poor, with a shorter journey to work, and with less exposure to other sources of environmental information, will naturally tend to have a local rather than a metropolitan orientation : something which will be buttressed by racial or ethnic segregation. Where language barriers further reinforce this introversion, the likely outcome is an extremely restricted image of the city, as in the Spanish-speaking neighbourhood of Boyle Heights (Fig. 4.22d).

One aspect of Lynch's technique which has been pursued separately for its own sake is the use of sketch maps. Although they do not lend themselves to the compilation of a composite image, sketch maps do help to illuminate the way in which people perceive the city. The images of New York portrayed in Figures 4.23 and 4.24 show very clearly how each person structures the city quite differently, with the organization and content of their sketch reflecting their own life-style and emotional concerns. These two sketches are part of the sample of 332 derived from a questionnaire in *New York* magazine and organized by Milgram, who found that, in additon to the idiosyncratic aspects of the sketches, many were drawn from the perspective of the individual's immediate neighbourhood (as in Fig. 4.23). On the other hand, many respondents made Manhattan the central feature, even though they lived and worked in one of the city's other boroughs (Duncan 1977).

Appleyard (1970) has suggested that the kinds of map

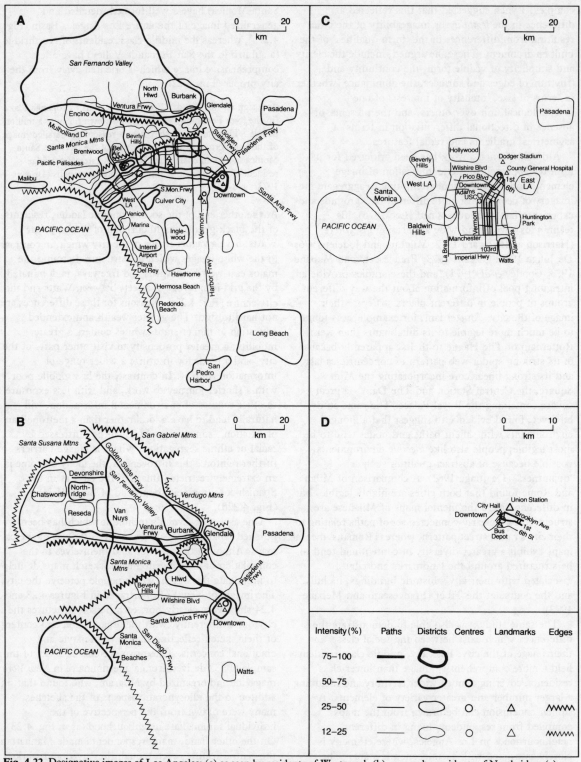

Fig. 4.22 Designative images of Los Angeles: (a) as seen by residents of Westwood; (b) as seen by residents of Northridge; (c) as seen by residents of Avalon; (d) as seen by residents of Boyle Heights.
Source: Orleans (1973), pp. 120–123.

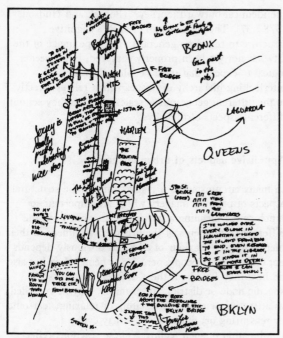

Fig. 4.23 A mental map of New York City drawn by a 29-year-old writer from the West Side. *Source*: Duncan (1977), p. 53. © 1977, News Group Publications Inc.

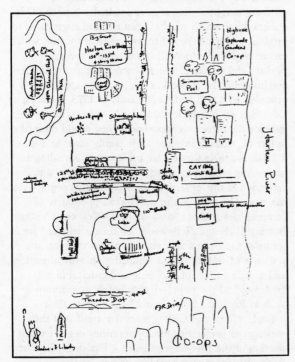

Fig. 4.24 A mental map of New York City drawn by a teacher in her forties and living in Harlem. *Source*: Duncan (1977), p. 53. © 1977, News Group Publications Inc.

people draw can be categorized according to their *accuracy* and the *type of element* emphasized, with a basic division between those who emphasize 'sequential' elements (such as roads and pathways) and those who emphasize 'spatial' elements (such as individual buildings, landmarks and districts). His eight-fold typology has been used in a number of studies (Goodchild 1974; Pocock 1975; Spencer and Lloyd 1974), and it appears that the overall tendency is for a sequential structuring, with working-class and female respondents tending to draw the least sophisticated maps. Most researchers have also noted, like Milgram, the tendency for people's mental maps to be oriented around the home neighbourhood or city centre, while Pocock (1976) has emphasized the tendency for people to 'better' the environment, recording a structure more uniform and less haphazard than the real world – a tendency which evidently increases with familiarity with the city concerned.

Cognitive distance

Underlying the organization of people's mental maps is the *cognitive distance* between image elements, and this is another aspect of imagery which has been shown to exhibit interesting and important regularities. Cognitive distance is the basis for the spatial information stored in cognitive representations of the environment. It is generated from a variety of mechanisms which includes the brain's perception of the distance between visible objects, the use-patterns and structure of the visible environment, and the impact of symbolic representations of the environment such as maps and road signs (Briggs 1973). For the majority of people, intra-urban cognitive distance is generally greater than objective distance, regardless of city size and their usual means of transport (Canter and Tagg 1975; Gollege *et al*. 1969; Lee 1970), although there is evidence to suggest that this over-estimation declines with increasing physical distance. Thus in both London and Dundee distances were in fact reported as being shorter than they were in reality (Canter 1975; Pocock 1972). Interestingly, the break-point in the relationship was much greater in London than in Dundee, suggesting that the overall scale and layout of the environment is itself an important determinant of cognitive distance. Gollege and Zannaras have argued that people's images and cognitive distance estimates are a function of the number and type of environmental stimuli, or *cues*, they encounter along the paths, or *supports*, that they normally use, and that the actual form of the city is of greater importance in determining the cue selection process than any personal characteristics, including length of residence. They have also suggested that different types of urban structure will result in the

105

selection of different cues, thus generating a different metric of cognitive distance and produccng different kinds of mental maps. Residents of concentrically-zoned cities might be expected to respond more to changes in land use, for example, than residents of sectorally-structured cities, who might be expected to respond more to traffic-related cues along the typical path from suburb to city centre and back (Gollege and Zannaras 1970, 1973).

Another interesting feature of cognitive distance is that it appears to be dependent upon orientation in relation to the city centre. Lee, for example, drew the conclusion from a study of Cambridge housewives' imagery that the 'schema of the whole city includes a *focal orientation*, built up by the satisfactions of the centre. These satisfactions . . . have a dynamic effect on the perceptual process, causing a foreshortening of perceived distances in the inward direction' (Lee 1970: 41). To see if this tendency operated on a wider basis, Lee conducted an experiment in which 171 students from the University of Dundee were asked to estimate the walking distance from a fixed focal point to 22 well-known locations within the city. These were paired so as to be approximately the same distance inward to the centre or outward to the periphery; but the cognitive distances derived from the students for inward destinations were significantly shorter than those for outward destinations (Lee 1970). Pocock and Hudson (1978) point out that this tendency is consistent with research findings from other studies which have related cognitive distance to the characteristics of 'origins' and 'destinations' in mental maps : cognitive distance tends to shrink with the perceived utility or attractiveness of the 'destination'. Thus a general survey of neighbourhood characteristics in Baltimore, Maryland, revealed that desirable elements such as parks, post offices, and libraries were felt to be closer to respondents' homes than they actually were, while less desirable elements such as parking lots and expressway interchanges were thought to be further away than they actually were (Lowery 1973). Similarly, socially desirable neighbourhoods are often felt to be nearer than they really are (Eyles 1968; Watson 1972); and the attractions of shopping centres tend to foreshorten the real distance between the home and the shop (Brennan 1948; Klein 1967; Thompson 1963).

Given the distorting effect of the values attached to different 'origins' and 'destinations', it seems likely that people possess a basic image of the city consisting of the branching network of their 'action space' which undergoes topological deformation, perhaps hourly, as they move about the city from one major node – home, workplace, city centre – to another. 'Who, for instance, has not experienced a homeward trip to be shorter than

the identical outward journey?' (Pocock and Hudson 1978 : 57). The relationship of such a cognitive structure to the more general Lynch-type image of the city has not yet been properly explored, but it seems logical to expect that most people will possess an interlocking hierarchy of images which relates directly to the different geographical scales at which they act out different aspects of their lives.

Appraisive aspects of urban imagery

In many circumstances it is not so much the structural aspects of people's imagery which are important so much as the meaning attached to, or evoked by, the different components of the urban environment in their mental map. Behaviour of all kinds obviously depends not only on *what* people perceive as being *where* but also on how they *feel* about these different elements. A specific node or district, for example, may be regarded as attractive or repellent, exciting or relaxing, fearsome or reassuring or, more likely, it may evoke a combination of such feelings. These reactions reflect what Pocock and Hudson (1978) have called the *appraisive* aspects of urban imagery.

In overall terms, the appraisive imagery of the city is reflected by the desirability or attractiveness of different neighbourhoods as residential locations. This is something which can be measured and aggregated to produce a map of the collective image of the city which can be regarded as a synthesis of all the feelings, positive and negative, which people have about different neighbourhoods. A good example of this approach is provided by Clark and Cadwallader's (1973) work on Los Angeles, in which respondents were asked to indicate the three neighbourhoods they would most like to live in, bearing in mind their family income. Fig. 4.25 shows their first-choice preferences, revealing an interesting geography which is by no means a simple reflection of the 'objective' socio-economic geography of the city. Thus, while the widespread popularity of communities such as Santa Monica, Westwood Village, Beverly Hills and Hollywood could be accounted for in terms of their physically attractive environment, the presence of several well-developed employment centres, and a wide variety of shopping and entertainment facilities, and the popularity of 'beach' communities such as Redondo Beach could be related to their lifestyle, Clark and Cadwallader point out that the widespread preference for communities in the eastern portion of the Los Angeles basin – Pasadena, Monterey Park, Alhambra and Arcadia – is 'less easily understood'. The inclusion of large parts of the San Fernando Valley in the least-preferred category is also

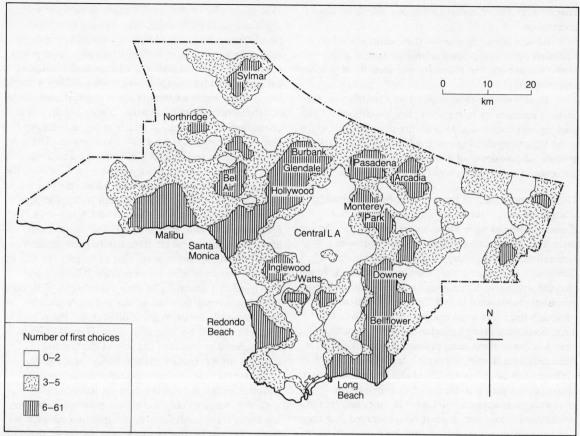

Fig. 4.25 Residential desirability of Los Angeles neighbourhoods.
Source: Clark and Cadwallader (1973), p. 697.

puzzling, since it has been one of the most rapidly-growing residential regions of the Los Angeles metropolitan area.

The cognitive dimensions of the urban environment
Given that people are able to make these overall evaluations of residential desirability, the question arises as to their derivation. In other words, what are the components of people's overall evaluation of a given place or neighbourhood, and how do they feel about these particular aspects of the environment? Johnston (1973d), in an attempt to explain the process of neighbourhood evaluation, has investigated the perceived attributes of eleven different suburbs in Christchurch, New Zealand. His analysis suggests that neighbourhood preferences are based on three underlying evaluative dimensions which are invariant with area of residence in the city:

1. the 'impersonal environment', composed mainly of the physical attributes of the neighbourhood;

2. the 'interpersonal environment', composed mainly of the social attributes of the neighbourhood;

3. the locational attributes of the neighbourhood.

Another recent analysis of the cognitive dimensions of the urban environment which asked respondents to consider the relevance of 100 different items to their *own* neighbourhood (in the San Francisco Bay area) found as many as 20 'meaningful' dimensions. These include:

1. aspects related to the *aesthetics* of the neighbourhood – its general appearance, tidiness, colourfulness, and level of maintenance, and the 'spaciousness' and general level of service provision in the area;

2. aspects related to *neighbours* – their friendliness, helpfulness, or snobbishness; and the feelings of contentment, happiness, pride, power, loneliness and safety which stem from living among them;

3. aspects related to *noise* – these include noise from the immediate environment (neighbours' children or

107

lawnmowers, for example) as well as noise from aircraft and trains;

4. aspects related to *safety* – these centred on two distinctive dimensions, one related to danger from traffic and the other to the safety and security of people and property;

5. aspects related to *accessibility* and mobility – these include accessibility to freeways, neighbourhood parking conditions, and accessibility to public transport;

6. aspects regarded as *annoyances*, such as the lack of privacy, the incidence of door-to-door salesmen, and the presence of animal nuisances (Carp *et al*. 1976).

Generalizations such as these should be treated with caution, however. Both the Christchurch and San Francisco studies were based on analyses of data which were aggregated across different neighbourhoods. Cadwallader (1979), using a methodology similar to Johnston's in an analysis of Madison, Wisconsin, found that the evaluative dimensions associated with different neighbourhoods were in fact 'far from identical', although there was some evidence that similar neighbourhoods evoked similar cognitive responses and that Johnston's three main evaluative dimensions were 'generally identifiable' in people's feelings about different neighbourhoods. There clearly remains a good deal of investigation to be undertaken before the composition of appraisive imagery in cities can be fully understood. Moreover, it must be recognized that there are some important aspects of appraisive imagery which extend beyond the context of residential desirability, having been derived from people's evaluations of the urban environment in less specific circumstances. This is illustrated by the results of a survey of residents of Bath, Somerset (Harrison and Sarre 1971). Using a methodology based on the repetory grid, an interview technique which ensures a minimum of interference from the researcher's ideas, Harrison and Sarre found that people's appraisive imagery tended simply to contrast places which were liked and beautiful (especially the Georgian areas of the city) with whose which were disliked and ugly (mainly the working-class, industrialized areas of the lower Avon valley). A second dimension was found to contrast places in which respondents were involved (the city centre and the middle-class residential areas) with places where they felt out of place (notably the Georgian areas); while a third dimension contrasted places with a wide significance and which had been known for a long time with recently-discovered places of only local significance.

Other, more specific aspects of appraisive imagery have been elicited by researchers pursuing particular themes. Ley (1972), for instance, has illustrated the local geography of perceived danger in an inner-city neighbourhood in Philadelphia, showing how most people recognized – and avoided – the danger points near gang hang-outs, abandoned buildings, and places where drugs are peddled. On a larger scale, Milgram has compiled a 'fear map' from a survey of New Yorkers (Fig. 4.26), which highlights the rather different kinds of urban environment – Harlem, Times Square, Wall Street, and Central Park – which generate feelings of fear or oppression among a city's inhabitants (Duncan 1977). Tranter and Parkes (1979) have pointed out that such imagery is often time-dependent: public parks, for example, may be felt to be tranquil and safe places by day but might induce quite different feelings at night. This points to an area of research which has yet to be fully explored; and there are still other aspects of appraisive imagery which have barely been touched upon by geographic research. One of these is the way in which some areas of some large cities (Glasgow and Liverpool, for example) become stigmatized, with their inhabitants being labelled as 'work-shy', 'unreliable', or 'troublesome', thus making it difficult for them to compete in local housing and job-markets (McGregor 1977). Another concerns the role of clothes and personal objects (rather than buildings and social characteristics) in contributing towards our feelings about different parts of the city. As Raban (1975) observes, many of our clothes and personal possessions are used, consciously or not, to communicate what we like or believe in: the pair of shoes, the book, the wall poster and the cut of a pair of jeans become 'briefly exhibited signs and badges' which not only help their owners to say something about themselves but which also help others to attach meaning and significance to their owners and to *their owners' environment*. Raban (1975 : 168) gives his own reaction to the people he associates with different Underground routes in London:

People who live on the Northern Line I take to be sensitive citizens; it is a friendly communication route where one notes commuters reading proper books and, when they talk, finishing their sentences. But the Piccadilly Line is full of fly-by-nights and stripe-shirted young men who run dubious agencies, and I go to elaborate lengths to avoid travelling on it. It is an entirely irrational way of imposing order on the city, but it does give it a shape in the mind, takes whole chunks of experience out of the realm of choice and deliberation, and places them in the less strenuous context of habit and prejudice.

Yet another under-investigated area concerns the way in which perception of the city in influenced by symbolism which has been culturally developed and which appears to exist collectively on a sub-cognitive level (Lasswell 1979). Obvious examples include the

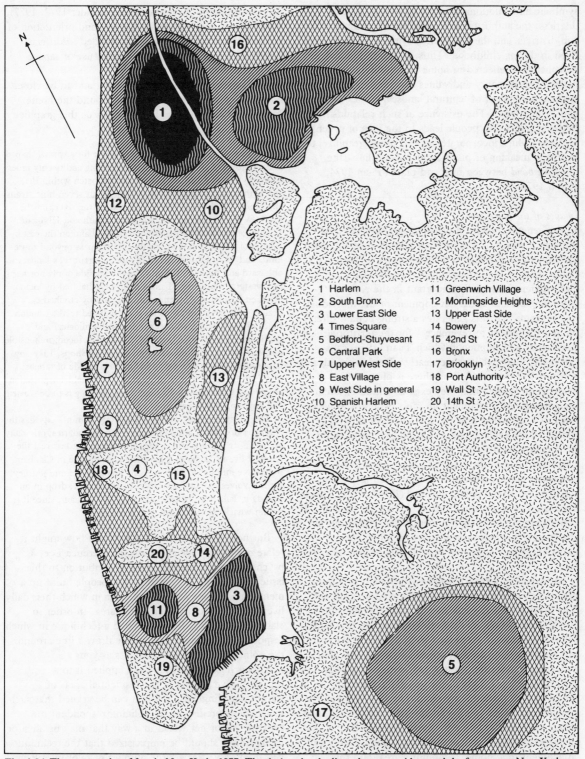

Fig. 4.26 The topography of fear in New York, 1977. The darker the shading, the more widespread the fear among New Yorkers of that particular part of town. The numbered locations list, in rank order, the 20 'most fearsome' neighbourhoods in the city. *Source*: Duncan (1977), p. 57. © 1977, News Group Publications Inc.

The legend within the figure reads:

1 Harlem
2 South Bronx
3 Lower East Side
4 Times Square
5 Bedford-Stuyvesant
6 Central Park
7 Upper West Side
8 East Village
9 West Side in general
10 Spanish Harlem
11 Greenwich Village
12 Morningside Heights
13 Upper East Side
14 Bowery
15 42nd St
16 Bronx
17 Brooklyn
18 Port Authority
19 Wall St
20 14th St

symbolic and emotional potency of special historic districts, the authoritarian symbolism of administrative sub-districts, and the sentimental symbolism of the area lived in during childhood. Thus, just as individual personality is reflected in home and possessions, so collective personality and values are translated into the wider environment of 'cultural landscapes' (Lowenthal and Prince 1964). The existence of such relationships between places and people leads to the idea of a 'sense of place', which incorporates aspects of imageability, the symbolic meaning of places, and 'topophilia' – the affective *bond* between man and place (Tuan 1974; Relph 1976).

Images of the home area

In the general context of urban geography, the most important aspect of this sense of place is probably the attachment people feel to their *home area*. There is no doubt that the immediate physical and social environment is crucially important in the early psychological and social development of the individual, and it seems that this generates a strong bond – often amounting almost to reverence – for the territorial homeland: a phenomenon which Tuan (1976) calls 'geopiety'. Such feelings are clearly related to the idea of territoriality (see p. 48), and there is plenty of evidence to suggest that they exist as a kind of latent 'neighbourhood attachment' in most people who have lived in a particular area for any length of time. The most striking evidence of such feelings emerges after people have been forced to leave their home neighbourhood in the cause of redevelopment of renewal schemes, when many report feelings of grief at the loss of their old neighbourhood (Fried 1963). This is because, as Pocock and Hudson (1978 : 85) observe: 'It is not only the built environment that is razed but also the contextual environment, the symbol of life's experience: part of people's roots, part of *themselves* is lost.'

Most people seem to have an attachment to a home area which they mentally 'recognize' and identify with. The most convincing evidence for this comes from the Royal Commission on Local Government in England (1969), which contracted Research Services Ltd to carry out a survey of a carefully stratified sample of 2,000 in order to ascertain the most appropriate size of local government units. One of the questions asked in the study was: 'Is there an area around here, where you are now living, which you would say you belonged to, and where you feel "at home"?' Approximately 80 per cent of the respondents claimed to possess some feelings of attachment to a 'home' community area, and this tendency tended to increase with length of residence. Similar findings have emerged from a survey of Los Angeles residents (Everitt and Cadwallader 1972, 1977), where it was also found that the size and orientation of husbands' and wives' home areas tended to differ, largely as a result of their differential use of sapace around the home.

The home area thus seems to exist and to be closely related to people's 'activity space' around the home. Jonathan Raban (1975 : 166–7) gives us this graphic description of his own 'home area':

The Greater London Council is responsible for a sprawl shaped like a rugby ball about twenty-five miles long and twenty miles wide; my city is a concise kidney-shaped patch within that space, in which no point is more than about seven miles from any other. On the south, it is bounded by the river, on the north by the fat tongue of Hampstead Heath and Highgate Village, on the west by Brompton cemetery and on the east by Liverpool Street station. I hardly ever trespass beyond those limits and when I do I feel I'm in foreign territory, a landscape of hazard and rumour. Kilburn, on the far side of my northern and western boundaries, I imagine to be inhabited by vicious drunken Irishmem; Hackney and Dalston by crooked car dealers with pencil moustaches and goldfilled teeth; London south of the Thames still seems impossibly illogical and contingent, a territory of meaningless circles, incomprehensible one-way systems, warehouses and cage-bird shops. Like any tribesman hedging himself in behind a stockade of taboos, I mark my boundaries with graveyards, terminal transportation points and wildernesses. Beyond them, nothing is to be trusted and anything might happen.

The constrictedness of this private city-within-a-city has the character of a self-fulfilling prophecy. Its boundaries, originally arrived at by chance and usage, grow more not less real the longer I live in London. I have friends who live in Clapham, only three miles away, but to visit them is a definite journey, for it involves crossing the river. I can, though, drop in on friends in Islington, twice as far away as Clapham, since it is within what I feel to be my own territory.

But how typical is this imagery, and how might it relate to people's social behaviour? Terence Lee, a psychologist, has made a major contribution to this issue (Lee 1968). He suggests that people build up a mental model, or *schema*, of the area in which their daily lives are played out – their home area. In order to elaborate this idea, Lee developed a technique in which respondents were asked to 'please draw a line around the point which you consider acts as your neighbourhood or district', and applied it to a representative sample of the residential areas of Cambridge, England. While it can be argued that such instructions predispose an obliging respondent to construe his or her world in a way that may be alien or unnatural, it should be emphasized that the technique was used only after a large number of pilot interviews had suggested that some kind of neighbourhood structuring of the city was widespread, and that people described their area mainly by delineating its boundaries in a variety of ways. As in the Royal Commission survey, Lee found that about 80 per cent of the people could delineate a home area. What is interesting, however, is that these turned out to be highly personal and idiosyncratic, with a map of superimposed home areas resembling 'a plate of spaghetti'. Nevertheless, there were also several interesting and significant regularities in the data. Firstly, the *area* covered by people's schemata tended to be fairly consistent: about 100 acres (40 ha.). Secondly, it was found that this size was quite unrelated to changes in population density, so that the home areas or schemata of suburban residents tend to extend over the same amount of territory as the home areas of inner-city residents. Lee suggests that this is probably because the home area is dependent on an action space based on walking distance and argues that this is of spatial significance to urban planning, since his findings suggest that it is possible to achieve the necessary number of consumers to support basic neighbourhood services and facilities within the kind of territory that appears to correspond with people's perception of a meaningful home area. From a closer examination of the 165 schemata produced by his respondents, Lee has also proposed a typology of neighbourhoods:

1. *The social acquaintance neighbourhood*: a small area in which people 'keep themselves to themselves' and where the main support in times of trouble is from kin rather than neighbours. This kind of neighbourhood is much more a function of people than locality. That is, it could be found in a variety of localities but only amongst a certain kind of person.

2. *The homogeneous neighbourhood*: here the schema includes greater awareness of physical aspects of the environment as well as people. An underlying principle is that the neighbourhood is comprised not only of 'people like us' but also of 'people who live in houses like ours'.

3. *The unit neighbourhood*: a territory which approximates to planners' conceptions of 'neighbourhood' – larger, with a heterogeneous population and a balanced range of amenities.

Further analysis of people's schemata was achieved by computing a 'neighbourhood quotient' which measured the size and complexity (in terms of the content of houses, shops and amenities) of neighbourhoods while holding constant the physical area in which they were drawn. The mean value of these quotients for a particular social or spatial group thus reflects its overall level of 'socio-physical involvement' in the locality, while the range of values serves as a measure of that group's agreement or, as Lee calls it, 'consentaneity'. Using this technique, Lee found evidence to support the classic planning axiom that a neighbourhood with well-defined boundaries will have an associated high level of social participation; and he also found that participation tends to increase with the social heterogeneity of an area's population: something which also has relevance to planning practice.

The very existence of these schemata, of course, is highly relevant to the debate on communities and neighbourhoods outlined in Chapter 3, and several researchers have attempted to relate functional neighbourhoods (based on patterns of social interaction and economic behaviour) to the perceived neighbourhood or home area. Buttimer (1972), for example, has demonstrated the rather variable relationship between the size and orientation of people's 'micro-service' activity spaces, 'macro-service' activity spaces, 'social participation' spaces and perceived home areas in different parts of Glasgow; while Everitt (1976) has demonstrated the broad congruence between the perceived home areas of a sample of Los Angeles residents and their activity patterns in relation to workplace, friends' residences, and clubs. Perhaps the most useful work in this context is the re-analysis by Berry and Kasarda (1977) of the Royal Commission data. They found that community sentiments, including the ability to identify a 'home area', are primarily influenced by participation in local social networks, and that this participation, in turn, is influenced mainly by length of residence in the area. This relationship held true even when population size, density, socio-economic status and life-cycle factors were held constant, suggesting that the 'systemic model' of community organization – based on length of residence and the strength of local social networks – is more appropriate than the 'linear development' model based on population size and density and stemming from the ideas of Tonnies and Wirth.

Chapter 5

HOUSING DEMAND, RESIDENTIAL MOBILITY AND URBAN RESIDENTIAL STRUCTURE

Although there are several important aspects of urban social geography which are concerned with people's behaviour outside the home, the mosaic of residential neighbourhoods is clearly the central concern of the subject. Having outlined the social dimensions of urban life and described the spatial configuration of the residential mosaic from several perspectives, attention is now turned towards the mechanisms and processes which produce these patterns.

As will already be apparent, it is possible to identify a large number of different influences on the residential structure of the city. What is more difficult, however, is to establish an overall perspective of their relative importance and the way in which they interact in shaping the residential environment. Several theoretical perspectives have been developed to complement or challenge the conventional wisdom of Wirthian and ecological theories and their derivations; and each tends to embrace several different schools of thought. Neo-classical economic theory, behaviouralist models, 'managerialist' approaches and structuralist analyses derived from Marxist theory all merit attention, since the central concern of all of them is the interpretation of the workings of urban land and housing markets. In this chapter, the focus of attention is on *demand-based* explanations of residential differentiation, following the 'mainstream' tradition of research which has highlighted the behaviour of households in competing for land, a dwelling and an 'address' within the city. An introductory consideration of neoclassical economic land-use theory is followed by a detailed examination of the determinants of housing demand and a summary of the behavioural aspects of residential mobility, leading to an evaluation of the cumulative effects of mobility processes on residential differentiation and the socio-spatial structure of the city.

The neoclassical economic approach

Models of urban structure based on neoclassical micro-economic theory stand with Burgess's ecological model as the most widely-known approaches to explaining the internal structure of cities. Originally developed to illuminate intra-urban patterns of land values and the relative location of different urban land-uses, these models are essentially elaborations of the von Thünen agricultural land-use model. They stem from a tradition of land economics which can be traced to Haig (1926), Hurd (1903) and Ratcliff (1949), but their full exposition dates from the more recent work of Alonso (1960, 1964), Wingo (1961), Mills (1967), Kain (1962), Muth (1969) and A. Evans (1973). The cornerstone of the approach is an attempt to determine the pattern of land consumption through an analysis of the pricing mechanism, with a central role being given to the relationship between location, ground rent and transport costs. It describes a process through which households and firms compete for space in a way that maximizes satisfaction, within budget constraints, for every competitor; thus also maximizing the 'efficiency' of the urban spatial economy. The end result is a static equilibrium which simultaneously explains the aggregate pattern of land uses, house prices (or rents) and population densities.

Assumptions

Such analysis is subject to a number of initial assumptions. Most models assume an urban area located within a uniform plain, so that all sites are homogeneous apart from their relative distances from one another. The CBD is assumed to be located centrally within this area and is therefore the single most accessible point. It is also assumed to be the only employment centre in the whole city. Transport is assumed to be ubiquitous, with transport costs being a direct function of the linear distance between places. The city is assumed to be inhabited by 'economic man': a rational being whose behaviour is geared to maximizing profits, utility and satisfaction. Competition between firms and households is assumed to be perfect, with no restrictions on land or buildings and no buyers or sellers with sufficient resources to affect the state of the market by their own activities.

The theory

Given these conditions, the argument is basically as follows: the most central sites will be more attractive than others for all types of land users; they are most desirable for shops because their accessibility enables retailers to tap the largest possible potential market; they are most desirable for manufacturers because their centrality minimizes the aggregate costs of assembling raw materials and distributing finished products; and they are most desirable for householders because their proximity to jobs minimizes the costs of commuting. However, the geometry of the city means that there are relatively few central sites in relation to the total space available. As a result, competition for central sites will be intense, and the prices offered for them will be higher than those offered for more peripheral sites. The ground rent accruing to each site may thus be seen simply as a charge for the utility of accessibility.

Nevertheless, it is recognized that different types of land users will place different financial evaluations on the utility of centrality, depending upon their particular budget constraints. It is, for example, logical to expect shops to be both able and willing to outbid households for central sites because the extra income accruing to a centrally-located shop through increased custom is likely to outweigh the savings in commuting costs obtained at the same site by a household – or even by several households living in the same dwelling. Similarly, it is recognized that the utility of progressively less central sites will decline at different rates for different land users, with the marginal losses from decreased accessibility being greater for retailing and commercial users than for residential users. Because of this, Alonso (1960) suggested, each type of land user can be thought of as having a characteristic *bid-rent curve*, reflecting the prices they are prepared to pay for sites at different distances from the CBD (Fig. 5.1). These curves are similar to the indifference curves of neoclassical economics in that each point on the curve represents a location of equal utility for that particular type of land user. Thus, for retailing, lower sales further out are offset by lower rents; and for households the

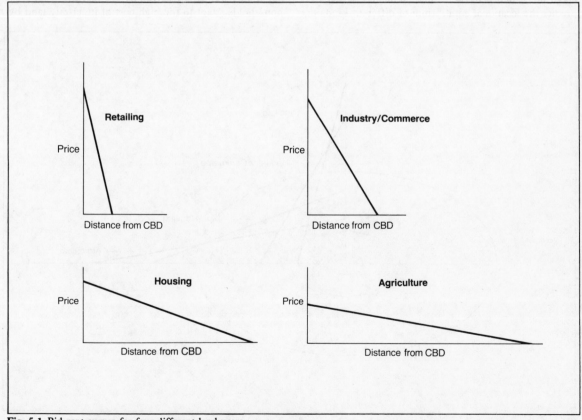

Fig. 5.1 Bid-rent curves for four different land users.

lower rents of peripheral locations are balanced by the higher costs of commuting. In theory, therefore, each land user should be indifferent to locating anywhere along its bid-rent curve.

What does this mean in terms of the structure of the city? Juxta-posing the bid-rent curves of different users (Fig. 5.2) reveals that those with steeper curves – retailing and commercial activities – capture the more central sites while those with shallower curves – residential users – are left with peripheral sites. This locational equilibrium is reflected in a simple pattern of concentric zones: a 'doughnut city' consisting of a CBD surrounded by a residential ring. As Ratcliff (1949: 375) concluded: 'in summary one might say that the structure of the city is determined through the dollar evaluation of the importance of convenience'.

A more detailed breakdown of land-use types would provide a more detailed picture of urban spatial structure, with more zones. It might be determined, for example, that under conditions of perfect competition the outer reaches of the CBD would consist of successive zones of offices, food stores and warehouses. This, however, does not tell us a great deal about *residential* differentiation. In fact, further assumptions about household behaviour must be made in order to predict the locational equilibrium of different kinds of

household. The usual assumption, following Alonso (1960; 1964), is that different households will bid for different-sized sites in different locations according to their relative preferences for living space and accessibility, subject to their overall budget constraints. Assuming also that expenditure on other goods and services remains (proportionally) constant for every household, the issue becomes one of balancing 'the costs and bother of commuting against the advantages of cheaper land with increasing distance from the center of the city and the satisfaction of more space for living' (Alonso 1960: 154). In other words, residential locations represent a *trade-off* between land and commuting costs. For this reason, neoclassical economic models of the sort described here are commonly referred to as 'trade-off' models.

Given two types of household, 'rich' and 'poor', most trade-off models proceed on the assumption that the rich have a preference for living space and that they can, moreover, afford to pay the recurring costs of commuting. It follows from this that rich households will tend to live in the suburbs, consuming relatively large amounts of cheaper land, while poor households are confined to more expensive inner-city sites. This apparent paradox is resolved by the fact that poor households adapt to the high cost of inner-city land by

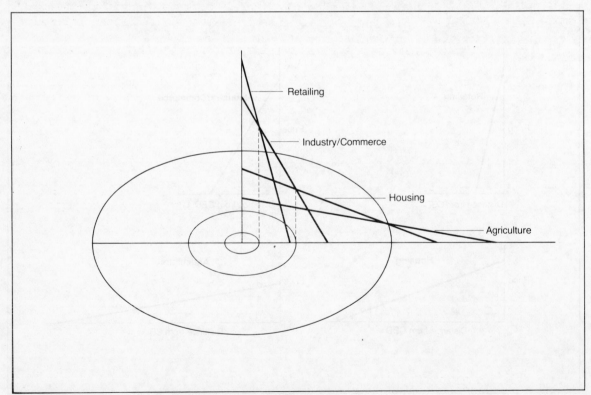

Fig. 5.2 The zonal urban structure suggested by the basic trade-off model.

consuming less of it, and so living at higher densities. In spatial terms then, trade-off models project a locational equilibrium in which higher socio-economic groups occupy successively more peripheral zones of the basic 'doughnut' city. At the same time, it is possible to show that population densities decrease regularly with distance from the city centre while residential lot sizes increase steadily with distance in the same direction. In morpholigical terms, one might therefore expect to find a succession of:

1. large multi-family dwelling-units (which spread the high cost of central sites over as large as possible a number of purchasers or renters);

2. low-rise apartment buildings;

3. terrace housing and/or single-storey apartment blocks;

4 semi-detached single-family dwellings; and

5. detached single-family dwellings standing in large lots;

with each type of housing being occupied by different socio-economic groups.

Extensions of the trade-off model

Such prognoses have sufficient resemblance to the reality of many cities to have encouraged researchers to extend the basic model, relaxing some of the more restrictive assumptions and introducing new variables. By allowing for secondary centres of employment and shopping and introducing the influence of major routeways, for example, it is possible to obtain a much more 'realistic' model of urban structure (Fig. 5.3). De Leeuw (1972), Papageorgiou (1976) and Romanos (1976) have elaborated the idea of multicentric urban areas in some detail, while others have extended the model in other ways. Among these are attempts to incorporate a choice of housing tenure (Doling 1973), to include a fuller range of housing services (Olson 1969; Isler 1970), and to account for the effects of variations in environmental quality (Kain and Quigley 1970), of different types of transport (Lave 1970), of local variations in housing taxes and subsidies (Beckmann 1973), and of racial discrimination (Kain and Quigley 1972). Moreover, the basic trade-off model has also been used to underpin the 'New Urban Economics', which attempts to integrate urban economics and welfare economics within a general equilibrium framework, using mathematical methods to derive generalized, qualitative results (Mills and MacKinnon 1973; Richardson 1977).

One of the most comprehensive attempts to extend the trade-off model is represented in the work of Evans (1973). Having set out the basic model in some detail, Evans introduces the assumption that households in a given socio-economic group will prefer to locate in the same neighbourhood as others of the same status, with the result that the model takes on a *sectoral* dimension in relation to socio-economic residential differentiation. Subsequently, Evans extends the model further. First, allowance is made for the phenomenon of 'gentrification', whereby higher-status people – from teaching, architecture or similar professions but not,

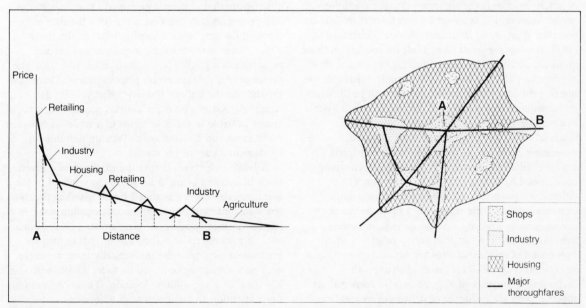

Fig. 5.3 The trade-off model modified to take into account the effects of major thoroughfares and additional nodes of shops and industry.

usually, from the business world – invade inner-city areas, upgrading and renovating housing previously occupied by low-income households. Second, the effect of variations in economic activity rates is introduced, with the result that households with non-working wives and children of school age or less are shown to be more likely to live further from the CBD than households with no children, where the wife is likely to be in paid employment and the demand for space is likely to be less. Third, the effect of transport improvements is evaluated, and it is demonstrated that among the likely effects are: (a) a 'flight to the suburbs' by high-income households, and (b) the emergence of an inner-city ring of old, high-density housing which it is unprofitable to demolish. Finally, the effects of relaxing the assumption of a monocentric city are examined and it is shown that, among other things, the existence of employment sub-centres is likely to reinforce the sectoral dimension of urban structure. These elaborations illustrate what Evans clearly regards as the potency and flexibility of the trade-off approach, not only as a positive theory of residential location but also as a normative model with which to evaluate the effects of public policy on urban spatial structure.

Criticisms of trade-off models

In contrast, many observers view such extensions merely as further wrinkles and twists to an analytical framework which is basically unsatisfactory. At the root of much criticism is the argument that the conditions of perfect competition assumed by neoclassical models are not even approached in the real world. Richardson (1971) has vigorously attacked trade-off models on these grounds, detailing the inconsistencies between their assumptions and the way people actually behave in the housing market. As he stresses, and as will be illustrated in subsequent sections of this chapter, people do not behave like 'economic man', always minimizing financial costs, travelling the shortest distance, possessing perfect knowledge, and choosing freely between different locations. Rather, their behaviour is conditioned by habit, convention, experience, deference, ignorance and, sometimes, downright irrationality; and their search for a place to live is constrained by limited time and money, imperfect information and the fact that only a relatively small proportion of residential sites are available for changes in occupancy in the short term. Moreover, the increasing dominance of large, powerful corporations, together with the influence of urban governments and their bureaucracies has led many to regard the 'free

market' in land as something of a myth; and the housing market is clearly partitioned into distinct submarkets – all of which are imperfect (Bourne 1976).

More specific criticism of neoclassical models includes the charge that they rest too heavily on the assertion that people's preference for increased space rather than for the convenience of short journeys will lead them to purchase more space as they grow richer. In fact, very little is known in a systematic, quantitative way about the way in which households make the complex trade-offs between housing expenditures, travel expenditure and the many other household budget items – holidays, clothing and so on – which loom large in many people's lives but which tend to be overlooked in most trade-off models. What empirical evidence there is, however, suggests that accessibility to workplaces is of minor importance in the household location decision (Short 1978a). In contrast, other less tangible environmental qualities and externalities (which would be difficult to build in to trade-off models) have been shown to be important determinants of the choice of residential environment (Michelson 1977).

Another weakness of the trade-off model to which Kirby (1976) has drawn attention is that whereas the analysis is based on the clearly established phenomenon of negative *land* price gradients, very few households do in fact purchase land. Most purchase (or rent) a *dwelling* from the existing stock and, because of the typical nature of this stock, the suburban dweller *must* purchase a large amount of surplus land in order to gain a roof over his head. As Kirby points out, 'This space, although perhaps cheaper per square foot than in the city proper, will *in toto* cost more than the flats or terraced housing more typically found in the inner city . . . Therefore, despite the existence of certain negative price gradients, emphasis must rest upon the presence of a positive house price/distance relationship throughout the bulk of the city' (Kirby 1976: 3). Accepting Kirby's point, of course, means that it is no longer possible to think in terms of a trade-off between travel costs and housing costs, thus undermining a fundamental part of the model.

A related objection is that the existence of a given stock of housing of different kinds (as opposed to the homogeneous surface assumed by neoclassical theory) tends to confound the instantaneous equilibrium implied in most models. As Richardson (1971) points out, such a concept is difficult to introduce into an established city since the theoretically most desirable sites may already be occupied by users whose inertia has left them in a sub-optimal location. These observations draw attention to a more general objection to neoclassical models: their ahistorical nature. Apart from overlooking the legacy of the past which is represented in the contemporary housing stock, neoclassical models, as Walker (1978: 167) observes, 'provide no insight into the process of historical change of the qualitative, rather than quantitative, sort and thus help not at all in developing an understanding of how we came to our present urban condition, whether it need be as it is, and from what direction change is likely to spring'.

A final and most damaging criticism concerns the failure of neoclassical models to deal adequately with the supply of land and housing. Under the assumptions of profit maximization and perfect competition, supply follows automatically from the structure of demand. In reality, however, the supply of urban land and housing is constrained by national and even international economic fluctuations, by planning regulations and fiscal controls, by the intervention of special interest groups such as conservationists and tenants' associations, and by the actions of key professionals and power-holders such as building society (i.e. savings and loan) managers, real estate agents and developers. The influence of such factors is examined in detail in subsequent chapters, and it is sufficient to note here that their combined effect on residential location is, to say the least, considerable.

In spite of these criticisms, it is generally accepted that trade-off models do offer some valuable insights into the pattern of urban structure, albeit as descriptive rather than explanatory models. Empirical tests of the model and its various extensions have provided a certain amount of support for the postulates of the approach, but the explanatory power of the model, in statistical terms, has been weak; and the nature of the results has varied from study to study (see, for example, Ball 1973; Evans 1973; Kain and Quigley 1970; Muth 1969). The fact is that even the most elaborate models must lead to an impasse because of the number of unknown parameters relating to household preferences and market behaviour. Nevertheless, the approach does provide a useful starting-point for the analysis of residential location, and in this respect its main value has been in stimulating alternative avenues of research. Among these are the 'New Urban Economics', urban development models (Chapin and Weiss 1968; Wilson 1974) and residential location models (Cripps and Foot 1969; Wilson 1970), all of which – like Alonso's model – concentrate upon the interactions between residences and workplaces, giving prominence to accessibility. The most fruitful area of research for urban geographers, however, has been the exploration of the cumulative effects of residential mobility on the overall structure of the city, and it is this field of enquiry to which attention is now turned.

Housing demand and residential mobility

Although it is widely accepted that the movement of households from one residence to another plays an important part in shaping and reshaping urban social areas, the relationship between residential structure and patterns of residential mobility are only imperfectly understood. In part, this is because intra-urban mobility, despite accounting for some two-thirds of all migration in most western countries, was, until recently, a neglected topic. But it is also a reflection of the complexity of these relationships. While migration creates and remodels the social and demographic structure of city neighbourhoods, it is also conditioned by the existing ecology of the city. Moreover, the process is undergoing constant modification, as each household's decision to move (or not to move) has repercussions for the rest of the system. Chain reactions of vacancies and moves are set off as dwellings become newly available, and this movement may itself trigger further mobility as households react to changes in neighbourhood status and tone.

The basic relationship between residential mobility and urban structure is outlined in Fig. 5.4, which emphasizes the circular and cumulative effects of housing demand and urban structure on each other. Mobility is seen as a product of *housing opportunities* – the new and vacant dwellings resulting from suburban expansion, inner-city renewal and rehabilitation, etc. – and the housing *needs* and *expectations* of households, which are themselves a product of income, family size and lifestyle. Given a sufficient amount of mobility, the residential structure of the city will be substantively altered, resulting in changes both to the 'objective' social ecology and to the associated neighbourhood images which help to attract or deter further potential movers. Households, then, may be seen as decision-making units whose aggregate response to housing opportunities is central to ecological change. It therefore seems logical to begin the task of disentangling the relationship between movement and urban structure by seeking to establish the fundamental parameters of household mobility. How many households do actually move in a given period? Do particular types of household have a greater propensity to move than others? And are there any spatial regularities in the pattern of migration?

Patterns of household mobility

In fact, the amount of movement by households in Western cities is considerable. Between 7 and 12 per

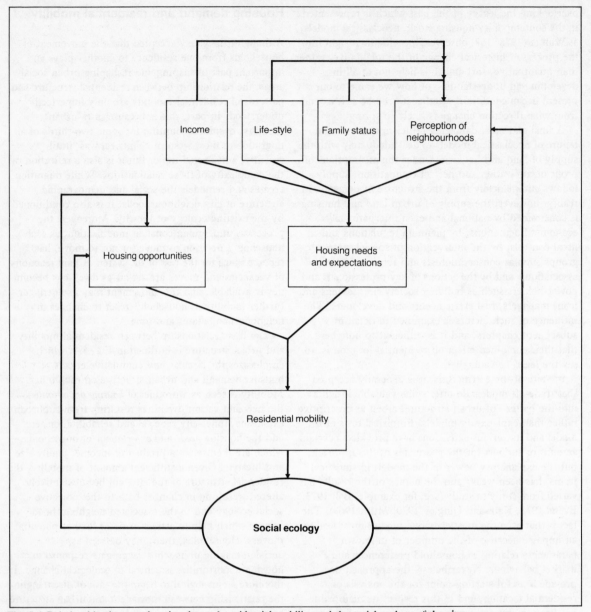

Fig. 5.4 Relationships between housing demand, residential mobility and the social ecology of the city.

cent of European households move each year, while in Australia, New Zealand and North America the figure is closer to 20 per cent. Having said this, it is of course important to recognize that some cities experience much higher levels of mobility than others. Adams and Gilder (1976), for example, point out that cities in the fast-growing West, South and Gulf Coast of the United States – Reno, Colorado Springs, Las Vegas and Anaheim/Santa Ana/Garden Grove, for instance – have an annual turnover of population which is double that of the likes of Scranton, Johnstown and

Wilkes-Barre/Hazleton in the more stable North East. It is also important to recognize that the magnitude of this movement stems partly from economic and social forces which extend well beyond the housing markets of individual cities. One of the most important determinants of the overall level of residential mobility is the business cycle which is endemic to capitalist economies. During economic upswings the increase in employment opportunities and wages leads to an increase in the effective demand for new housing which, when completed, allows whole chains of households to change homes. Changes in social organization – particularly those involving changes in family structure and the rate of household formation, dissolution and fusion – also affect the overall level of mobility by exerting a direct influence on the demand for accommodation. Long-term changes in the structure of the housing market itself are also important. In many European countries, for example, the expansion of owner-occupied and public housing at the expense of the privately rented sector has led to a general decrease in mobility because of the higher costs and longer delays involved in moving (Short 1978a).

Notwithstanding these general factors, it is clear that residential mobility is a selective process. Households of different types are not equally mobile. Some have a propensity to move quite often; others, having once gained entry to the housing system, never move at all, thus lending a degree of stability to the residential mosaic. This basic dichotomy between 'movers' and 'stayers' (Wolpert 1966) has been identified in a number of studies, and it has been found that the composition of each group tends to be related to the lifestyle and tenure characteristics of households. In particular, younger households have been found to move more frequently than older households; and private renters have been found to be more mobile than households in other tenure categories. In addition, there appears to be an independent duration-of-residence effect whereby the longer a household remains in a dwelling the less likely it is to move. This has been termed the principle of 'cumulative inertia' (Cave 1969; McGinnis 1968), and is usually explained in terms of the emotional attachments which develop towards the dwelling and immediate neighbourhood (Land 1969) and the reluctance to sever increasingly strong and complex social networks in favour of the 'unknown quantity' of the pattern of daily life elsewhere (Moore 1972). In contrast, the actual experience of moving home probably reinforces the propensity to move. As Van Arsdol *et al.* found, movers 'are more oriented to future mobility than are persons who have not moved in the past and are better able to actualize a moving plan and choice' (Van Arsdol, Sabagh and Butler 1968: 266).

Spatial regularities in the migration patterns of movers have proved difficult to establish, partly because of the problems involved in obtaining and analyzing migration data. Census data, although reliable, rarely include sufficient information about the origin of migrants; and few countries outside the Netherlands and Scandinavia have registers of households which can be used to plot household movements. Questionnaire surveys provide an obvious alternative, but they involve the expenditure of a large amount of time and money in order to obtain a sufficiently large sample of migrants.

In North America, many researchers have resorted to data based on changes of address worked out from telephone directories; but European researchers, faced with large numbers of households who do not have telephones, have often had to rely on town directories and electoral lists, both of which are known to be rather incomplete sources of information. Difficulties have also been experienced in analyzing migration data. In addition to the pitfalls of the ecological fallacy, these include the statistical problem of multi-collinearity and the practical problems involved in handling the large, complex data sets associated with migration studies (Clark and Moore 1978).

Patterns of in-migration

Nevertheless, it is possible to suggest a number of important regularities in people's migration behaviour. At this stage it is useful to distinguish between the spatial behaviour of intra-urban movers and that of in-migrants from other cities, regions and countries. Furthermore, in-migrants can be usefully divided into high- and low-status movers. The latter, as seen in Chapter 2, were particularly influential in shaping the residential structure of cities earlier this century. There are some cities, however, where low-status in-migrants continue to represent a significant component of migration patterns. Johnston's study of population movements in London, for example, showed that in-migrants from foreign countries and from Scotland and Ireland (the majority of whom can safely be assumed to have been of low socio-economic status) were still making a significant contribution to the city's residential structure, with large numbers moving to cheap housing in the western sector of the inner city (Johnston 1969b). Substantial flows of low-status in-migrants have also been shown to be directed to fairly narrowly defined inner-city districts in other cities: Cincinnati, for example, where the in-migrants are mainly poor whites from Appalachia (Hyland 1970); and Australian cities such as Melbourne and Sydney, where the in-migrants are mainly foreign born (Burnley 1972a; Stimpson 1970). It should be noted, however, that the impact of these in-migrants on urban social ecology is often finely tuned in relation to the national and regional origins, religion and ethnic status of the migrants involved: a process which is explored in detail in Chapter 7.

High-status in-migrants are similar to low-status in-migrants in that the majority are drawn into the city in response to its economic opportunities. Their locational behaviour, however, is quite different. The majority constitutes part of a highly mobile group of the

better-educated middle classes whose members move
from one city to another in search of better jobs or
career advancement. Some of these moves are voluntary
and some are made in response to the administrative fiat
of large companies and government departments. The
vast majority, though, follow the same basic pattern,
moving to a rather narrowly defined kind of
neighbourhood: newly-established suburban
developments containing housing towards the top end of
the price range. Such areas are particularly attractive to
the mobile élite because the lack of an established
neighbourhood character and social network minimizes
the risk of settling amongst neighbours who are
unfriendly, too friendly, 'snobbish' or 'common':
something which may otherwise happen very easily,
since out-of-town households must usually search the
property market and make a housing selection in a
matter of days. Moreover, housing in such areas tends
to conform to 'conventional' floor and window shapes
and sizes, so that there is a good chance that furnishings
from the previous residence will fit the new one.
Nevertheless, once established in the new city, it is
common for such households to make one or more
follow-up or 'corrective' moves in response to their
increasing awareness of the social ambience of different
neighbourhoods and the quality of their schools and
shops.

Intra-urban moves

This brings us conveniently to the general category of
intra-urban moves which makes up the bulk of all
residential mobility and which therefore merits rather
closer consideration. Indeed, a good deal of research
effort has been devoted to the task of searching for
regularities in intra-urban movement in the belief that
such regularities, if they exist, might help to illuminate
the relationships between residential mobility and urban
ecology.

One of the most consistent findings of this research
concerns the *distance moved*. In virtually every study,
the majority of moves has been found to be relatively
short, although the distances involved clearly depend to
a certain extent on the overall size of the city concerned.
In a national sample of United States movers between
1960 and 1966, almost 45 per cent had moved within
the same central city, with half of these moves taking
place within the same neighbourhood (Butler *et al*.
1969). Results from studies of individual cities,
including Minneapolis (Adams 1969), Philadelphia
(Rossi 1955), Providence, Rhode Island (Speare *et al*.
1975), Melbourne (Johnston 1969c), Glasgow (Forbes
and Robertson 1978) and Swansea (Herbert 1973), are

consistent with these findings. Within Minneapolis, for
example, the longest moves made by relocating
households in 1970–71 were over 20 miles (32 km); but
the modal distance moved was nearer to one mile
(1.6 km) and about 30 per cent of all the moves
involved distances of less than one mile (Nordstrand
1973). This tendency for short moves notwithstanding,
variability in distance moved is generally explained best
by income, race and previous tenure, with
higher-income white owner-occupier households
tending to move furthest.

Directional bias has also been investigated in a
number of migration studies, but with rather less
consistent results. While it is widely recognized that
there is a general tendency for migration to push
outward from inner-city neighbourhoods towards the
suburbs, reverse flows and cross-currents always exist to
complicate the issue. Adams (1969) has suggested that
the strong orientation of the urban system towards the
jobs and shops of the CBD tends to suppress lateral
flows, leaving a mixture of inward and outward moves
to dominate the pattern of intra-urban mobility.
Johnston's (1969c) analysis of Melbourne lends some
support to this idea, although he found that little of the
short-distance movement originating in the inner city
exhibited any strong directional bias. However, of the
moves terminating in the suburbs, 54 per cent were
found to stay within the sector of origin, and moves
from residences in outer zones were found to be even
more likely to end within the same sector than those
from inner zones, suggesting that once households have
lived in one segment of suburbia they are reluctant to
leave it for another. A broadly similar directional bias is
reported by Clark (1971), who found that households
from suburban neighbourhoods relocating within
Christchurch, New Zealand, tended to move towards
the CBD, while inner-city movements, like those in
Melbourne, were essentially random.

The most significant regularities in intra-urban
movement patterns, however, relate to the relative
socio-economic status of origin and destination areas. As
Simmons (1968) noted in his review of intra-urban
mobility, a vast majority of moves – about 80 per cent in
the USA – take place within census tracts of similar
socio-economic characteristics. A parallel and related
tendency is for a very high proportion of moves to take
place within tenure categories (Murie, Niner and
Watson 1976). In other words, relocation within
'community space' and 'housing space' usually involves
only short distances. These tendencies were first
documented for the Providence, Rhode Island,
metropolitan area (Goldstein and Mayer 1961), and have
since been observed in sufficient cities to suggest that
the phenomenon is universal (Brown and Longbrake

1970; Clark 1976; Short 1978b; Speare, Goldstein and Frey 1975). It follows from these observations that, while intra-urban mobility may have a significant impact on the spatial expression of social and economic cleavages, the overall degree of residential segregation tends to be maintained or even reinforced by relocation processes.

Putting together these empirical regularities in an overall spatial context, we are presented with a three-fold zonal division of the city. The innermost zone is characterized by high levels of mobility, which are swollen by the arrival of low-status in-migrants. Similarly, high levels of mobility in the outermost zone are supplemented by the arrival and subsequent follow-up mobility of higher-status in-migrants. Between the two is a zone of relative stability containing households whose housing needs are evidently satisfied. Here, turnover is low simply because few housing opportunities arise, either through vacancies or through new construction. It is probably the existence of such a zone which accounts for longer-distance moves and which helps to explain the sectoral 'leap-frogging' of lower-middle class and working class households to new suburban estates and dormitory towns. In an attempt to throw further light on these patterns, several researchers have undertaken analyses of the spatial correlates of mobility rates. Moore (1969; 1971), for example, has investigated the ecological correlates of population turnover in Brisbane, and Herbert (1973a) has analyzed the ecological correlates of residential mobility in Swansea. In general, however, the results of such studies have been inconclusive. Herbert was able to demonstrate that in-migration had a much greater impact on Swansea's affluent suburbs than on inner-city areas, but he found no statistically significant correlations between intra-urban mobility and urban structure. Moore, on the other hand, did establish significant associations between population turnover and several socio-economic variables, but he was not satisfied that these justified any causal inferences, largely because of the well-known fallibilities of ecological analysis.

Finally, it should be emphasized that the generalizations made here must be qualified by a measure of caution. In particular, patterns of movement within many European cities are complicated by the presence of significant amounts of public sector housing for which the entry and transfer rules are completely different from the rest of the housing market (see pp. 149–153). In general this does not distort the overall pattern of household movement, although it is likely that different elements of the pattern will be linked to particular sectors of the housing market. In Glasgow, for example, where the privately-rented and owner-occupied sectors are truncated by a massive public sector (in 1971, 54 per cent of the city's households lived in publicly-owned dwellings), the overall pattern of residential mobility still exhibits the 'typical' components of short-distance relocation within the neighbourhood of origin and of outward sectoral movement over larger distances. But a closer examination of migration flows reveals that these components are derived in composite fashion from the various flows within and between the main tenure categories. Thus, while short-distance moves dominate both the owner-occupied and public sector (see Figs. 5.5 and 5.6), longer-distance sectoral movements stem from:

1. outward flows of owner-occupiers and council tenants from first-tier suburban neighbourhoods towards peripheral locations outside the city boundary;
2. outward flows of households from inner-city slum-clearance areas to suburban public housing estates; and
3. a smaller, inward flow of households moving from public housing to older, owner-occupier tenement property nearer the centre of the city (Forbes and Robertson 1978).

The determinants of residential mobility

If the outward configuration of intra-urban mobility is difficult to pin down, its internal dynamics are even more obscure. The flows of mobility which shape urban structure derive from aggregate patterns of demand for accommodation which in turn spring from the complex deliberations of individual households. An understanding of how these deliberations are structured is thus likely to provide some insight into the relocation process, and a considerable amount of attention has therefore been given by geographers to two important aspects of household behaviour:

1. the decision to seek a new residence;
2. the search for and selection of a new residence.

This two-stage approach is adopted here. First, attention is focused on the personal, residential and environmental circumstances which appear to precipitate the decision to move, and a conceptual model of the decision to move is outlined. Subsequently, attention is focused on how this decision is acted upon, highlighting the bias imposed on locational behaviour by differential access to, and use of, information.

Reasons for moving
In any consideration of migration it is important to make a distinction between *voluntary* and *involuntary*

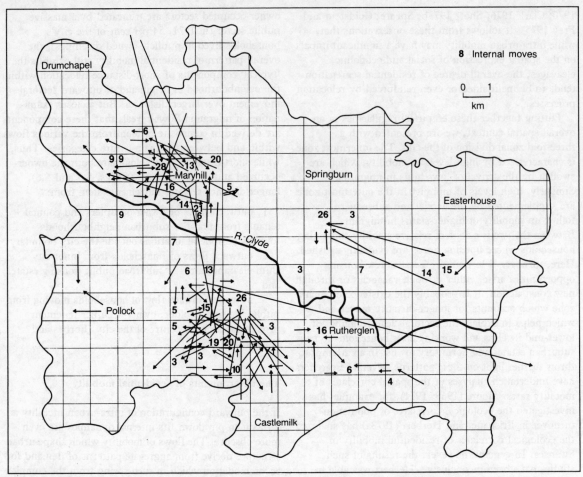

Fig. 5.5 Moves within the owner-occupied sector of Glasgow District involving three or more households, 1974. Numbers represent the number of internal moves in each grid square.
Source: Forbes and Robertson (1978).

moves. As Rossi (1955) showed in his classic study of migration in Philadelphia, involuntary moves make up a significant proportion of the total. In Philadelphia, almost a quarter of the moves were involuntary, and the majority of these were precipitated by property demolitions and evictions. Similar findings have been reported from studies of other cities, but remarkably little is known about the locational behaviour of affected households. In addition to these purely involuntary moves is a further category of 'forced' moves (Moore 1972) arising from marriage, divorce, retirement, ill-health, death in the family, and long-distance job changes. These frequently account for a further 15 per cent of all moves, leaving around 60 per cent as voluntary moves.

Survey data show that the decision to move home voluntarily is attributed to a number of quite different factors. It must be acknowledged, however, that the

reasons given for moving in the course of household interviews are not always entirely reliable. Some people have a tendency to rationalize and justify their own decisions, others may not be able to recollect past motivations; and most will inevitably articulate reasons which are simpler and more clear-cut than the complex of factors under consideration at the time of the move. Nevertheless, survey data are useful in indicating the major elements which need to be taken into consideration in explaining movement behaviour. Table 5.1 presents the reasons given for moving – both voluntarily and involuntarily – by a large sample of recently-moved British households, revealing a mixture of housing, environmental and personal factors. Among the more frequently-cited housing factors associated with voluntary moves are complaints about dwelling and garden space, about housing and repair costs and about style obsolescence. Environmental factors encompass

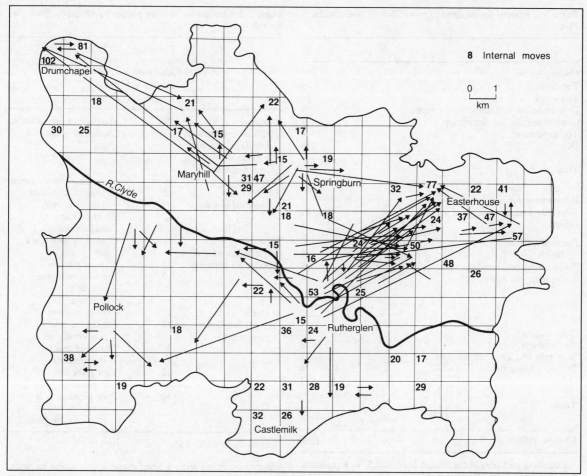

Fig. 5.6 Moves into and within local authority and Scottish Special Housing Association housing in Glasgow District involving 15 or more households, 1974. Numbers represent the number of internal moves in each grid square.

complaints about the presence of noxious activities such as factories, about noisy children, and about the incidence of litter, garbage and pet dogs. Personal factors are mostly associated with forced moves, but some voluntary moves are attributed to personal factors, such as a negative reaction to new neighbours. These generalizations hold true for sample populations in North America, Australia and New Zealand, as well as Britain (Barrett 1973; Butler *et al*. 1969; Clark 1970; Rossi 1955). Important variations do exist, however, between population sub-groups, with equally important implications for the social ecology of the city. The General Household Survey, for example, shows that only 36 per cent of British professionals, employers and managers who moved house in 1976 did so for 'housing' reasons, compared to 55 per cent of skilled manual workers and 50 per cent of semi-skilled and unskilled manual and personal service workers (Office of Population Censuses and Surveys 1978). Not

surprisingly, therefore, moves from different types of neighbourhood tend to be prompted differentially by different factors. In Swansea, for instance, Herbert (1973a) found that the high-status district of Derwen Fawr was distinctive in that a much larger proportion of movers than elsewhere gave employment as their main reason for having moved; and a comparison of four different neighbourhoods in Bristol shows clearly the differential importance of factors such as troublesome neighbours, housing costs and the physical condition of housing (Table 5.2).

Residential mobility and the family life-cycle
Of the more frequently cited reasons for moving, it is generally agreed that the most important and widespread is related to the household's need for dwelling space. More than half of the movers in Rossi's study cited complaints about too much or too little living space as contributing to their desire to move (with

123

Table 5.1 Reasons for wishing to move: British households, 1976

	%
Housing reasons	
Too large	6
Too small	16
Poor amenities or standard/poor repair	8
Condemned/due for demolition	3
Too expensive	4
Other	10
Total	47
Environmental reasons	
Job/study reasons (change of job, etc.)	21
Other	7
Personal reasons	
Ill health	3
To join relatives/friends	5
Retirement and other	4
Total	12
Other reasons	
To be nearer work †	3
Been asked to leave (by landlord)	2
To buy a house/flat	4
Other	3
Total	12
Base (= 100%)	1040

* Excluding members of the Armed Forces, full-time students, and those who have never worked
† Excluding a change of job
Source: General Household Survey 1978: 164.

Table 5.2 Reasons for moving house, by neighbourhood, in Bristol

	Percentage of households in each sample	Reason given
Bedminster	70	Marriage/to own a house
(19th-century terraced dwellings, manual households, owner-occupied)	13	Change in household size
St George	66	Marriage/to own a house
(Cheaper new owner-occupied housing)	12	Change in houshold size
	12	Troublesome neighbours
Westbury	28	Change in household size
(High status owner-occupied housing)	23	To own a house
	10	Previous residence was only temporary
St Pauls	21	Forced to move
(Mixed, run-down inner-city)	21	Setting up new household
	20	Changing space requirement
	12	Last place too expensive
	10	Poor physical condition of previous dwelling

Source: Short 1978: 538.

44 per cent giving it as a primary reason). Subsequent surveys have confirmed the decisive importance of living-space in the decision to move and, furthermore, have established that the crucial factor is not so much space *per se* but the relationship between the size and composition of a household and its *perceived* space requirements. Because both of these are closely related to the family life-cycle, it is widely believed that life-cycle changes provide the foundation for much of the residential relocation within cities. Moreover, the attractions of the family life-cycle as an explanatory variable are considerably reinforced by its relationships with several other frequently cited reasons for moving, such as the desire to own (rather than rent) a home and the desire for a change of environmental setting. Abu-Lughod and Foley (1960) have proposed a model which links all these factors together rather succinctly (Table 5.3).

According to their scheme, the typical family life-cycle begins with a brief stage living alone or with friends after leaving home to study or find work. The first year or two of marriage, when wives generally remain at work, may be regarded as a continuation of this phase. Whereas the physical size of the dwelling is unlikely to be important, accessibility to jobs and social amenities is often a major consideration in choosing a home, so that central locations are favoured. With the birth of a child, the household's real and perceived needs change considerably, reversing the relative importance of dwelling-space and accessibility and placing a premium on safe, quiet residential environments. However, the loss of one income during this 'child-bearing' stage tends to prevent an immediate move to the suburban ideal. Instead, it is more likely that a series of adjusting moves will be made as household income increases and the space requirements of the growing family increase. By the time the children are of secondary school age, access to neighbourhood facilities – especially social facilities and schools – becomes increasingly significant. Meanwhile, the earning power of the household is likely to be at a peak, so that – for middle-class families at least – it is common

Table 5.3 Simplified representation of Abu-Lughod and Foley's family-cycle model

Stage	Access	Space	Median tenure	Housing age	Mobility	Locational preference
Pre-child	Important	Unimportant	Rented flat		1 move to own home	Centre city
Child-bearing	Less important	Increasingly important	Rented house	Old	High 2–3 moves	Middle and outer rings of centre city
Child-rearing	Not important	Important	Owned	Relatively new	1 move to owned house	Periphery of city or suburbs
Child-launching	Not important	Very important	Owned	New	1 move to second home	
Post-child	Not important	Unimportant	Owned	New when first bought	Unlikely to move	
Later life	Not important	Unimportant		Widow leaves owned house to live with grown child		

Source: Morgan 1976: 86.

to move to a larger new suburban home. Later, when the children have left home, the space requirements of the household decrease considerably. At this stage, however, it is recognized that neighbourhood ties and sentimental attachments will prevent many couples from moving to smaller accommodation. The final residential change for many people, therefore, comes at the 'later life' stage, with a move to live with a son or daughter, to institutionalized accommodation, or to specialist retirement communities.

Evidence from Michelson's comprehensive analysis of housing in Toronto lends some general support to this process, showing a significant movement of childless families into the downtown area, with larger families moving to suburban areas from more central locations and from out of town (Table 5.4). Only families of six or more persons were not tending to move towards the suburbs, but this was because they were there already (Michelson 1977). A recent study of *intending* migrants

Table 5.4 Residential relocation in Toronto
Location change (%)

Number in Household	Downtown to downtown	Centralizing and outside Toronto to downtown	Suburbs to suburbs	Decentralizing and outside to suburbs
2	27.9	26.0	10.6	35.6
3	11.5	7.7	17.3	63.5
4	7.4	5.2	28.7	58.7
5	6.9	11.9	36.6	44.6
6 or more	10.8	9.2	46.2	33.8

Source: Michelson 1977: 140.

in the inner London borough of Lambeth also provides some support for life-cycle related mobility. Over half of those who wanted to move out from Lambeth to the suburbs were families with children, whereas of those wanting to stay in inner London only a third were families with children and over a quarter were single people (Department of the Environment 1978).

It follows from these observations that a marked residential segregation will emerge as households at similar stages in the family life-cycle respond in similar ways to their changing circumstances. This, of course, fits conveniently with the results of the many descriptive studies (including factorial ecology studies) which have demonstrated a zonal pattern of family status. The generally accepted sequence of these zones runs from a youthful inner-city zone through successive zones of older and middle-aged family types to a zone of late youth/early middle-age on the periphery (Morgan 1976). It must be acknowledged, however, that such a pattern may be the result of factors other than those associated directly with the dynamic of the family life cycle. As Adams and Gilder (1976: 165) observe: 'Households often undergo changes in their family status at the same time as they experience changes in income and social status', so it is dangerous to explain mobility exclusively in terms of one or the other. Quite different factors may also be at work. North American and Scandinavian developers, for example, knowing that many households prefer to live among families similar to their own in age and composition as well as socio-economic status, have reinforced family status segregation by building apartment complexes and housing estates for

125

specific household types, with exclusionary covenants and contracts designed to keep out 'non-conforming' residents. It is thus quite common for entire condominiums to be inhabited by single people or by childless couples. The extreme form of this phenomenon is represented by Sun City, a satellite suburb of Phoenix, Arizona, where no resident under the age of 50 is allowed, and where the whole townscape is dominated by the design needs of the so-called 'grey panthers', who whir along the quiet streets in golf caddy-cars, travelling from one social engagement to the next. In contrast, much of the family status segregation in British cities with large amounts of public housing can be attributed to the letting policies of local authorities, since eligibility for public housing is partly a product of household size (see pp. 164–165).

It should also be stressed that the correlation between the family life-cycle and family status segregation is in any case by no means perfect or universal. The relevance of the life-cycle model to British cities has been questioned by Morgan (1976), whose study of family status segregation in Exeter showed that progression through the family life-cycle was not significantly associated with relative location or changes in housing tenure. Rather, households were found to be associated with housing built at the time of, or soon after, their formation. In other words, the segregation of family status groups in Exeter is best understood in terms of the inertia of ageing cohorts of households. Even in North American cities, where the higher overall levels of mobility seem more closely aligned to the life-cycle model, much of the movement postulated by the model is suppressed by a series of intervening factors. For one thing, by no means every household is 'typical'. Many, including an increasing number of voluntarily childless couples, experience a life-cycle whose major stages and associated housing needs bear only a loose resemblance to those in the Abu-Lughod/Foley model. More important is the fact that many of the households which do want to relocate because of housing needs related to the idealized life-cycle are prevented from doing so either because suitable accommodation is not available or because they cannot afford it.

A conceptual framework: 1. The decision to move

An alternative approach to residential mobility is provided by behaviouralist work which, rather than invoking specific processes such as the family life-cycle to explain the relocation process, emphasize the individual decision to move within a general conceptual framework. Brown and Moore (1970) have outlined the

basis of a widely accepted scheme (Fig. 5.7) in which the first major decision – whether or not to move home – is viewed as a product of the *stress* generated by discordance between the household's needs, expectations and aspirations on the one hand and its actual housing conditions and environmental setting on the other.

While the nature of the stresses associated with housing and environmental conditions should be clear, it is necessary at this point to elaborate upon the idea of people's housing *expectations* and *aspirations*. Basically, these are thought by behaviouralists to stem from the different frames of reference which people adopt in making sense of their lives and, in particular, in interpreting their housing situation. These frames of reference are the product of a wide range of factors which includes age, class background, religion, ethnic origin, and past experience of all aspects of urban life. What they amount to is a series of *life styles* – privatized, familistic, cosmopolitan, and so on – each with a distinctive set of orientations in relation to housing and residential location. Bell (1958; 1968) has suggested that there are in fact three main lifestyles, whose adherents may be termed familists, careerists and consumerists.

Family-oriented people are also home-centred and tend to spend much of their spare time with their children. As a result, their housing orientations are dominated by their perceptions of their children's needs for play space, a clean, safe environment, proximity to child clinics and schools, and so on. Bell found that 83 per cent of the households in his sample who had moved to suburban locations in Chicago had done so 'for the sake of the children'.

Careerists have a life style centred on career advancement. Since movement is often a necessary part of this process, careerists tend to be highly mobile; and since they are, by definition, status conscious, their housing orientations tend to be focused on prestige neighbourhoods appropriate to their jobs, their salary and their self-image.

Consumerists are strongly oriented towards enjoying the material benefits and amenities of modern urban society, and their housing preferences are therefore dominated by a desire to live in downtown areas, close to clubs, theatres, art galleries, discotheques, restaurants, and so on.

To these, Moore (1972) has added *community seekers*, who stress a lifestyle which is centred on social interaction with other people with the same kind of group-oriented values. Examples include members of 'alternative' lifestyles and cultures, who tend to gather in cheaper inner-city areas; and some of the more affluent elderly population, who seek the companionship of suburban retirement communities.

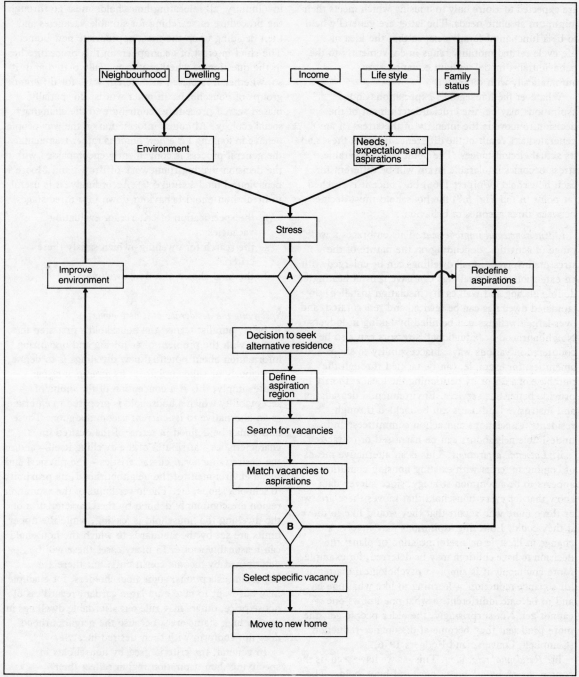

Fig. 5.7 A model of residential mobility.
Source: Robson (1975), p. 33.

Bell's typology can be criticized for its middle-class tenor, since it overlooks the 'lifestyle' of the large number of households whose economic position reduces their housing aspirations to the level of survival. As Rainwater (1966) has shown, many working-class households view their homes as havens from the outside world rather than as platforms for the enactment of a favoured lifestyle. This limitation, however, is allowed for by the behaviouralist model outlined in Fig. 5.7. Quite simply, households with more modest incomes are expected to aspire only to housing which meets their minimum absolute needs. The latter are generally held to be a function of family size, so that the idea of life-cycle related mobility plugs in conveniently to the behaviouralist model without equating stress automatically with mobility.

Whatever the household's expectations and aspirations may be, the crucial determinant of the decision to move is the intensity of the stress (if any) generated as a result of the difference between these and its actual circumstances. The point where tolerable stress becomes intolerable strain will be different for each household (Wolpert 1966) but, once it is reached (at point 'A' on Fig. 5.7) the household must decide between three avenues of behaviour:

i. *Environmental improvement*. This embraces a wide range of activities, depending on the nature of the stressors involved. Small dwellings can be enlarged with an extension, cold dwellings can have central heating, double glazing and wall cavity insulation installed, dilapidated dwellings can be rewired and redecorated, and over-large dwellings can be filled by taking in lodgers. Neighbourhood or 'situational' stressors can also be countered in various ways: inaccessibility to shops and amenities, for example, can be tackled through the purchase of a car or by petitioning the local authority to provide better bus services. Environmental degradation and intrusive land-users can be tackled through residents' associations and action committees; and undesirable neighbours can be harrassed or ostracized.

ii. *Lowering aspirations*. This is an alternative means of coming to terms with existing housing conditions. It appears to be a common strategy, since survey data show that for every household that moves there are two or three more who report that they would like to move if they could. Lowering aspirations may involve a change in lifestyle or a reformulation of plans: the decision to have children may be deferred, for example. More commonly it is simply a psychological matter of 'dissonance reduction' – learning to like what one has and to become indifferent to what one knows one cannot get. Not surprisingly, the older people get, the more proficient they become at dissonance reduction (Campbell, Converse and Rodgers 1976).

iii. *Residential relocation*. This, as we have seen, is the course chosen by a large minority of households. The decision to move, however, leads to a second important area of locational behaviour: the search for and selection of a new residence.

2. The search for a new residence

Whether the decision to move is voluntary or involuntary, all relocating households must go through the procedure of searching for suitable vacancies and then deciding upon the most appropriate new home. The chief interest of geographers in this procedure lies in the question of whether it is spatially biased and, if so, whether it is biased in different ways for different groups of households. In other words, do spatially biased search procedures contribute to the changing social ecology? Although information on the way people behave in looking for a new home is rather fragmentary, the general process is conveniently encompassed within the decision-making framework of Brown and Moore's behavioural model (Fig. 5.7). Accordingly, it is useful to break household behaviour down into three stages:

1. the specification of criteria for evaluating vacancies;
2. the search for dwellings which satisfy these criteria;
3. the final choice of a new dwelling.

Specifying the desiderata of a new home

In behaviouralist terms, the household's first step in coping with the problem of acquiring and organizing information about potential new dwellings is to define, consciously or subconsciously, its *aspiration region*. Quite simply, this is a conception of the limits of acceptability which a household is prepared to entertain as an alternative to its current accommodation. These limits may be defined in terms of the desired *site* characteristics – attributes of the dwelling itself – and/or the desired *situational* characteristics – the physical and social environment of the neighbourhood, its proximity to schools, shops, etc. The lower limits of the aspiration region are commonly defined by the characteristics of the dwelling the household is leaving, while the upper limits are set by the standards to which the household can reasonably aspire. In many cases these will be determined by income constraints, but there are important exceptions: some householders, for example, may not want to take on a large garden, regardless of house price; others may rule out affordable dwellings in certain high status areas because the neighbourhood does not conform with their desired lifestyle.

In general, the criteria used by households in specifying their aspiration region reflect their motivations in deciding to move. We can thus expect living-space, tenure, dwelling amenities, environmental quality and social composition to be amongst the more frequently used criteria. This is confirmed by Table 5.5, which compares the reasons given for moving with those given for selecting a new residence by a sample of Toronto households. But, in addition to the broad correspondence between the two, it is worth noting that

Table 5.5 Motivations associated with intra-urban mobility, Toronto

Reasons*	For move away from current home (%)	For a choice of new residence (%)
Unit interior size and layout	17.0	23.7
Unit interior features	3.1	4.7
Exterior setting	16.8	17.3
Dwelling unit	20.2	10.2
Neighbourhood	12.4	19.0
Access	7.1	17.4
Family composition	15.0	1.3
Interaction with people	1.1	0.2
Leisure activities	0.6	0.4
Fiscal considerations	8.0	6.0
Other	0.8	0.1
Total reasons	2,658	4,019

* Up to but not necessarily four reasons per person

Source: Michelson 1977: 115 and 122.

some of the criteria used in evaluating the new residence are largely unrelated to the problems encountered in the previous residence. Interior aspects of the dwelling, the social characteristics of the neighbourhood and accessibility to various facilities are more important in attracting people to a new home than in propelling them away, for example. It also appears that movers of different types tend to differ quite a lot in the criteria they use. In Toronto, households moving to houses are evidently more likely to be concerned with situational characteristics than those moving to apartments. Furthermore, those moving to suburban houses tend to be particularly concerned with the layout of the dwelling and its potential as an investment, whereas for those moving to downtown houses the aesthetics of dwelling style and the neighbourhood environment tends to be a more important criterion (Michelson 1977). The existence of differently conceived aspiration regions is, of course, a function of the different needs and aspirations which prompt households to move in the first place. Their significance to the spatial outcome of the relocation process lies not only in the consequent variability in the evaluation of particular housing opportunities, but also in the fact that households set out from the very start to look for vacancies with quite different housing goals in mind.

Searching for vacancies

The general objective of the search procedure is to find the right kind of dwelling, at the right price, in the time available. It must be acknowledged that there are some households that do not have to search deliberately because their decision to move has come after accidentally discovering an attractive vacancy. Rossi (1955), who termed these 'windfall' moves, found that as many as 25 per cent of the movers in his sample had done so in this way. The majority of movers, though, must somehow organize themselves into finding a suitable home within a limited period of deciding to relocate. According to Brown and Moore (1970), most households organize the search procedure in locational terms, focusing attention on particular neighbourhoods which are selected on the basis of (a) their perceived *situational* characteristics and (b) the household's evaluation of the probability of finding vacancies satisfying their *site* criteria. Moreover, faced with the problem of searching even a limited amount of space, it is natural that households will attempt to further reduce both effort and uncertainty by concentrating their search in areas which are best-known and most accessible to them (Silk 1971).

The upshot is that households concentrate their house-hunting activities within a limited *search space* which is spatially biased by their familiarity with different districts. In behaviouralist terminology, this search space is a subset of a more general *awareness space*, which is usually regarded as a product of (a) people's *activity space* or *action space* (the sum of all the places with which people have regular contact as a result of their normal activities) and (b) information from secondary sources such as radio, television, newspapers, and even word-of-mouth. Both elements, as we have seen (pp. 100–111) are subject to a mental filtering and coding which produces a set of imagery which constitutes the operational part of the individual's awareness space. The subset of this space which constitutes the search space is simply the area (or areas) which a household feels to be relevant to its aspiration region, and it is spatially biased because of the inherent bias in both activity spaces and mental maps. It follows that different sub-groups of households, with distinctive activity spaces and mental maps, will tend to exhibit an equally distinctive spatial bias in their search behaviour. In particular, we may expect the more limited activity spaces and more localized and intensive images of the home area to limit the search space of low-income households to a relatively small area centred on the previous home, while more mobile, higher-income households will have a search space which is more extensive but focused on the most familiar sector of the city between home and workplace. What empirical evidence there is tends to support this proposition. Brown and Holmes (1971), for example, have demonstrated that patterns of social contacts and vacancies visited in the search for a new home were much more compact and localized around the former residence for low-income, inner-city residents (of Cedar Rapids, Iowa) than for higher-income suburban dwellers, who searched over a wider area and displayed both directional bias, towards the CBD, and sectoral bias, towards the sector of their previous residence. This, it will be observed, ties in neatly with the regularities in actual migration patterns outlined above.

The *information sources* used to find vacant dwellings within the search space can also exert a significant spatial bias. Moreover, since different types of households tend to rely on different combinations of sources, there results a further process of socio-spatial sorting. Overall, the most frequently-used sources of information about housing vacancies are newspaper advertisements, real estate agents, friends and relatives, and personal observation of 'for sale' signs, although their relative importance and effectiveness seems to vary somewhat from one city to another (see, for example, Barrett 1973; Herbert 1973b; Rossi 1955). Although little research has been done on these information sources, it is clear that each tends to be biased in a different way. Personal observation, for example, will be closely determined by personal activity space, while the quantity and quality of information from friends and relatives will depend a lot on social class and the structure of the searcher's social networks. Estate agents also exert a considerable spatial bias in their role as mediators of information. Risa Palm (1976a; 1976b) has shown that this operates in two ways: first, each business tends to specialize in limited portions of the housing market in terms of both price and area; second, while most estate agents were found to have a fairly accurate knowledge of the city-wide housing market, they tended to over-recommend dwellings in the area in which they were most experienced in selling and listing accommodation and with which they were most familiar. As a result, 'households which are dependent on realty salesman for information . . . are making use of a highly structured and spatially limited information source' (Palm 1976b: 28).

The critical issue in the present context, however, is the relative importance and effectiveness of different information sources for different households. Again, empirical evidence is rather patchy, but survey data from Swansea and Toronto do show a marked variation in the emphasis that different movers put on different sources. In Swansea, migrants from a high-cost housing area used estate agents and newspaper advertisements much more than migrants from a low-cost area, though informal sources of information were dominant for both groups (Herbert 1973b). In Toronto, where Michelson (1977) used a more detailed breakdown of movers, several sharp differences emerged. Newspaper advertisements were a much more effective source of

information for households searching for an apartment than for those searching for a house. Conversely, estate agents were consulted mainly about houses, proving a very effective source (in the sense that a high proportion of movers eventually found their new homes as a result of information obtained from estate agents rather than from other sources), particularly for housing in the downtown area. Personal observation (in the form of 'driving around'), on the other hand, was a more popular and effective source of information for suburban house-hunters.

This differential use and effectiveness clearly serves to increase the degree of socio-spatial sorting arising from the migration process, while at the same time making it more complex. Another important compounding factor in this sense is the constraint of *time* in the search procedure. Both search space and search procedures are likely to alter as households spend increasing amounts of time and money looking for a new home. When time starts to run out, the search strategy must change to ensure that a home will be found. Anxiety produced by a lack of success may result in a modification of the household's aspiration region, a restriction of their search space, and a shift in their use of information sources; and the pressure of time may lead people to make poor choices. On the other hand, the longer the search goes on, the greater the household's knowledge of the housing market. Each household therefore has to balance the advantages of searching and learning against the costs – real and psychological – of doing so. This dilemma is analogous to the so-called 'marriage problem', which has been stated by Lindley (1961: 47), from a male point of view, as follows:

A known number, n, of ladies are presented to you one at a time in random order. After inspecting any number r ($1 \leqslant r \leqslant n$) of them you are able to rank them from best to worst and this order will not be changed if the $(r + 1)$th lady is inspected; she will merely be inserted into the order. At any stage of the 'game' you may either propose to the lady *then being inspected* (there is no going back!), when the game stops, or inspect the next lady; however, if you reach the last lady you have to propose. All proposals are accepted. What is the optimum strategy?

Statistical probability models have been developed in order to devise the optimal 'stopping rule' for this type of problem. Evidently the optimal strategy in the marriage problem is to pass by all opportunities (of marriage!) until the age of 26, and then propose to the first 'lady' who compares favourably with the best of those encountered before. The probability of marrying the 'best' possible partner in this way is, rather dauntingly, estimated at just over 36 per cent (Lindley 1961). No such bold conclusions have yet been derived for house-hunting, although Flowerdew (1976) has outlined the bases of a relatively sophisticated stopping-rule model for house-hunting. One of the difficulties in operationalizing such models, however, is the variability of personality and psychological factors in decision-making. Conservative households, for example, may tend to take an acceptable vacancy instead of pushing on to find a better deal. Survey data in fact show a consistent tendency for the majority of households to seriously consider only a few vacancies (usually, only two or three) before selecting a new home, an observation which may appear to undermine the utility of developing elaborate models and theories of search behaviour. Nevertheless, this phenomenon can itself be explained within a behaviouralist framework. As Barrett (1973) points out, households are able to reduce the element of uncertainty in their decision-making by restricting serious consideration to only a few vacancies. Moreover, as Short (1978a) observes, most households begin with an aspiration region which is quite narrowly defined (either because of income constraints or locational requirements), so that what appears to be an inhibited search pattern is in fact a logical extension of the decisions formulated in the preceding stage of the search procedure.

A useful example of the aggregate patterns of searching arising from these influences is provided by Barrett's (1973) work on Toronto. Using an index of the 'temporal intensity' of the search for housing calculated from the number of vacancies examined divided by the time spent searching, Barrett found a generally low intensity, with few vacancies searched within a short period, and a random spatial distribution of vacancies. It was found that households with a temporally intensive search pattern were mainly associated with the central city area, where keen competition for accommodation had created a sellers' market. Households taking time to view more vacancies tended to be those searching the suburban house market. A second index was used to measure the 'spatial intensity' of household search patterns. This was calculated as the mean distance to all searched vacancies from the mean centre of their locations. For over 90 per cent of the households, this turned out to be three miles (4.8 km) or less, compared to an urban area radius of 13 miles (20.8 km). The lowest values of all were found amongst households of below-average socio-economic status. Dividing the first index by the second gave an index of the concentration of search. High values, suggesting casual and erratic search patterns, were found to be associated with central-city searchers; while low values, suggesting more intensive and thorough search behaviour, were common in newer suburban housing estates.

Choosing a new home

Those households which do find two or more vacancies which fall within their aspiration region must eventually make a choice. Theoretically, this kind of choice is made on the basis of household *utility functions* which are used to give a subjective rating to each vacancy. In other words, vacancies are evaluated in terms of the weighted sum of the attributes used to delineate the aspiration region. These weights reflect the relative importance of the criteria used to specify the aspiration region, and so they will vary according to the preferences and predilections of the household concerned. Difficulties arise, however, in attempting to operationalize the theory for more than one household at a time, when non-transitive preferences and the 'paradox of majority rule' (Arrow 1951) wreak havoc with the theoretical elegance of utility functions.

Nevertheless, it is clear that some criteria are given greater weight than others. The national survey of United States movers, for example, discovered an overall tendency for people to value neighbourhood quality more than housing quality and accessibility, to value interior style and appearance more than the exterior style and appearance of a dwelling, and to prefer neighbourhoods with better-than-average schools and relatively high local taxes to those with lower taxes but poorer schools (Butler *et al.* 1969). What is not yet known, though, is whether there are consistent differences in the housing preferences of different demographic and socio-economic groups. Without this kind of information, few inferences can be made about the nature of socio-spatial outcomes, if any, associated with the choice of housing. Lyon and Wood (1977) have suggested that the constraints of time, coupled with the limitations of human information-processing abilities and a general lack of motivation, mean that a real choice of the kind implied in behaviouralist theory is seldom made: people are happy to take any reasonable vacancy, so long as it does not involve a great deal of inconvenience. The fact that their sample was drawn from a modern housing estate in south London goes some way towards explaining their conclusions, however, for there certainly seems little to choose between amongst the cautious architectural variations which are typical of post-war British housing. Nevertheless, it remains for behaviouralists to suggest the exact nature of spatial bias resulting from the actual choice between alternative vacancies.

Finally, it should be noted that the basic behavioural model allows for those households which are unable to find vacancies within their aspiration region in the time available to them (point 'B' on Fig. 5.7) to change their strategy to one of the two options open to them at point 'A' on the diagram: environmental improvement or a redefinition of aspirations. Although the basic model stops at this point, it is a simple matter to extend the behaviouralist perspective to treat mobility as a continual process. Kennedy (1975), for example, has outlined a model involving:

1. a comparison of the new dwelling with the household's prior expectations of it; and
2. a comparison of the new dwelling with the household's previous dwelling.

In the light of this reflection, Kennedy points out, some households will experience satisfaction and decide to stay, while others, dissatisfied with their new dwelling, will find themselves once more at the equivalent of point 'A' on Figure 5.7.

Residential mobility and neighbourhood change

Although the behavioural approach provides important insights into the spatial implications of mobility, the emphasis on individual decision-making tends to divert attention from the aggregate patterns of neighbourhood change which result 'as like individuals make like choices' (Rees 1970: 313). In this section, therefore, some consideration is given to the macro-scale generalizations which have been advanced about processes of mobility and neighbourhood change.

One scheme which has already been introduced and discussed is the zonal pattern of family status associated with moves arising from family life-cycle changes (see above, pp. 123–126). Another is the zonal patterning of socio-economic status associated with the sequence of invasion-succession-dominance postulated by Burgess in his model of ecological change (see pp. 37–40). The dynamic of this model, it will be recalled, was based on the pressure of low-status in-migrants arriving in inner-city areas. As this pressure increases, some families penetrate surrounding neighbourhoods, thus initiating a chain reaction whereby the residents of each successively higher status zone are forced to move further out from the centre in order to counter the lowering of neighbourhood status. Notwithstanding the criticisms of ecological theory *per se*, with its heavy reliance on biotic analogy, the concept of invasion-succession-dominance provides a useful explanatory framework for the observed sequence of neighbourhood change in cities where rapid urban growth is fuelled by large-scale in-migration of low-status families. The classic example, of course, is Chicago during the 1920s and 1930s, although many of the industrial cities in Britain had undergone a similar process of neighbourhood change during the nineteenth century. More recently, the postwar flow of overseas

immigrants to London, Paris and larger Australian cities such as Melbourne and Sydney has generated a sequence of change in some neighbourhoods which also fits the invasion/succession model. Nevertheless, this model is of limited relevance to most modern cities, since its driving force – the inflow of low-status migrants – is of diminishing importance; the bulk of in-migrants is now accounted for by middle-income families moving from a suburb in one city to a similar suburb in another (Johnson, Salt and Wood 1974; Schwind 1971).

High status movement, filtering and vacancy chains

An alternative view of neighbourhood change and residential mobility stems from Hoyt's (1939) model of urban growth and socio-economic structure. Hoyt's ideas were derived from a detailed study of rental values in 142 US cities which was undertaken in order to classify neighbourhood types according to their mortgage lending risk. This study led him to believe that the key to urban residential structure is to be found in the behaviour of high status households. These, he argued, pre-empt the most desirable land in the emerging city away from industrial activity. With urban growth, the high-status area expands axially along natural routeways, in response to the desire amongst the well-off to combine accessibility with suburban living. This sectoral movement is reinforced by a tendency amongst 'community leaders' to favour non-industrial waterside sites and higher ground; and for the rest of the higher-income groups to seek the social cachet of living in the same neighbourhood as these *prominenti*. Further sectoral development occurs when dissatisfaction with their existing housing prompts a move outwards to new housing in order to maintain standards of exclusivity. In the wake of this continual outward movement of high-status households, the housing they vacate is occupied by middle-status households whose own housing is in turn occupied by lower-status households. At the end of this chain of movement, the vacancies created by the lowest-status groups are either demolished or occupied by low-status in-migrants. Subsequently, as other residential areas also expand outwards, the sectoral structure of the city will be preserved, with zonal components emerging as a secondary element because of variations in the age and condition of the housing stock.

The validity of Hoyt's sectoral model has been much debated. Empirical studies of the emerging pattern of élite residential areas and tests of the existence of sectoral gradients in socio-economic status have provided a good deal of general support for the spatial configuration of Hoyt's model (see, for example, Johnston 1970, 1971; Murdie 1976), although the relative dominance of sectoral over zonal components in urban structure is evidently by no means a simple or universal phenomenon. In particular, emphasis has been given to the persistence of élite neighbourhoods in the innermost zone of many cities (Johnston 1966, 1969d), a phenomenon to which Firey first drew attention in 1945.

It is the *mechanism* of neighbourhood change implied in Hoyt's model which is of interest here, however. The basis of this mechanism is the chain of moves initiated by the construction of new dwellings for the wealthy, resulting in their older properties *filtering down* the social scale while individual households *filter up* the housing scale. In order for this filtering process to operate at a sufficient level to have any real impact on urban structure, there has to be more new construction than that required simply to replace the deteriorating housing of the élite. According to Hoyt, this will be ensured by the *obsolescence* of housing as well as its physical deterioration. For the rich, there are several kinds of obsolescence which may trigger a desire for new housing. Advances in kitchen technology and heating systems and the innovation of new luxury features such as swimming pools, saunas and solaria may cause 'functional obsolescence', while more general social and economic changes may cause obsolescence of a different kind: the trend away from large families combined with the relative increase in the cost of domestic labour, for example, has made large free-standing dwellings something of a white elephant. Changes in design trends may also cause obsolescence – 'style obsolescence' – in the eyes of those who can afford to be sensitive to architectural fads and fashions. Finally, given a tax structure which allows mortgage repayments to be offset against taxable income (as in Britain and many other Western countries), dwellings may become 'financially obsolescent' as increases in household income and/or inflation reduce the relative size of mortgage repayments (and therefore of tax relief). Driven on to new housing by one or more of these factors, the wealthy will thus create a significant number of vacancies which the next-richest group will be impelled to fill through a desire for a greater quantity and/or quality of housing. This desire can be seen not only as the manifestation of a general preference for better housing but also as a result of the influence of changing housing needs associated with the family life-cycle. In addition, Harvey (1973) has suggested that the social and economic pressures resulting from proximity to the poorest groups in society may prompt those immediately above them to move as soon as the opportunity presents itself, either by moving into vacancies created by the construction of new housing for others or by moving out into new subdivisions specially constructed for the lower-middle classes. Harvey calls this the 'blow-out' theory and suggests that 'the dynamics of the housing market can probably best be viewed as a combination of 'blow-out' and 'filter down'' (Harvey 1973: 173).

In practice, however, the dynamics of the housing market are rather more complex than this. To begin with, vacancy chains may start in other ways than the construction of new housing, whether for the rich (as in Hoyt's model) or for middle-income families (as in Harvey's blow-out theory). A substantial proportion of vacancies arise through the subdivision of dwelling units into flats and the conversion of non-residential property to residential uses. Even more occur through the death of a household, through the move of an existing household to share accommodation with another, and through emigration outside the city. Similarly, vacancy chains may be ended in several ways other than the demolition of the worst dwellings or their occupation by poor in-migrants. Some vacancies are rendered ineffective through conversion to commercial use, while others may be cancelled out by rehabilitation or conversion schemes which involve knocking two or more dwellings into one. Vacancy chains will also end if the household which moves into a vacant dwelling is a 'new' one and so leaves no vacancy behind for others to fill. This may arise through the marriage of a couple who had both previously been living with friends or parents, through divorced people setting up separate homes, or through the splitting of an existing household with, for example, a son or daughter moving out to their own flat.

A closer examination of the filtering process between the start and finish of vacancy chains also reveals a certain amount of complexity. This is not helped by the lack of agreement on how to measure the process, despite a lengthy and often bitter debate in the literature. Conceptions of filtering have involved notions of change in price and housing quality as well as changes in occupancy. Ratcliff (1949) described the filtering process as the changing of occupancy as the housing that is occupied by one income group becomes available to the next lower income group as a result of a decline in price. Smith (1964) also regarded filtering as a change in the occupancy of dwellings by different income groups. Others, notably Fisher and Winnick (1951) and Lowry (1960), have proposed definitions based solely on changes in the price of housing, although the issue is further complicated by the several ways in which price changes can be measured – against changes in the prices and rentals of all dwellings, for example; or against consumer prices. Amongst the narrower definitions of filtering is that proposed by Grigsby, who suggests that 'filtering only occurs when value declines more rapidly than quality so that families can obtain either higher quality and more space at the same price or the same quality and space at a lower price than formerly' (Grigsby 1963: 97). This clearly comes close to the conception of filtering in Hoyt's model. It is also useful in emphasizing the role of filtering not just as a mechanism of intra-urban mobility but also as a means of facilitating a general improvement of housing conditions as new houses filter down the social scale.

This aspect of filtering has attracted more attention than any other because of its policy implications, since it can be argued that facilitating new housebuilding for higher income groups will result in an eventual improvement in the housing conditions of the poor through the natural process of filtering, without recourse to public intervention in the housing market. This argument has a long history, dating to the paternalistic logic of the nineteenth century housing reformers who used it to justify the construction of model housing for the 'industrious' and 'respectable' working classes rather than the poorest sections of society to whom their efforts were ostensibly directed (Tarn 1973). Subsequently, it became the central plank of government housing policy in many countries. Up to the 1930s, Britain relied almost entirely on the filtering process to improve the housing conditions of the working classes (Kirby 1979), while it still remains the basis of US housing strategy.

Empirical studies of vacancy chains
The general validity of the filtering concept is not disputed, apart from the obvious exception of movement into and within the public sector. Many of the once-fashionable quarters of the rich, now sub-divided into flats and bedsitters, can be seen to be occupied by distinctly less prosperous families, students, single-person households and the aged. What is not clear, however, is the impact of this process on different social groups and different neighbourhoods. Relatively few studies have been able to furnish detailed empirical evidence, and their results are rather inconclusive. One of the most comprehensive analyses of vacancy chains so far undertaken is that by Lansing, Clifton and Morgan in the United States. They sought to answer a series of questions, including 'what is the economic level of people who move into new housing? If rich people move into new housing, do poor people benefit directly by moving into vacancies further along in the sequence? Or do the sequences stop before they reach low income people?' (Lansing, Clifton and Morgan 1969: 111). An examination of over 1,100 vacancy chains generated by the construction of new dwellings showed that while the average sequence of moves thus initiated was 3.5, those resulting from the

construction of more expensive houses ($30,000 or more) were roughly twice as long as those resulting from the construction of cheaper houses (less than $15,000) and rental units costing less than $150 per month. It was also found that a majority of the families moving into a dwelling had a lower income and socio-economic status than the previous occupants. At the same time, almost two-thirds of the moves resulted in an increase in dwelling space. It is also interesting to note in relation to both Hoyt's model and the family life-cycle model that the average distance from the centre of the city was found to decrease with each successive link in the chain, and that whereas over 40 per cent of the households moving into a house were at an 'earlier' stage in the life-cycle than families moving out, only 28 per cent were at a later stage.

These results seem to suggest that an upward filtering of households does arise from the construction of new homes for the wealthy. Nevertheless, closer inspection of the results shows that the benefits to poor families (in terms of vacant housing opportunities) are not in proportion to their numbers, suggesting that filtering is unlikely to be an important agent of neighbourhood change in poor areas. Moreover, the fact that a large proportion of the vacancy chains ended through the formation of 'new' households while only a small proportion ended through demolitions also suggests that the filtering mechanism rarely penetrates the lower spectrum of the housing market to any great extent. We must therefore set aside the idea of a general upward filtering of social classes in favour of a more selective process of movement. This is also the conclusion of a recent study of moves arising from the construction of single-family dwellings in Windsor, Ontario (Dzus and Romsa 1977). The general pattern of vacancy chains in Windsor is evidently very much the same as in other cities (see, for example Adams 1973; Grigsby 1963; Watson 1974), with higher-priced homes generating rather larger chains of movement and the bulk of all terminations being caused by the formation of new households. However, a close examination of the individual moves revealed a complex and highly segmented pattern of movement arising from the new construction. In particular, the spatial distribution and directional flow of moves was found to be highly localized, with little upward filtering originating from poorer inner-city neighbourhoods or the more stable upper-income neighbourhoods of the city's southern suburbs. The conclusion drawn from this is that the construction of new single-family housing 'will only affect the urban structure of middle class areas' (Dzus and Romsa 1977: 232).

In summary then, filtering offers a useful but nevertheless partial explanation of patterns of neighbourhood change. Amongst the factors which can be identified as inhibiting the hypothesized sequence of movement arising from new high status housing are:

1. the failure of high income housing construction to keep pace with the overall rate of new household formation and in-migration;
2. the structure of income distribution which, since higher-income groups constitute a relatively small class, means that the houses they vacate in preference for new homes are demanded by a much larger group, thus maintaining high prices and suppressing the process of filtering;
3. the inertia and non-economic behaviour of some households. This includes many of the behavioural patterns discussed above (see pp. 121–132), although the most striking barrier to the filtering process is the persistence of élite neighbourhoods in symbolically prestigious inner-city locations;
4. the existence of other processes of neighbourhood change whose dynamic is unrelated to the construction of new, high-income housing. Reference has already been made to the process of invasion/succession, the 'blow-out' process identified by Harvey (1973), and the process of neighbourhood change associated with changes in the family life-cycle. In addition, two other processes merit consideration: the abandonment of slum housing and the 'gentrification' of more solid inner-city neighbourhoods.

Abandonment and contagion
It should be stressed at the outset that the abandonment of housing is a much less widespread phenomenon than any of the other processes of neighbourhood change so far discussed. It is mainly encountered in the worst-off neighbourhoods in the largest cities, and it is much more common in North American cities than elsewhere. Nevertheless, it must be recognized as an increasingly important agent of neighbourhood change. Large-scale localized abandonment is a phenomenon which emerged during the 1960s in most of the larger American cities of the eastern seaboard and midwest. Kristoff (1970) calculated that about 100,000 housing units had been withdrawn from the market in New York City alone between 1965 and 1968, displacing as many as 275,000 persons; while Grigsby and several associates indicated that Baltimore was losing up to 4,000 units per year during the 1960s (Grigsby *et al*. 1970). By the end of the decade, concern over this trend led the United States Department of Housing and Urban Development (HUD) to commission a study of abandonment in Chicago, New Orleans, Oakland and St Louis. At the same time, the National Urban League undertook a survey of housing abandonment encompassing seven

more cities. From the resultant reports (Linton, Mields and Coston 1971; National Urban League 1971) it became clear that not only was the incidence of abandonment increasing but also that its increasing localization was triggering marked changes in the social, economic and demographic composition of whole neighbourhoods.

There appear to be several contributing factors to this process. The reduction in the flow of low-income in-migrants to inner-city areas has inevitably meant the abandonment of a certain amount of housing as the lowest income groups get the opportunity to filter up the housing scale, leaving unwanted and difficult-to-let dwellings behind. But this alone is not a sufficient explanation of the intensity of abandonment in cities like Chicago, Detroit and Newark: it has already been shown that relatively few inner-city households get the chance to filter out of slum housing in this way. What seems to have been behind the particularly high levels of abandonment in parts of these cities is a combination of factors related to the general decline of the inner city within metropolitan areas. The loss of much of the employment base traditionally associated with these areas, combined with a steady deterioration of property, has taken the heart out of the private market for low-income housing. Landlords, faced with escalating maintenance costs and unable to increase revenue because of rent controls and the depressed state of the inner-city housing market, have simply written off their least attractive property by abandoning it to long-term vacancy. *In desperation*, some New York 'slumlords' have reportedly resorted to arson in an attempt to at least salvage insurance moneys.

Given this general propensity for abandonment in the inner city, the localization of abandonment in particular neighbourhoods and the consequent change in neighbourhood character seems to be best explained in terms of a *contagion* effect. This, at least, is the conclusion drawn from a recent study of abandonment in the Tioga district of central Philadelphia, where the incidence of abandoned residential structures increased from 3.7 per cent to 4.6 per cent between 1969 and 1971 (Dear 1976). An examination of the spatial distribution of these structures led Dear to suggest that abandonment can be viewed as a contagious process having at least two distinct stages. Initially there emerges a broad scatter of loosely-defined clusters of abandoned structures, each consisting of several 'microgroups' of two or three abandoned units. 'With the passage of time, the pattern is intensified: the broad scatter is maintained, although the small groups now contain a greater number of structures' (Dear 1976: 65). The reasons for this intensification through contagion are closely related to the depressing effects of long-term vacancy on the value and desirability of adjacent property. The fact that abandoned structures make good sites for crime and vandalism provides a further stimulus for the abandonment of nearby property, and this downward spiral is reinforced by what Dear calls the 'psychological abandonment' of the wider area by estate agents, financiers, landlords and urban governments who, having seen the writing on the wall (*sic*), accelerate the decline of the area through disinvestment and cutting back on maintenance and municipal services. The effect of this process on the structure of the city is a polarization of neighbourhood status and environmental quality within the inner city. Where abandonment takes hold, decay accelerates to the point where a residual population of the city's losers is left in an environment downgraded beyond rehabilitation. Elsewhere, the remainder of the shrinking inner-city population regroups and consolidates in neighbourhoods where the physical fabric has not yet reached the critical point at which both residents and owners lose confidence in the neighbourhood's capacity for self-regeneration.

Gentrification

In contrast, gentrification involves a sequence of residential mobility the end result of which is an improvement of the socio-economic status and environmental quality of inner-city neighbourhoods. Put simply, gentrification is 'the invasion of traditionally working class areas by middle and upper income groups' (Hamnett 1973: 252). This process usually begins with the movement of young couples from the arts, design and teaching professions into older, run-down working-class areas. By renovating such property, these 'pioneer' middle classes are able to obtain proximity to the city centre at a reasonable cost. In addition, they are likely to be given credit with their friends for going to live among the working classes, thus generating a 'trendiness' which soon ensures that the pioneers acquire a substantial number of middle-class neighbours of similarly adventurous and liberal outlook to themselves. Meanwhile, of course, their initial investment in the house will have reassuringly risen in value. As this invasion continues, the status of the area also rises and it becomes socially acceptable for young business executives and lawyers to move in, thereby escalating rents and property values even further and edging out the working-class families who had previously occupied the neighbourhood.

The areas which have been most intensively gentrified are those which are near both the city centre and acknowledged areas of high social status within the inner city. As Hamnett observes, many of these areas

were originally built for the middle classes and have subsequently undergone invasion and succession in an almost classical ecological fashion. They are now experiencing a reversal of this sequence as the excess of demand over supply in adjacent high-status neighbourhoods creates a 'price shadow' which makes rehabilitation and renovation a worthwhile undertaking. The success of the middle classes in wresting these areas from the working classes stems largely from their ability to operate and manipulate the mechanisms of the housing market and to satisfy the requirements of the financiers of house purchase and rehabilitation. Williams (1976a), for example, has written of the reluctance of building societies to lend funds for house purchase and/or improvement in Islington (London) until the feasibility of 'reclaiming' old property had been demonstrated by the financially reliable middle classes. Similarly, the middle classes have been shown to be better able to exploit the availability of government grants for the improvement and conversion of property (Hamnett 1973; Pearson and Henney 1972), even though these grants are ostensibly designed to facilitate the self-regeneration of declining working-class neighbourhoods.

Examples of gentrified neighbourhoods can be found in most large cities. The best-known examples include Barnsbury and Canonbury in Islington and Georgetown in Washington, D.C., sought out early on for their attractive Georgian and Victorian terraced town houses. Gentrification has now spilled over into neighbourhoods where the original housing was built for artisans rather than the middle classes but which nevertheless offers scope for internal redesign and renovation, with a potential environmental and aesthetic appeal – a 'raffish chic' – which attracts the inverted snobbery of the pioneering young professionals. In London for example, gentrification has penetrated to Clapham. As Angela Carter observes, 'You can't walk home from the tube, these days, without seeing somebody moving their Swiss-cheese plants into a white-painted room, probably with a chrome and glass coffee table and maybe spotlight fittings' (Carter 1977: 189). Apart from the changing social status of the affected areas, the manifestations of neighbourhood change resulting from this movement are striking, although they do not always lend themselves to the protocol of 'scientific' investigation. In Clapham, the 'seedy respectability of soiled net curtains', the 'well-attended dancing classes, classical and tap, held in bay-windowed front rooms', and the 'jellied eels and mashed potatoes consumed in white-tile eel-and-pie shops' have been joined, if not entirely replaced, by the trappings of life necessary to young professional couples:

A health food shop has opened to sell them black beans. The bookshop has display cases of Picador Books, the publications of Pluto Press, *Spare Rib*, and God knows what else besides... Kids called Gareth and Emma [play] with their Galt toys on the floor of the bank while – *at the same time* – down the road, an old lady in the pub removes her teeth in order to sing *Some of these days* with passion and vibrancy, to tumultuous applause (Carter 1977: 189).

One study which has documented the neighbourhood changes associated with gentrification in a more systematic way is that by Cybriwsky (1978) of the Fairmount area of central Philadelphia. Cybriwsky points out that the gentrified part of Fairmount is adjacent to a district of townhouses and high-rise flats occupied by upper- and middle-income whites and buffered from the declining property values, urban decay and hostility of black working-class neighbourhoods of northern Philadelphia by a 'defended neighbourhood' occupied by working-class whites. Between 15 and 20 per cent of the residents of this gentrified area moved in during the 1970s. They are mostly young 'singles' and childless couples in their twenties and thirties earning 'comfortable' salaries. Unlike the host population, they are politically liberal and home- rather than neighbourhood-oriented; and they have brought a radically different lifestyle, commercial structure and social organization to the neighbourhood. Renovation has contrived an ambience of 'Colonial Philadelphia', together with a proliferation of roof gardens and patios. Changes in the neighbourhood's commercial structure include the replacement of several 'Ma and Pa' stores with an art gallery, an antique shop and two house-plant shops, and the arrival of a film studio and the headquarters of the Pennsylvania Ballet in former industrial premises. Not surprisingly, Cybriwsky found that the social networks of the newcomers seldom extended to the host population, in spite of their having moved in 'to be amongst the people'. They find themselves rejected by Fairmounters, a rejection which is sometimes expressed in terms of petty vandalism of newcomers' property by the neighbourhood youth and which has brought about the emergence of increased policing and formal residents' 'block associations', replacing the close-knit social networks and informal social controls of the 'urban village' of pre-gentrification Fairmount.

	Neighbourhoods experiencing change in selected population characteristics	Neighbourhoods experiencing stability in selected population characteristics
Neighbourhoods experiencing high mobility	**I** (a) Rapid change resulting from ethnic, social or racial conflict within area (b) Change resulting from area being assigned high social value by specific subgroup (c) Change resulting from rapid deterioration of physical environment (particularly due to location of public facilities)	**II** (a) Inflexible housing catering to small range of household types (b) Neighbourhood is a transit point for in-migrants from rural and from other urban areas
Neighbourhoods experiencing low mobility	**III** (a) Flexible housing catering to many household types. Slow ageing of population and selective outmigration by age (b) Deteriorating housing with selective inmigration by socio-economic status	**IV** (a) Tightly structured social networks, particularly for ethnic communities, tie individual to neighbourhood

Fig. 5.8 A typology of neighbourhood change.
Source: Moore (1972), p. 33.

Typologies of neighbourhood change

Recognizing that there is no single mechanism linking residential mobility to ecological change, several attempts have been made to set out a typology of the neighbourhood changes associated with the various ebbs and flows of residential mobility. Moore (1972), for example, has set out a four-fold typology which is intended to be 'illustrative rather than exhaustive' of the relationships between the mobility characteristics of neighbourhoods and their socio-economic and demographic characteristics (Fig. 5.8). Moore points out that Type II situations, with stable characteristics yet high levels of mobility, are probably more common than Type I situations (high mobility and rapid change), an observation which is clearly related to the tendency for most moves to take place within the same 'community-space'. *Type I* situations include the classic invasion/succession sequence which is probably most frequently encountered where an ethnic or racial minority is invading the territory of another group. Other Type I situations include both the gentrification and the abandonment of inner-city neighbourhoods, as well as the high mobility and rapid social change associated with the intrusion into middle-class neighbourhoods of undesirable features such as motorways, factories and residential homes for juvenile delinquents.

Type II situations are typified by neighbourhoods which specifically cater for a transient population, such as the districts of small rented flats close to the CBD occupied by young single persons or newly married couples as a stepping stone to home ownership in the suburbs. Other examples of this type of situation include the slum district which serves as a receiving area for low-income in-migrants and the newer suburbs which serve as ports of entry for successive waves of middle-class in-migrants. *Type III* situations, where neighbourhood change is associated with low levels of mobility, are generally the product of steady selective in- or out-migration. This includes a large selection of middle-class neighbourhoods whose socio-economic composition steadily changes as the housing stock filters down the social ladder. In addition, neighbourhoods which experience a gradual demographic change as a cohort of 'stayers' ages together also fall into this category. *Type IV* situations, where low rates of mobility are accompanied by stability of neighbourhood characteristics, find their strongest expression in the tightly-knit ethnic neighbourhoods and urban villages of the inner city, together with some of the most affluent white suburbs. All such areas derive their stability from the lack of incentive for members of their distinctive communities to move elsewhere in the city, to 'alien' and potentially hostile environments.

A more comprehensive typology is represented by Bourne's (1976) attempt to link both physical and socio-economic changes to residential mobility within the concept of a *neighbourhood life-cycle* (Table 5.6). This provides a useful descriptive summary although, as Bourne points out, it would be very difficult to test its validity empirically, let alone extend the typology into a model or theory of residential mobility and neighbourhood change. Nevertheless, the idea of neighbourhood life-cycles can provide a useful explanation of urban residential structure, as Webber (1975) has shown in his analysis of social areas in Liverpool. Webber emphasizes the point that large new housing subdivisions tend to be located at the edge of the currently built up area, to contain dwellings of a similar type or size, to be designed to meet the require- ments of a specific and relatively homogeneous socio- economic group, and to be populated by families at an early stage of the family life-cycle. With the passage of time, Webber recognizes three major aspects of change:

1. the gradual ageing of the original colonizing cohort;
2. the structural obsolescence of buildings; and
3. the technical obsolescence of dwellings.

Table 5.6 Summary of neighbourhood life-cycles

Stage	Physical changes	
	Dwelling type (predominate additions)	Level of construction
1. Suburbanization (new growth) 'homogeneity'	Single-family (low-density multiple)	High
2. In-filling (on vacant land)	Multi-family	Low, decreasing
3. Downgrading (stability and decline)	Conversions of existing dwellings to multi-family	Very low
4. Thinning out	Non-residential construction- demolitions of existing units	Low
5. Renewal	(a) Public housing	High
	(b) Luxury high-rise apartment	Medium
	Townhouse conversions	Low

Source: Bourne 1976: 139.

He also points out that the periodicity of the ageing cycle is shorter than that of structural obsolescence, so that the period between the dying-off of the original colonizing cohort and the eventual abandonment or demolition of housing may take up to 50 years, during which time the social composition of the neighbourhood will change through invasion and filtering. Meanwhile, the effects of technical obsolescence will result in some neighbourhoods being more vulnerable to change than others: 'Large villas, of the type which characterize the rooming house area for instance, are clearly less adaptable in an age without service than the Victorian artisan terraces. This type of housing responds to technical change by attracting a different household type as well as a different socio-economic class' (Webber 1975: 95).

The residential structure of Liverpool lends itself easily to an interpretation based on this conception of neighbourhood life-cycles. Thus the inner-city public housing estates correspond to those areas which have already experienced one cycle of structural obsolescence and which have now been redeveloped. Where the original inner-city housing was built to a higher standard – to house prosperous Victorian merchants – the cycle of structural obsolescence is somewhat longer, and these dwellings remain as a radial neighbourhood

which has now filtered down the social scale to become a rooming-house area, with the technical obsolescence of large units being resolved by subdivision and multi-occupation. Beyond these areas are neighbourhoods of older terrace housing whose colonizing cohort has died off and which have become technically obsolescent for most families because of their lack of basic amenities like inside lavatories. As a result, successive zones of terrace housing have been invaded by the very lowest socio-economic group, producing local concentrations of the unskilled, the unemployed, and New Commonwealth immigrants.

Further out still are the city's middle-class neighbourhoods which, since they date from the interwar period, have not yet suffered particularly from either structural or technical obsolescence. Moreover, most still contain a large proportion of the original colonizing population. The exceptions are the oldest, innermost middle-class neighbourhoods – which have reached the stage at which a large number of young families are moving in – and the newest, outermost neighbourhoods – which are still under development and colonization. Similarly, most of the suburban public housing estates have pronounced concentrations of particular age groups, reflecting the period of their original development.

	Social changes			*Other changes*
Population density	*Family structure*	*Social status income*	*Migration mobility*	*Other characteristics*
Low (but increasing)	Young families, small children, large households	High (increasing)	High net in-migration, high mobility turnover	Initial development stage; cluster development; large-scale projects, usually on virgin land
Medium (increasing slowly or stable)	Ageing families, older children, more mixing	High (stable)	Low net in-migration, low mobility turnover	First transition stage– less homogeneity in age, class, housing first apartments; some replacements
Medium (increasing slowly), population total down	Older families, fewer children	Medium (declining)	Low net out-migration, high turnover	Long period of depreciation and stagnation; some non-residential succession
Declining (net densities may be increasing)	Older families, few children, non-family households	Declining	Higher net out-migration, high turnover	Selective non-residential succession
Increasing (net)	Young families, many children	Declining	High net in-migration, high turnover	The second transition stage– may take either of two forms depending on conditions
Increasing (net)	Mixed	Increasing	Medium	
Decreasing (net)	Few children	Increasing	Low	

Chapter 6

HOUSING SUPPLY: OPPORTUNITIES AND CONSTRAINTS

Although the analyses of housing demand and residential mobility discussed in the previous chapter provide some understanding of the process of residential differentiation, their emphasis on choice rather than constraint has tended to divert attention away from the effects of housing supply agencies. It is now recognized that the supply of housing is at best only indirectly responsive to demand, and an increasing amount of attention is being given to the social stratification and residential differentiation arising from the regulation and manipulation of housing supply by various institutions, interest groups and individuals. Indeed, the prominence given to constraints on housing opportunities in contemporary urban research has reached the point where 'The rising tide of interest in residential mobility may well be sweeping onto a deserted beach' (Short 1978a: 421).

It will be clear to the reader by now that the supply of housing is derived from several sources, including the creation of vacancies through the dissolution or migration of households, the subdivision or conversion of dwellings, and the construction of new dwellings – which is, of course, the chief source of supply in the long run. None of these sources of supply, however, is directly responsive to demand in the way that most other goods are. In part, this is due to the special nature of housing as a commodity. As Harvey (1972: 16) observes, 'It is fixed in geographic space, it changes hands infrequently, it is a commodity which we cannot do without, and it is a form of stored wealth which is subject to speculative activities in the market . . . In addition, the house has various forms of value to the user and above all it is the point from which the user relates to every other aspect of the urban scene.' These qualities make for a highly complex housing market in which the needs and aspirations of different socio-economic groups are matched to particular types of housing by a series of different market arrangements. In short, there exists in each city a series of distinctive sub-markets for housing. To the extent that these

sub-markets are localized, they have a direct expression in the residential structure of the city. Moreover, it is now evident that the spatial outcome of each sub-market is significantly influenced by the actions of key decision-makers and mediators such as landowners, developers, estate agents and housing managers, whose motivation and behaviour effectively structures the supply of housing from which relocating households make their choice. Before going on to examine the ramifications of this behaviour in detail, however, it is essential to expand upon the nature of the major sub-markets for housing in contemporary cities.

Housing sub-markets and the housing stock

It is important to bear in mind that the 'housing' available in any particular sub-market is a complex package of goods and services which extends well beyond the shelter provided by the dwelling itself. Housing is a primary determinant of personal security, autonomy, comfort, well-being and status, and the ownership of housing itself structures access to other scarce resources, such as educational, medical and leisure facilities. Harvey (1972: 15) has listed the services a person obtains by renting or purchasing a house or flat as follows:

1. Shelter.
2. A quantity of space for the exclusive use of the purchaser or renter . . . .
3. A relative location which is:
   (a) Accessible to –
      (i) workplace;
      (ii) retail opportunities;
      (iii) social services (schools, hospitals, etc.);
      (iv) entertainment and recreational facilities;
      (v) family and friends (people you like);
   (b) Proximate to:
      (i) sources of pollution (noxious facilities);
      (ii) areas of congestion;

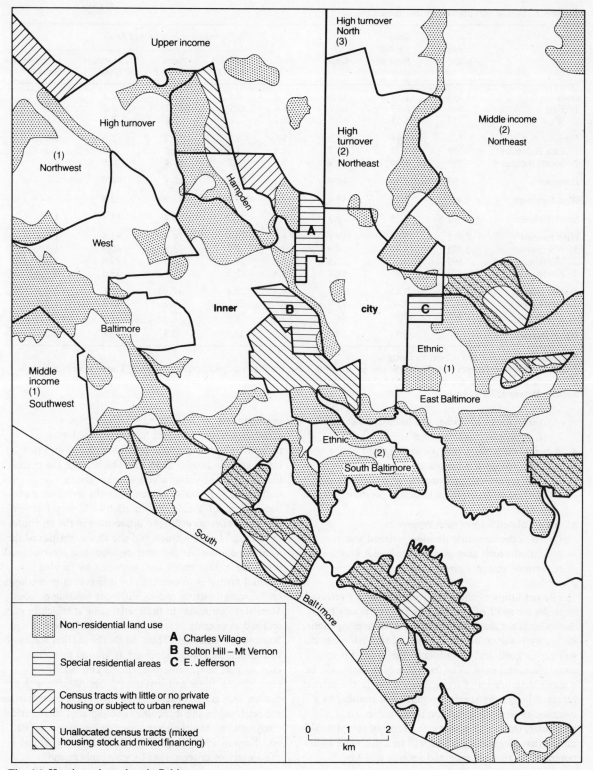

Fig. 6.1 Housing sub-markets in Baltimore.
Source: Harvey (1974), p. 246.

Table 6.1 Housing sub-markets in Baltimore City

	Total houses sold	Sales per 100 properties	Cash	pvt	% Transactions by source of funds:			
					Federal S. & L.	State S. & L.	Mortgage Bank	Community Bank
Inner city	1,199	1.86	65.7	15.0	3.0	12.0	2.2	0.5
1. East	646	2.33	64.7	15.0	2.2	14.3	2.2	0.5
2. West	553	1.51	67.0	15.1	4.0	9.2	2.3	0.4
Ethnic	760	3.34	39.9	5.5	6.1	43.2	2.0	0.8
1. East Baltimore	579	3.40	39.7	4.8	5.5	43.7	2.4	1.0
2. South Baltimore	181	3.20	40.3	7.7	7.7	41.4	0.6	—
Hampden	99	2.40	40.4	8.1	18.2	26.3	4.0	—
West Baltimore	497	2.32	30.6	12.5	12.1	11.7	22.3	1.6
South Baltimore	322	3.16	28.3	7.4	22.7	13.4	13.4	1.9
High turnover	2,072	5.28	19.1	6.1	13.6	14.9	32.8	1.2
1. North-west	1,071	5.42	20.0	7.2	9.7	13.8	40.9	1.1
2. North-east	693	5.07	20.6	6.4	14.4	16.5	29.0	1.4
3. North	308	5.35	12.7	1.4	25.3	18.1	13.3	0.7
Middle income	1,077	3.15	20.8	4.4	29.8	17.0	8.6	1.9
1. South-west	212	3.46	17.0	6.6	29.2	8.5	15.1	1.0
2. North-east	865	3.09	21.7	3.8	30.0	19.2	7.0	2.0
Upper income	361	3.84	19.4	6.9	23.5	10.5	8.6	7.2

* Assumed mortgages and subject to mortgage
† Ground rent is sometimes included in the sale price and this distorts the averages in certain respects. The relative differentials differentials between the sub-markets are of the right order, however
Source: Harvey 1974: 264.

(iii) sources of crime, fire hazard, noise, etc.;
(iv) people you don't like.
4. A neighbourhood which is characterized by:
(i) people of a certain sort;
(ii) a physical environment of a certain sort;
(iii) an address which indicates prestige or social status.
5. An absolute location with respect to:
(i) other absolute locations around you;
(ii) the total transport network as it exists around you at a given point in time.

The net utility of these services is generally referred to as the *use value* of housing. As Harvey points out, this value is not fixed by the attributes of housing alone, for utility is very much in the eyes of the beholder and will vary a good deal according to life-cycle, lifestyle, social class, and so on. The use value of housing will be a major determinant of its *exchange value* in the market place, although the special properties of housing as a commodity tend to distort the relationship. In particular, the role of housing as a form of stored wealth means that its exchange value will be influenced by its potential for reaping unearned income and for increasing capital.

This complexity in the nature of housing services is compounded by differences in tenure, type of accommodation (detached house, terrace house, maisonette, etc.), physical condition, location, price range and method of financing which make the precise identification of sub-markets a rather tricky undertaking. It is also evident that the structure and composition of housing sub-markets will vary from one city to another according to differences in the attributes of the local housing stock and the characteristics of the local population. At the inter-regional and international scale, these differences are sharpened by varying cultural attitudes to housing, by differences in methods of financing housing and by different housing policies. Moreover, variations in the spatial scale at which buyers and sellers operate defy any neat categorization of housing sub-markets. Thus, while the market for most households and some suppliers is limited to a single city, or part of it, some households and many construction firms and investment companies see their market in regional or national terms. These complexities are reflected in the difficulties encountered in empirical analyses of intra-urban variations in house prices (Ball and Kirwan 1977; Palm 1978; Straszheim 1975) and in the variety of criteria used by geographers and economists to classify housing sub-markets in different cities (Bourne 1976). So, while it is generally agreed that

Savings Bank	Other*	FHA	VA	Average sale price ($)†
0.2	1.7	2.9	1.1	3,498
0.1	1.2	3.4	1.4	3,437
0.4	2.2	2.3	0.6	3,568
0.9	2.2	2.6	0.7	6,372
1.2	2.2	3.2	0.07	6,769
—	2.2	0.6	0.6	5,102
3.0	—	14.1	2.0	7,059
3.1	6.0	25.8	4.2	8,664
4.0	9.0	22.7	10.6	8,751
5.7	6.2	38.2	9.5	992
2.9	4.5	46.8	7.4	9,312
5.6	5.9	34.5	10.2	9,779
15.9	12.7	31.5	15.5	12,330
8.7	9.0	17.7	11.1	12,760
10.8	11.7	30.2	17.0	12,848
8.2	8.2	14.7	9.7	12,751
21.1	2.8	11.9	3.6	27,413

% Sales insured

ownership which is chiefly financed by small, community-based savings and loan associations (the North American equivalent of building societies).

3. Black residential areas (particularly West Baltimore) where a large proportion of home ownership has been financed by costly 'land-instalment contracts' – the only way in which low- or moderate-income blacks could become home owners in the early 1960s.

4. Areas of high turnover and racial change where house purchase is serviced by a combination of mortgage banker finance and Federal Housing Administration (FHA) guarantees (often requiring no downpayment) as a result of government policies aimed at creating a socially stable class of home owners amongst blacks and the poor.

5. White middle class areas which were originally financed by earlier FHA programmes (i.e. in the 1930s) and where house purchase is now financed through federal savings and loan associations, together with some FHA guarantees.

6. Affluent areas where house purchase is achieved by way of savings banks and commercial banks, without the assistance of FHA guarantees.

As Harvey and Chatterjee observe, this geographical structure of sub-markets forms a 'decision environment' in the context of which individual households make housing choices. Most of these choices, they suggest, are likely to conform to the structure and to reinforce it. But in the long term the geographic structure 'is continuously being transformed by the ebb and flow of market forces, the operations of speculators and realtors, the changing potential for homeownership, the changing profitability of landlordism, the pressures emanating from community action, the interventions and disruptions brought about by changing governmental and institutional policies, and the like' (Harvey and Chatterjee 1974: 25). Furthermore, they suggest that this process of transformation 'must be the focus for understanding residential differentiation' (Harvey and Chatterjee 1974: 25).

Research undertaken in the London Borough of Southwark provides a rather different perspective on the nature of sub-markets which exist within inner London. Here, the interaction between a series of *housing groups* and a number of *housing agencies* is seen as the chief determinant of the structure of housing supply. Table 6.2 shows the six major housing groups identified within Southwark classified according to income, socio-economic status and national origin – variables which are used jointly as proxy measures of housing needs and aspirations and of the 'capacity' to realize these needs and aspirations. The latter, in turn, is regarded as a product of employment status, income,

sub-markets do exist, it is clear that they do not form neat, discrete compartments within an overall housing system. For this reason, the nature of housing sub-markets is best illustrated by reference to specific examples rather than by the construction of an all-embracing model or typology.

The first of the two examples taken here is drawn from David Harvey's work on the city of Baltimore, in which the major housing markets are identified in terms of the nature of housing finance available to different population sub-groups (Harvey 1974; Harvey and Chatterjee 1974). For Harvey and Chatterjee, the major feature of the Baltimore housing system is the highly structured relationship between household characteristics (particularly income) and the availability of mortgage funds. The spatial manifestation of this relationship is identified in terms of 13 sub-markets (Fig. 6.1), each having a distinctive mix of financing sources (Table 6.1). The main features of these sub-markets are:

1. An inner-city area consisting of low-priced rented dwellings, occupied mainly by low-income black families, where property sales are dominated by cash and private transactions.

2. White 'ethnic areas' dominated by home

Agencies ▶ Housing groups ▼	Owner occupation purchase	Local authority	Housing association	Estate	Small estate landlord	New landlord
Upper income	✓					✓
Indigenous middle income	✓	✓	✓	✓	✓	✓
Indigenous lower income		✓	✓	✓		✓
Immigrant middle income coloured	✓	✓	✓			✓
Immigrant middle income non-coloured		✓	✓		✓	✓
Immigrant lower income		✓				✓

Fig. 6.2 Housing supply agencies in inner London.
Source: London Borough of Southwark (1973), p. 40.

Housing groups ▼	Upper income	Indigenous middle income	Indigenous lower income	Immigrant middle income coloured	Immigrant middle income non-coloured	Immigrant lower income
Upper income		AB	B	A	B	
Indigenous middle income	A		ABC	AB	AB	B
Indigenous lower income		C		C	C	C
Immigrant middle income coloured	A	AB	BC		BC	BC
Immigrant middle income	C	C		C		C
Owner occupier		C	C	C	C	

Fig. 6.3 Competition between different groups for housing in inner London. A = competition for owner occupation of similar property, B = rented property bought for owner occupation; C = competition for the same rented property.
Source: London Borough of Southwark (1973), p. 42.

capital, intelligence, education, knowledge about housing, and social acceptability (London Borough of Southwark 1973). As indicated in Table 6.2, these characteristics lead different housing groups to seek accommodation of different kinds (distinguished chiefly by tenure) within varying geographical limits. Thus, for example, the housing opportunities of indigenous lower-income households encompass both furnished and unfurnished privately-rented accommodation, publicly-rented accommodation and owner-occupation; although they are rather limited geographically. Table 6.3 shows the major housing supply agencies operating in Southwark; and an indication of their relationship with the main housing groups is given in Fig. 6.2, which is effectively a summary of the housing sub-markets within the borough. It can be seen that each housing group enjoys access to a different range of housing opportunities through different combinations of supply agencies offering different degrees of security of tenure. Much of the potential choice implied in Fig. 6.2, however, is negated by competition for accommodation between housing groups and by competition between housing supply agencies for the acquisition and management of property. A more sensitive portrayal of the submarkets within this part of London therefore requires recognition of the effects of this competition. This is attempted in Figs. 6.3 and 6.4, which show the major areas of effective competition between housing groups and supply agencies respectively. A more detailed investigation of these areas of conflict revealed several important consequences, including:

1. The loss of privately rented accommodation to owner-occupation and local authority redevelopment, resulting in fierce competition for the remaining privately-rented stock amongst the worst-off housing groups;

Agencies ▶	Developer	Small landlord	Estate landlord	New landlord	Local authority	Housing association	Owner occupier
Developer		B				A	AB
Small landlord	C			C	C	C	C
Estate landlord				C	C		
New landlord		B			A	A	A
Local authority		B	B	A		A	AB
Housing association		B		A	A		AB
Owner occupier	B	B				C	

Fig. 6.4 Competition between different housing supply agencies in inner London. A = competition to buy and redevelop or convert the same property; B = one agency seeking to buy property from another; C = one agency under pressure to sell to another.

Table 6.2 Housing groups in Southwark

Housing groups	Socio-economic groups	Housing opportunities in terms of tenure	Location
1 Upper income	Primarily professional, managerial and self-employed	Permanent: owner occupation, (high cost unfurnished) Temporary: furnished preceding ownership	Degree of flexibility in location, throughout London
2 Indigenous, middle income	Skilled and semi-skilled	Permanent: owner occupation unfurnished, local authority	Owner occupied throughout London, tenants mainly Inner London and locally
3 Indigenous, lower income	Semi-skilled and unskilled	Permanent: unfurnished, local authority, long-standing owner occupation. Temporary: furnished	Mainly Inner London, emphasis on Southwark
4 Immigrant, middle income, coloured, (West Indian, Pakistani, Greek etc.)	Skilled and semi-skilled	Permanent: furnished, owner occupation. Temporary: furnished	London area, often in immigrant community, may be temporary UK resident
5 Immigrant, middle income non-coloured (mainly Irish)	Skilled, semi-skilled and unskilled	Permanent: unfurnished, local authority furnished. Temporary: furnished	Mainly Inner London for jobs, may be temporary UK residents
6 Immigrant, lower income coloured and non-coloured.	Semi-skilled and unskilled	Permanent: furnished, local authority, temporary: furnished	Mainly Inner London, many with their own communities

Note: (a) Location preference is noted to indicate the degree to which Southwark might be substituted for any other housing location, assuming jobs, schools etc. to be satisfactory

(b) Only the main housing groups and their housing opportunities are noted

Source: *London Borough of Southwark* 1973: 29–30.

Table 6.3 Provision and goals of housing agencies

Agency	Provision	Goal
Developers	Providing mainly new houses and flats for sale, little new renting is provided	Profit from the development process is capitalized
Landlords	Providing unfurnished and furnished lettings on a small scale, lettings often controlled or regulated	May be to retain interest, may wish to sell
Large established (estate) landlords	Providing large numbers of unfurnished lettings, concentrated in certain areas	Tradition and responsibility to community, limited profit
Small and large new landlords	Providing mainly furnished renting; (quality variable, better with larger landlords)	Profit, perhaps service to particular groups
Local authorities	Providing unfurnished lettings in new buildings or conversions	Service to the community, better environment
Housing associations	Providing unfurnished lettings	Service to the community, and professional fees
Housing societies	Providing co-ownership 'renting'	Provision of a transition tenure between renting and ownership; and professional fees
Owner occupiers	Householders seeking owner occupation are their own agency	Accommodation that is an investment

Source: *London Borough of Southwark* 1973: 33.

2. The increasing reliance of lower income groups on housing supplied by housing associations and the local authority; and

3. The precipitation of a residuum of homeless families as a result of an overall deficiency of housing (London Borough of Southwark 1973).

In Harvey and Chatterjee's terms, these outcomes are part of the transformation process which they maintain is crucial to the understanding of residential differentiation. As we shall see, Southwark's experience in this respect is fairly typical of many central city areas throughout the Western world. In the remainder of this chapter, detailed consideration is given to the implications of the dynamics of housing supply, beginning with a summary and explanation of the major trends in the transformation of the urban housing stock: the increase in the construction of dwellings for home ownership, the decrease in the availability of cheaper privately-rented dwellings, and the increase (in many countries) in the construction and letting of dwellings by public authorities.

The growth of home ownership

The growth of home ownership is characteristic of all Western countries and it has had a market effect not only on residential differentiation but also on the whole space-economy of urbanized societies. In the United States, the overall proportion of owner-occupied dwellings rose from 20 per cent in 1920 to 44 per cent in 1940 and 65 per cent in 1974; while in Britain the proportion of owner-occupied dwellings rose steadily from 10.6 per cent in 1914 to 28 per cent in 1953 and then accelerated to reach 45 per cent by 1963 and 52 per cent in 1973. As shown in Chapter 2, the socio-spatial manifestations of this trend include the development of extensive tracts of low-density suburban sprawl, with an associated increase in residential differentiation according to households' ability to pay for different grades of housing and for transport between home and work. It is not necessary to reiterate these developments in detail; nor should it be necessary to emphasize the relationship between suburban home ownership and the imperatives of the family life-cycle, the filtering process, and the general residential preferences of a majority of households. The point which must be made here, however, is that the growth in home ownership has not been entirely the result of increasing affluence among a progressively wider section of society. In other words, supply has not simply followed demand.

What has happened in most countries is that the supply of owner-occupier housing has been deliberately stimulated by government policies. No doubt part of the motivation for these policies can be attributed to the notion of giving the electorate what it wants. But it is more likely that political and social stabilization has been the major motive for government intervention. One of the principal areas of state intervention has been the fostering of the institutions – building societies, savings and loan associations, and the like – which finance the purchase (and ultimately, therefore, the supply) of private housing. These institutions originated in Britain in the late eighteenth century as savings clubs and friendly societies which used the proceeds of their efforts to build houses for members. The first such organization to appear in the United States was the Oxford Provident Building Association, set up in Philadelphia in 1831. By the early twentieth century, organizations in both countries had proliferated and grown into substantial institutions controlling large amounts of capital. Because of their role in financing home ownership amongst the middle and upper-working classes, they soon came to be regarded as an essential mechanism in the promotion of a property-owning democracy. This objective assumed considerable importance to Western governments in the light of the political unrest of the time, and so home ownership was actively fostered as a 'Bulwark against Bolshevism'. In other words, governments sought to defend the property system by giving as many people as possible a stake in it. Financing this ownership by way of long-term loans from organizations such as building societies provided a further source of social and political stability, since the widespread debt encumbrance represented by mortgage repayments committed home 'owners' to oppose any changes to the social and economic structure of society which might endanger the value of their property or make it more difficult for them to pay off their debt (Boddy 1976a; Stone 1978).

One of the first significant steps towards promoting home ownership in Britain came soon after the First World War with the establishment of concessionary tax rates – a quarter of the standard rate – on interest received from investments in building societies. This rapidly swelled the resources of the societies and, together with low interest rates and the relatively low costs of labour and materials in the 1930s, facilitated the housebuilding boom which spawned the extensive interwar sprawl and ribbon development which revolutionized the social geography of British cities. Although this boom was interrupted by the Second World War and, briefly, by the postwar Labour government's strong committment to cheap working-class housing for rent, the promotion of home ownership was again pursued vigorously from the 1950s onwards with the return of a Conservative government and, later, under the Labour administrations of Wilson and Callaghan. Among the various policy instruments which have been used to encourage home ownership are:

1. Grants to building societies in order to keep interest rates below market rates and to encourage the purchase of pre-1919 dwellings which were formerly rented;

2. The abolition of taxation on the imputed income from property while preserving the tax payer's right to deduct mortgage interest repayments from gross taxable income;

3. The exemption of homes from capital gains taxes;

4. The provision of mortgages by local authorities;

5. The sale of local authority dwellings to 'sitting tenants' or newly-married couples at a substantial discount from the market price;

6. The introduction of the 'option mortgage' scheme to provide cheap loans for first-time housebuyers from lower income groups; and

7. The utilization of public powers of compulsory purchase to acquire development land on which owner-occupier houses could be built (Boddy 1976a; Cullingworth 1979; Nevitt 1978).

In the mid-1970s, the cash subsidies accruing to owner-occupier households as a result of these policies was, on average, £141.00: slightly more than the average subsidy enjoyed by tenants of public housing (Department of the Environment 1977; Morton 1977).

Similar developments have occurred in other countries. In Belgium, for example, owner-occupation is encouraged by a mixture of state-subsidized mortgages, guarantees covering that part of a mortgage exceeding the normal loan of 60–75 per cent of the purchase price, and subsidized reductions in sales duties and legal fees (Watson 1971). In the United States, the growth of home ownership has been encouraged by a variety of mortgage guarantees and subsidies. One of the earliest programmes was the Federal National Home Loan Bank System, set up in the 1930s to insure savings accounts in the wake of the uncertainty created by the Depression. After the Second World War, further assistance was given to private house financing, partly in response to the mounting disorder in larger cities. As the US National Committee on Urban Problems (1968: 401) observed, 'Home ownership encourages social stability and financial responsibility. It gives the homeowner a financial stake in society ... It helps eliminate the 'alienated tenant' psychology.' Among the major programmes which have been initiated are the Federal Housing Administration and Veterans Administration mortgage guarantee schemes, together with the Government National Mortgage Association,

the Federal Home Loan Mortgage Corporation and various state housing finance agencies created to channel more funds into the owner-occupied sector.

The decline of the privately rented sector

The corollary of the growth in home ownership has been the decline of privately rented housing. In cities everywhere as recently as the 1920s, between 80 and 90 per cent of all households lived in privately-rented accommodation, whereas the equivalent figure now stands at between 30 and 40 per cent in North American cities and between 10 and 20 per cent in European cities. Nowhere has this decline been more marked than in Britain, where only 12 per cent of the housing stock is now rented from private landlords, compared to around 60 per cent in 1947 and 90 per cent in 1914. In general terms, this decline reflects the response by landlords to changes in the relative rates of return provided by the ownership of rental accommodation and by households to the artificial financial advantages associated with home ownership and (in Europe) public tenure. Put another way, it is not related to any decline in the demand for privately-rented accommodation as such: it is the product of wider economic and political changes (Mellor 1973).

It is not difficult to understand the landlord's desire to disinvest in rental accommodation. Before 1914, investment in rented property produced an income which was almost double the return of gilt-edged securities, even allowing for maintenance and management costs; but by 1970 landlords in Britain could only obtain around 6 per cent on their investment, compared to the 9 per cent obtainable from long-dated government securities (Department of the Environment 1977; Eversley 1975). Moreover, investments in rental accommodation compare unfavourably with other forms of property investment, particularly in industrial, commercial and retail property. Ambrose (1976) suggests that the average annual revenue derived from privately rented housing is exceeded by a factor of 2.5 by the average revenue derived from a similar-sized parcel of land given over to factories or warehouses, by a factor of 7.5 for shops, and by a factor of 40 for offices in provincial cities.

One of the major factors influencing the relatively low returns on investment in rental housing (thus impeding its supply) has been the existence of *rent controls*. These were introduced in many countries to curtail profiteering by landlords in the wake of housing shortages created by the lack of housebuilding during the First World War. Once introduced, however, rent controls have tended to persist because of government

147

fears of unpopularity with urban electorates. The effect of such controls has been to restrict the ability of landlords to cover loan charges, maintenance and management costs as well as extracting an adequate profit. This situation has been exacerbated by taxation policies which do not allow landlords to deduct depreciation costs from taxes and by the introduction and enforcement of more rigorous building standards and housing codes. Landlords have responded to these pressures by selling their property, either to owner-occupiers or to developers interested in site redevelopment. In some neighbourhoods, as we have seen, the deterioration of the housing stock has reached the stage where landlords can find no buyers and so are forced to abandon their property (Palm 1979). In other areas, where there is a high level of demand for accommodation, specialist agencies have moved in to expedite disinvestment. This has been especially noticeable in London, where large numbers of purpose-built flats in interwar suburbs like Ealing, Chiswick and Streatham and in some central areas – Kensington, Chelsea and Westminster – have been sold by specialist 'break-up' companies on behalf of large landlords such as property companies and insurance companies (Hamnett 1979a).

Overall, 2.6 m. dwellings were sold by landlords to owner-occupiers in Britain between 1938 and 1975 (Short 1979). Moreover, little new property has been built for private renting in the last 50 years, so that what is left of the privately rented sector is old (nearly 70 per cent of the existing stock in England and Wales was built before 1914) and, because of a succession of rent controls, most of it has deteriorated badly. This deterioration has itself led to a further depletion of the privately rented stock in many inner-city areas, as urban renewal schemes have demolished large tracts of housing. It is also worth noting that many European cities suffered a considerable loss of privately-rented housing through bomb damage during the Second World War.

This decline in the quantity and quality of privately-rented accommodation has affected the social geography of the city in several ways. In general terms, it has clearly hastened the decay of inner-city areas whilst reinforcing the shift of a large proportion of the lower-middle and more prosperous working classes to owner-occupied housing in the suburbs. It has also led to a resorting and realignment of inner-city neighbourhoods and populations as the various groups requiring cheap rented accommodation are squeezed into a smaller and smaller pool of housing. These groups encompass a variety of 'short stay' households, including young single persons and young couples for whom private rental accommodation is a temporary but essential stepping-stone to either owner-occupied or public housing. In addition there are the more permanent residents who have little chance of obtaining a mortgage, saving for a house or being allocated a house in the public sector. These include some indigenous low-income households, low-income migrants, transient individuals, single-parent families, and elderly households on fixed incomes. Fierce competition for the diminishing supply of cheap rental housing between these economically similar but socially and racially very different groups inevitably results in an increase in social conflict which in turn leads to territorial segregation and the development of 'defended neighbourhoods'.

Finally, it should be noted that the shrinkage of the privately-rented sector has been selective. In larger cities, the demand for centrally-situated luxury flats has been sufficient to encourage investment in this type of property. Thus, in cities like London, Paris, Brussels and Zurich, the more expensive element of the privately-rented sector has been preserved intact, if not enhanced, by the dominance of pure rent over housing and tax legislation. It must also be recognized that in some of the larger and more affluent cities of Australia and North America the privately-rented sector has maintained its overall share of the housing stock through the expansion of high-income rental apartments, even though low-income rental accommodation has been rapidly disappearing. Bourne, for instance, has drawn attention to the occurrence of this sub-market in Toronto during the 1960s in response to the interplay of several supply factors. These included the rising costs of purchasing suburban land and providing the infra-structure of roads, drains and other services, the consequent increase in the costs of home ownership, and the structure of local tax and education costs (Bourne 1968). Combined with a shift in personal attitudes towards living in flats, these factors have led to an increase in the proportion of flats in the city's housing stock from 42 per cent in 1958 to 73 per cent in 1967, altering both the structure and location of the city's housing stock away from 'traditional' patterns. More recently, continuing shortages in the supply of land and capital in the faster-growing cities of North America has further restored the position of rental housing. Basically, what has happened is that the cost of financing low density owner-occupier housing has risen beyond the pocket of many potential housebuyers, with the result that the development and construction industry has turned to the production of multiple-unit structures for sale or rent, creating an 'apartment boom' which has ringed the *edges* of American cities with apartment complexes and terrace houses for the middle classes: a development which completely flies in the face of traditional land-use patterns (Vance 1976).

The development of public housing

Like the other major changes in the long-term pattern of housing supply, the emergence of public housing is a product of wider economic and political factors rather than the result of secular changes in the underlying pattern of housing need or demand. Public housing is supplied in a variety of ways. In Britain, the bulk of all public housing is purpose-built by local authorities; in the Netherlands, Denmark and Sweden most public housing is supplied by way of co-operatives; while in West Germany the public housing programme is almost entirely organized by *Neue Heimat*, an adjunct of the trades union movement (Fuerst 1974). But, whatever the organizational framework, the quality and extent of public housing supply is ultimately dependent upon the resources and disposition of central and local governments and public institutions. For this reason, it is difficult to make sense of trends in the provision of public housing without recourse to specific examples. Here, attention is focused on the two very different histories of public housing in Britain and the United States.

Britain
As we have seen, public sector housing accounts for a large proportion of the housing stock in British cities: 25 to 30 per cent on average, rising to over 50 per cent in Scottish cities. The provision of low-rent public housing dates from the late nineteenth century, when it emerged as part of the reformist public health and town planning movements (see Chapter 2). Nevertheless, public housing was slow to develop. The nineteenth century legislation was permissive: local authorities could build housing for the poor but were under no obligation to do so, and there was no question of financial support from the central government. Not surprisingly, most local authorities did nothing, preferring to rely on the activities of philanthropic and charitable housing trusts. The first major step towards large-scale public housing provision came in 1919, when the acute housing shortage which had developed because of the virtual cessation of building during the war years was made even more pressing by Lloyd George's highly publicized promise of 'Homes fit for Heroes'. As Bowley (1945: 9) observed 'It was politically necessary to make some effort to control and organize the supply of new houses, particularly of working class houses to let.' The response was to give local authorities the responsibility and the funding to provide such housing. Subsequently, although public housing became something of a political football, the level of exchequer subsidies was steadily raised, and a succession of legislation gave local authorities increasing

powers and responsibility to build public housing for a wider section of the community.

After the Second World War there was again a backlog of housing, this time exacerbated by war damage. Moreover, the incoming Labour government was heavily committed to the public sector and in 1949 passed a Housing Act which removed the limitation restricting local authorities to the provision of housing for the 'working classes'. From this date, local authorities have been free to gear the supply of public housing to the more general needs of the community. The immediate result was a surge in housebuilding to make up the postwar backlog – the so-called 'pack 'em in' phase. Later, with the return of the Conservatives to power, the supply of public housing was more closely tied to slum clearance programmes and the needs of specific groups such as the elderly and the poor. By the mid-1960s, however, it had become evident that there was a continuing 'housing problem' of considerable proportions, and the Labour government which took office in 1964 initiated a new phase of 'general needs' housebuilding with a target of 500,000 houses a year. While this target was never reached (the peak was reached in 1967 when 204,000 dwellings were completed), the housing stock of every British city was substantially altered during the 1960s by the addition of large amounts of public housing. During the 1970s the supply of public housing continued to increase, albeit at a somewhat diminished rate in response to changing political and economic circumstances. The unusual combination of inflation and economic recession which followed the rise in petroleum prices in Western countries in the mid-1970s, together with the cut-backs in public expenditure imposed by the 1979 Thatcher government, have considerably reduced the supply of new public housing. Moreover, the stock of existing public housing is now being eroded by the Conservatives' policy of encouraging the sale of local authority housing to sitting tenants and newly married couples.

The legacy of these public housing policies has had a profound effect on the morphology and social geography of British cities. Tracts of public housing are to be found throughout the urban fabric, with a particular concentration in suburban locations: as illustrated by the examples of Bristol, Edinburgh, Leeds and Leicester shown in Fig. 6.5. In general terms, and certainly in comparison with the location of public housing in North American cities, the location of public housing in British cities is remarkable for its integration with owner-occupied housing and for its occupation by a wide band of the socio-economic spectrum (Cox and Agnew 1974). The former is partly explained by the extensive planning powers of British local authorities;

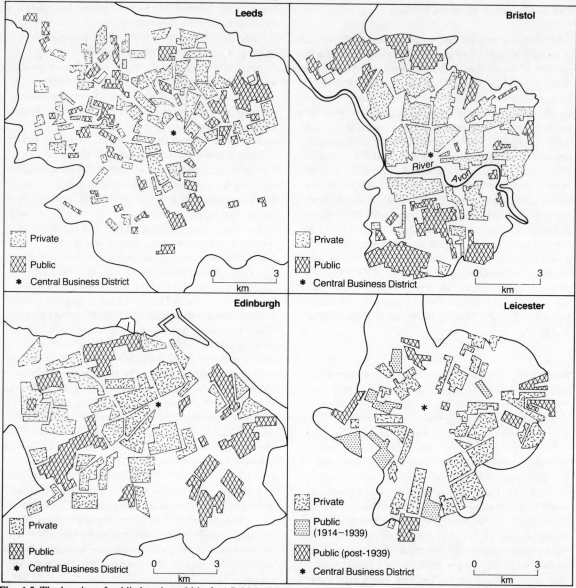

Fig. 6.5 The location of public housing within four British cities.

and the latter by standards of construction which compare favourably with those found in the lower end of the private market – a factor which is especially important when the costs of renting public housing and buying private housing are compared. This broad social and spatial integration fits conveniently with Sopher's (1972) proposition that societies with a high degree of social stratification (like Britain) require only a symbolic distancing of social groups, in contrast to the more overt territorial segregation of social groups required in more 'open' societies like the United States. It is interesting to speculate on the role of architecture in this respect for,

as Nevitt (1978) points out, the aesthetic sterility of much local authority housing seems far in excess of any limitations on design imposed by financial constraints alone.

This image of spatial and social integration should not be exaggerated, however. Public housing developments do not find a ready welcome near established owner-occupier neighbourhoods because the general perception of their morphological and social characteristics leads to fears among owner-occupiers of a fall in their existing quality of life and (perhaps more significantly) in the future exchange value of their houses. Vigorous opposition is therefore common, as exemplified by the episode of the Cutteslowe Walls (see p. 47); and despite the legislative power of urban governments to override such opposition, it is usually deemed to be politically wiser to seek out the least contentious locations for public housing. Moreover, financial pressures on local authorities tend to encourage the purchase of cheaper land whenever possible (Ambrose 1977). For these reasons, many public housing developments tend to be located on extremely peripheral sites, thus effectively isolating their residents from the rest of the city, at least until residential infill and the general socio-economic infra-structure catch up with the initial housing construction.

It must also be recognized that a considerable amount of differentiation exists *within* the stock of public housing. As English (1976) observes, public housing in Britain is highly stratified, providing accommodation and environments which range from excellent to appalling. Much of this differentiation can be explained in the context of the chronology of the supply of public housing. Thus whereas most of the early public housing estates (i.e. those built during the 1920s) were 'cottage-style' semi-detached dwellings, the succeeding generation of council estates built in the 1930s was dominated by 3- and 4-storey walk-up flats built for slum clearance families. These acquired a social character quite different from the earlier estates and have subsequently developed a poor reputation in the popular imagination, even if not always justified in practice (Niner and Watson 1978). A different character again was produced by the postwar boom in public housing construction. The accommodation provided at this time – in the face of waiting lists of tens of thousands in every city and in the context of strict financial constraints and a severe shortage of conventional building materials – created vast tracts of functional but austere housing on the outskirts of cities, much of it in the form of low-rise multi-occupation units. Moreover, because these peripheral estates were catering for those at the top of the waiting list (and who were therefore deemed to be most needy), there developed a sequential segregation along socio-economic lines. The first estates to be completed were thus dominated by the unskilled and semi-skilled who were the least able to compete in the private sector, and with large families whose previous accommodation was overcrowded. As these families were siphoned from the top of the waiting list, later estates were given over to relatively smaller and more prosperous families. After the backlog had been cleared, architectural and planning experiments provided further differentiation of the public housing stock, leading specific housing schemes to acquire varying levels of popularity and,

therefore, of status. The public housing boom of the 1960s brought yet another set of distinctive housing environments, this time dominated by maisonettes and high-rise blocks of flats, most of which were located in inner-city areas on slum-clearance sites. As Ambrose (1977b) has pointed out, the heavy emphasis on high-rise developments in the 1960s was the product of several factors in addition to the infatuation of architects and planners with the 'modern movement' in architectural design and the doctrine of high-rise solutions to urban sprawl (Malpass 1975). Ambrose specifically mentions:

1. the pattern of government subsidies, which favoured the construction of high-density, high-rise housing schemes; and
2. the tendering policies of large construction and civil engineering companies, who were anxious to obtain contracts for high-rise buildings in order to recoup the considerable investment they had made in 'system' building.

To these we should add a third factor: the feeling on many city councils that large high-rise buildings were 'prestige' developments with which to display civic pride and achievement – another example of the interaction of 'spirit and matter'. Since 1968 there has been a rapid retreat from this kind of development, partly as a result of the publicity given to the damaging effects of high-rise living on family and social life, partly because of shortcomings in the design and construction of high-rise buildings (the partial collapse of the Ronan Point flats in east London were crucial in this respect), and partly because the big construction firms began to turn their attention to the 'office boom' which began in the late 1960s. Having experienced the consequences of low-cost, high-rise, high-density living, the current trend is towards the development of low-rise, small-scale housing schemes with 'vernacular' architectural touches and the provision of at least some 'defensible space'. There is, therefore, a considerable stratification of the public housing stock which is reflected in the morphology and social geography of the city as a whole and which forms the basis for further segregation as a result of the actions of housing managers and other local authority officials (see below, pp. 164–166).

The United States
The history of public housing in the United States represents the polar opposite to that of Britain. Although public housing programmes have been operating for over 40 years, and although a succession of studies have established that about one-third of all families in American cities require basic housing which they cannot afford (Fuerst 1974), the supply of public

housing units has been restricted to a very narrow clientele. This is the obverse of a national housing policy which is orientated towards the encouragement of owner-occupation on the premise that the process of filtering will eliminate the housing problem at the lower end of the market. Vance (1976) suggests that this approach can be attributed to the 'geographical' characteristics of US cities: the widespread availability of low-cost development land coupled with cheap and flexible intra-urban transport, which facilitates the free-market provision of housing via suburban expansion. While this may be so, it does not take into account the failure of filtering mechanisms to provide housing for the poor. We must, therefore, look to wider economic and political forces in explaining the failure of US public housing programmes to match the expansion experienced in most Western European countries.

The initial public housing legislation (1937) was a product of the Depression and the political climate created by the New Deal, and much of the rationale for the first low-rent public housing was couched in terms of its utility as an employment programme. But although it was significant in establishing a federal presence in the housing market its effects were curtailed by the Second World War. Afterwards, the supply of public housing was invigorated by the Housing Act of 1949 which linked construction with slum clearance programmes and expressed a committment to subsidized housing for the poor. Bollens and Schmandt (1975: 173) suggest that the Act managed to get past strong opposition because the various interested parties, 'like the blind men feeling the elephant, made entirely different assumptions about the purpose of the legislation'. Whilst liberals saw it as a means of eliminating slums and rehousing the poor, businessmen saw it as a means of bolstering waning property values in and around CBDs; and fiscally-oriented administrators looked upon it as a means of bolstering the tax base and luring back some of the more affluent consumers and taxpayers who had moved to the suburbs. The Act authorized the construction of 810,000 low-rent units over six years, and has since been amended and reinforced by a series of programmes (Aaron 1972). The conventional method of supplying this housing has been for the federal government to underwrite the bonds issued by local public housing authorities to finance land and construction costs; but in 1965, in an attempt to provide a wider range of housing opportunities, provision was made for housing authorities to lease dwellings from private owners for rent at low rates to families who are eligible for public housing. The private owner receives market rental rates, with federal contributions covering the difference. More recently, the emphasis has been on the construction of multi-unit projects to house the lower-middle and low-income elderly by providing cheap loans to local authorities, non-profit organizations and consumer co-operatives.

The success of these programmes has been derisory. The 810,000 units called for in the 1949 legislation took 25 years to materialize, and although the pace of subsidized housing construction has increased since Lyndon Johnson's Housing and Redevelopment Act of 1968 (itself a response to the riots and civil disorder of the 1960s), the net contribution of public housing programmes to the low-rent housing stock of most cities has been insignificant (Downs 1973). Several reasons may be advanced for this poor record. Above all, it must be recognized that the aggressively free-enterprise social and political climate of the United States makes a poor environment for housing reform. In addition to widespread public antipathy towards any form of 'creeping socialism', the political clout of vested interests within the urban business lobby has effectively retarded the fruition of public housing programmes. Spearheading the opposition to the generosity and coerciveness of national legislation have been the National Association of Real Estate Boards, the National Association of Home Builders and the United States Savings and Loan League, backed up by the powerful support of the US Chamber of Commerce, the Mortgage Bankers Association of America and the American Bankers Association. It is also significant that the major postwar debate about public housing took place during the McCarthy era, with the inevitable charges of communist infiltration (Cox and Agnew 1974). The effectiveness of this opposition is reflected in the poverty of US public housing programmes. Moreover, even where public funds have been appropriated for housing construction, the organization and tactics of local business interests and the corruption of key housing officials and FHA inspectors has ensured that 'free enterprise' has emerged as the winner, with most of the benefit of federal subsidies being siphoned off by the local construction industry, its professionalized handmaidens – the so-called 'exchange professionals' such as mortgage brokers and estate agents – and the somewhat less professional 'quick buck artists' (Boyer 1973; Fried 1971).

It should also be borne in mind that the imperative for housing reform has been less pressing in the United States than in most Western European countries. The housing stock of most cities is much younger, and none were subject to war damage. In addition, levels of investment in private housing have traditionally been higher in the United States than in Europe (Vance 1976). Nevertheless, there has for a long time been a chronic housing problem for a large minority of the

American urban poor. The decisive factor in the continued rejection of public housing as a solution to this problem has probably been the failure of existing public housing projects to effect a substantial improvement of the urban housing problem, just as its opponents predicted. To a large extent this has been a self-fulfilling prophecy, because most of the shortcomings of public housing can be traced to restrictions on the financing and allocation of public housing built into the relevant legislative framework by its opponents. The most important factor in this respect is the existence of strict means-testing for households wishing to rent public housing. This takes the form of an established maximum income which varies locally but which is generally only marginally above the officially-defined poverty line. Only families with incomes below this level are admitted and, more important, as soon as their incomes rise 25 per cent above it they are required to leave. Thus public housing is effectively treated as a receptacle for the economically incompetent. The residents themselves, with no security of tenure, have no reason to care for their homes and no reason to expect to be able to develop local ties. Not surprisingly, such an environment is conducive to the intensification of a wide range of social problems; a situation exacerbated by the low quality of the dwelling units themselves. Between 1949 and 1965 a dollar limit on construction costs (it was $2,400) meant that many homes were handed over to tenants without doors on the lavatory, without seats on the toilet, and without either a bath or a shower. As a result, many large public housing projects rapidly deteriorated to the point where they were more of a liability to the community than a solution to its housing problems, and a number have gone the way of the celebrated Pruitt-Igoe project in St Louis: dynamited by the housing authority to forestall further increases in the incidence of murder, arson robbery and vandalism.

Restrictions on location have also contributed to the poor reputation of public housing. Local housing authorities have no powers of compulsory purchase, and the process of site selection is frequently decided by default. A study of site selection processes in Chicago, San Francisco and Oakland came to the conclusion that middle-class communities were able to intervene so successfully that there was effectively little chance for public housing outside existing slum areas (Peel *et al*. 1971). Thus, to the extent that public housing can be said to have any real impact on the spatial structure of the American city, its effect is to reinforce economic and racial segregation, compounding social problems by localizing them. In Chicago, the housing authority's various projects fan outwards from the CBD in three linear belts (Fig. 6.6). Almost all the conventional

housing projects (92 per cent) are situated within low-income black neighbourhoods. One project alone – Taylor Homes – contains over 4,300 units, with 75 per cent of its residents officially classed as 'broken families' and many of its 25,250 inhabitants being the perpetrators or the victims of crime, vandalism and alcoholism (Mercer and Hultquist 1976). Attempts to disperse public housing and thereby reduce the intensity of such problems through the federally-sponsored leased housing programme have met with limited success, since only in a few neighbourhoods are private landlords willing to enter into such an arrangement. Consequently, leased housing units are concentrated in areas such as Woodlawn-Englewood, a black neighbourhood on Chicago's south side (Mercer and Hultquist 1976). Mercer and Hultquist also point out that litigation has also been unsuccessful, so far, in achieving a less segregated distribution of public housing. In response to a court action by the American Civil Liberties Union in 1969, the Chicago Housing Authority was ordered to build 700 public housing units in white residential areas immediately and thereafter to build three units in white neighbourhoods for every one in non-white areas. When the Authority's proposals were presented to the city council two years later they were found to be politically unacceptable, and a much smaller and less dispersed list of sites was re-submitted as a result of the ensuing political uproar. Not surprisingly, progress in the actual construction of these dwellings has been slow, and there appears to be no prospect of any real expansion, territorially or numerically, in the city's supply of public housing.

Managerialism and social gatekeepers

The consideration of housing sub-markets and the changing structure of housing supply suggests that any search for universal laws and straightforward economic determinants of housing supply is unlikely to succeed. What does seem to offer considerable potential, however, is the exploration of the housing circumstances of particular groups within the major sub-systems of the housing market. This involves the identification, first, of groups of households in the same kind of situation in relation to housing opportunities and, second, the investigation of the way these opportunities are shaped and constrained by the various agencies and professional mediators of housing supply. Such an approach stems largely from the view of class relations and social differentiation developed by Max Weber, whose writings have been very influential in shaping the nature of conventional sociological inquiry.

153

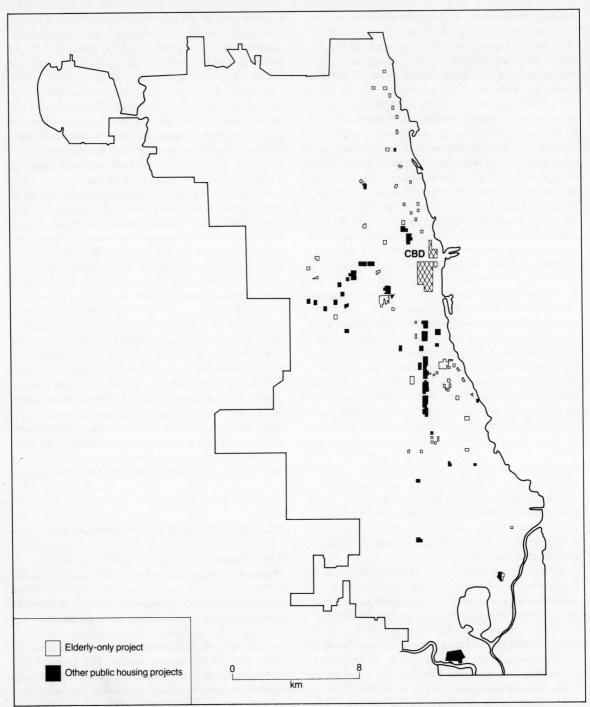

Fig. 6.6 Chicago Housing Authority Public Housing Projects, 1972.
Source: Mercer and Hultquist (1976), p. 126.

Weberian analysis centres on an 'action frame of reference' which puts 'man as the actor' on the centre of the stage and seeks to explain social systems in terms of the people who make and sustain them. The focus of

this approach is the conflict of interests arising from the variety of orientations, aspirations and motivations which people have, and it describes a society 'where interest groups collide, collude and cohere in the control of institutions, where privilege and status are negotiated, where, in short, power becomes the crucial variable' (Lambert, Paris and Blackaby 1978: 6). Institutional arrangements and key 'actors' are therefore studied in order to explain the outcome of competition between conflicting social groups.

The development of this approach in relation to housing can be traced to the work of Rex and Moore (1967) in their study of the inner-city districts of Birmingham. Dissatisfied with the explanatory powers of ecological orthodoxy, they turned to a consideration of the underlying pattern of social relations in order to explain, rather than merely describe, the nature of residential differentiation. In doing so, they explicitly followed Weber, 'who saw that class struggle was apt to emerge whenever people in a market situation enjoyed differential access to property' (Rex and Moore 1967: 273). According to Rex and Moore, this struggle over the use of housing is the central process of the city as a social unit. Moreover, they suggest that it is not necessarily linked to economic power, for 'men in the same labour market may come to have differential degrees of access to housing' (Rex and Moore 1967: 273). There thus emerges the idea of *housing classes* as the basis of conflict: groups of households with common housing opportunities structured by bureaucratic and political forces as well as economic ones. The housing classes identified by Rex and Moore each had a territorial distribution and were ranked according to their power to achieve access to scarce and desired housing resources. Two criteria were identified as governing these housing opportunities. The first was the size and stability of household income, since this is crucial in obtaining mortgage finance; the second was the ability to meet the 'need' and length-of-residence qualifications laid down by the local authority as entry rules for the public housing sector. Rex (1968) has described the housing classes as:

1. the outright owners of large houses in desirable areas;
2. mortgage payers who 'own' whole houses in desirable areas;
3. local authority tenants in houses built by the local authority;
4. local authority tenants in slum houses awaiting demolition;
5. tenants of private house owners;
6. house owners who must take lodgers to meet repayments;
7. lodgers in rooms.

It should be remembered that these housing classes are specific to central Birmingham. Indeed, they should not be thought of as definitive in any way. The problems of identifying groups of people in a similar 'market situation' are considerable, and Rex and Moore themselves were by no means dogmatic as to the classification. Their objective was merely to suggest a classification which might 'pose questions' and 'point the way' towards a more precise delineation of the social structure and conflicts of the city. The central focus of their research was not so much the refinement of the concept of housing classes so much as the exploration of the opportunities and constraints facing one particular group (low-income immigrants) who enjoyed neither high incomes and secure employment nor could fulfill the eligibility rules of the local authority and who were therefore obliged to seek shelter in the declining and decaying private rented accommodation located in the inner city 'zone of transition'.

Nevertheless, the concept of housing classes and its emphasis on housing opportunities has stimulated widespread interest which has in turn triggered some important contributions to the analysis of residential differentiation. Haddon's (1970) critique of Rex and Moore's work has been influential in this context. He drew attention to the problem of defining housing classes according to *current* housing situations: it does not follow that those who share a common housing situation at any one time also share a common capacity to obtain better housing in the future. It thus becomes necessary to distinguish between those who are trapped in a given housing situation and cannot move out, those who choose to live in a particular area and type of housing but who could move out if they wished, and those who, in time, will move up the housing ladder once they have satisfied the requirements of the housing institutions, whether in the private or the public sector. As Haddon puts it, 'The emphasis of the analysis ought to be on the *means and criteria of access* to desirable housing, and the ability of different people to negotiate the rules of eligibility' (Haddon 1970: 129). This brings us to a focus on the relationships between different households and the key actors in the various institutions and agencies concerned with housing supply.

This approach was developed in a wider context by Ray Pahl. In a provocative and influential essay (Pahl 1969) he argued that the proper focus of urban research should be the interplay of spatial and social constraints which determine opportunities of access to urban resources and facilities – transport, education and so on, as well as housing. Furthermore, he suggested, the key to understanding the social constraints could be found in the activities, policies and ideologies of the managers or controllers of the urban system. Very broadly, this is the basis of what has become known as the 'managerialist thesis'. In the context of housing, the managers of scarce resources (or the 'middle dogs' or 'social gatekeepers' as they are sometimes called) include key personnel from the spheres of:

1. *finance capital*, e.g. building society and savings and loan association managers and others engaged in lending money for house purchase, housing development and housing improvements;
2. *industrial capital*, e.g. developers and builders;
3. *commercial capital*, e.g. exchange professionals such as estate agents, lawyers and surveyors engaged in the market distribution of housing; and
4. *landed capital*, e.g. landowners and rentiers such as private landlords.

To the extent that city *planners* control certain aspects of the housing environment they may also be regarded as 'managers' within the housing system. And, of course, there are influential managers to be found within the *public sector*: housing managers *per se* and their related staff of lettings officers and housing visitors. As Norman (1975) observes, what these groups have in common is a job at the interface between available resources and a client (or supplicant) population. 'It is in terms of the day-to-day decision-making of these groups that individual access to resources is determined' (Norman 1975: 76). And it is in terms of their cumulative day-to-day decision-making that socio-spatial differentiation takes place.

It should be made clear at this point that urban managerialism is not a theory nor even an agreed perspective (Williams 1978). Indeed, Pahl himself has reformulated his own position more than once and now seems unsure of the utility of managerialist analyses in the wider context of urban political economy (see p. 200). It is instead a framework for study, and at this level it offers 'a useful way of penetrating into the complex of relationships that structure urban areas' (Williams 1978: 240). A succession of empirical studies has left no doubt that there are managers in every sphere of housing supply whose activities exert a considerable impact on urban residential differentiation. (Moreover, their influence can be shown to extend beyond day-to-day decision-making, for such is the power of the institutions of housing supply that they not only shape people's actual opportunities but also their *sense* of possibilities). The following sections illustrate the effects of particular types of managers and social gatekeepers on residential structure. The managerial role of city planners, which spans the whole housing system, is considered in Chapter 8, where a broader view is taken of their part in mediating conflict between different social groups.

Landowners

Landowners stand at the beginning of a chain of key actors and decision-makers whose activities, like the households they ultimately supply, are governed by a variety of objectives and orientations, not all of which are framed in 'rational' economic terms. As Kaiser and Weiss and their associates at the University of North Carolina have shown, it is possible to construct a behavioural model of the process of residential development and redevelopment in much the same way as others have built models of households' residential location decision process (Kaiser and Weiss 1970; Weiss *et al*. 1966). Landowners exert a significant influence on the outcome of this process, though it must be acknowledged that this influence is less now than it was, largely because of the lattice of public policy constraints on the use of urban land and housing. Following Robson (1975) it is possible to recognize two main ways in which land ownership can influence the course of residential development. First, the pattern of land ownership, particularly in relation to the *size* of the parcels of land held by different owners, can influence the *nature* of development. We have already seen (Chapter 2), for instance, how the pattern of land holdings helped to guide the location of railway infrastructure as well as that of the larger and more comprehensively planned residential developments in nineteenth-century cities. More recently, the location of interwar local authority housing estates was guided by the availability of large parcels of land (Mortimore 1969; Ward 1962); and the pattern of speculative suburban development in Los Angeles has been shown to have followed the layout of the old *ranchos* and mission lands (Banham 1973). In contrast, small and fragmented parcels of land, which do not allow developers to benefit from economies of scale, give rise to haphazard and piecemeal development whose quality depends a great deal on their relative location.

Equally important is the influence which landowners can exert through imposing their wishes as to the *type* of development which takes place and, indeed, whether it takes place at all. Some owners hold on to their land for purely speculative reasons, releasing the land for urban development as soon as the chance of substantial profit is presented. This can have a considerable effect on the morphology of cities, not least in the way that plots tied up in speculation schemes act as barriers to development (Sargent 1976) and in the sequence that land is released. In addition, a study of suburban development by Harvey and Clark found that the manipulation of the tax system by landowners was having a distinct effect on the nature of the development. Since owners were taxed less if they sold their land in small parcels over a period than if they sold it all at once, they favoured the operation of 'instalment contracts' with developers, who took up agreed portions of land at convenient intervals. This forced other developers to find land in other neighbourhoods, thus increasing what appeared to be 'random' urban sprawl (Harvey and Clark 1965). However, because of the special properties of land as a commodity, many landowners are reluctant to sell unless they need to raise capital. Moreover, for many of the 'traditional' large land holders, land ownership is steeped in social and political significance which makes its disposal a matter of some concern. Spring (1951), for instance, has detailed the determination of the landed gentry of the nineteenth century to hold on to their land even when considerable financial gains could be achieved by selling. The reason, of course, was to maintain the status and political influence deriving from land ownership.

When landowners do sell, they sometimes limit the nature of subsequent development through restrictive covenants, either for idealistic reasons, or, more likely, to protect the exchange value of land they still hold. Such covenants usually discriminate in favour of high-status groups, although they are generally framed in a rather oblique way: by stipulating certain minimum plot sizes, for example, or by forbidding the construction of public houses (as in Dundee's Edwardian exurb of Wormit) in the hope that this will ensure development for a 'better' class of person. Robson (1975) cites the contrasting examples of, on the one hand, middle-class suburbs in North London which resulted from the insistence on high standards of construction and layout by the landowner (Eton College) and, on the other, the slums in Sheffield built on land whose owner (the Duke of Norfolk) allowed building to take place without restriction. Other, well-documented examples include the close control exerted by the Fitzwilliam family on the quality and extent of residential development on their Bierlow estate in Sheffield (Rowley 1975) and the differential residential and commercial development within Scunthorpe resulting from the various policies of the major landowners in the town (Pocock 1970). The use of restrictive convenants is less common nowadays, partly because of an increase in land-use regulations, and partly because some have been successfully challenged in the courts (Haar 1963).

Builders and Developers

Considering the very important role of private-sector builders and developers, surprisingly little is known about the way decisions are made in individual firms or the effect these may have on the pattern of housing opportunities within the city. Some research has been conducted into the process of site selection and housing type, notably by Bather (1976) in Reading, by Craven (1975) in the metropolitan fringe of Kent, by Harloe, Isacharoff and Minns (1974) in London, by Bourne (1969) and Chamberlain (1972) in Toronto, by Neutze (1971) in Melbourne and Sydney, and by Clawson (1971) in New York and Philadelphia. What emerges from these studies is a fairly consistent pattern of activity in response to the search for profitability. Prime amongst the economic considerations facing builders and developers is the cost of urban land and its sheer scarcity, as well as the need for speed of operation (because they have to finance land preparation and construction long before receiving income from the sale of completed dwellings). On the other hand, the market for new housing tends to be a sellers' market in which the builder has a reasonable latitude in what he produces, knowing that it is likely to be sold quickly. Together, these factors shape the rather distinctive patterns of operation pursued by builders and developers. In Craven's words, the developer becomes 'a catalyst who interprets, albeit innacurately, major forces in the urban environment; an initiator of action based on this interpretation and a challenger of public policies which obstruct such action' (Craven 1975: 124).

To begin with, builders and developers may play an important part in shaping the pattern and direction of residential growth; and since they are catering mainly for a middle-class market, this really means that they exert an important influence on the location of middle-class neighbourhoods. Larger companies, with an urgent need to acquire land at a rapid rate in order to keep their organization fully employed, search out and bid for suitable land even before it has been put on the market: a strategy known as 'bird-dogging' in the United States. The outcome of this activity, of course, does not always coincide with the ideas of planners as to the most desirable location for new residential development, so that developers should not be regarded as completely independent actors in this context (Bather 1976). Nevertheless, the profits to be made from land speculation gives developers a strong incentive to proceed, and the size of the larger companies enables them to exert strong economic and political pressure on local governments. Harvey (1972) cites the example of developers in Baltimore who, having had proposals turned down by the city Planning Board, found that their applications were approved by councilmen whose political campaign had previously been supported by large donations from the developers. Other, more subtle strategies on the part of British developers have been

157

reported by Craven (1975) and Harloe, Isacharoff and Minns (1974).

Having secured the land they need, developers are able to exert a considerable influence on the physical and social character of the housing they build. Because they are operating in a sellers' market they are able to build what they think the middle-class public wants, and what is easiest and safest to produce. Given their need for plentiful supplies of cheap land and for speed of construction, together with the advantages to be derived from economies of scale and standardization, the net result is a propensity to build large, uniform housing estates on peripheral sites. Moreover, the imperatives of profitability ensure that the housing is built at relatively high densities and to relatively low standards: the resultant stereotype being epitomized in Pete Seeger's song about 'little boxes made of ticky-tacky . . . (that) all look just the same'. In Britain, houses at the lower end of the private market have for some time been of poorer quality and less generous space standards than the statutory minima governing public housing, but attempts by the National House Builders Registration Council to upgrade the minimum standards of private house construction have been resisted 'in the interests of the consumer', who would have to bear the extra cost. Housing opportunities for the broad spectrum of middle classes thus tend to be rather limited in scope. In North America, the well-tried norm of detached, single-storey, single-family dwellings has now been joined, because of the rising costs of suburban land, by suburban apartment blocks. Variety is provided through deviations in facades and architectural detail: mock-Georgian doors and porticoes, mock-Tudor leaded windows and brick chimneys, and mock-Spanish Colonial stucco and wrought iron. Thrown together on a single housing development, these 'personalized' features can sometimes create an unfortunate Disneyland effect. In contrast, British estates tend to be uniform down to the styling of doors, windows and garden furniture. More important from the point of view of housing opportunities, however, is the uniformity of size of house. In Britain, the norm is a 3-bedroom, 2-storey, semi-detached or terraced house, while the lower end of the market is dominated by two-bedroom maisonettes and flats (Murie, Niner and Watson 1976). Whole estates are built to this tried-and-trusted formula, with perhaps a sprinkling of larger houses in order to increase sales through raising the potential social status of the estate. Consequently, substantial numbers of 'atypical' middle-class families – single persons and large families – are effectively denied access to the new owner-occupier sub-market and so must seek accommodation either in the older owner-occupier stock or in the privately rented sector.

On the other hand, 'typical' families become increasingly localized – and isolated – in suburban estates.

Finally, it should be noted that the nature of building companies' activities has been found to be related to their size and internal organization. In general, larger companies tend to build larger developments of more uniform housing further towards the periphery of the city, leaving small firms with more detailed local knowledge to scavenge for infill sites which by definition tend to be less peripheral and smaller in size. Medium-sized companies find it difficult to build one-off houses on small sites because of labour diseconomies but, unlike the larger companies, they cannot afford to take risks on land for which they might not secure permission to build, or to pay the interest on large parcels of land which take a long time to develop. When they do get sites of suitable size, they therefore seek to maximize profits either by building blocks of flats at high densities or by catering for the top end of the market, building low-density detached houses in 'exclusive' subdivisions. In this context it is significant for the future pattern of housing opportunities that although the building industry in most countries tends to be dominated by small firms, the tendency everywhere is for an increasing proportion of output to be accounted for by a few large companies with regional or national operations.

Mortgage financiers

The allocative decisions of mortgage finance companies represent one of the more striking examples of social gatekeeping in the housing system, and there is now a small body of literature documenting the outcome of mortgage financiers' activities. Much of the empirical research has been conducted in Britain and directed towards the role of the branch managers of building societies, who are responsible for financing the bulk of all house purchasing by private households. Nevertheless, what evidence there is from elsewhere suggests that it is safe to assume that the managers of mortgage finance companies in other countries exert a broadly similar influence on the social geography of the city in similar ways to their British counterparts. It should be stressed at the outset that building society managers are not independent decision-makers. Much of their activity is closely circumscribed by head office policy, while many of their day-to-day decisions are dependent upon the activities of lawyers, estate agents, surveyors, bank managers and the like. Nevertheless, building society managers enjoy a pivotal position in this 'magic circle' of exchange professionals, and although the self-image of the trade is that of a passive broker in the supply of housing, the mortgage allocation system 'exerts a decisive influence over who lives where, how much new housing gets built, and whether neighbourhoods survive' (Stone 1978: 190).

In order to be properly understood, the activity of building society managers must be seen against the general background of their commercial objectives. Although building societies are non-profit making organizations, their success depends upon financial growth and security and the maintenance of large reserve funds. Their chief allegiance, therefore, is to the investor rather than the borrower. Not surprisingly, societies operate a fairly rigid system of rules to protect their operations and encourage an ethos of conservative paternalism among their staff. Indeed, there is some evidence to support the idea of building society managers as a rather narrowly-defined breed: an 'ideal type' with a uniformity of attitudes resulting from the recruitment of a certain group (white Anglo-Saxon Protestant moderately-educated family men) and the absorption of society traditions and lending policies through a career structure with a high degree of internal promotion which rewards personnel with a 'clean' record of lending decisions (Ford 1975; Harloe, Isacharoff and Minns 1974). As a group, then, building society managers tend to have good reason to be cautious, investment-oriented, and suspicious of unconventional behaviour in others. Likewise, the ground rules of society lending policy are cautious, devised to ensure financial security both in terms of the 'paying ability' of potential borrowers and the future exchange value of dwellings they are willing to finance.

In operating these ground rules, building society managers effectively act as social gatekeepers – wittingly or unwittingly – in a number of ways. It is normal practice for societies to lend only 80 to 90 per cent of the total cost or valuation of a house (whichever is the less), and for the maximum loan to be computed as a multiple of the household's main income (although some societies also take into consideration a proportion of a second income, if there is one). This means that people need to raise a certain amount of capital in order to qualify for a mortgage in the first place, and it has been suggested (Robson 1975) that this might discriminate against people with lower earnings who may be less able or less predisposed to accumulate the necessary savings. While this may be so, it is in the evaluation of potential borrowers' ability to maintain the flow of repayments that the first major stratification by building society managers takes place. Because of their desire for risk-minimization, branch managers give a lot of weight to the general creditworthiness of applicants. Credit register searches are used to reveal previous

financial delinquency, which normally results in the refusal to advance a loan. Having passed this test, applicants are then judged principally in terms of the *stability* of their income and their future *expectations*. This, of course, tends to favour white-collar workers since their pay structure commonly has a built-in annual increment and is not subject to the ups and downs of overtime and short-time working. Conversely, several groups will find that their chances of obtaining a mortgage are marginal, including the self-employed, the lowly-paid and single women. The importance of this factor is borne out by the findings of a study of new private housing in outer London, where clerical workers were able to obtain higher mortgages, and buy more expensive houses, than skilled manual workers *whose average earnings were higher* (Barbolet 1969).

Further allocation procedures operate to the disadvantage of the marginally qualified in situations where building society funds are oversubscribed. Many societies give priority to existing clients who are selling their houses in order to buy another; and for first-time buyers it is often essential to have saved with the society for some time before getting a loan. In addition, quotas of finance may be allocated to estate agents, solicitors and brokers, so that the chance of getting a loan may depend on the applicant's connections with these other professionals. Harloe, Isacharoff and Minns (1974) point out that it is also important for 'marginal' households to choose the right building society to approach for a loan, since lending policies, although broadly similar, tend to vary in the way that marginal cases are dealt with. In Lambeth, for example, one particular society prided itself in attempts to encourage a wide spectrum of the community to become owner-occupiers and was one of the first societies to introduce 35-year mortgages.

There is also evidence that purely subjective factors influence managers' decisions. Managers appear to categorize applicants in terms of a set of operational stereotypes ranging from bad risks to good ones, although it has proved difficult to pin down these operational stereotypes in detail and to establish their generality within the profession. As Ford (1975) found, it is difficult even for the managers themselves to articulate something which is an unconscious activity. Nevertheless, the criteria they employ in making subjective judgements about people seem to be closely related to their values of financial caution and social conventionality. Harloe, Isacharoff and Minns (1974) quote one manager who was impressed by people who had 'worked things out', suggesting that the prospective buyer who did not display this ability might be at a disadvantage in securing a loan; and Ford quotes managers as saying 'I always try and assess the ability and willingness of the wife to work' and 'Those people who do not perceive that they must live an English way of life would be treated with caution' (Ford 1975: 298). This last quote is an oblique reference to coloured immigrants, who seem to be particularly disadvantaged by managers' subjective judgements. Duncan (1976: 310) quotes one manager in Huddersfield as saying that 'From a building society point of view, they [blacks] do not have satisfactory status' and another who observed that 'whether we like it or not, the coloured people are here, and we have to be very careful. There's no doubt coloured gentlemen are good savers, but we're very careful.'

Socio-spatial sorting also takes place through managers' evaluation of the *property* for which funds are sought. With any loan, the manager's first concern is with the liquidity of the asset, so that if the borrower defaults and the society is forced to foreclose, the sale of the property will at least cover the amount advanced. The assessment of this liquidity ultimately rests with professional surveyors, but building societies tend to have clear ideas as to the 'safest' property in terms of price range, size and location, and surveyors tend to anticipate these criteria in formulating their survey reports (Lambert 1976). Many managers evidently assume that market demand for properties which deviate from their ideal (a postwar, suburban house with three or four bedrooms) is very limited, and therefore regard them as greater risks and are more cautious about advancing funds for them (Williams 1976b). Managers tend to be particularly concerned with the *size* of dwellings because of the possibility of multiple occupation and the consequent problem of repossession if the borrower defaults. Their concern with *age* is related to the possibility that the property will deteriorate before the mortgage is fully redeemed; and their concern with *location* is related to the possibility of property values being undermined by changes in neighbourhood racial or social composition. Their concern with *price* reflects their anxiety that applicants should not overstretch themselves financially.

Managers thus effectively decide not only who gets loans but also what kinds of property they can aspire to. Households with more modest financial status, for example, will find it more difficult to buy older property even though the overall price may not be beyond their means, since loans for older property generally have to be repaid over a shorter period, thus increasing the monthly repayments. The most striking aspect of the gatekeeping activities of building society managers in this context is their practice of refusing to advance funds on any property within neighbourhoods which they perceive to be bad risks – usually inner-city areas,

as in Birmingham (Fig. 6.7). This practice is known as *redlining* and has been well documented in a number of studies on both sides of the Atlantic (Boddy 1976a; Duncan 1976; Vitarello 1975; Weir 1976). In British cities, the key indicators of 'risky' neighbourhood status seem to be the presence of black people and students. Weir (1976: 113) quotes the example of a library assistant in Leeds who was informed by the Northern Rock building society that 'it was doubtful if a mortgage would be available' on a Headingley property 'owing to the nearness of the "blue zone", i.e. high proportion of students and immigrants'. Another company operating in the same city, London Life, explained to a lecturer that they could not make a loan because 'immigrants were moving into the area . . . with the probable effect of depressing the value of property there'. The lecturer objected that eminent people such as Lord Boyle lived in one of these areas. The London Life man replied: 'One swallow doesn't make a summer.' Although redlining may be an understandable and legitimate business practice, it has several consequences for the social geography of the city:

1. It puts cheaper housing beyond the reach of low-income residents wanting to become owner-occupiers unless they are either willing to pay punitively high rates of interest to 'back-street' financiers or fortunate enough to obtain a mortgage from the local authority.

2. Denial of funds to neighbourhoods over a long period also encourages urban decay and tends to undermine the effectiveness of government-sponsored neighbourhood improvement programmes (Boddy 1976a; Lambert 1976).

3. At the same time, by creating a shortage of owner-occupied houses, it increases prices elsewhere and stimulates the demand for new construction in the suburbs. Building societies are quite happy to finance the purchase of this type of property; and where they are heavily involved in financing and controlling the activities of construction companies it is clearly in their best interests to do so. Boddy (1976b) points out that such involvement is commonly reinforced by organizational connections. Thus, in the north of England, Boddy found that the Northern Rock building society had directors in common with Bellway Holdings, a major house-building company, while William Leech (Builders) Ltd had directors in common with both Northern Rock and Bellway Holdings.

4. As writers such as Harvey (1977) have emphasized, a substantial proportion of the capital used to finance suburban house construction and purchase is derived from small investors in inner-city areas, so that the net effect of building society policies is to

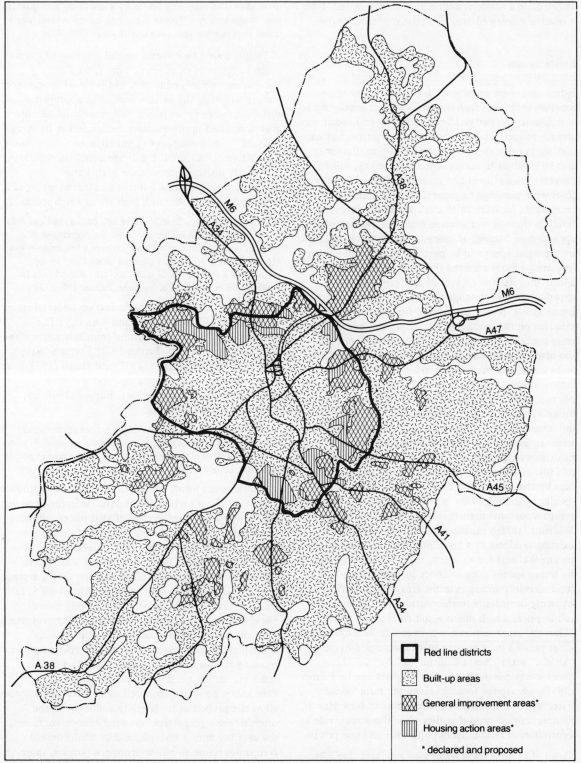

Fig. 6.7 The 'red line' district in Birmingham in relation to the city's inner area improvement programme.
Source: Weir (1976), p. 111.

Red line districts
Built-up areas
General improvement areas*
Housing action areas*
* declared and proposed

redistribute a scarce resource (investment capital) from a relatively deprived area to a relatively affluent one.

Estate agents

Estate agents are responsible for a wide range of activities connected with the exchange and management of residential property. They find houses and sometimes arrange finance for buyers; they attract purchasers and transact paperwork for sellers. In addition, they may also be involved in surveying, auctioneering, valuation, property management and insurance. They have close links with mortgage financiers, collecting mortgage repayments for companies and channelling investment funds to them. The mortgage financiers reciprocate by apportioning a quota of mortgage funds to be allocated by the estate agent and by paying a small commission on investment funds received through the agent. Estate agents then use their quota of mortgage funds to expedite the sale of properties on their books. Since estate agents' profits are derived from percentage commissions on the purchase price of houses, one of their chief concerns is to maintain a high level of prices in the market whilst encouraging a high turnover of sales.

In many countries of Western Europe and North America, estates agents account for between 50 and 70 per cent of all house sales. They are not simply passive brokers in these transactions, however, for they influence their social and spatial outcome in several ways. In addition to the bias introduced in their role as mediators of information (Palm 1976a, 1976b; see also p. 130), estate agents sometimes introduce a deliberate bias by channelling households into, or away from, specific neighbourhoods in order to maintain what they regard as optimal market conditions (Palm 1979). Williams (1976b) explains this activity as follows: existing residents in a given neighbourhood represent potential clients for an agent, and if an agent is seen to be acting against their interests by introducing 'undesirable' purchasers to the area, he may suffer both by being denied any further custom and through any fall in prices which might result from panic selling. 'Thus the safest response is to keep like with like and to deter persons from moving to areas occupied by persons "unlike" themselves' (Williams 1976b: 58). This process was demonstrated over 25 years ago by Palmer (1955), who seems to have coined the term 'social gatekeeper'. His study of estate agents in New Haven, Connecticut, showed that they clearly saw their role as controllers of residential opportunities. As one put it:

People often try to get in higher class areas than they'll be accepted in. We just don't show them any houses in those areas. If they insist, we try and talk them out of it in one way

or another. I've purposely lost many a sale doing just that. It pays in the long run. People in the community respect you for it and they put business your way (Palmer 1955: 77).

Palmer found that agents carefully evaluated clients' status in terms of race, ethnic origin, religion, occupation, income, education and personal appearance. Failure to satisfy the agent's notions of appropriate social attributes for a specific neighbourhood nearly always resulted in diversionary tactics, either by lying – 'its sold' – or by warnings of unhappiness – 'you won't fit in'. Even small social handicaps could (in the 1950s) apparently disbar a person from high-status neighbourhoods. Palmer quotes one agent as saying of a person seeking a house in a high-status neighbourhood:

What does he do for a living. Maybe he's on the road and sells – well let's call them rubber goods for the prevention of disease . . . like a fellow who drove up here a few months ago. He didn't tell me that but I checked around and found out . . . well a man who'd fit into a top area around here just wouldn't be in that kind of business (Palmer 1955: 79).

But the most widespread discrimination undertaken by estate agents is based on race and ethnicity. The segregation in US cities resulting from this activity has been well documented (Brown 1972; Forman 1971; Helper 1969), and Burney (1967) and Hatch (1973) have shown that a similar process also operates on a significant scale in British cities. Burney (1967: 39) quotes one agent as saying:

I would do my best to head off black buyers from a good suburban area or new estate. In fact it would be my duty to do so in the interests of the community and for the sake of people who have bought houses in good faith.

On the other hand, estate agents sometimes introduce black families to a white neighbourhood in the hope that whites will sell up quickly at deflated prices, allowing the agents to buy houses and then resell them to incoming black families at a much higher price. In Edmondson Village, Baltimore, houses which were purchased from departing white families for an average price of $7,500 were sold to incoming blacks for $12,500 (Harvey 1972). A similar process – usually called *blockbusting* – involves the purchase of older properties in prime development sites. These properties are subsequently given over to low-income apartments or rooming houses and promptly neglected. As other residents see the neighbourhood beginning to deteriorate, more and more sell up to estate agents, who allow the properties to deteriorate along with the original 'seed' properties. 'As deterioration continues, the area becomes a fire risk, and as fire insurance companies refuse to renew insurance policies, more owners are persuaded to sell out' (Holmes 1976: 411). When a sufficient number of dwellings have been acquired, the agents themselves are able to sell out at a considerable profit to developers seeking large plots of land for redevelopment schemes.

This kind of opportunism has also been shown to have been involved in the process of *gentrification*. Williams (1976a) suggests that gentrification in parts of Islington, London, can be attributed as much to the activities of estate agents as to the incomers themselves. He found that it was often estate agents who persuaded mortgage financiers to give loans for the purchase and renovation of old working-class dwellings. In addition, some agents purchased and renovated property themselves before selling to incoming young professionals. The role of estate agents in manipulating housing supply and shaping social geography in this context is well illustrated by these quotes from the *London Property Letter*, which is written by cells of estate agents:

The fascinating thing about London is that it throws up an endless supply of new possibilities for the property pioneer and Brixton is about as near to the Klondike as you can get without actually digging.

Nestling down at the bottom of the Archway area is a distinctly working class area which presents possibilities for reclamation.

Grubby Kennington has been providing rich killings for sharp hunters. But the best parts of the carcass are disappearing fast leaving late comers only the bones to pick over. Where next will the South Bank hunt turn. Our money goes on the Stockwell Vauxhall sector where prices are at last starting to skip in anticipation of the Victoria Line's arrival.

(quoted in Williams 1976b: 60.)

Finally, it should be noted that estate agents also operate as gatekeepers in the privately rented sector. Estate agents act as property managers for both large and small property owners, collecting rents, attending to paperwork, and overseeing the maintenance of property. In order to minimize management problems many agents are selective in their choice of tenants, discriminating quite subjectively against people they feel will cause problems in one way or another, whether through rent arrears, maltreatment of property, or anti-social behaviour. It is also worth noting that in university towns it is common for university accommodation officers to take upon themselves the role of gatekeepers in a similar way, 'shutting out' students they perceive to be somehow undesirable in order to preserve good relations with landlords in the longer term (McDowell 1978).

Private landlords

On the face of it, there are few formal 'qualifications' for access to privately-rented housing: all that is needed – in theory, at least – is an ability to pay the rent and to respond quickly to vacancies in a sub-market where housing is usually in short supply. In practice, however, access to privately-rented housing is often constrained by the gatekeeping activities of landlords. 'Through their ability to select or reject tenants, through their ability . . . to set the conditions of letting, they have power over those who rent and their many individual decisions combine to produce obvious and well-established differences in the social composition of neighbourhoods' (Elliot and McCrone 1975: 541).

This sorting of households can take several forms. Some landlords deliberately set out to manage their stock of accommodation in a 'socially responsible' way. Thus, for example, two of the large institutional landlords operating in Southwark – Alleyn's College Estate and the Church Commissioners – allocate vacancies in favour of Southwark residents, with preference being given to friends and relatives of existing tenants (London Borough of Southwark 1973). Similarly, institutional landlords (the Duchy of Cornwall and the Church Commissioners) operating in Lambeth were found to be maintaining a proportion of low-income housing in their stock as a gesture of 'social concern' rather than for economic reasons, with priority again being given to relatives of existing tenants (Harloe, Isacharoff and Minns 1974). More often, letting policies are formulated for the benefit of the landlord. Given the strength of demand compared with supply in the private rented sector, landlords – even the small landlord with poor quality property in the inner city – are in a position to deny access to 'unsuitable' individuals or families. It is quite common for landlords to demand character references and to scrutinize rent books for evidence of financial instability. In Bristol, Short (1979) found that most of the small-scale landlords were concerned to select 'good' tenants: those who do not make undue noise, who pay the rent regularly and who generally give the landlord a trouble-free source of income. In contrast, most of the larger individual and corporate landlords were attempting to allocate vacancies to short-stay tenants. According to Short, there were three reasons for this narrow letting policy. First, some landlords felt that short-stay tenants were unlikely to apply to the city Rent Officer to get the rent fixed at a 'fair' level. Secondly, a continual turnover of tenants allows rent increases to be made more easily; and, if the rent has previously been fixed, a high turnover will allow the full fixed rent to be charged to new incoming tenants irrespective of any previous phasing arrangements. Thirdly, having short-stay tenants has the advantage that obtaining vacant possession for subsequent sale is relatively easy. Without vacant possession, it is impossible to sell to owner-occupiers, and the price received from selling to another landlord may be depressed by as much as a half. As Short points out, the net result of this discrimination in favour of short-stay tenants is that households with children find it particularly difficult to gain access to privately-rented accommodation. 'They are seen as the type of tenants who want long term accommodation and are felt to be likely to go to the Rent Officer to get the rent level fixed.' As one landlord put it: 'My policy is to let to under-30s, students, single people and young married couples with no children – I steer clear of couples over thirty with children; by this age they should have a house of their own' (Short 1979: 71).

Elliot and McCrone (1975) emphasize that the nature of landlordism tends to vary from one neighbourhood to another according to the dominance of different types of landlord. One important contrast is between the activities of individual landlords (whether large or small) and corporate landlords: allocation by the former may involve more subtle, non-economic elements of personal judgement; while the latter tend to operate in a more formal, bureaucratic way. There are, however, several other categories of landlord, each with rather different motivations and letting policies. In Edinburgh, for instance, Elliot and McCrone identified six main types of landlords: individuals, property companies, trusts, welfare organizations, commercial firms such as brewery companies which had diversified into property, and institutions such as churches and universities. Relatively little, however, is known about the particular effects of these specific types of landlord on the structure of residential opportunities.

Public housing managers

Within the public sector the principal gatekeepers are the housing managers and their staff who operate the housing authority's admissions and allocation policies. In Britain, the discretion given to local authorities in formulating and operating such policies is very broad and is encumbered by the minimum of legal regulation. There is a requirement to rehouse families displaced by clearance or other public action as well as those officially classed as overcrowded, but otherwise it is only necessary to give 'reasonable preference' to households in 'unsatisfactory' housing conditions. Since demand for public housing often exceeds supply, housing managers in most cities are in a position of considerable power and importance in relation to the spatial outcome of public housing programmes.

Research has shown that the rationing of available

housing is carried out through a wide variety of eligibility rules and priority systems (Niner 1975; Welsh Consumer Council 1976). Most local authorities operate waiting lists, although these vary in practice from a simple first-come first-served basis to sophisticated queueing systems using 'points schemes' to evaluate need for a specific type of dwelling: points may be awarded, for example, for overcrowding, ill-health or disability, sub-standard accommodation, marital status, length of time on the waiting list and so on, together (in some authorities) with discretionary points awarded by housing managers to enable priority to be given to 'special cases'.

Not surprisingly, different schemes have different outcomes, and families in identical circumstances may find themselves with quite different degrees of access to council housing, depending on the local authority within whose jurisdiction they live (Murie, Niner and Watson 1976). In general, those households with least access to public housing in British cities include young single people without dependents, newcomers to the area, and former owner-occupiers. Conversely, the letting policies of most authorities tend to favour households from slum clearance and redevelopment areas, households living in overcrowded conditions, small elderly households, new households who lack their own accommodation and are living with parents or in-laws, and households with young children (Niner and Watson 1978).

But in addition to the question of whether or not a household is offered accommodation there is the question of *what sort* of accommodation is offered, and in *what area*. For housing managers it makes sense not only to allocate households to dwellings according to size characteristics but also to match 'good' tenants to their best housing in order to minimize maintenance costs, to ensure that the aged and 'problem families' are easily supervised, and (some would argue: see Byrne 1974) to punish unsatisfactory tenants (those with records of rent arrears and unsociable behaviour in their previous accommodation) by sending them to 'dump' estates. In this situation, problem families are often doubly disadvantaged by living in low-grade property whilst having to pay rent at comparable levels to families in more attractive housing schemes. The isolation of problem families in this way can be traced to the policy of housing 'socially weak' families in specially-designed austere and durable public housing schemes in France and the Netherlands in the 1930s (Scobie 1975; Vance 1976). Since 1945, many local authorities in Britain have been pursuing similar, if less well publicized, policies using obsolescent housing stock rather than purpose-built developments. By the 1960s, the segregation and localization of 'problem families' as well as the grading of other tenants according to their worthiness for particular housing vacancies was commonplace, exciting little or no attention (Lewis 1976). In 1969, however, the 'moralistic' attitudes of local authorities were condemned (in suitably diplomatic language) by the Central Housing Advisory Committee:

the underlying philosophy seemed to be that council tenancies were to be given only to those who 'deserved' them and that the 'most deserving' should get the best houses. Thus, unmarried mothers, cohabitees, 'dirty' families and 'transients' tended to be grouped together as 'undesirable'. Moral rectitude, social conformity, clean living and a 'clean' rent book . . . seemed to be essential qualifications for eligibility – at least for new housing
(Central Housing Advisory Committee 1969, para 96).

The process of screening tenants and allocating them to vacancies according to their 'suitability' has been described by several writers (Byrne 1974; Corina 1976; Damer and Madigan 1974; English 1979; Gray 1976a; Means 1977). Central to the whole procedure is the housing visitor's report, and it is here that the temptation to succumb to value judgements derived from impressionistic grounds is strongest, as illustrated by the following excerpts from housing investigators' reports in Hull:

'Excellent tenant, suitable for new property'
'Good type of tenant, every effort made, suitable for any
    property offered'
'Good type of O.A.P. Suitable for new or post-war re-let'
'Fairly good type – suitable for post-war re-let or pre-war
    property'
'Poor type, will need supervision – suitable for old
    property . . . seems to have taken over the tenancy of this
    house and sat back until rehoused'
'Fair only – suitable for pre-war property'
'Condition of furniture good, applicant also in good order'
'A good type of applicant – this is not a long-haired person.
    Suitable for a post-war re-let' (Gray 1976a: 41).

Similarly, Damer and Madigan (1974) found that the grading of tenants in Glasgow was 'arbitrary and subjective'. At the time of their research, the Glasgow housing department classified its stock of housing into eight groups, ranked roughly in order of physical attractiveness, desirability to the public, and rent. At the top end were two kinds of estate: older developments which had withstood the test of desirability over time 'and now exhibit an air of embourgoisement – mature trees, well-manicured lawns, and beautifully-appointed houses' (Damer and Madigan 1974: 226), and newly-constructed housing (usually multi-storey flats) which remains in the top grade until such time as popular demand falls off. At the other end of the scale, Group 8 accommodation tended 'to have a blitzed, semi-derelict and thoroughly depressing appearance' (Damer and Madigan 1974: 226) and to be 'difficult to let' because of its image. In order to match tenants to these carefully graded housing estates, Glasgow corporation employed seven housing visitors – all middle-aged married women – to search council records and electricity and gas board records for evidence of debt on the part of tenants and to interview them in their homes in order to inspect the house and its occupants and, subsequently, grade them. The official grading was arrived at by way of three five-fold classifications of 'cleanliness', 'furniture', and 'type of person'. According to Damer and Madigan, households faring best on this grading system were those who were most articulate, grateful and deferential. Those who fared worst were debtors, the 'wilfully' unemployed, and previous tenants who had either done 'moonlight flits' leaving rent arrears or who had been evicted. The result, of course, is that the Group 8 estates rapidly became 'ghettos' of socially unacceptable (by middle-class standards) families. Damer and Madigan found that such families included many single-parent households and families with a husband/father who was either chronically unemployed, in prison, or suffering from an incapacitating illness.

It is now recognized that the localization of such families in dump estates sets in motion a labelling process which results in the stigmatization of both the estate and its residents (Damer 1974; Taylor 1978). Because of this stigmatization, accommodation in such areas becomes difficult to let, and housing officials eventually tend to admit households who would normally be ineligible for public housing but who are desperate for any vacancy, thus reinforcing the initial grading process (English 1976). Means (1977), following Cohen's (1973) model of deviancy amplification, suggests that the problem is further exacerbated by societal reaction to dump estates, with media coverage helping to dramatize the situation and to reinforce 'moral panic' through the creation of sensational and sometimes distorted stereotypes. This, in turn, polarizes attitudes and behaviour both inside and outside dump estates, leading to an increase in anti-social behaviour on the part of the inhabitants, and therefore to a confirmation of the stereotypes and a further reinforcement of the area's undesirable character.

Finally, it should be noted that the socio-spatial segregation resulting from allocation policies is constantly reinforced by applications by existing tenants for *transfers* from one dwelling to another. This provides further opportunities for screening and grading, allowing 'deserving' and 'respectable' households to maintain or improve their housing status rather than having to remain in accommodation which may be ageing.

A final comment: managerialism in perspective

In concluding this chapter it is important to set managerialist rsearch against the wider perspective of the urban system. Pahl (1975, 1977, 1979) has warned of the dangers of ascribing too much power to the managers of the system (and too little to political power-holders), and Norman has suggested that the managerialist approach lacks a theory of the distribution of power 'which would solve the problem of which groups are the most significant gatekeepers in given localities' (Norman 1975: 66). This question of the relative power of gatekeepers is important, and it is essential to recognize that 'managerial' decisions are themselves subject to constraints determined by the wider economic, political and ideological structure of society and that there are forces completely beyond the control of the managers which exert a significant influence on urban patterns.

In his earlier writings, Pahl (1969, 1970a) recognized the importance of spatial constraints and ecological limitations but, as Saunders (1979) has observed, he failed to explain how these factors are articulated with the activities of urban managers to produce what he called the 'socio-ecological system' as a whole; and he under-emphasized the significance of other factors such as the control exercised by central government and the constraints imposed on urban managers by the reliance of the system on continued capital accumulation. Thus the managerial approach 'in concentrating on studying the allocation and distribution of "scarce resources", fails to ask why resources are in scarce supply' (Gray 1976b: 81). Urban managers, then, should be seen as actors of significant but limited importance in the context of an urban system in which economic, social and political processes set the limits for their activities whilst their professional *modus operandi* determines the detail of the resulting patterns (Johnston 1979a). In the remaining chapters of this book, attention is turned towards the relationships between urban structure and the forces – spatial, social, political and economic – which derive from this wider context.

Chapter 7

SPATIAL ORGANIZATION AND LOCATIONAL CONFLICT

Urban residential structure is not merely the result of the interplay of housing demand and supply. As we saw in Chapter six, housing provides a relative location which confers access to a package of neighbourhood and community attributes including health services, educational facilities, recreational amenities and environmental quality as well as a social and cultural milieu. Competition in the housing market, of course, has much to do with gaining access to these geographically-restricted packages of facilities, but the spatial structure of the city cannot be fully understood without reference to the *group* competition and *group* conflict which occurs over the organization of city neighbourhoods and the location and allocation of services and amenities.

The 'groups' involved in such conflict are themselves a product of the differential wealth, power and prestige derived from people's position in the occupational structure – a position which is in part determined by ethnic status. Much of the conflict between these socio-economic and ethnic groups is set in a spatial framework and derives from their desire to maximize the net *externalities* of urban life. Externalities, sometimes called 'spillover' or 'third-party' effects, are unpriced by-products of the production or consumption of goods and services of all kinds. An externality effect exists if the activity of one person, group or institution impinges on the welfare of others. The classic example is the factory which pollutes local air and water supplies in the course of its operations, bringing *negative* externalities to nearby residents. In contrast, well-kept public parks produce *positive* externalities for most nearby residents. The behaviour of private individuals also gives rise to externality effects (Cox 1973). These can be divided into 'public behaviour' externalities and 'status' externalities. The former include people's behaviour in relation to public comportment (e.g. quiet, sobriety, and tidiness), the upkeep of property and the upbringing of children. Status externalities relate to the 'reflected glory' (or otherwise) of living in a socially or

ethnically distinctive neighbourhood. Externality effects therefore can take a variety of forms. They are, moreover, very complex in operation. Consider, for example, the behaviour of a householder in adding an imitation stone facade to the exterior of his house, adding new coach lamps as finishing touches to his work. For one neighbour this activity may generate a positive externality in the form of improved environmental quality; but for another, with different tastes in design, it may produce an equally strong negative externality effect.

For the geographer, much of the significance of externality effects stems from the fact that their intensity is usually a function of relative location. In other words, externalities may be regarded as having a spatially limited 'field'. Thus, the socially undesirable family and the noisy factory impose the greatest disutilities on their immediate neighbours, while the indirect benefits of parks, gardens and fire stations are greatest for those living nearby and diminish with increasing distance from them. In this context, Harvey (1973) makes a useful distinction between the *price of accessibility* to desirable urban amenities and the *costs of proximity* to the unwanted aspects of urban life. Both, however, are a product of relative location, and it is clear that the spatial organization of social groups in relation to one another and to the urban infrastructure therefore determines the net intensity of the externality effects which they enjoy. As a general rule, of course, those with the greatest wealth, the most power and the best knowledge will be best placed to reap the benefits of positive externalities and to fend off activities which generate negative externalities. As Pahl puts it, 'The unequal distribution of power, wealth and prestige created by the occupational structure may be simply reinforced in a given locality – so that the less privileged are made even more "less privileged" by differential access to facilities' (Pahl 1970a: 113). The location of public facilities such as transport routes, hospitals, and sports centres is often intended to ameliorate the regressive nature of locational advantage resulting from private competition but, as Harvey (1973) has shown, the 'hidden mechanisms' of group conflict tend to ensure that the inhabitants of the richest and most powerful neighbourhoods enjoy a large net benefit as a result of decisions affecting the location of public goods and the organization of public services.

It is clear, then, that the pattern of externality fields can exert a powerful influence on people's welfare. Because of this, many commentators regard the social geography of the city as the outcome of conflicts which are worked out in society as a whole between unequally endowed groups seeking to obtain more or less exclusive access to positive enternalities and to deflect negative externality fields elsewhere. As Harvey puts it, 'much of what goes on in a city . . . can be interpreted as an attempt to organize the distribution of externality effects to gain income advantages' (Harvey 1973: 58). Harvey is particularly concerned to show that the form, location and focus of such conflict depends, ultimately, on long-term urban structural changes, a point which is also emphasized by Janelle and Millward (1976). Their model (Fig. 7.1) illustrates the variety of locational conflicts which might be expected within a city exhibiting the classic concentric pattern of land uses and socio-demographic characteristics and with a propensity

for outward expansion and internal reorganization. Thus, conflict over transportation is expected to exhibit a bi-modal distribution, with peaks of conflict intensity in areas of peripheral expansion and in the region immediately surrounding the expanding and reorganizing city centre. On the other hand, conflict over 'cultural' issues – such as the encroachment of one ethnic group upon the territory of another – are expected to decline in number and intensity with increasing distance from the city core, reflecting the lower population densities and increased ethnic homogeneity.

In the long run, one of the principal outcomes of the resolution of locational conflicts is the creation of a set of *de facto* territories on the basis of income and ethnicity as people respond by relocating to neighbourhoods where they can share their positive externalities with one another and are able to avoid, as much as possible, those who impose negative externalities (Cox 1973). The residents of such territories also attempt to improve and preserve their quality of life through collective action: competing through formal and informal neighbourhood groups and local political institutions to attract the utility-enhancing and keep out the utility-detracting. One of the most common community strategies in this context is that of

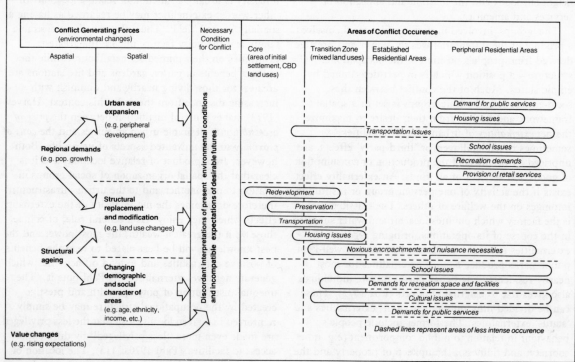

Fig. 7.1 A model of locational conflict within the city.
Source: Janelle and Millward (1976), p. 103.

voicing claims over a particular issue (Dear and Long 1978; Hirschman 1970), whether by organizing petitions, lobbying politicians and bureaucrats, writing to newspapers, forming local resident groups, picketing, or distributing handbills and posters. As Dear and Long (1978) point out, this sometimes extends to *illegal activities*, such as personal violence, damage to property, sit-ins and deliberate violations of anti-discrimination laws. Alternatively, some communities are able to use formal channels of *participation* as a profitable strategy when they find themselves in conflict with other communities or institutions. Another 'strategy' available to communities is that of *resignation* to the imposition of negative externalities. This is especially common where communities feel that voicing strategies are regularly ignored or over-ruled and that participation is ineffective. Many people who disapprove of city plans, for example, simply resign themselves to the 'inevitable' because they feel unable, individually or collectively, to exert any real influence on policy-makers. The final strategy is that of re-location, or *exit*, which is a household rather than a community strategy, and brings us back to the idea of a continually evolving geography of *de facto* territories.

Not all intra-metropolitan conflict is acted out at the level of *de facto* territories, however. A good deal of inter-group conflict is associated with the *de jure* organization of space which determines many aspects of the quality of neighbourhood life (Coates, Johnston and Knox 1977; Massam 1975; Smith 1977). Much of the intra-metropolitan variation in levels of community welfare stems from variations in the overall level of public service provision in different jurisdictions and on the particular packages of public services available for a given level of taxation. It follows that each social group will tend to seek out the jurisdiction which maximizes its *fiscal surplus* and, once established, will compete with residents of other jurisdictions to attract the fiscally desirable – those whose demands for public services are small relative to the tax revenues they contribute – and to exclude the fiscally undesirable. In this way, inter-group conflict becomes institutionalized and is resolved through the activities of local governments and their representatives. One of the most important strategies in this context, for example, is the use of local authority controls over land use through zoning regulations which, if they are carefully drawn up, can effectively exclude specific social, ethnic or demographic groups from an entire jurisdiction.

The geometry of specialized *de jure* territories also serves to accentuate intra-metropolitan variations in community well-being and to provide the basis for further inter-community conflict. School catchment areas, for example, are often designed to maximize the homogeneity of school pupil compositions with respect to social class, thus accentuating local variations in 'public behaviour' externalities (Cox 1973). Where such districts have their own powers to raise revenues – as American school districts do – there is a direct relationship between the location of district boundaries and the relative welfare of communities on either side of the boundary line (Herbert 1976c). Conflict over resources and the use of space is also reflected in the way that space is organized into electoral subdivisions, and there is now a good deal of evidence documenting the manipulation of political boundaries by particular groups seeking to enhance their political power and, therefore, their ability to influence the intra-urban distribution of public resources (Johnston 1979b; Taylor and Johnston 1979).

The social geography of the city can thus be seen as the product of inter-group conflict over the organization and use of urban space and resources. In the remainder of this chapter, attention is focused on three important aspects of this conflict: the organization of ethnic minority groups into distinctive *de facto* territories, the location and allocation of services and amenities, and the organization and manipulation of *de jure* political and administrative boundaries.

The spatial segregation of ethnic groups

The residential behaviour of ethnic groups in Western cities provides a useful example of the way in which group conflict is resolved through the housing market. The utility of a 'conflict' interpretation of ethnic residential segregation has been stressed by Boal (1972; 1976; 1979), whose analysis of the field provides the framework for this section. Following the work of Duncan and Lieberson (1959) and Lazarus (1969), Boal suggests that ethnic segregation is inversely related to the process of assimilation with the host society, a process which is itself governed by different forms of group behaviour designed to minimize real or perceived threats to the group from outsiders. But before going on to examine this behaviour and its spatial consequences in detail, it is first necessary to clarify the meaning of terms such as 'ethnic group', 'host society', 'segregation' and 'assimilation'.

Quite simply, the term 'ethnic group' is used to mean any group which is defined or characterized by race, religion, nationality or culture. Implicit in its use is the idea that ethnic groups are minority groups whose presence in the city stems from a past or continuing stream of in-migration. Ethnic groups in this sense therefore include blacks, Puerto Ricans, Italians, and Jews in American cities; West Indians, Asians and Irish in British cities; Algerians in French cities; Turks and Yugoslavs in West German cities; and so on. While the host society may not be ethnically homogeneous, it always contains a *charter group* which represents the dominant matrix into which new ethnic groups are inserted. In North America, Australasia and Britain the charter group in most cities is white, with an 'Anglo-Saxon' culture. The degree to which ethnic groups are spatially segregated from the charter group varies a good deal from city to city according to the group involved. *Segregation* is taken here to refer to situations where members of an ethnic group are not distributed absolutely uniformly in relation to the rest of the population. This clearly covers a wide range of circumstances, and it is useful to be able to quantify the overall degree of segregation in some way. Several indexes of segregation are available (see, for example, Duncan and Duncan 1955a; Taeuber and Taeuber 1965), although the sensitivity of all of them depends on the scale of the areal units employed (Jones and McEvoy 1978; Woods 1976).

One of the most widely used methods of quantifying the degree to which an ethnic group is residentially segregated is the index of dissimilarity, which is analogous to the Gini index of inequality and which produces a theoretical range of values from 0 (no segregation) to 100 (complete segregation). Index values calculated from census tract data in US cities show that blacks are generally the most segregated of the ethnic minorities in America. A study by Taeuber (1965) found the median index value to be 88, while Van Valey *et al.* (1977) found that over half of the 237 cities they examined had index values of 70 or more, with Chicago, Dallas, Fort Lauderdale, Las Vegas, Monroe (La.), Oklahoma City, Orlando (Fla.) and West Palm Beach having index values of over 90. Puerto Ricans, Mexicans and Cubans have also been found to be very highly segregated in American cities, with index values at the tract level commonly exceeding 70. By comparison, ethnic residential segregation in European cities is relatively low. In Britain, for example, index values calculated for major coloured immigrant groups – West Indians, Pakistanis, Bangladeshis, Indians and Africans – at the enumeration district level range between 40 and 70 (Jones 1979; Peach 1975; Winchester 1974; Woods 1976); although at more detailed levels of analysis the degree of segregation can be much higher. Jones and McEvoy (1978), for example, computed an index value of 81.6 for Asians in Huddersfield at the scale of individual streets. This emphasizes the vulnerability of statistical indexes, and makes inter-city comparisons difficult. Another practical difficulty in making precise statements about the degree of residential segregation is that ethnic groupings may subsume important internal

differences. Statements about the segregation of Asians in British cities, for instance, overlook the tendency for Indians, Pakistanis and Bangladeshis to exist in quite separate communities, even though these communities may appear to outsiders to be part and parcel of the same community.

What is clear enough from the available evidence, however, is that most ethnic minorities tend to be highly segregated from the charter group. Moreover, this segregation has been shown to be greater than might be anticipated from the socio-economic status of the groups concerned. In other words, the low socio-economic status of ethnic groups can only partially explain their high levels of residential segregation (Berry 1972; Lee 1977; Taeuber 1965). The maintenance of the ethnic in-migrant group 'as a distinctive social and spatial entity' will depend, as Boal (1976: 43) observes, 'on the degree to which assimilation occurs'. This process can take place at different speeds for different groups, depending on the perceived social distance between them and the charter group. Moreover, behavioural assimilation – the acquisition by the ethnic group of a cultural life in common with the charter group – may take place faster than structural assimilation – the diffusion of members of the ethnic group through the social and occupational strata of the charter group society. In general, the rate and degree of assimilation of an ethnic minority group will depend on two sets of factors: (1) external factors, including charter group attitudes and 'fabric' effects, and (2) internal group cohesiveness. Between them, these factors determine not only the degree and nature of conflict between ethnic groups and the charter group, but also the spatial pattern of residential segregation.

External factors

Ethnic groups which are perceived by members of the charter group to be socially undesirable will find themselves spatially isolated through a variety of mechanisms. One of the most obvious and straightforward of these is the 'blocking' strategy by existing occupants of city neighbourhoods in order to resist the 'invasion' of ethnic groups. Established tightly-knit ethnic clusters tend to be the most resistant to invasion, actively defending their own territory in a variety of ways (ranging from social hostility and the refusal to sell or rent homes to petty violence and deliberate vandalism) against intruding members of ethnic groups of inferior status. Perhaps the best-known example of this is the resistance by residents of the 'Polish Principality' of Hamtramck in Detroit to the residential expansion of blacks (Clark 1964). Where this strategy of 'voicing' opposition is unsuccessful, or where the territory in question is occupied by socially and geographically more mobile households, the charter group strategy commonly becomes one of 'exit'. The invasion of charter group territory generally precipitates an outflow of charter group residents which continues steadily until the critical point is reached where the proportion of households from the invading ethnic group precipitates a much faster exodus. This is known as the 'tipping point'. The precise level of the tipping point is difficult to establish, although Rose (1970) suggests that for whites facing 'invasion' by blacks the tipping point may be expected to occur when black occupancy reaches a level of about 30 per cent. The subsequent withdrawal of charter group residents to other neighbourhoods effectively resolves the territorial conflict between the two groups, leaving the ethnic group spatially isolated until its next phase of territorial expansion.

The spatial isolation of ethnic groups is also contrived through discrimination in the housing market, thus limiting ethnic groups to small niches within the urban fabric. Although formal discriminatory barriers are illegal, ethnic minorities are systematically excluded from charter group neighbourhoods in a variety of ways. As we have seen (pp. 158–164), the role of estate agents and mortgage financiers in the owner-occupied sector is particularly important, while the general gatekeeping role of private landlords also tends to perpetuate ethnically segregated local sub-markets (Daniel 1968). There is also a considerable weight of evidence to suggest that immigrants and ethnic minorities are discriminated against in the public sector. In Britain, a report by Political and Economic Planning (1967) enumerated the ways in which the allocation of public housing could operate to the disadvantage of such groups. These included unintentional discrimination, such as the residential requirements associated with eligibility rules, as well as more deliberate discrimination through the personal prejudice of housing visitors who may have little or no understanding of the cultural background and family life of immigrant households. More recently, a study of housing allocation in London found that coloured tenants on Greater London Council estates were being disproportionately allocated to older, poorer-quality lettings in unpopular 'flatted' estates in inner London, thus intensifying the localization of the non-white population in the inner city (Parker and Dugmore 1976). This type of discrimination is exacerbated by the discriminatory policies of city planners. Again, some of this discrimination is unintentional, as in the omission of ethnic neighbourhoods from urban renewal and rehabilitation schemes (Rex and Moore 1967); but much

is deliberate, as in the manipulation of land-use plans and zoning regulations in order to exclude non-whites from suburban residential areas (Foley 1973).

The net effect of this discrimination is to render much of the housing stock unavailable to members of ethnic groups, thus trapping them in privately-rented accommodation and allowing landlords to charge inflated rents while providing little security of tenure. In an attempt to escape from this situation, some householders reluctantly become landlords, buying large deteriorating houses and sub-letting part of the house in order to maintain mortgage repayments and/or repair costs (Haddon 1970; Hiro 1973). Others manage to purchase smaller dwellings which are shared with another family or a lodger, but many can only finance the purchase through burdensome and unorthodox means. Asians, in particular, have been found to exhibit a strong propensity towards home ownership in preference to tenancy, notwithstanding the extra financial costs (Dahya 1974). The localized nature of cheaper accommodation (whether for sale or rent) is another important 'fabric' effect which serves to segregate ethnic minority groups from the rest of the population by channelling them into a limited niche. Moreover, since many ethnic groups have an atypical demographic structure, with a predominance of young adult males and/or large, extended families, their housing needs – single-room accommodation and large dwellings respectively – can be met only in very specific locations. In many cities, therefore, the distribution of ethnic clusters is closely related to the geography of the housing stock (Jones 1979; Kearsley and Srivastava 1974; Rose 1969).

Underlying both charter group discrimination and the localization of ethnic groups in particular pockets of low-cost housing is their position in the overall social and economic structure of society. Rex and Moore, for example, suggest that while some of the discriminatory behaviour they found in Sparkbrook, Birmingham, may have been due to innate tendencies or personality disturbances, a great deal of it could be explained by Birmingham's social structure and by conflicts of interests and roles which were built into Birmingham society (Rex and Moore 1967). This approaches the Marxist analysis of race relations in Britain, which holds that 'the position of immigrants in society is not one of an "outgroup" cut off from society by the "factor of colour"; rather it recognizes that the subordinate, oppressed position of such groups is conditioned by their racial distinctiveness and *reinforced by their concentration in the working class*, leading to their super-exploitation in society' (Doherty 1973: 50, emphasis added). In this context, discrimination by working-class members of the charter group is related to the role attributed to ethnic groups in job and housing markets as competitors whose presence serves to depress wages and erode the quality of life. In short, ethnic groups are treated as the scapegoats for the shortcomings of the economic system.

But it is the concentration of ethnic groups at the lower end of the occupational structure which is the more fundamental factor in their localization in poor housing. Because of their lack of skills and educational qualifications, members of ethnic minority groups tend to be concentrated in occupations which are unattractive to members of the charter group, which are often unpleasant or degrading in one way or another, and which are usually associated with low wages (Unit for Manpower Studies 1976). The majority of such occupations are associated with the CBD and its immediate surrounds, and the dependence of ethnic groups on centralized job opportunities is widely cited as a prime determinant in the location of ethnic residential clusters (Lee 1977; Morrill 1965; Rose 1971). This factor, in turn, is reinforced by the location of suitably cheap accommodation in inner-city neighbourhoods surrounding the CBD. Moreover, the isolation of ethnic groups in this sector of the housing and labour markets is increasingly exacerbated by the suburbanization of job opportunities which effectively become inaccessible to the inner-city poor because of their inability to meet the necessary transportation costs (Bederman and Adams 1974; de Vise 1976).

Internal group cohesiveness

While charter group attitudes, fabric effects and occupational status go a long way towards explaining residential segregation, they do not satisfactorily explain the clustering of ethnic groups into discrete, ethnically homogeneous territories. According to Boal (1976), such clusters are basically defensive and conservative in function, partly in response to the external pressures outlined above. As he puts it:

Conflict situations in cities lead people to feel threatened. This will particularly apply to recent in-migrants, who may vary culturally and indeed racially from the 'host' population . . . The perceived threat may materialize in the form of physical violence or remain as a psychological threat. At the same time, and indeed sometimes because of the threat, the ethnic group may have a strong urge to internal cohesion, so that the cultural 'heritage' of the group may be retained (Boal 1976:45).

Boal suggests that the clustering of ethnic groups serves four principal functions: defence, support, preservation and attack.

The *defensive* role of ethnic clusters is most prominent when charter group discrimination is

extremely widespread and intense, so that the existence of a territorial heartland enables members of the ethnic group to withdraw from the hostility of the wider society. Jewish ghettos in medieval European cities functioned in this way, and Boal himself has vividly demonstrated the way in which working-class Catholic and Protestant communities in Belfast have become increasingly segregated from one another in response to their need for physical safety (Boal 1974; 1978). Nowhere has this phenomenon been more marked than on the Shankhill-Falls 'Divide' between the Protestant neighbourhood of Shankhill and the Catholic neighbourhood of Clonard/Springfield. Transitional between the two, and marking the Divide between the two ethnic groups, is the Cupar Street area, which had acquired a mixed residential pattern in the years up to 1968. When the 'troubles' broke out in 1969, however, the territorial boundary between the two groups took on a much sharper definition. Sixty-five households moved to the relative safety of their own religious heartland from Cupar Street alone during August/September 1969 in response to the mounting incidence of physical attacks in the district. It is estimated that within the following seven years between 35,000 and 60,000 people from the Belfast area relocated for similar reasons, thus reinforcing the segregation of Protestants and Catholics into what have become known in army circles as 'tribal areas' (Boal 1978).

Closely related to the defensive functions of ethnic clusters is their role as a haven, providing *support* for members of the group in a variety of ways. These range from formal ethnic-oriented institutions and businesses to informal friendship and kinship ties. Clustered together in a mutually supportive haven, members of the group are able to avoid the hostility and rejection of the charter group, exchanging insecurity and anxiety for familiarity and strength. This 'buffer' function of ethnic clusters has been documented in a number of studies, including Raveau's (1970) description of the segregation of black Africans in Paris, Deakin's (1970) analysis of coloured groups in British cities, and Kramer's (1970) discussion of ethnic minorities in American cities. The existence of ethnic institutions within the territorial cluster is one of the most important factors in protecting group members from unwanted contact with the host community. Hiro (1973), for example, describes how Sikh temples and Moslem mosques in British cities have become the focus of Sikh and Pakistani local welfare systems, offering a source of food, shelter, recreation and education as well as being a cultural and religious focus.

More generally, most ethnic immigrant groups develop informal self-help networks and welfare organizations in order to provide both material and social support for group members. At the same time, the desire to avoid outside contact and the existence of a local concentration of an ethnic population with distinctive, culturally-based needs serve to provide what Hannerz (1974) calls 'protected niches' for ethnic enterprise, both legitimate and illegitimate. One example given by Hannerz is the success of the Cosa Nostra in Italian-American communities; but it is clear that ethnic enterprise is an important component of community cohesion in ethnic neighbourhoods everywhere, providing an expression of group solidarity as well as a means of economic and social advancement for successful entrepreneurs and an alternative route by which ethnic workers can bypass the white-controlled labour market. In their classic study of the black community in Chicago, Drake and Cayton (1962) describe the doctrine of the 'double-duty dollar', according to which members of the community should use their money not only to satisfy their personal needs but also to 'advance the race' by making their purchases in black-owned businesses. In Britain, the most distinctive manifestations of ethnic enterprise are the clusters of banks, butchers, grocery stores, travel agencies, cinemas and clothing shops which have developed in response to the food taboos, specialized clothing styles and general cultural aloofness of Asian communities (Cater and Jones 1978).

This brings us to a third major function of ethnic residential clustering: that of *preserving* and promoting a distinctive cultural heritage. Ethnic group consciousness may result from external pressure, but for many groups there exists an inherent desire to maintain a distinctive cultural identity rather than to become completely assimilated within the charter group. Residential clustering helps to achieve this not only through the operation of ethnic institutions and businesses but also through the effects of residential propinquity on marriage patterns. Several writers have emphasized the self-segregating tendencies of Asian communities in British cities in this context (Dahya 1974; Kearsley and Srivastava 1974), while Rosenthal (1961) has suggested that the persistence of Jewish residential clusters in Chicago is closely related to the knowledge among Jewish parents that residence in a Jewish neighbourhood confers a very high probability of their children marrying a Jewish person. The residential clustering of some ethnic groups is also directly related to the demands of their religious precepts relating to dietary laws, the preparation of food, and attendance for prayer and religious ceremony. Where such mores form an important part of the group's culture, they are clearly followed more easily where the group is territorially clustered. On the other hand, where group consciousness is weak and the group culture is not

especially distinctive, ties between group members tend to be superficial – sentimental rather than functional – with the result that residential clustering as well as group solidarity is steadily eroded: a process which Dench (1975) has tellingly documented in relation to the Maltese in London.

The fourth major function of ethnic spatial concentration is the provision of a 'base' for action in the struggle of its members with society in general. This *attack* function, as Boal calls it, is usually both peaceful and legitimate. Spatial concentrations of group members represent considerable electoral power and often enable ethnic groups to gain official representation within the institutional framework of urban politics. This has been an important factor in the political power base of blacks in the United States, where the Black Power movement has been able to exploit the electoral power of the ghetto with considerable success – to the extent that black politicians now constitute an important (and sometimes decisive) voice in the urban political arena (Brunn 1974). Ethnic clusters also provide a convenient base for illegitimate attacks on the charter group. Insurrectionary groups and urban guerrillas with ethnic affiliations are able to 'disappear' in their own group's territory, camouflaged by a relative anonymity within their own cultural milieu and protected by a silence resulting from a mixture of sympathy and intimidation. An obvious example of this is the way in which the IRA and loyalist para-military organizations have taken advantage of their respective territorial heart-lands in Belfast; and, indeed, the way in which the IRA has used Irish communities in Birmingham, Liverpool, London and Southampton as bases for terrorist attacks.

Spatial outcomes

The spatial expression of ethnic group/charter group conflict is determined by the interplay of charter group attitudes, fabric effects, and the strength of internal group cohesion. Where the perceived social distance between the ethnic group and the charter group is relatively small, the effects of both charter group discrimination and internal cohesion are likely to be minimized and so ethnic residential clusters are likely to be only a temporary stage in the assimilation of the group into the wider urban socio-spatial fabric. Such clusters may be termed *colonies*. They essentially serve as a port-of-entry for members of the ethnic group concerned, providing a base from which group members are culturally assimilated and spatially dispersed. Their persistence over time is thus dependent on the continuing input of new ethnic group members.

Examples of this type of pattern include the distribution of European ethnic groups in North American cities during the 1920s and 1930s, of similar groups in Australasian cities during the 1950s and 1960s, and of the Maltese in London during the 1950s (Duncan and Lieberson 1959; Burnley 1972; Dench 1975).

Ethnic clusters which persist over the longer term are usually a product of the interaction between discrimination and internal cohesion. Where the latter is the more dominant of the forces, the resultant residential clusters may be termed *enclaves*; and where external factors are more dominant, the residential clusters are generally referred to as *ghettos*. In reality, of course, it is often difficult to ascertain the degree to which segregation is voluntary or involuntary, and it is more realistic to think in terms of a continuum rather than a two-fold classification. Boal (1976) has identified several distinctive spatial patterns in relation to this enclave/ghetto continuum. The first of these is exemplified by Jewish residential areas in many North American cities, where an initial residential clustering in inner-city areas has formed the base for the subsequent formation of new suburban residential clusters (Fig. 7.2). The fact that this suburbanization represents a general upward shift in socio-economic status and that it is usually accompanied by the transferral of Jewish cultural and religious institutions to the suburbs suggests that this type of pattern is largely the result of voluntary segregation.

The second distinctive expression of the enclave/ghetto takes the form of a concentric zone of ethnic neighbourhoods which has spread from an initial cluster to encircle the CBD. Such zones are often patchy, the discontinuities reflecting variations in the urban fabric in terms of house types and resistant social groups. Anderson (1962) has suggested that the growth of black areas in American cities tends to conform to this pattern, while other examples include the distribution of Asians, Irish and West Indians in Birmingham (Jones 1979), of Asians in Glasgow (Kearsley and Srivastava 1974) and of West Indians in London (Fig. 7.3: see Lee 1977). It should be noted, however, that the same pattern may occur in different places for different reasons. In the case of the Glasgow Asians, for example, Kearsley and Srivastava suggest that the concentric pattern derives from a process of 'uncontested filtering' into tenement housing which has been made available by the out-migration of indigenous Glaswegians. In contrast, the concentric pattern of black neighbourhoods in certain American cities seems to be related more to the twin effects of occupational status and racial discrimination (Rose 1971).

Where an ethnic group continues to grow numerically, and provided that a sufficient number of its population are able to afford better housing, residential segregation is likely to result in a sectoral spatial pattern. The distribution of blacks in many of the more prosperous and rapidly expanding cities of the United States tends towards this model although, as Boal (1976) points out, sectoral development is often truncated because of economic constraints operating at the suburban margin. The distribution of the black population in Oklahoma City provides a good example of this type of pattern. As Fig. 7.4 shows, the city's

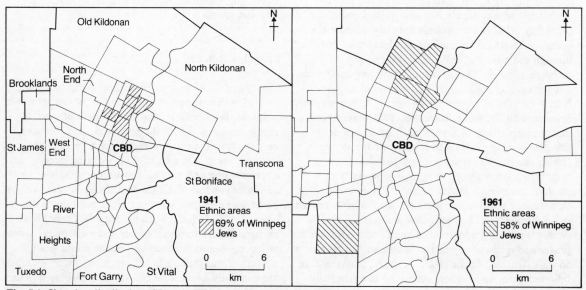

Fig. 7.2 Changing distribution of Jews in Winnipeg, Manitoba, 1941–1961.
Source: Driedger and Church (1974), pp. 38 and 40.

black population is almost entirely confined to the north-eastern sector: few census tracts outside this area contain even 1 per cent of black persons. Other examples of this sort of spatial pattern include the distribution of blacks in Grand Rapids, Michigan (Boal 1976) and of Catholics in Belfast (Poole and Boal 1973). Finally, it should be noted that, whatever the overall spatial pattern, most ethnic groups display an internal differentiation on a social class basis. Gordon (1964) has suggested that a series of sub-societies is created by the intersection of the vertical stratification of ethnicity with the horizontal stratification of social class. These sub-societies – what Gordon calls 'ethclasses' – are explicit in the integrated model of urban factorial ecology put forward by Berry and Rees (1969), where ethnic social stratification is associated with a zonal spatial pattern (Fig. 4.13). Such a pattern has also been demonstrated by Frazier (1967) in his study of black residential patterns in Chicago. As Table 7.1 shows, almost all the indices of family life, social organization

and economic and family status display clear zonal trends. It must be emphasized, however, that this pattern of zonal ethclass segregation is relevant only to ethnic groups whose overall residential pattern is sectoral. Where concentric patterns or nodal enclaves form the overall spatial framework, other patterns will emerge.

Location and accessibility

The importance of relative location and accessibility to the quality of life of different social and ethnic groups is to a large degree the product of the overall trend of modern urban development outlined in Chapter 2. The ascendancy of the automobile as the dominant means of personal transportation, together with the consequent spread of low-density suburban development, has brought to an end the traditional notion that jobs, shops, schools, health services and community facilities

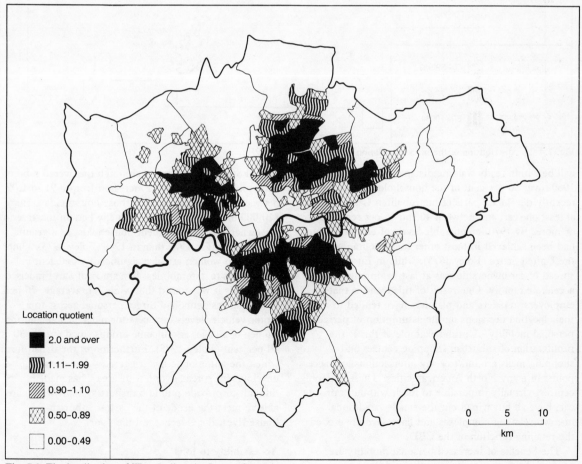

Location quotient

■ 2.0 and over

▩ 1.11–1.99

▨ 0.90–1.10

▧ 0.50–0.89

□ 0.00–0.49

0 5 10
km

Fig. 7.3 The localization of West Indians in Greater London.
Source: Lee (1977), p. 24.

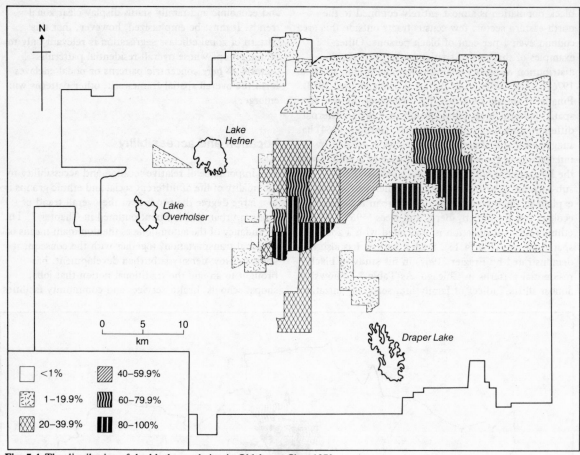

Fig. 7.4 The distribution of the black population in Oklahoma City, 1970.

will be within ready walking distance of homes. Even by 1960, over 90 per cent of the households in the most recently developed parts of metropolitan California had at least one car, and between 40 and 45 per cent had two or more. By 1970, comparable levels of car ownership had been achieved in most other metropolitan areas of the United States (Foley 1975), while in Europe the spread of car ownership was at last beginning to accelerate rapidly. One result of this trend is that employers, retailers and planners have tended to make their location decisions on the assumption of perfect personal mobility. A prime example of this is the proliferation of suburban shopping centres and shopping malls around freeway intersections and access points in many North American cities. These shopping centres, virtually impossible to reach without a private car, have all but wiped out the smaller traditional in-town retailing complexes and have severely eroded the retailing function of the CBD.

The benefits of increased personal mobility are enjoyed disproportionately by the middle-class, the middle-aged and the male population, however. In the United States, for example, although the overall ratio of automobiles to households increased from 0.91 to 1.09 between 1960 and 1970, only those households earning $10,000 or more per annum actually had an increase in car ownership. Less affluent households, as a group, were worse off in 1970 than in 1960 (Foley 1975). Older people and women are also significantly deficient in their access to automobiles. In a study of San Francisco households it was found that while, on average, 70 per cent of all residents had direct personal access to a motor vehicle, levels of access for older people and for women of all ages and income groups stood at only 30 or 40 per cent (Foley 1975). Furthermore, the urban form which the automobile has triggered – low-density development spread over a wide area – has made it very difficult to provide public transport systems which are able to meet the needs of the carless suburban housewives, the elderly, and the poor.

Accessibility to jobs

One aspect of this trend which has received some

Table 7.1 Zonal patterns in Chicago's black community

	Zone						
	I	*II*	*III*	*IV*	*V*	*VI*	*VII*
Per cent illiterate[1]	13.4	4.6	3.2	2.3	3.3	2.9	2.7
Per cent males professional and white collar	5.8	5.5	10.7	11.2	12.5	13.4	34.2
Per cent family heads born in South	77.7	77.0	74.7	73.8	72.6	69.0	65.2
Per cent illegitimate	2.3	1.1	1.2	0.9	0.6	0.4	0.2
Per cent families with female heads	22.0	23.1	20.8	20.4	20.5	15.2	11.9
Per cent owner occupiers	0.0	1.2	6.2	7.2	8.3	11.4	29.8
Rate of family desertion[2]	2.5	2.6	2.1	1.5	1.1	0.4	0.2
Adult crime rate[2]	9.4	6.7	3.8	2.5	2.9	3.2	1.2
Juvenile delinquency rate[2]	42.8	31.4	30.0	28.8	15.7	9.6	1.4

[1] of persons aged 10 and older
[2] per 100 base population

Source: Frazier 1967: 227–31.

attention from geographers is the residential location of the poor and the unemployed in relation to job opportunities. Many jobs have moved out to the suburbs along with the general trend towards urban decentralization. The city of Chicago, for example, lost 211,300 jobs between 1960 and 1970 while its suburbs gained 548,000 jobs (de Vise 1976). Similar trends have been reported in Indianapolis by Davies and Albaum (1973) and in Atlanta by Bederman and Adams (1974). All three studies have also found that the poor – especially blacks – tend to remain trapped in the inner city, separated from the suburbanized job opportunities by distances of between 15 and 45 kilometres. In Chicago, jobs suburbanized twice as fast as the labour force between 1960 and 1970. This meant, as in cities elsewhere, that a large number of workers became involved in 'reverse commuting'. It has also meant that carless job-seekers have been at a considerable disadvantage, being forced to find employment either within walking distance of their homes or along the routes of public transport systems. Given the decreasing employment base of the inner city and the tendency for

urban bus services to operate along radial routes with few crosstown connections, the net effect is an intensification of the problems of unemployment and deprivation in the inner city (Falcocchio *et al.* 1972; Stutz 1976). Even when new jobs are brought into the inner city, they are often inappropriate to the local labour force. In Britain, Ambrose (1977a) and others have drawn attention to the effects of inner-city redevelopment schemes which displace unskilled manual and service jobs with office jobs. Without the qualifications to secure these new job opportunities, inner-city residents are left to search elsewhere for employment whilst their position in the local employment market is taken by suburban commuters.

In most American cities the situation has been exacerbated by the lack of an open housing market for the black population. De Vise (1976) has calculated that the number of blacks working in Chicago suburbs is less than half the number that would be expected from their occupational, industrial and earning characteristics. Although this can be partially explained by the paucity of information about suburban housing and job opportunities reaching black inner-city neighbourhoods (Bernstein 1973), the chief reasons for their exclusion from suburban job markets seem to be associated with racial discrimination and the residential segregation of blacks. Transport-based solutions to this particular accessibility problem are therefore of doubtful value. One scheme designed to link the ghetto with outlying suburban trading estates in St Louis, for example, failed because the industrialists were reluctant to employ blacks and because many of the ghetto residents were unwilling to work in white suburbia (Muller 1976b). The roots of black inner-city unemployment thus go deeper into the social and economic fabric of society than the spatial disposition of homes and jobs. This point certainly emerges from the study of Atlanta undertaken by Bederman and Adams (1974). Having demonstrated that the inner city is in fact the area from which accessibility to the city's jobs is greatest, they conclude that 'Atlanta's critically underemployed are mainly black female heads of families, and no matter where they live in the metropolitan area they have neither the skills to qualify them for most of the new jobs being created, nor the opportunity to acquire marketable skills' (Bederman and Adams 1974: 386).

Accessibility to facilities

After employment considerations, accessibility to facilities and services is probably the most important source of use value attached by people to their place of residence. Some of these facilities, such as shops and restaurants, are located by private decision-makers; but it is the location of public and semi-public goods such as schools, clinics, parks, sewage plant and airports which is increasingly important in determining the real income of local communities in cities everywhere. Within the last ten years, geographers and political scientists have begun to investigate the way in which accessibility to particular facilities and services serves to reinforce disparities in the quality of life enjoyed by different communities. Studies of shopping opportunities (Bunge 1975; Johnston and Rimmer 1969), the provision of police protection (Bloch 1974; Smith 1977; Weicher 1971), street maintenance and sewage disposals (Antunes and Plumlee 1977; Boots *et al.* 1972; Lineberry 1977), dental care (Bradley *et al.* 1978), primary medical care (Barnett 1978; Knox 1978b), recreational facilities (Lyon 1970) and educational resources (Cox 1973; Kirby 1979b) and the incidence of nuisances such as air pollution and aircraft noise (Wood *et al.* 1974; Wolpert *et al.* 1972) have all revealed a tendency for inequitable spatial distributions, although not always in a simple or straightforward way. Nevertheless, the overall trend is evidently for the externality effects of facility locations to be regressive. In the private market, location is normally determined by potential profit, so that wealthier communities are likely to attract more private facilities and services – and of better quality – than are poorer communities. Public provision could affect this advantage, but the ability of wealthy groups to organize political campaigns and to manipulate bureaucratic machinery means that they are often able to attract a disproportionate share of public services. Similarly, the rich are often able to ensure that undesirable activities are banished to poorer neighbourhoods.

In relation to the spatial allocation of educational resources in American cities, for example, Cox (1973) has illustrated how variations in teacher quality and in the provision of capital equipment tend to favour more affluent neighbourhoods. Thus 'children attending schools in the whiter and more middle-class areas ... tend to be taught in newer, more up-to-date buildings and to use the newest and least worn-out text books and equipment' (Cox 1973: 77). In Britain, Kirby (1979b) has described the way in which the concentration of manpower and physical resources in élite middle-class schools within Newcastle upon Tyne has effectively limited the educational opportunities of pupils in other schools. Moreover, he also notes that the school which was least accessible to its pupils also had the highest non-attendance figures. Such disparities ultimately serve to reinforce localized patterns of social and economic deprivation, for there exists a clear relationship between educational achievement and

educational resources, notwithstanding variations in pupils' home environment and the social mix in their school. Low educational achievement makes for a vulnerability to unemployment, which in turn constrains opportunities in relation to most other aspects of life.

Accessibility to medical care

Patterns of accessibility to health care facilities provide a particularly good example of the way in which the spatial allocation of resources serves to intensify disparities in the quality of neighbourhood life. In countries like the United States and Australia, where health care delivery systems are essentially run on *laissez-faire* principles, wide variations exist between neighbourhoods in the availability and quality of medical care. In the United States, the best-documented city in this respect is Chicago, where geographers such as Earickson, Morrill, Pyle and Rees have been involved in the lavish Chicago Regional Hospital Study (see de Vise 1973). Working papers from the Study have described Chicago's hospital system as 'apartheid', discriminating on the basis of race, residence and age not only in terms of the relative location of hospitals but also in terms of waiting time, quality of care, and cost. In general, the spatial arrangement of hospital services tends to follow the intra-urban commercial hierarchy, except that there is rarely the same degree of suburbanization of facilities. As a result, there tends to be an excess of capacity in the central city and a shortage in the suburbs, especially the less prosperous black and working-class suburbs. Such a pattern has been demonstrated by Megee (1976), and Shannon and Dever (1974) in other North American cities, and by Morris (1976), Cleland *et al.* (1977), and Stimpson (1978) in Australian cities. In relation to Adelaide, South Australia, for example, Cleland *et al.* (1977: 50) conclude that:

the overall pattern is one of a marked hierarchical system of hospital provision ... with high concentration of facilities in the inner city locations ... with lower order facilities, almost always of the private type, located in the higher status areas or at locations that are old settlement nodes ... As a result, patients and the friends and relatives visiting them will have relatively long journeys to make to gain access to a hospital.

The spatial organization of primary care in cities also tends to be regressive. In addition to the important limitations on people's accessibility to primary care imposed by income constraints and socio-psychological barriers, home-to-surgery distance is especially important because of its repercussions on local patterns of health and well-being, due to the deterrent effect of distance in relation to 'therapeutic behaviour' – the seeking of medical advice. In cities where large sectors of the population are still without private transport, the actual distance from home to the family doctor's surgery is particularly critical. About 0.75 kilometres – 'pram-pushing distance' – is often regarded as the upper limit for mothers with pre-school children and for the elderly; and travelling much more than this by public transport may involve a long wait or a change of bus unless both home and surgery lie conveniently near a bus route. Class differences in car ownership are also exacerbated by the time constraints of the working classes, who are normally subject to much more inflexible working hours than the middle classes. The disutility of travelling to the surgery can thus act as a substantial barrier to proper care, influencing therapeutic behaviour just as educational, religious and class-related barriers do (Mechanic 1968; Phillips 1979). Patients living further away will tend to make light of symptoms and put up with discomfort, gambling that their condition is not serious rather than making the effort to travel to their doctor. Distance has already been shown to have a marked negative effect on consultation rates (Girt 1972), and it seems reasonable to suppose that this will eventually exercise a direct effect on local patterns of morbidity and mortality. It is also worth noting that blue-collar workers are, in general, less inclined to consult family doctors and much less concerned than white-collar workers with preventive medicine, with the likely result that distance will affect the delivery of medical care differentially by social class, notwithstanding class differences in personal mobility. Moreover, such effects do not appear to be attenuated by increased requests for home visits: Hopkins *et al*. (1968), for example, found that patients living further away from the surgery not only had lower utilization rates than others, but were more reluctant to call out their doctor for home visits.

In this context, intra-urban variations in the provision of primary care are alarming. Where primary care is provided on a competitive fee-for-service basis – as in Australia and the United States – the locational behaviour of general practitioners is influenced primarily by local effective demand and the propensity for people to want (rather than need) medical care (Lankford 1971; Shannon and Dever 1974). Other factors which have been identified as influencing the location of surgeries include neighbourhood ethnicity (Lieberson 1958), the availability of office space (Elesh and Schollaert 1971), the proximity of specialist hospital facilities, the availability of manpower to cover illness and vacations, the approval of the neighbourhood by the doctor's spouse (Diseker and Chappell 1976), and the pull of local family ties (Bible 1970). The result is a gross imbalance between medical needs and resources, with physicians tending to be clustered around nodes of commercial activity (Earickson 1970) and in affluent white suburbs (Rees 1967; de Vise 1973). Recent studies of the distribution of general practitioners (GPs) in Sydney, Australia, have established a positive correlation between neighbourhood status and the incidence of primary care facilities, although the dominant spatial pattern is one of declining access to facilities with distance from the city centre (Freestone 1975; Donald 1978). This maldistribution is also typical of Adelaide (Cleland, Stimpson and Goldsworthy 1977), and Melbourne (Morris 1976). Similar patterns are evident in North American cities, although the most striking feature of the distribution of GPs in many US cities is the lack of primary care resources in black neighbourhoods. In Chicago, the aversion of private physicians to poor black neighbourhoods has meant that the ratio of physicians to population in the city's ten poorest communities – which were mostly black – deteriorated from 0.99 per 1,000 in 1950 to 0.26 per 1,000 in 1970, whilst in the ten most affluent communities the ratio improved from 1.78 to 2.10 per 1,000 (de Vise and Dewey 1972). This has left welfare physicians to serve an average of 7,000 people rather than 700, to see 80 patients a day rather than 80 a week and to cease home visits altogether (de Vise 1968).

Even in countries such as the United Kingdom and New Zealand, where nationalized health services make adequate health care a legitimate expectation for all, the maldistribution of GPs within cities has given cause for concern (Barnett 1978; Barnett and Sheerin 1977; Knox 1978b, 1979a, 1979b, 1980b). In Britain, the locational inertia of GPs has meant that their distribution is much as it was at the inception of the NHS in 1948, with a concentration of surgeries in the older and more central neighbourhoods, particularly those of higher socio-economic status where large dwellings can be used to incorporate both surgery and residence. Although controls and incentives have been introduced under the NHS in order to regulate the spatial distribution of GPs, these policies have rarely operated at a scale below that of whole towns or cities, so that these intra-urban disparities have been reinforced by the natural tendency for family doctors to live and work in well-established high-status areas where there often exists the possibility of earning extra income with fees from private patients (Knox and Pacione 1980). At the same time, the structure and ideology of the medical profession in Britain has discouraged the location of GPs in working-class areas, since not only is working in blue-collar neighbourhoods held to be unglamorous and unsatisfactory (Cartwright 1967), but time spent in general practice in such areas is regarded as almost certain disqualification for any further career advancement (Hart 1971). Having said this, however, it is important to point out that the locational behaviour of GPs has also been influenced by 'fabric' effects, which have tended to reinforce the relative advantages enjoyed by older middle-class neighbourhoods. There is, for instance, an almost complete lack of accommodation suitable for use as doctors' surgeries in the large housing estates – both public and speculatively built – which have encircled most British cities since 1945. The net result is a maldistribution of medical resources which is part of what Hart (1971) has called the *inverse care law*: the tendency for medical care to vary inversely with the need of the population served.

This tendency is evident in the distribution of primary care resources in Edinburgh and Glasgow (Figs. 7.5 and 7.6), although neither pattern conforms exactly with the notion of an inverse care law. In Glasgow, for example, the localization of surgeries in the older central areas of the city tends to favour several

of the more deprived inner-city neighbourhoods. The most favoured areas are in fact the relatively compact communities of New Commonwealth immigrants – mainly Asians – occupying tenement housing near the large health centre at Woodside. But at the other extreme ware neighbourhoods consisting of public housing estates which, between them, house over two-thirds of the city's population. These neighbourhoods – especially the likes of Easterhouse, Drumchapel, Barmulloch and Garthamlock on the periphery of the city, containing many of the city's most notorious 'problem estates' – have very few local surgeries at all. In addition, levels of personal mobility are very low (typically, over three-quarters of the households in these neighbourhoods do not have a car); and bus services to other parts of the city are infrequent and expensive. Large numbers of people have to face return journeys of over four miles in order to see their GP, and the problem is particularly acute for families rehoused from substandard tenement dwellings in the

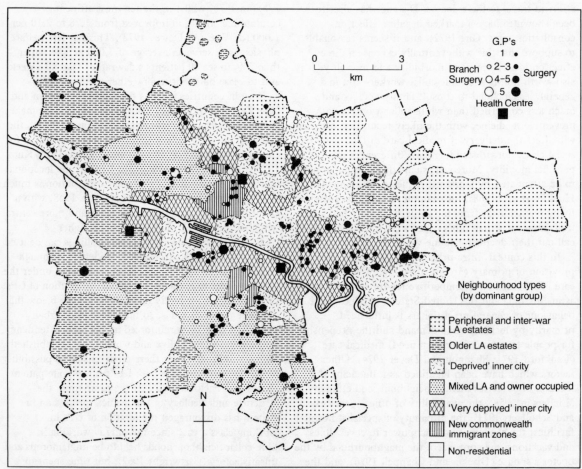

Fig. 7.5 The distribution of general practitioners in Glasgow, 1974.

inner city, since the shortage of surgeries in peripheral estates often means that they have no alternative but to remain on the list of their inner-city GP, thus facing return journeys of up to eight miles. Similarly, it is the peripheral housing schemes in Edinburgh which are worst served by the spatial distribution of GPs, the great majority of whom are to be found in a series of clusters encircling the CBD (Fig. 7.6), in areas of older but sound and much sought-after housing of varying social status.

The regressive nature of these patterns is rather more apparent when local variations in car ownership are taken into account. Fig. 7.7 shows the results of an index which takes into account the relative size and location of general practitioner services, local levels of car ownership, and the relative speed of public and private transport (Knox 1980a). Scores of more than 100 on the index indicate that a neighbourhood has more

than its fair 'share' of accessibility to the city's primary care facilities. In Glasgow, there are several less affluent inner-city neighbourhoods which still enjoy high levels of accessibility to primary care services even when these additional factors are taken into consideration. But these areas excepted, accessibility corresponds systematically and inversely to the social geography of the two cities. This is most pronounced in Edinburgh, where there is a Y-shaped area of 'over-doctored' neighbourhoods. All these are middle-class, owner-occupied neighbourhoods, the best-served of which – Morningside-Merchiston, Murrayfield, the New Town and Clermiston – also contain some of the most prestigious districts in terms of income and social status. Conversely, the city's worst-served areas correspond depressingly with 'deprived' local authority estates: Granton-Pilton-Drylaw in the south, Sighthill-Stenhouse in the west, and a large

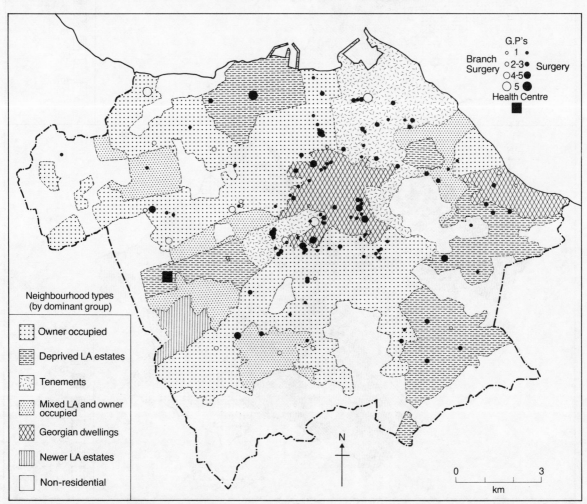

Fig. 7.6 The distribution of general practitioners in Edinburgh, 1973.

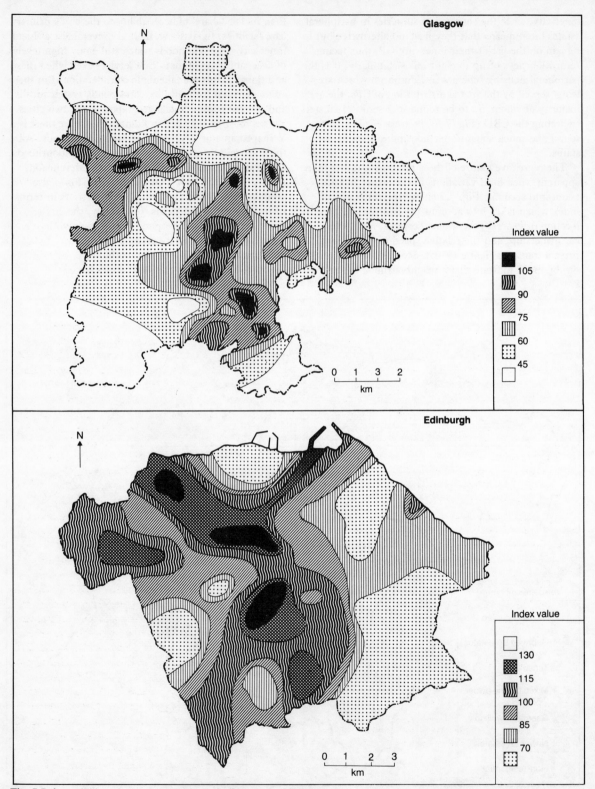

Fig. 7.7 Accessibility to primary medical care in Glasgow and Edinburgh.

uninterrupted tract in the east stretching from Lochend through Duddingston, Craigmillar, Ferniehill and Gilmerton to Liberton.

Physical inaccessibility to GPs, however, is only one aspect of medical deprivation in urban areas, and other aspects of the geography of primary care lend still more support to the idea of an inverse care law, with the deprived areas of the inner-city emerging as the worst off in terms of the quality, if not the availability, of primary care facilities. A good example is provided by Glasgow's East End, one of the harshest and most brutalized urban environments in Britain, with a population of over 150,000 and where the extent and intensity of unemployment, housing stress, environmental deprivation and social pathology is practically unrivalled in north-west Europe (Knox 1979a). It has a large and increasingly elderly population and contains high proportions of vagrants, in-migrants, one-parent families, students and other indigent and vulnerable groups with special medical needs; but it has not attracted medical manpower in proportion to these needs. Almost 75 per cent of the East End's GPs are aged over 45, and 17 per cent over 65, reflecting the persistent unattractiveness of the area since the late 1940s, when a post-war glut of newly qualified doctors forced many of them to take jobs in depressed areas like the East End. Moreover, the organization of the area's doctors has remained static, with a lack of teamwork and group practices: over 40 per cent of East End practices are single-handed. Equally disturbing is the condition of many of the surgeries, for many of the lock-up premises have deteriorated at a rate which matches that of the East End as a whole. In addition to the damage these poorly equipped, damp and grubby premises inflict on the morale of both doctors and patients there is also a perceived threat to people's health (local conventional wisdom holds that 'you go in with the 'flu and come out with pneumonia'), which probably acts as a further barrier to proper health care.

The situation in other large cities is little different. Melanie Phillips (1978) has described the reality of primary care in the Vauxhall area of Liverpool in these terms:

There are no chairs [in the waiting room]. From the ceiling a large piece of wallpaper hangs down limply. Unshaded light bulbs, coated in grime, hang among drooping coils of lighting flex. Nearby, three GPs hold their surgeries in a converted pair of shops. The windows are boarded up and one of the few panes of glass is smashed. The waiting area smells damp. It contains chairs – red plush, former cinema seats, torn and losing their stuffing, and wooden benches arrayed around the walls.

Complaints by patients of cursory and unsympathetic treatment by doctors are rife. In such areas it is the conditions in which primary care is presented – what Dutton (1978) describes as a 'dehumanising ambience' – which constitute the major barrier to therapeutic behaviour, and not distance between home and surgery. Nevertheless, there are many patients who are subject to both deterrents. As in Glasgow, patients who move out – or are moved – to suburbs such as Speke and Netherley as part of urban renewal schemes are often forced to remain on the list of the GP in the area from which they were rehoused. As a result, many patients must face journeys of over 30 minutes by car each way; or a total of at least four bus journeys, taking much longer and costing up to £2.00.

In London, a detailed survey of primary care in Thornhill – a deprived inner-city area between Kings Cross and Barnsbury – provides an equally depressing story (Thornhill Neighbourhood Project 1978). Thornhill has above average levels of infant mortality, malnutrition and tuberculosis in a population which contains above average numbers of young children, pensioners, members of ethnic minority groups, alcoholics, vagrants, and physically and mentally handicapped people. The health care needs of the area are also swollen by the local workforce, many of whom register with a Thornhill GP even though they live outside the neighbourhood. As in Glasgow's East End, physical accessibility to primary care is high: there are 21 GPs practising from 13 surgeries in the 1.5 square mile area, and the average number of patients per doctor in this part of London is 2,162, a low enough figure for the Medical Practices Committee to restrict the area to all new practitioners on the grounds of overdoctoring. But Thornhill is medically deprived. Like their counterparts in Liverpool and Glasgow, Thornhill people must attend poorly-equipped surgeries to consult doctors who are mostly working single-handedly and who therefore find it difficult to employ a nurse or receptionist, to attend in-service courses, and to find a deputy familiar with their patients and their needs. One in three of the area's doctors in 1978 were over 70, and this included two practitioners of over 80 years of age: whose training took place ten years before the discovery of penicillin. Whatever the value of experience, it must be doubtful whether people of this age can effectively tackle a full workload in an area whose medical needs are as intense and specialized as Thornhill's. In fact, many of the older GPs have deliberately restricted their catchment areas and pruned their lists. Thus, what appears to be a local abundance of manpower turns out to be a rather depleted group of GPs working in an uncoordinated way from under-equipped surgeries.

Time budgets and effective accessibility

Recent work by geographers such as Hagerstrand (1970), Pred (1973) and Carlstein, Parkes and Thrift (1978) has emphasized that questions of accessibility to jobs, services and amenities must be carefully qualified in terms of people's time budgets. Since most people's daily lives follow a variety of closely constrained and well-worn paths through time and space, it follows that *effective accessibility* to particular locations will depend not only on their physical proximity but also on whether they are free to make the journey in the first place. Hagerstrand (1970) has outlined a framework for the study of *time geography* which is based on the environment of resources and opportunities (including jobs, goods, services and social contacts) which surrounds each individual. According to Hagerstrand, the individual's capacity to move from one place or activity to another within this environment is defined by three different sorts of constraint:

1. *Capability constraints* – which include the need for a minimum amount of sleep (which limits the time which can be spent travelling) and the kind of transportation which is available (which will determine the radius of the territory which can be included in the daily life path).

2. *Authority constraints* – which include laws, rules and customs which limit accessibility to certain places and curtail participation in certain activities. Some restaurants, for example, require women to have an 'escort'.

3. *Coupling constraints* – which stem from the limited periods during which particular opportunities are available for access. As Hagerstrand points out, people's daily activities are highly dependent on the opening hours of shops and offices, the scheduling of public transport, and the timing and duration of 'rush hours'.

The *time budget* of any individual within his or her

environment can be depicted graphically by representing distance along a horizontal axis, and time along a vertical axis: the effective range of a person during the day is then described by a 'prism'. As Fig 7.8 shows, the shape of the prism depends on the available mode of transport. It may also vary from day to day, depending on the places and activities involved. Moreover, every stop, for whatever reason, causes the range of the prism (or subprisms) to shrink in proportion to the length of stay ((c) on Fig. 7.8).

The time budgets of some population sub-groups will clearly make for more effective accessibility to the city's opportunities than will those of others. One group which is particularly vulnerable to time-related constraints on locational accessibility is women. Allan Pred and Risa Palm (1974, 1978) have argued that even the suburban housewife with teenage children, access to a car and a relatively leisurely daily schedule is limited in her opportunities because of the limits of the subprisms that are sandwiched between her fixed 'duties' as a housewife: providing breakfast for the family and driving the children to school, preparing lunch, picking up the children from school, chauffeuring them to sporting or social engagements and preparing dinner. In addition, she may have to be home to accept deliveries, supervise repair workers or care for a sick child. This fragmentation of time gives rise to coupling constraints which limit her quality of life by effectively barring her from much of her environment. Women without cars, of course, suffer much greater restrictions on their quality of life. As we have seen, women do not, in general, enjoy very high levels of accessibility to cars, even in the United States. As Pred and Palm put it, the daily prism of the car-less suburban housewife

is restricted to those opportunities which can be reached on foot or by the use of a bus service (which in many suburbs is inconvenient and in some nonexistent) ... Even routine shopping becomes a chore. Socializing is limited to the

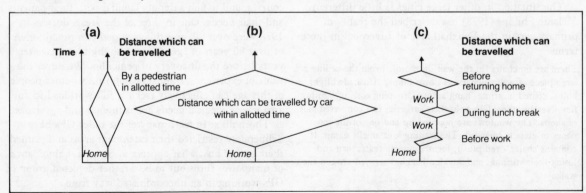

Fig. 7.8 Time budgets and daily prisms.
Source: Pred and Palm (1978), p. 103.

neighbourhood in which she lives... With children under school age she is virtually locked into a world of very limited physical space because of coupling constraints and societal expectations concerning her family role. Viewed from a time-geographic perspective, she has the greatest number of leisure hours and yet little opportunity to invest leisure time in personal fulfilment (Pred and Palm 1978: 108).

It is not only the suburban woman who lacks effective accessibility. Unmarried, divorced and widowed women with young children face particular hardship wherever they live because the coupling constraints imposed by the opening hours of day-care centres, nurseries and schools tend to limit job opportunities to a very narrow range (Pickup 1976; Pred and Palm 1978).

Spatial organization, community conflict and the quality of life

The geo-political organization of metropolitan areas has become an important determinant of the quality of neighbourhood life. To a large extent, the magnitude and composition of the 'social wage' – the benefits derived from public expenditure – is decided by the policies of local governments and their administrative bureaucracies. Moreover, the *de jure* territories in which these institutions operate can be seen to serve as a framework for the resolution of inter-community conflict over the resources which constitute the social wage (Cox and Reynolds 1974). In this section, therefore, we examine the evolution of *de jure* spaces at the intra-metropolitan level and discuss some of the major implications of the way in which space has been partitioned for political and administrative purposes.

Metropolitan fragmentation and the evolution of special districts

Modern metropolitan areas are characterized by a complex partitioning of space into multi-purpose local government jurisdictions and a wide variety of special administrative districts responsible for single functions such as the provision of schools, hospitals, water and sewage facilities. This complexity is greatest in Australia and North America, where the ethic of local autonomy is stronger, and it reaches a peak in the United States, where in 1972 the 33 largest metropolitan areas had an average of 268 separate jurisdictions. The most prolific city of all was Chicago, with 1,172 units, followed by Philadelphia (852), Pittsburgh (698) and New York (538) (Bollens and Schmandt 1975). While never reaching these levels of complexity, the same phenomenon can be found in Europe. In Britain, for

example, the Birmingham, Manchester, Merseyside and Tyneside conurbations were all under the control of at least four major multi-purpose local authorities until the whole system of local government was reorganized in the mid-1970s; the government of the London conurbation is still fragmented between 32 boroughs, with the Greater London Council presiding over them all as an extra tier of government; and in every city there are special district authorities which are responsible for the provision of health services and water supplies.

Much of this complexity can be seen as the response of political and administrative systems to the changing economic and social structure of the metropolis. In short, the decentralization of jobs and residences from the urban core has brought about a corresponding decentralization and proliferation of local jurisdictions (Soja 1971). New local governments have been created to service the populations of new suburban and exurban dormitory communities, resulting in the 'balkanization' of metropolitan areas into competing jurisdictions. In the United States, this process has been accelerated by policies which, guided by the principle of local autonomy, made the annexation of territory by existing cities more difficult while keeping incorporation procedures 'outlandishly easy' (Bollens and Schmandt 1975). New single-function special districts, on the other hand, have proliferated throughout metropolitan areas, largely in response to the failure of existing political and administrative systems to cope with the changing needs and demands of the population. Between 1942 and 1972, the number of non-school special districts in the US increased from 6,299 to 23,885 (Coates, Johnston and Knox 1977). As Stetzer (1975) points out, new spatial districts are an attractive solution to a wide range of problems because they are able to avoid the statutory limitations on financial and legal powers which apply to local governments. In particular, a community can increase its debt or tax revenue by creating an additional layer of government for a specific purpose. Special districts also have the advantage of corresponding more closely to functional areas and, therefore, of being more finely tuned to local social organization and participation. Another reason for their proliferation has been the influence of special interest groups, including (a) citizen groups concerned with a particular function or issue and (b) business enterprises which stand to benefit economically from the creation of a special district.

Although fragmentation can be defended on the grounds of fostering the sensitivity of politicians and administrators to local preferences, it can also be shown to have spawned administrative complexity, political disorganization, fiscal imbalance and an inefficient distribution of public goods and services. Not least of these problems is the sheer confusion resulting from the functional and spatial overlapping of different jurisdictions. Decentralized decision-making leads to the burgeoning of costly bureaucracies, the duplication of services and the pursuit of conflicting policies. Of course, not all public services require metropolitan-wide organization: some urban problems are of a purely local nature. But for many services – such as water supply, planning, transport, health care, housing and welfare – economies of scale make large areal units with large populations a more efficient and equitable base.

Problems of policy co-ordination and economic efficiency notwithstanding, Yeates and Garner (1976) suggest that the proliferation of special districts has in fact led to an attenuation of public control over public policy. Their argument is that the public is simply not aware of the numbers of different units of local government which influence their daily lives and that this lack of awareness leaves the control of most authorities to a self-selected knot of individuals and special interest groups. The balkanization of general-purpose government in the United States has also led to the suppression of political conflict between social groups. As Newton (1978: 84) observes:

Social groups can confront each other when they are in the same political arena, but this possibility is reduced when they are separated into different arenas. Political differences are easier to express when groups occupy the same political system and share the same political institutions, but this is more difficult when the groups are divided by political boundaries and do not contest the same elections, do not fight for control of the same elected offices, do not contest public policies for the same political units, or do not argue about the same municipal budgets.

This erosion of democracy means in turn that community politics tend to be low-key affairs, while the politics of the whole metropolitan area are often notable for their absence. The balkanization of the city means that it is difficult to make, or even think about, area-wide decisions for area-wide problems. 'The result is a series of parish-pump and parochial politics in which small issues rule the day for want of a political structure which could handle anything larger' (Newton 1978: 86).

Another unfortunate aspect of metropolitan political fragmentation arises from the competition between neighbouring governments seeking to increase revenue by attracting lucrative taxable land users. Cox and Dear (1975), who call this competition *fiscal mercantilism*, point out that its outcome has important implications for residential segregation as well as the geography of public service provision. In a fiscal context, desirable households include those owning large amounts of

taxable capital (in the form of housing) relative to the size of the household and the extent of its need for public services. Low-income households are seen as imposing a fiscal burden, since they not only possess relatively little taxable capital but also tend to be in greatest need of public services. Moreover, their presence in an area inevitably lowers the social status of the community, thus making it less attractive to high-income households. In competing for desirable residents, therefore, jurisdictions must offer low tax rates while providing good schools, high levels of public safety and environmental quality and pursuing policies which keep out the socially and fiscally undesirable.

Tiebout (1956), noting the different 'bundles' of public goods provided by different metropolitan jurisdictions, suggested that households will tend to sort themselves naturally along municipal lines according to their preferences for particular services and their ability to pay for them. It is now increasingly recognized, however, that a good deal of socio-spatial sorting is deliberately engineered by local governments pursuing mercantilist policies (Kasarda 1972; Newton 1975; Young and Kramer 1977). The most widespread strategy in the US involves the manipulation of land-use zoning powers, which can be employed to exclude the fiscally undesirable in several ways. Perhaps the most common is 'large lot zoning', whereby land within a jurisdiction is set aside for housing standing on individual plots of a minimum size – usually at least half an acre (0.2 ha.) – which precludes all but the most expensive housing developments and so keeps out the fiscally and socially undesirable. More than two-thirds of suburban Philadelphia, for example, is zoned for occupation at not less than one acre per dwelling (Johnston 1979b). Other exclusionary tactics include zoning out apartments, the imposition of moratoria on sewage hook-ups, and the introduction of building codes calling for expensive construction techniques (Babcock and Bosselman 1973; Danielson 1976). As Cox and Dear (1975) observe, the existence of large tracts of undeveloped land within a jurisdiction represents a major asset, since it can be zoned to keep out the poor and attract either rich households or fiscally lucrative commercial activities such as offices and shopping centres. Inner metropolitan jurisdictions, lacking developable land, have to turn to other, more expensive strategies in order to enhance their tax base. These include urban renewal projects designed to replace low-yielding slum dwellings with high-yielding office developments – projects which also have the effect of displacing low-income families to other parts of the city, often to other jurisdictions.

One of the most detrimental consequences of

metropolitan fragmentation and fiscal mercantilism is the *fiscal imbalance* which leaves central city governments with insufficient funds and resources relative to the demands for the services for which they are responsible. The decentralization of jobs and homes, the inevitable ageing of inner-city environments and the concentration of low-income households in inner-city neighbourhoods has led to a narrowing tax base accompanied by rising demands for public services (Muller 1975). The ageing, high-density housing typical of inner-city areas, for example, requires high levels of fire protection; high crime rates mean higher policing costs; and high levels of unemployment and ill-health mean high levels of need for welfare services and health care facilities. As a result of these pressures, many central cities in the United States have experienced a *fiscal squeeze* of the type which led to the near-bankruptcy of New York City in 1975 (Coates, Johnston and Knox 1977; Tabb 1978). Some have suggested that such problems are aggravated by additional demands for public services in central city areas which stem from suburbanites working or shopping there. This is the so-called 'suburban exploitation' thesis (Neenan 1972), although its validity remains in some doubt. There is no question that the presence of suburban commuters and shoppers precipitates higher expenditures on roads, parking space, public utilities, policing, and so on; on the other hand, it is equally clear that the patronage of downtown businesses by suburbanites enhances the central city tax base whilst their own suburban governments have to bear the costs of educating their children. The extent to which these costs and benefits balance out has not yet been conclusively demonstrated (Bollens and Schmandt 1975).

Fiscal crises of the sort epitomized by the plight of New York City in the mid-1970s are seen by Hill (1978) as an important catalyst for change in the political economy of central cities. He is not, however, optimistic as to the eventual outcome. One particularly gloomy scenario, which Hill suggests can be recognized in the central areas of cities like Newark and St Louis, is the emergence of what he calls a 'pariah city', a form of 'geographical and political apartheid – a "reservation" for the economically disenfranchised labour force' (Hill 1978: 228). Those left behind in the 'pariah city', he suggests, will be the poor, the deviant, and the unwanted, together with those who make a business or career of managing them for the rest of society. Scenarios such as this have prompted widespread interest in local government reform. The problem facing reformists, of course, is to reconcile demands for local self-determination and equity of service provision whilst ensuring that jurisdictions are large enough to realize the advantages of economies of scale. This problem is difficult enough to resolve without the resistance of existing jurisdictions to change: as Soja (1971) observes, the reaction of many to the prospect of consolidation or reform resembles that of nineteenth-century nation states encountering a challenge to their sovereignty. This attitude of 'sacred inviolability', fostered by bureaucrats and politicians with vested interests in the *status quo*, has been one of the biggest stumbling-blocks to local government reform. In England and Wales, for example, the administrative reforms carried out in 1974 did not embody the full recommendations of the preceding Royal Commission (the Redcliffe-Maud Commission) because of the political pressure exerted by those who had most to lose from the revision of geographical boundaries. Thus, for example, much of suburban north–eastern Cheshire, which is functionally part of the Manchester conurbation, was kept separate from Manchester as much on the grounds of tradition as anything else. Similarly, when Scottish local government was reformed in the mid-1970s, the Dundee area was denied its fiscally lucrative exurbs on the southern bank of the Tay estuary on the grounds that they were part of the ancient 'Kingdom' of Fife.

In the United States, local government reform has been more piecemeal, lacking the coherence of a nationally formulated framework. Honey (1976) lists a wide range of approaches to metropolitan governance which have been advanced as solutions to the problems of fragmentation and decentralization. These include: (1) the acquisition of extra-territorial powers; (2) the transfer of functions to a higher tier of government; (3) the institution of inter-governmental agreements whereby one sells a service to another or they jointly perform a function; (4) the creation of councils of governments; (5) the federation of governments within a clearly structured hierarchy; and (6) the consolidation of two or more jurisdictions into a unitary, multi-function authority. In addition, there are purely fiscal strategies which do not involve any territorial or administrative reorganization. The best-known of these is the 'revenue sharing' programme introduced by the Nixon administration in 1972, which provided for the allocation of $30.2 billions of federal funds over a 5-year period to state and local governments in an attempt to alleviate the worst consequences of metropolitan fiscal imbalance. Many observers, however, are sceptical of the effectiveness of these strategies. To date, spatial and administrative reforms have been rather tentative (Honey 1976; Reynolds 1976), and there are fears that fiscal programmes such as the revenue sharing scheme will be abused by local officials spending the money to satisfy their most influential constituencies rather than in the pursuit of a more equitable distribution of public services.

Metropolitan fragmentation and territorial justice

The extent of territorial disparities in public service provision in a fragmented metropolitan area can be illustrated with reference to the example of the provision of social services for the elderly in Greater London. From a geographical point of view, the 'ideal' distribution of such resources might be one that is in direct proportion to the levels of need in each of the 32 Greater London boroughs: a situation which represents what Davies (1968) has called 'territorial justice'. An examination by Pinch (1979) of the provision of home helps, meals-on-wheels, home nurses and residential accommodation for the elderly, however, found evidence of considerable variability in the extent to which territorial justice has been achieved. In order to quantify local levels of need for social services for the elderly, Pinch used an index of social conditions based on a mixture of variables measuring local levels of health, housing conditions, unemployment and socio-economic status, as well as the incidence of pensioners living alone. Levels of provision were measured both in terms of the *financial input* committed to each service by the local authorities and in terms of the *extensiveness* and *intensity* of the services provided by this expenditure. The extensiveness of service provision is taken to be the proportion of those eligible for a service who actually receive it (e.g. the percentage of the elderly who receive home helps or meals-on-wheels), while the intensity of service provision is evaluated in terms of the average amount of monetary or physical resources provided per recipient of the service.

Correlations between the index of need and a series of measures of service provision (Table 7.2) show that although the overall trend is for a positive relationship between need and provision, the situation falls a long way short of the criterion of territorial justice. Indeed, there are some aspects of the home nursing and health visiting services for the elderly for which the overall spatial distribution is regressive, as shown by the negative correlation coefficients in Table 7.2. This, of course, represents yet another facet of the 'inverse care law' discussed in the previous section (pp. 178–183). Most of the domiciliary services for the aged are distributed more equitably, although the correlation between needs and provision is far from perfect. This is illustrated by Fig. 7.9, which shows the relationship between Pinch's index of social conditions and the average net expenditures on residential accommodation for the elderly. Not surprisingly, several of the

Table 7.2 Correlations between Social Conditions Index and indices of provision of social services for the elderly in Greater London boroughs

	Correlations with Social Conditions Index
(A) Residential accommodation	
1. Average net expenditure on residential accommodation for the elderly and disabled provided directly by London boroughs and registered voluntary and private agencies on their behalf between 1965 and 1968 (per 1,000 population)	0.45
2. Number of persons (excluding staff) in residential accommodation for the elderly and disabled provided directly by London boroughs and registered voluntary and private agencies on their behalf on 31 December 1971 per 1,000 population of pensionable age in 1971	0.65
(B). Home-helps service	
3. Average net expenditure by London boroughs on home helps between 1971 to 1972 per 1,000 population	0.76
4. Number of home helps employed by London boroughs per 1,000 population of pensionable age in 1971	0.68
5. Number of persons aged 65 or over on first visit by a home-help during 1971 per 1,000 population aged 65 and over	0.81
(C). Meals-on-wheels service	
6. Number of persons aged 65 and over served with meals-on-wheels by London boroughs and voluntary agencies in a one week period in 1970 per 1,000 population aged 65 and over	0.67
7. Number of meals-on-wheels served to persons aged 65 and over by London boroughs and voluntary agencies in a one week period in 1970 per 1,000 population aged 65 and over	0.72
(D). Home nursing	
8. Average net expenditure on home nursing by London boroughs between 1965 and 1968 per 1,000 population	0.15
9. Number of home nurses employed by London boroughs in 1969 per 1,000 population aged 65 and over	−0.03
10. Number of persons aged 65 and over first visited by a home nurse during the year 1971 per 1,000 population aged 65 and over	−0.25
(E). Health visiting	
11. Average net expenditure on health visiting by London boroughs between 1965 and 1968 per 1,000 population	0.55

12. Number of persons aged 65 and over
    first visited by a health visitor in 1971
    per 1,000 population aged 65 and
    over   − 0.44

Source: Pinch 1979: 213– 18.

boroughs with poor social conditions (i.e. high levels
of need) and relatively low levels of provision are inner-
city jurisdictions – the likes of Islington, Lambeth and
Lewisham, where the fiscal squeeze has been most
severe. On the other hand, there are several needy
inner-city boroughs which provide a relatively high
standard of service – Camden, Hammersmith and
Southwark, for example. The explanation for this is
likely to be rooted in local political disparities which,
like the local resource base, are very closely influenced
by the spatial configuration of local government
boundaries.

Malapportionment and gerrymandering

The interdependence of local service provision, local
needs and local resources with administrative and

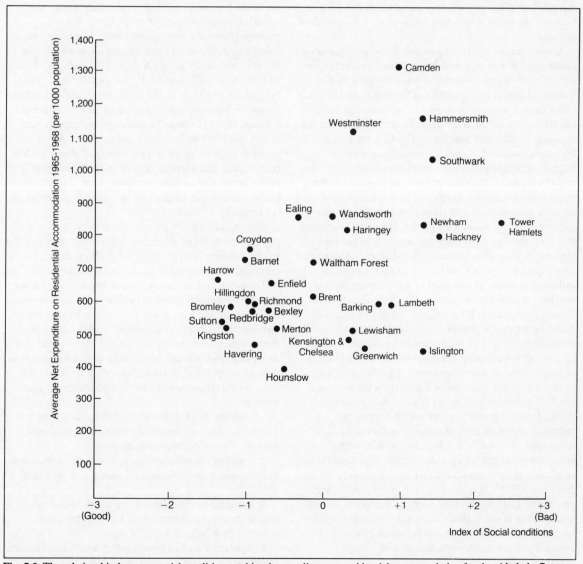

Fig. 7.9 The relationship between social conditions and local expenditure on residential accommodation for the elderly in Greater
London.
Source: Pinch (1979), p. 214.

political boundaries is by now clear enough. It must also be recognized, however, that the provision of local authority services is at least partially determined by the results of local government elections; and that these results are in turn influenced by the size and shape of electoral districts in relation to the distribution of the electorate. Put another way, a vote can be regarded as a resource whose value varies according to the degree to which it permits the voter to secure preferred policies (Cox 1973). This value tends to vary from one neighbourhood to another according to the individual voter's relative numerical importance within his own constituency. At the same time, it is a function of the marginality of his constituency in terms of the balance between the major conflicting social groups and political parties.

Evaluating the effects of geo-political organization on community power and well-being in this context is not easy, since systems of electoral representation and their associated spatial frameworks can be very complex. This complexity is compounded by the existence, in most countries, of a hierarchy of governments responsible for a variety of different functions. The Greater London boroughs discussed above, for example, are both independent multi-purpose jurisdictions and constituencies for the Greater London Council, which is responsible for certain aspects of strategic planning, housing management and slum clearance. They also happen to be constituencies for the House of Commons and they are themselves divided into wards for the election of their own political office-holders. A person may therefore find his vote much more effective in influencing policy at one level of government than at another. A further complicating factor is the electoral system itself which, for any given set of constituencies may operate on the basis of: (1) a single-member plurality system; (2) a multi-member plurality system; (3) a weighted plurality system; (4) preferential voting in single-member constituencies; (5) preferential voting in multi-member constituencies; or (6) a list system in multi-member constituencies (Taylor and Johnston 1979). It is not possible to do justice here to the potential effects of each of these systems on the geography of social well-being, nor to deal with their effectiveness in providing a democratic and equitable resolution of inter-group conflict (see, however, Johnston 1979b). Rather, attention is directed towards two of the more widespread ways in which the spatial organization of electoral districts has been engineered in favour of particular communities, social groups and political parties: malapportionment and gerrymandering.

Malapportionment refers to the unequal population sizes of electoral subdivisions. Quite simply, the electorate in smaller constituencies will be over-represented in most electoral systems, while voters in larger-than-average constituencies will be under-represented. Deliberate malapportionment involves creating larger-than-average constituencies in the areas where opposing groups have an electoral majority. Some of the best-known examples of malapportionment have been at the expense of metropolitan areas and in favour of rural-based interest groups in Australia and the United States (Johnston 1979b). In the United States, malapportionment of congressional, state senatorial and state assembly districts was ended by the Supreme Court in a series of decisions between 1962 and 1965 which began the so-called 'reapportionment revolution'. But malapportionment continues to exist at the city council level, and deviations in constituency size as large as 30 per cent are common in Chicago, Philadelphia, Atlanta and St Louis (O'Loughlin 1976). Deviations of this magnitude also exist at the intra-metropolitan level in Britain, effectively disenfranchising large numbers of citizens. If, as is often the case, the malapportioned group involves the inner-city poor, 'the problem assumes an even more serious nature. Policies such as rent control and garbage collection, and questions such as the location of noxious facilities or the imposition of a commuter tax will be decided in favour of the outer city' (O'Loughlin 1976: 540).

Gerrymandering occurs where a specific group or political party gains an electoral advantage through the spatial configuration of constituency boundaries. Not all gerrymanders are deliberate, however: some groups may suffer as a result of any system of spatial partitioning because of their geographical concentration or dispersal. Gerrymandering by a party for its own ends is usually termed 'partisan gerrymandering' and it occurs most frequently where – as in the United States – the power to redraw constituency boundaries lies in the hands of incumbent political parties. According to Orr (1969), partisan gerrymandering can be undertaken in four main ways:

1. creating *stacked districts* which usually have a grotesque shape designed to encompass pockets of support for the gerrymandering party;
2. creating *packed districts*, in which the opposition party's voters are concentrated into a few very safe seats;
3. creating *cracked districts*, in which opposition voting strength is fragmented, leaving them as a minority in a large number of seats;
4. operating a *silent gerrymander*, which involves the preservation of constituency boundaries over a long period, thereby creating malapportionment as the distribution of population changes.

It is very difficult to prove that gerrymandering has taken place: all that is usually possible is to produce strong circumstantial evidence. The curious boundaries used in Cleveland for the 1960 congressional elections, for example (Fig. 7.10) seem to be a deliberate attempt by Cleveland Democrats to concentrate Republican strength in district 23 (Busteed 1975). There is also considerable evidence of gerrymandering against blacks in US cities. O'Loughlin (1976) suggests that in cities with relatively small black neighbourhoods the most common type of racial gerrymander involves the creation of cracked districts, while in cities with black neighbourhoods large enough to warrant two or more elected representatives it is common for the electoral map to include only one black majority district, with the rest of the black area subdivided into white majority districts. Examples of the latter given by O'Loughlin

include the US congressional districts of New York City and Chicago, the state senatorial districts of Philadelphia and Milwaukee, and the city council districts of Atlanta. Finally, it should be noted that although the definition of constituency boundaries is left to non-partisan Boundary Commissions in Britain and some other countries, their efforts often result in an unintentional gerrymander which favours the majority party, thus reinforcing its dominance in the electoral assembly. Taylor and Gudgin (1976), for example, have shown how the application of the rules for the creation of parliamentary constituencies from an amalgamation of city wards by the fiercely neutral English Boundary Commission tends to produce a packed gerrymander in favour of the majority party simply because of the marked spatial segregation of the social classes which provide the support for the principal political parties.

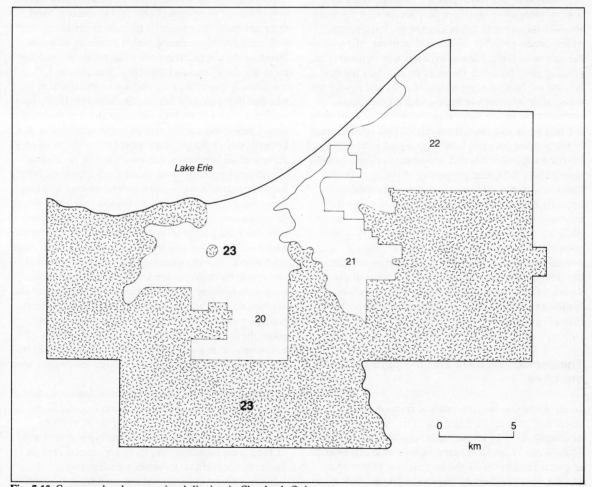

Fig. 7.10 Gerrymandered congressional districts in Cleveland, Onio.
Source: Busteed (1975), p. 10.

Chapter 8

POLITICS, PLANNING AND SOCIETY

Consideration of inter-group conflict over the location and allocation of urban goods and the spatial organization of the city leads inevitably to an examination of the wider political context. Indeed, a large number of geographers now accept that there is virtually no aspect of urban change or development which can be properly understood without reference to the nature and operation of urban power structures and political processes. For the most part, urban political systems are based on agreed sets of rules and procedures which effectively reduce inter-group conflict and confrontation to the routine and unspectacular ritual of the ballot box and council chamber. This routinization of the political process, however, should not be allowed to obscure the fundamental importance of local power structures to the social geography of the city. In this chapter, attention is focused on the relationships between different interest groups, paying particular attention to the links between the political process, the planning process and the structure of the city – both physical and social. We begin, however, with a consideration of the motivation and relative influence of the principal protagonists in the urban political process: voters, office holders, bureaucrats, business élites, organized labour, citizen organizations and special interest groups.

The democratic base and the para-political structure

In all Western cities, the political framework is structured around the democratic idea of power resting, ultimately, with an electorate in which all citizens have equal status. The outstanding feature of urban politics in practice, however, is the low turnout of voters at election time. Seldom do more than 50 per cent of the registered voters go to the polls in municipal elections: the more likely figure is 30 per cent, and it is not uncommon for the vote to drop to less than 25 per cent

of the electorate. Moreover, although data on voting behaviour at municipal elections is rather fragmentary, it seems probable that about a fifth of the electorate never vote at all. This passivity can be attributed to two very different perspectives on life. On the one hand there are those who feel that their interests are well-served by the existing power structure and who therefore do not feel the need to act; and on the other there are those who feel that their interests are consistently neglected or sacrificed by government but who feel they can do little about it (Saunders 1979). Such passivity is clearly undesirable from the standpoint of civic vitality; even more serious is the consequent lack of sensitivity of the political system to the interests of all sectors of society, since non-voters are by no means distributed randomly throughout the population. People living in rented accommodation tend to vote less than home owners; women tend to vote less than men; young people and retired people are less likely to go to the polls than are people in intervening age groups; people with lower incomes and lower educational qualifications tend to vote less than the rich and the well-educated; and recent in-migrants are less inclined to vote than long-term residents. This amounts to a distortion of the democratic base which inevitably leads to a bias in the political complexion of elected representatives; and, given the overall composition of voters compared with non-voters, it is logical to expect that this bias will find expression in municipal policies which are conservative rather than radical.

In addition to this bias, the formal democracy of urban politics is also subject to imperfections in the behaviour of the elected holders of political office. Although city councillors are ostensibly representative of their local communities, there are several reasons for doubting their effectiveness in pursuing their constituents' interests within the corridors of power. Apart from anything else, councillors are by no means representative in the sense that their personal attributes, characteristics and attitudes reflect those of the electorate at large. Even in large cities the number of people who engage actively in local politics is small and, as Hampton has observed in relation to Sheffield, they tend to form a community of interest of their own: 'they meet each other regularly, share common interests, and denounce public apathy towards their activities with a vehemence only matched by the suspicion they sometimes evidence towards those who seek to contest their authority' (Hampton 1970: 49). Moreover, those who end up as councillors tend to be markedly more middle-class and older than the electorate as a whole, and a large majority are men (see, for example, Hill 1970).

Notwithstanding these differences between councillors and their constituents, it is in any case doubtful whether many councillors are able – or, indeed, willing – to act in the best interests of their constituents all the time. Councillors with party political affiliations, for example, may sometimes find that official party policy conflicts with constituency feelings. Alternatively, some councillors' behaviour may be influenced by the urge for personal gain or political glory. A graphic though perhaps extreme example of this is provided by the politicians of the Democratic 'machine' in Chicago described by Rakove (1975). Their approach to politics and public office, coloured heavily by economic self-interest and the desire for power, leaves little room for the broader considerations of community well-being:

They have little concept of broad social problems and social movements. They deal with each other, and with the problems of the community, on a person-to-person, individual basis. They shrink from striking out in new directions, have no interest in blazing new trails, abhor radical solutions to problems, and, in general, resist activism of any sort about anything. 'I got two rules', 29th Ward Committeeman Bernard Neistein confided when asked how he operated so successfully in politics in Chicago for most of his adult life. 'The first one is "Don't make no waves". The second one is "Don't back no losers"' (Rakove 1975: 11).

Another doubt about the effectiveness of councillors as local representatives stems from the conflicting demands of public office. In particular, it is evident that many councillors soon come to view their public role mainly in terms of responsibility for the city as a whole or in terms of their duties as committee members rather than as general spokesmen for specific communities (Batley 1972; Newton 1976). Moreover, after election, 'a councillor's preceptions become increasingly socialized into ways of looking at things dominated by other councillors, and his views become more similar to others in his stratum of the political elite' (Davies 1976: 352). It is therefore not surprising to find that empirical evidence suggests that there is a marked discrepancy between the priorities and preoccupations of local electorates and those of their representatives (Table 8.1; see also Bryant 1975). At least part of this gap between councillors' perceptions and those of their constituents must be attributable to the dearth of mutual contact: one survey of 1,235 local councillors in England and Wales found that almost half of them had contact with less than nine electors over a four week period (Committee on the Management of Local Government 1967). Moreover, the bulk of this contact tends to take place in the rather uneasy atmosphere of councillors' advice bureaux and clinics, where discussion is focused almost exclusively on personal grievances of one sort or another – usually connected with housing (Helco 1969: Newton 1976). Personal links within the constituency

Table 8.1 Assessment by councillors and electors of the importance of local issues in Sheffield

		Proportion placing issue 1st, 2nd, or 3rd in importance						
		Total		Cons. supporters		Lab. supporters		Others
		Cllrs.	Electors	Cllrs.	Electors	Cllrs.	Electors	Electors
Issue:	*Base:*	108	584	48	198	59	300	86
		%	%	%	%	%	%	%
Provision of housing		62	49	46	55	76	45	52
Comprehensive education		52	25	35	22	66	26	29
Rent rebate scheme		43	37	54	30	34	43	31
Provision of education		35	27	38	29	34	24	31
Redevelopment		32	42	31	38	34	44	49
Roads and Traffic		19	53	31	56	10	53	50
Recreation and social facilities		15	13	2	11	25	14	12
Utility services		11	21	15	26	8	18	21
Closed shop for council employees		11	4	23	4	2	5	5
Local airport		7	16	17	21	0	13	12
Local radio station		1	6	2	6	0	6	3

Source: Hampton 1970: 207.

also appear to be weak. In Hampton's (1970) survey of Sheffield councillors for instance, only one-third were found to live within their own constituency, while less than one-sixth reported that a majority of their friends lived in their constituency. In short, it seems that the 'communion' with a district often claimed by councillors is more mystical than actual.

Bureaucrats Rule OK

Some writers have also questioned the effectiveness of councillors inside the city hall, especially in relation to committee work. Harrison, for example, suggests that many councillors overlook the wider implications of policy and resource allocation whilst devoting undue amounts of time to detail; and quotes an experienced development control planner as saying:

You get an old lady saying something . . . and everyone looks round and grins. They will spend half an hour discussing the extension to the back of a house and then an application worth a million pound goes straight through! (Harrison 1972: 265).

It is, however, the nature of the relationship between councillors and professional officers – city planners and the like – which concerns most commentators. Because of the increasing complexity and sophistication of urban administration, councillors have to feed on professional appraisal and know-how in a wide range of areas, thus placing the professional officers in an influential position. In theory, the expert professional is 'on tap' but not 'on top', but there are many who believe, like Max Weber (1947), that the sheer complexity of governmental procedure has brought about a 'dictatorship of the official'. Lineberry (1977), for instance, has argued that the influence of professional personnel and the decision rules by which they operate is so great as to effectively remove the allocation of most public services from the control of even the strongest political power groups. The crucial point here is that the objectives and motivations of professional officers are not always coincident with the best interests of the public nor in accordance with the views of their elected representatives. Although it would be unfair to suggest that bureaucrats do not have the 'public good' at heart, it is clear that they are all subject to distinctive professional ideologies and conventions; and their success in conforming to these may be more valuable to them in career terms than how they accomplish their tasks as defined by their clientele. The professional ideology of city planners, for example, centred on the trinity of Beauty, Health and Efficiency and with a veneer of technical sophistication, has encouraged some practitioners to become zealots, as if they believed they

were in possession of The Truth about urban systems; and it has given many more an evangelistic attitude towards the implementation of policies which emanate from the ideological fountainhead.

Some of the 'bureaucratic offensives' pursued in this way by professional planners are examined in the second half of this chapter. For the moment, however, the point at issue is the extent to which the democratic process is subverted by bureaucratic intervention and manipulation. Few would deny that a certain amount of essentially 'political' decision-making must be undertaken by professional officers because of the complexity and immediacy of urban administrative problems, but there is a growing body of opinion in support of the idea that the power of bureaucracy consistently outweighs that of the elected representatives. Dennis (1972), for example, concluded that the planners in Sunderland were quite out of control over most policy issues, while Gans (1972) and Goodman (1972) have written at length about the increasing influence of professional planners. There are several techniques which bureaucrats are able to use in getting their own way. Amongst the more widely recognized are: (1) 'swamping' councillors with a large number of long reports; (2) 'blinding councillors with science' – mainly by writing reports which are full of technicalities and statistics; (3) presenting reports which make only one conclusion possible; (4) withholding information or bringing it forward too late to affect decisions; (5) rewriting but not changing a rejected plan, and submitting it after a decent interval; and (6) introducing deliberate errors in the first few paragraphs of a report in the hope that councillors will be so pleased at finding them that they let the rest go through. In the graphic words of one councillor in Birmingham:

It's a subtle blend of bullshit and flannel and making sure things go their way. And writing reports. Report writing, I would say, is the most important part of their job. They put out so many reports that you get swamped by it all . . . Just look at this lot. That's for one committee. It's – what – about two inches thick. Well this thing may cost £200, and the other lot may cost three million. It may all be on the same size paper. Same size print. You've got to be on the watch for what's going on . . . It's all protective confetti to the officers (Newton 1976: 156–7).

The idea of politicians as part-time dilettantes, powerless to control ever growing regiments of highly-trained, technically expert and crafty officials is of course very close to the spirit of the 'managerialist thesis' outlined in Chapter six. But there is by no means common agreement as to the degree of autonomy enjoyed by professional officers. As pointed out in relation to housing managers, there are broad economic and social forces which are completely beyond the control of any urban 'manager' as well as strong constraints on their activities which derive from central government directives. In addition, it has been argued that the highest stakes in urban politics are won and lost in the budgetary process to which few professional officers are privy. Thus, 'having set the rules of the game', politicians 'can leave the calling of the plays to the bureaucratic referees' (Rich 1979: 148).

The para-political structure

Bureaucrats as well as politicians may in turn be influenced by elements of what Greer and Orleans (1962) called the *parapolitical structure* – informal groups which serve as mediating agencies between the individual household and the machinery of institutional politics. These include business organizations, trades unions and voluntary groups of all kinds, such as tenants' associations and conservation societies. Although relatively few such organizations are explicitly 'political' in nature, many of them are 'politicized' inasmuch as they occasionally pursue group activities through the medium of government. Indeed, there is a school of thought among political scientists which argues that, in American cities at least, private groups are highly influential in raising and defining issues for public debate (see, for example, Banfield and Wilson 1963; Kaplan 1967). According to this school of thought, politicians and officials tend to back off until it is clear what the alignment of groups on any particular issue will be and whether any official decision-making will be required. In essence, this gives urban government the role of umpiring the struggle among private and partial interests, leaving these outsiders to decide the outcome of major issues in all but a formal sense. The idea of a strong para-political structure is also central to the school of thought which subscribes to what Gale and Moore (1975) call the 'manipulated city' hypothesis. Here, the city is regarded as a distributive system in which coalitions of major private interests are able to operate the legal and institutional framework in order to obtain favourable resource allocations.

Business
Businessmen and business organizations have of course long been active in civic affairs. One of the more active and influential business organizations in most towns is the Chamber of Commerce, but it is by no means the only vehicle for private business interests. Lynda Ewen (1978), for example, has shown how the leading business families of Detroit are able to influence policy-makers and exercise social control through their presence on university, hospital and library committees,

and as prominent members of civic organizations such as the Detroit Urban League and New Detroit Inc. Because of its contribution to the city's economic health in the form of employment and tax revenues, the business community is in an extremely strong bargaining position and, as a result, its interests are often not so much directly expressed as *anticipated* by politicians and senior bureaucrats, many of whom seek the prestige, legitimacy and patronage which the business élite is able to confer.

The basic reason for business organizations' interest in urban politics is clearly related to their desire to influence the allocation of public resources in favour of their localized investments. In general, the most influential nexus of interests occurs in what Cox (1973) calls the 'downtown business élite': directors of insurance companies, department stores and banks, together with the owners and directors of local newspapers who rely heavily on central city business fortunes for the maintenance of their advertising revenue. The policies for which this group lobbies are those which can be expected to sustain and increase the commercial vitality of the central city. Given the widespread trend towards the decentralization of jobs and residences, one of their chief objectives has been to increase the accessibility and attractiveness of the CBD as a place in which to work and shop, and this has led business interests to support urban motorway programmes, improvements to public transport systems, urban renewal schemes and the construction of major amenities such as convention centres and theatres from public funds.

Labour
Organized labour, in the form of trades unions, represents the obvious counterbalance to the influence of the business élite in urban affairs. But, while organized labour is a major component of the para-political structure at the national level, it is rarely influential in the allocation of resources at the intra-urban level. It is true that union representation on civic organizations is widespread, and many union officials are actively engaged in local party political activities; but organized labour in general has been unwilling to use its *power* (the withdrawal of labour) over issues which are not directly related to members' wages and conditions. In Britain, Trades Councils provide a more community-based forum for trade unionists and are more likely to take a direct interest in housing and broader social problems, but they are concerned primarily with bread-and-butter industrial issues rather than those related to the size and allocation of the 'social wage' (Community Development Project 1976). The point is that organized labour in most

countries (France and Italy being the obvious exceptions) is essentially and inherently reformist. It has never posed a direct challenge to the interests of capital and the likelihood is that it never will. Occasionally, however, union activity does have direct repercussions on the urban environment. In Australia, for example, the Builders' Labourers Federation organized 'Green Bans' during the 1970s which held up over \$A 3,000 m. of development projects on the grounds that they were environmentally undesirable; and, on a rather different level, construction unions in the United States have resisted changes to building regulations which threatened to reduce the job potential of their members.

Citizen organizations and special interest groups
It is commonly claimed in the literature of political sociology that voluntary associations are an essential component of the democratic infrastructure, helping to articulate and direct the feelings of individuals into the relevant government channel (Almond and Verba 1965; Dahl 1967; Olson 1971). In spite of this, relatively little is actually known about the number of citizen organizations of different kinds in cities, whose interests they represent, and how many of them are ever politically active. There have been numerous case studies of pressure group activity over controversial issues such as fluoridation, school organization and motorway proposals, but these represent, as Newton (1976) puts it, only the tip of the pressure-group iceberg, leaving the remaining nine-tenths unexplored. This other nine-tenths encompasses a vast range of organizations, including work-based clubs and associations, church clubs, welfare organizations, community groups such as tenants' associations and parents' associations, sports clubs, social clubs, cause-oriented groups such as Shelter, Help the Aged, and the Child Poverty Action Group, groups which emerge over particular local issues (e.g. the 'Save Covent Garden' campaign) as well as political organizations *per se*.

Given the nature of local government decision-making, many of these are able to influence policy and resource allocation on the 'squeaky wheel' principle. This need not necessarily involve vociferous and demonstrative campaigns. The Los Angeles system of landscaped parkways, for example, is widely recognized as the result of steady lobbying by *Sunset* magazine, the official organ of obsessive gardening and planting in Southern California (Banham 1973). But not all organizations are politically active in any sense of the word. In his study of Birmingham, Newton (1976) found over 4,000 formally organized voluntary associations, from the local branch of Alcoholics Anonymous to the Zoroastrian society. Of these, only

30 per cent were considered to have been at all politically active, with social welfare, youth- and health-related organizations and trades unions being most active of all. It appears, therefore, that the bulk of the 'pressure-group iceberg' is in fact fairly passive. A typical example is provided by working-men's clubs, one of the most popular types of local voluntary organization in British industrial cities (Batley, 1972; Hampton, 1970). In Newcastle, Batley found that working-men's clubs firmly rejected the idea of involvement in community issues: 'It's not our job to get involved in politics. The members wouldn't stand for it.' Club committees were therefore expected, as Batley found, 'not so much to provide leadership as to manage the existing and traditional activities of the clubs. Even members' often-asserted pride in the co-operative self-government of their clubs seemed to carry with it a rejection of the outside world in which they were not masters.' Thus, 'In spite of their important social role in the local community, the workingmen's clubs were peculiarly defenceless' (Batley 1972: 103). Such passivity is of course a reflection of the passivity of the community at large. It should not be confused with neutrality, however, since passivity is effectively conservative, serving to reinforce the *status quo* of urban affairs. Moreover, this conservatism is not balanced by any real radicalism amongst the minority of citizens who are politically active. On the contrary, there is evidence to suggest that activists, like decision-makers, are generally more conservative than non-activists (Verba and Nie 1972).

Community power structures and the role of the local state

How are the relationships between these various groups and decision-makers structured? Who really runs the community and what difference does it make to the local quality of life? These are questions which have concerned political scientists and urban sociologists for some time and which have now caught the attention of urban geographers because of their implications for the socio-spatial structure of the city. There are two 'classic' types of urban power structure – monolithic and pluralistic – each of which has been identified in a wide range of cities since their 'discovery' by Hunter (1953) and Dahl (1961) respectively. In his study of 'Regional City' (Atlanta), Hunter found that nearly all decisions were made by a handful of individuals who stood at the top of a stable power hierarchy. These people, drawn largely from business and industrial circles, constituted a strongly entrenched and select group: with their blessing, projects could move ahead, but without their express or tacit consent little of significance was ever accomplished.

In contrast, the pluralistic model of community power advanced by Dahl in the light of his analysis of decision-making in New Haven, Connecticut, holds that power tends to be dispersed, with different élites dominant at different times over different issues. Thus, if the issue involves public housing, one set of participants will control the outcome; if it involves the construction of a new health centre, a different coalition of leaders will dominate. In Dahl's model, therefore, business élites of the kind Hunter found to be in control of Atlanta are only one among many influential 'power clusters'. As Dahl puts it, 'The Economic Notables, far from being a ruling group, are simply one of many groups out of which individuals sporadically emerge to influence the politics and acts of city officials. Almost anything one might say about the influence of the Economic Notables could be said with equal justice about half a dozen other groups in the New Haven community' (Dahl 1961: 72). Dahl argues that the system as a whole is democratic, drawing on a wide spectrum of the para-political structure and ensuring political freedom through the competition of élites for mass loyalty. When the policies and activities of existing power structures depart from the values of the electorate, he suggests, people will be motivated to voice their concerns and a new power cluster will emerge. According to the pluralist model, therefore, we may expect the interplay of views and interests within a city to produce, in the long run, an allocation of resources which satisfies, to a degree, the needs of all interest groups and neighbourhoods (Kirby 1979a): problems such as area deprivation are seen merely as short-term failures of participation in the political process (Eyles 1978). On the other hand, we might expect monolithic power structures to lead to polarization of well-being, with few concessions to the long-term interests of the controlling élite.

While the validity of both models has been widely debated, the central issue of 'who governs?' has been somewhat obscured by a lack of comparability in the techniques used to establish the nature of community power structures. Basically, studies using the 'reputational' type of analysis employed by Hunter have tended to conclude that community power resides in the hands of a business élite, whereas those using the 'power-in-action' analysis favoured by Dahl have tended to support the pluralist model (Curtis and Petras 1970). Moreover, a major weakness of both models is their failure to adequately deal with the relationship between the controlling élite(s) and the rest of the population. The crucial question here is whether the legitimacy of the élite(s) is in fact voluntarily ceded from below or imposed in some way from above. Both the classic models assume, implicitly or explicitly, that the passivity of the bulk of the population is a reflection of their voluntary acceptance of a relationship in which they follow the decisions of the leadership in return for the latter's pursuit of the 'common good', with the electoral system providing redress for any serious abuse of power. A number of observers, however, have rejected the view that political inaction is necessarily indicative of a consensus of interests between the controlling élite and society in general. Rather, it is suggested, this passivity is the net result of the suffocation of opposition within the political system. According to Bachrach and Baratz (1970), it is possible to recognize three main ways in which opposition to the policies of powerful élites may be defused:

1. the failure of disgruntled groups to press their demands, either because they *anticipate* a retaliatory response or because they believe it would be futile to do so;

2. the failure of those in powerful positions to respond to the articulation of political demands by less powerful groups. This may be achieved, for example, by establishing committees or inquiries which fail to report until years later;

3. the 'mobilization of bias'. This involves the manipulation by the powerful of the values, beliefs and opinions of the general public. Thus, for example, demands for change may be denied legitimacy by being branded 'communistic' or 'a threat to the freedom of the individual'. In this context, control over resources such as the mass media is particularly important. Given such control, the élite is able to restrict public consideration to those matters considered 'safe' and, as a result, the demands or grievances of some segments of the community may never be heard.

According to this view, therefore, the issues debated in local politics are no more than 'political crumbs strewn carelessly about by an élite with its hands clasped firmly round the cake' (Saunders 1979: 30–1). Such an interpretation suggests that we must look beyond the immediate apparatus of community power structures to the wider relationships within the organization of society itself in order to understand cities.

Marxist theory and the New Urban Sociology

In recent years an increasing number of scholars have turned to Marxist theories of political economy in response to the need to relate urban structure to the wider organization of society. This has led to the emergence of a 'New Urban Sociology', a 'New Urban Politics' and a 'radical' urban geography; although it should be acknowledged at the outset that the literature on the subject contains an eclectic mixture of views which sometimes disguises fundamentally opposed theoretical positions. This possibly derives from the fact that Marx himself was not especially sensitive to urbanism or spatial issues, and so it has been left to others to interpret and elaborate his work in the context of the modern city. It is, however, possible to outline those strands of Marxist theory and its derivatives which are more widely accepted as relevant to an understanding of the urban 'problematic'.

At its most fundamental level, Marxist theory turns on the contention that all social phenomena are linked to the prevailing mode of production. This is the material economic *base* from which everything else – the social *superstructure* – derives. In historical terms, the economic base is the product of a dialectical process in which the prevailing ideology, or 'thesis', of successive modes of production is overthrown by contradictory forces (the 'antithesis'), thus bringing about a *transformation* of society to a higher stage of development: from tribalism through feudalism and capitalism to socialism. Base in Western society is of course the capitalist mode of production and, like other bases, it is characterized by conflict between opposing social classes inherent in the economic order. The superstructure of capitalism encompasses everything which stems from and relates to this economic order, including tangible features such as the morphology of the city as well as more nebulous phenomena like legal and political institutions, the ideology of capitalism, and the counter-ideology of its antithesis.

As part of this superstructure, one of the major functions of the city is to fulfil the imperatives of capitalism, the most important of which is the circulation and accumulation of capital. Thus the spatial form of the city, by reducing indirect costs of production and costs of circulation and consumption, speeds up the rotation of capital, leading to its greater accumulation (Lojkine 1976). Another important role of the city, according to Marxist theory, is to provide the conditions necessary for the perpetuation of the economic base. In short, this entails the reproduction of the relationship between labour and capital and, therefore, the stabilization of the associated social structure. As Harvey has argued (1973; 1975), the social geography of the city helps to provide these conditions, so that we find 'a white collar labour force being "reproduced" in a white collar neighbourhood, a blue collar labour force being "reproduced" in a blue collar neighbourhood, and so on' (Harvey 1975: 363). An essential factor in this reproduction is the differential

access to scarce resources – especially educational resources – between neighbourhoods, since it helps to preserve class and neighbourhood differences in 'market capacity' – the ability to undertake certain kinds of function within the economic order – from one generation to another. The role of government is particularly important in this respect because of its control over the patterns and conditions of provision not only of schools but also of housing, shopping, leisure facilities, and the whole spectrum of 'collective consumption' (Castells 1977). Moreover, it can also be argued that urban neighbourhoods provide distinctive milieux from which individuals derive many of their consumption habits, moral codes, values and expectations. The resulting homogenization of life-experiences within different neighbourhoods 'reinforces the tendency for relatively permanent social groupings to emerge within a relatively permanent structure of residential differentiation' (Harvey 1975: 364). The division of the proletariat into distinctive, locality-based communities through the process of residential differentiation also serves to fragment class consciousness and solidarity whilst reinforcing the traditional authority of élite groups (Bell and Newby 1976), something which is also strengthened, as we have seen, by the symbolic power of the built environment. In short, the city is at once an expression of capitalism and a means of its perpetuation.

At the same time, however, it is recognized that the structure of the city reflects and incorporates many of the contradictions in capitalist society, thus leading to local friction and conflict. This is intensified as the city's economic landscape is continually altered in response to capital's drive towards the accumulation of profit. Residential neighbourhoods are cleared to make way for new office developments; disinvestment in privately-rented accommodation leads to the dissolution of inner-city communities; while the switch of capital to more profitable investment in private housing leads to an expansion of the suburbs; and so on. This continual tearing down, re-creation and transformation of spatial arrangements brings about locational conflict in several ways. Big capital, as Cox (1977) observes, comes into conflict with small capital in the form of retailers, property developers and small businesses in general. Meanwhile, conflict also arises locally between, on the one hand, capitalists (both large and small) and, on the other, those obtaining important use – and exchange– values from existing spatial arrangements. This includes conflict over the nature and location of new urban development, over urban renewal, road construction, conservation, land-use zoning, and so on: over the whole spectrum, in fact, of urban activity. Much of this conflict, of course, is formalized and routinized within the structure of institutional politics, but some writers have argued that crises in the provision and allocation by the state of various components of 'collective consumption' precipitate the development of 'urban social movements', or popular alliances (e.g. between tenants and shopkeepers) which operate outside orthodox political channels and which therefore, it is suggested, offer one of the principal sources of real social change in advanced capitalist society (Pickvance 1976a).

Underlying most Marxist analyses of the city is the additional hypothesis involving the role of the state as a legitimating agent, helping to fulfil the imperatives of capitalism in a number of ways. These include the defusion of discontent through the pursuit of welfare policies, the provision of a stable and predictable environment for business through the legal and judicial system, and the propagation of an ideology conducive to the operation and maintenance of the economic base through its control and penetration of socializing agencies such as the educational system, the armed forces and the civil service.

From these various strands of Marxist theory there has emerged a corpus of research which can collectively be termed the 'New Urban Sociology' (or, depending on disciplinary predilections, the 'New Urban Politics' or 'radical' geography). The principal contributors to this movement include David Harvey (1973; 1975; 1977) as well as members of the French 'school' of urban sociology such as Manuel Castells (1977; 1978), Jean Lojkine (1974) and Edmund Preteceille (1973), whose work has been introduced to the English-speaking world by Chris Pickvance (1976b) and Michael Harloe (1977). Some of this work has justifiably been criticized for its epistemological self-righteousness and a predilection for cryptic literary styles which all but an inner circle of *cognoscenti* find difficult to understand. But the overall contribution of the New Urban Sociology is clearly significant. It provides a clear break with earlier, narrower conceptions of urban socio-spatial relationships and a flexible theoretical framework for a wide range of phenomena. Much of this new work reflects national intellectual traditions as well as differences in the nature of national policies and urban development. A good deal of recent French and Spanish work has been concerned with the emergence of urban social movements (Castells *et al.* 1977; Olives 1976), whereas American research has tended to be concerned more with analyses of the fiscal crises of cities (Tabb and Sawers 1978) and British research has focused on questions of collective consumption at the local level (Lambert, Paris and Blackaby 1978). In general, however, one of the most fruitful themes to emerge from the New Urban Sociology is that of the role of the 'local state'.

The local state

Despite the clear importance of local government – even simply in terms of the magnitude of expenditure on public services – there is no properly developed and generally accepted theory of the behaviour and objectives of local government, or the 'local state'. Within the debate on this question, however, three principal positions have emerged :

1. that the local state is controlled by officials, and that their goals and values are crucial in determining policy outcomes (the 'managerialist' view);
2. that the local state is an adjunct of the national state, with both acting in response to the prevailing balance of class forces within society (the 'structuralist' view);
3. that the local state is an instrument of the business élite (the 'instrumentalist' view).

The first of these has, as we have seen (pp. 153–165) generated widespread interest and support, and it is clear that a focus on the activities and ideologies of professional decision-makers can contribute a lot to the understanding of urban socio-spartial processes. We have also seen, however, that the managerialist approach does not give adequate recognition either to the influence of local élites and pressure groups or to the economic and political constraints stemming from the national level.

Because of such shortcomings, attention has recently been focused on the structuralist and instrumentalist positions, both of which stem directly from Marxist theory. Although the flavour of discussion has been somewhat abstract and rarefied, it is possible to make some general statements about the putative role of the local state. Saunders (1979), following O'Connor (1973) and Cockburn (1977), suggests that the key functions of the local state are as follows:

1. The sustenance of private production and capital accumulation

(a) through the provision of an urban infra-structure of roads, sewage disposal, water supply, etc.;

(b) by easing spatial aspects of the reorganization of production through the planning process and the initiation of urban renewal programmes, etc.;

(c) by investment in 'human capital' through the provision of educational facilities in general and technical education in particular;

(d) through 'demand orchestration' which, through public works contracts etc., brings stability and security to markets which might otherwise be volatile and unpredictable.

199

2. The reproduction of labour power through collective consumption

    (a) by means of the material conditions of existence (e.g. low-rent public housing);

    (b) by means of the cultural conditions of existence (e.g. libraries, art galleries, parks).

3. The maintenance of order and social cohesion

    (a) through agents of coercion (e.g. the police);

    (b) through the provision of welfare programmes and social services to support the 'surplus population';

    (c) through the support of 'agencies of legitimation' such as schools, the social work system and public participation schemes.

Although this taxonomy of the functions of the local state draws heavily on Marxist analysis, it does not imply the acceptance of any particular theoretical position. Where the structuralist view differs from the instrumentalist view is not so much in the identification of the functions of the state as in the question of for whom or for what the functions operate, whether they are class-biased, and the extent to which they reflect external political forces (Saunders 1979).

One of the few detailed empirical analyses of the local state in this context is Cockburn's (1977) study of Lambeth, in London. She identified two dominant trends within the borough – corporate management and community development – and interpreted these as a reflection of the position of the local state in relation both to the national state and to business interests. As she points out, the trend towards corporate management was initiated by the central government in an attempt to replace the fragmented administrative structure of local authorities with a corporate approach borrowed from business. This meant the establishment of an integrated senior management team and a shift of power away from junior administrators and backbench councillors. But, while municipal efficiency was increased, the concentration of power at the top meant a decrease in contact between the local population and the power-holders. Apart from anything else, this reduced the feedback of information essential to the effective management of the corporate-style system. Moreover, the erosion of democracy, both real and perceived, tended to undermine the legitimacy of the local authority and encourage 'the managed' to seek sources of power outside the orthodox system of representative democracy. It was in order to remedy this situation, it is argued, that 'community development' (i.e. public participation) was encouraged, with the initiative again coming from central government. Meanwhile, the onset of the economic crisis in the mid-1970s revealed that the power of the corporate decision-makers in the town hall

was strictly limited, especially in comparison with the power of local property speculators and industrialists. Cockburn's interpretation of events thus generally supports the structuralist view that the local state, as a relatively autonomous adjunct of the national state, tends to safeguard the long-term interests of the dominant class (in this case, monopoly capital) while 'buying off' the working class through reformist strategies (Poulantzas 1973; Castells 1977).

The instrumentalist view of the local state derives from Miliband's work (1969; 1977), in which he emphasizes the significance of the class backgrounds of top decision-makers, presenting evidence to show that the social composition of senior positions in government, the civil service, the judiciary, the police, legislative assemblies and local governments is such as generally to ensure that the interests of capital will receive a sympathetic hearing. He also argues that the state itself is dependent upon continued capitalist accumulation, which it is therefore constrained to support. This, in turn, serves to enhance the leverage of the already powerful business élite which represents the interests of capital. These ideas have found some support in Saunder's (1979) study of community power in the London borough of Croydon, where 'the local authority's committment to private profitability is mediated by an interpersonal "community of interest and sentiment" which exists between leading politicians and top business leaders in the town' (Saunders 1979: 207).

In short, it seems that each of the three models of the local state – managerialist, structuralist and instrumentalist – contain useful insights which are relevant in some areas of explanation but less so in others. Put another way, none of the three models can be completely dismissed on the rather limited evidence available at present. Not surprisingly, some theorists have attempted to reconcile elements of the different models. One example of this is the work of Offe (1974, 1976), whose theorizing about the state in advanced capitalist economies contains elements of both instrumentalist and managerialist perspectives; but perhaps more relevant to the role of the local state is Pahl's later work on urban managerialism, which has led him to set managerialism within a general theory of the state. Pahl now distinguishes between local 'managers' in the private sector and those in the public sector, with the former being seen as gatekeepers in a very general sense, while bureaucrats in the local state are seen as performing crucial mediating roles both between the state and the private sector and between the state and various special interest groups (Pahl 1977). The details of these arguments need not detain us here, but it will be appreciated that the reconciliation of different theoretical perspectives is a difficult task. For the present, therefore, it seems reasonable to follow Kirby (1979a) and Saunders (1979) in suggesting that 'theoretical pluralism and epistemological tolerance' offer the most useful approach to the study of the city. It is in this spirit that we now turn to an examination of the implications and spatial outcomes of the relationships between the urban planning machine, the urban power structure and the community at large.

Planners, the city, and society

As Ruth Glass observes, cities are ' a mirror ... of history, class structure and culture' (Glass 1968: 48). The fact that cities are dominated by the huge buildings of commercial and state bureaucracies says something about the power of those bureaucracies; just as barracks-like public housing schemes say something about the relationship between those who put them up and those who live in them; and the range of facilities available in a neighbourhood says something about the economic and political importance of its inhabitants. At the heart of the relationship between power, society and the built environment in modern cities is the city planning profession which, through a mixture of default and intent, finds itself the arbiter between the interests of different classes.

The crucial feature of this role is that it has never been (and, indeed, cannot ever be) neutral. Although concerned mainly with improving the physical environment, city planning has for a long time been oriented towards certain people, even if only indirectly and implicitly. According to Gans (1969), these people have been the planning profession itself, its political supporters, and the middle-class citizen in general. Thus, he argues, just as architects often seem to design buildings with an eye more to professional acclaim than to the effects of their buildings on users, so planners have sought to create the kind of city they wanted. At the same time, the planners' ideal city reflects their own class-culture, leaning towards the promotion of solid, single-family dwellings and the creation of facilities catering to middle-class tastes. Finally, since planners have to work with an eye to the businessmen and civic leaders who sit on planning committees, they tend to work towards an 'efficient' city which is good for business. But

The planner did not realise he was planning for himself, his supporters and people of his class, however; he thought that by focusing on what he thought were desirable types of housing, business and industry, he was planning for everybody. As a professional he thought he knew what was best for the community and for people ... Because he was a descendant of a missionary reform cause, he never questioned his aims or his activities (Gans 1969: 36).

As a result, the planning profession has tended to proceed on the assumption of a value consensus when in reality society is made up of groups who stand to gain or lose differentially by different plans. A good example of this is the British green belt policy. Although it commands widespread public acceptance because of its conservationist aims, it has had a number of important side-effects conferring capital gains on property owners in or near green belts, increasing the need for long-distance commuter travel, increasing the housing costs of inner-city residents who are unable to commute, and so on. This, however, is not an isolated example. Simmie (1974) has argued convincingly that planning activity of all kinds is generally regressive in its effects.

Planning ideology and planning praxis

It follows from all this that, whatever the degree of autonomy ascribed to the profession as a whole (and this of course depends on the theoretical perspective one adopts), the key to the relationship between planning, society and urban structure is likely to be found in the motivation, ideology and *modus operandi*, or praxis, of professional planners. As we saw in Chapter two, the town planning movement in Britain grew from a coalition of sanitary reformers, garden city idealists, would-be conservers of Britain's countryside and architectural heritage, and farmers and politicians who were worried about the loss of agricultural land. Together, they had a bold and progressive vision which has subsequently been translated into a huge, powerful and professionalized machine. For all its progressivism, however, it was an essentially reactionary movement, in the sense that it aimed at containing the city and preserving the countryside from contamination by it. Patrick Geddes, the visionary inspiration of the emerging planning movement, saw cities as 'sprawling man-reefs', expanding like 'ink-stains and grease-spots' over the 'natural' environment, creating nothing but 'slum, semi-slum and super-slum' with social environments that 'stunt the mind' (Geddes 1915). Cities , therefore, were to be thinned out, tidied up, penned in by green belts, fragmented into 'neighbourhood units' and generally made as like villages as possible. In other countries, too, urban planning became a vehicle for the utopian and prophylactic strains of Western liberal thought, nurtured by a coalition of anti-urban interests. In the struggle to establish itself as a profession with intellectual standing as well as statutory powers, it

201

developed a 'great tradition', with heroes to match: Howard and Gedds were joined by Abercrombie, Unwin, Perry, Soria y Mata and, borrowed from architecture, Frank Lloyd Wright and Le Corbusier (Hall 1974). The assumptions which governed their approach to town planning and the arguments they employed in order to justify its practice have entered into the ideology of the profession, and their postulates form part of the mythology of planning to which all new recruits are introduced. *Ideology* in this context refers to the ideas derived from previous experience which are brought to bear on a situation in order to identify the 'correct' strategy in professional situations. The trainee is socialized into these ideas through formal education, meetings, journals and general day-to-day contact with fellow professionals. In relation to planning, for example, the descriptions of the trials, tribulations and final vindication of Geddes, Abercrombie, Unwin *et al*. given to planning students are not mere academic exercises in the history of the subject: they are the moral equipment of the professional planner, teaching him what to expect – which groups have been hostile to the growth of his profession in the past, why they were hostile, and what responses were successful in disarming them (Davies 1972).

In overall terms, the ideology of the profession constitutes the basic operating rationale by which the planner feels able to justify his own activities and to judge the claims of others for his sympathetic attention. It is also reflected in conventional planning praxis – the routine, day-to-day procedure for dealing with the problems which are considered to be within their sphere of competence. It is important, therefore, to identify the major strands of thought which contribute to planning ideology. Although these strands are closely intertwined, it is possible to identify five themes which have had a major influence on planning praxis everywhere: environmentalism, aesthetics, spatial determinism, the systems approach and futurism.

The theme of *environmentalism* in planning ideology can be traced back to the sanitary reformers, philanthropists and utopianists of the Victorian era. A brief outline of their background has been given in Chapter two and need not be reiterated here. Their major contribution to planning ideology has been the rather naïve assumption that the key to improvements in physical, moral and social welfare is to be found in the provision of facilities and the upgrading of the physical environment. As Gans rather disparagingly puts it, the belief is that

if poor people were provided with a set of properly designed facilities, ranging from model tenements to better work places and parks and playgrounds, they would not only give up their slum abodes but also change themselves in the process . . . The

founders of the playground movement believed that if the poor could be provided with playgrounds and community centres, they would stop frequenting the taverns, cafes, brothels and later the movie houses in which they spent their leisure time, and would desert the street corner gangs and clubs which they had created for social life (Gans 1969: 34).

Although crude environmental determinism no longer dominates planning ideology to the extent that it did in the early days of the profession, it remains a strong influence on planning praxis, not least in the prescription of all kinds of formulae and standards for achieving a satisfactory environment, both in the home and outside.

The concern with *aesthetics* also has a long history, stemming from the links between planning, civic design and architecture. Considerations of 'scale', 'harmony', 'townscape' and 'visual order' predominate here, together with a predilection for erasing blots on the urban landscape. Little emphasis is given to the economic or social implications of such objectives, however. An extreme example of the viewpoint is provided by Harrison, who quotes an exchange at one of the annual British Town and Country Planning Summer Schools. A speaker was asked if a planning application for a new factory in a stone-built village said to be dying for lack of employment should be turned down if it was not to be built in stone. The reply was that 'it was a question of the greatest good for the greatest number, and that particular village might have to forgo its industry if there were a greater number of people for whom the landscape provided something of eternal value' (Harrison 1975: 262). As with the environmentalist perspective, such attitudes are underlain by more than a little moral righteousness and professional paternalism. Opposition to the aesthetic judgement of the planner is derided as irrational or ill-informed, although how or why the planner himself should be superior is never explained, save for the invocation of professional experience. This, of course, is a flimsy and vulnerable qualification, since the criteria of quality in the built environment require constant redefinition. The 'ugly' may survive to become 'interesting' or 'significant'; what was once deemed to be 'harmonious and orderly' may later be seen as 'monotonous and mechanical', while the 'excessively vulgar' may become 'imaginitive and vital'. Nevertheless, the aesthetic strand of planning ideology has entered everyday planning practice in a variety of forms including controls over building height, the alignment of buildings and outhouses on residential streets, and even the colour of pigeon lofts and garages; while on a different scale it has undoubtedly influenced the way in which planners have approached slum clearance, redevelopment schemes and environmental improvement programmes. Perhaps more than anything else, however, it is reflected in the way in which the profession has embraced the *zeitgeist* of successive architectural messiahs such as Mies van der Rohe, Walter Gropius, Frank Lloyd Wright and Le Corbusier, allowing architectural fads and fashions to influence civic design at the expense of human use and scale. As Inglis puts it : 'Style for style's sake: the *zeit* for sore eyes' (Inglis 1975: 182).

Spatial determinism encompasses a wide range of planning wisdom whose common feature is an assumption that the imposition of spatial order brings social and economic benefits. This attitude is associated with a belief that one of planning's chief concerns should be with the 'best use' of the limited supply of land: hence the preoccupation with zoning, separating different kinds of land uses. A closely related theme is the concern with traffic and transport which, at least in Britain, was greatly fostered by the appointment of engineers to senior planning positions during the formative years of the profession. The logic here is that efficient traffic systems are fundamental to the welfare of all city users: businesses become more profitable, commuters become less frustrated and residents and pedestrians become less vulnerable to traffic hazards. Spatial determinism is also implicit in the concept of 'neighbourhood units' pioneered by Clarence Perry. The underlying assumption – and here there are clear links with environmentalism – was that the careful layout of roads, dwellings, precincts and amenities would lead to social interaction, the stimulation of feelings of security and stability, and the development of 'community'. Through this rudimentary social engineering, it was believed, the threats to social order implied by urbanization could be subverted by the creation of local social structures similar to those of traditional society (Bell and Newby 1976). Although the concept of the neighbourhood unit is now unfashionable, spatial determinism in general still remains a major component of planning ideology, partly because of the influx of geography graduates to the profession during the 1960s, bringing with them a whole kitbag of techniques of locational analysis and an academic tradition of concern with spatial organization.

Geographers have also been closely associated with the propagation of the *systems approach* in planning. According to this school of thought, the role of the planner lies in optimizing the performance of the city system, and the task is to be approached through the empirical analysis of inter-relationships and interactions (McLoughlin 1969). Stemming largely from the American planning vanguard, systems planning attempts to being together the all-round vision of the traditional planner and the techniques of operational research, systems analysis and cybernetics. Stimulated by the availability of new statistical techniques and computer hardware, the modelling and monitoring of urban economic, demographic and social systems have become objectives in their own right. Town planning is thus redefined as a distinctive method, a process of arriving at decisions rather than as a responsibility for a delimited field or as a substantive body of theory. It is an abstract process, which 'may be applied to many sets of circumstances, and is characterized by its analytical technique, its synoptic concern for the total environment, and its orientation towards problem-solving action' (Amos 1972: 305). Like spatial determinism, the systems approach has an aura of being rational, uncontroversial and 'scientific'. In reality, of course, it involves some of the biggest political questions of all, since it is concerned with the allocation of resources and opportunities.

An orientation towards the future is implicit in the very idea of planning, but the *futurism* of planning ideology involves something more than far-sightedness. It extends to a vision of a life-style based on planners' own class-culture and on an overly optimistic view of social and economic trends. Typically, this vision is dominated by the pursuits and concerns of the present-day rich, whose life-style is assumed to be aspired to – and attainable – by all. The resulting planning praxis is what Gladstone (1976) refers to as 'dream planning'. It is manifested in planning documents which are generously sprinkled with references to yachting marinas, golf courses and leisure centres, to the needs of households with second homes and second cars, to the problems of providing retailing complexes to cater for mass consumption on unprecedented scales, and to the urgency of remodelling the environment to match the spirit of the bright new future. Planning based on these conceptions is an expensive commodity, since it is the taxpayer of today who must pay for the planners' vision of the future. It can also be expensive in the wider sense for, in the urge to adapt society to its future rather than vice versa, planning has been seduced by newness, modernism, and technology *per se*. As a result, planning praxis tends to favour futuristic designs and schemes which exploit all the possibilities of the latest building and transport technology: as witnessed by the concrete slabs, girder grids and curtain facing of many of the city centres redeveloped during the 1960s and 1970s. Closely linked to this aspect of futurism is the profession's vulnerability to being 'captured' by one fashion after another: low densities; high rise apartments; urban motorways; no urban motorways; no high-rise apartments; renewal; rehabilitation; 'community'; high densities; low densities again; and so on.

Overlying all five major ideological strands is the mantle of what Davies (1972) has dubbed the 'Evangelistic Bureaucrat'. According to Davies, this mantle has been acquired by the profession in order to immunize itself against the persistent criticisms levelled against its members as a result of the conflicts which inevitably arise from the pursuit of their trade. It is related to a self-image of imaginative far-sightedness, selflessness, fairness and humanitarianism, 'beset by the carping criticisms of narrow-minded rate payers, greedy speculators, parochial councillors, apathetic citizenry, calculated vested interests . . . irresponsible young people, jealous rival professionals, reluctant legislators and twittering academics' (Davies 1972: 94–5). The mantle of evangelism allows the planner to turn a deaf ear to these criticisms. But it can also lead to what Cox (1976) has called 'bureaucratic aggression' – the relentless pursuit of their policies at the expense of 'defenceless citizens'. Such behaviour is compounded by the fact that once an idea or strategy has been floated it tends to acquire an almost autonomous life of its own. As Cox points out, once some actor in a situation decides to support an idea, he has in effect made an investment in it: an investment of his own prestige which he will be reluctant to see lost. At the same time, others will tend to judge the idea in the light of the support it has gathered as much as by its intrinsic merits, thus bolstering the momentum of potentially faulty policies.

Bureaucratic offensives: land use and urban renewal

Doctors, according to the old adage, bury their mistakes, while lawyers hang theirs. Those at the receiving end of the mistaken prescriptions and unanticipated side-effects of the bureaucratic offensives launched by planners suffer a variety of maladies. Urban motorways are a case in point. As Simmie observes, they penalize low-income groups in several ways:

In the first place they tend to destroy more poor homes than rich ones while at the same time employing funds which, among other things, means the forgoing of other opportunities such as the building of more local authority housing. After they are built, they do not serve the poor unless they possess private transport. Such is not often the case among the unemployed, the low paid , the chronically sick, the old and children (Simmie 1974:146).

It would be naïve and misleading to suggest that the net effect of town planning is consistently regressive, or that the sole explanation of those policies which are regressive is to be found in the inexorable machinations of a bureaucracy guided inflexibly by its professional

ideology. Town planning can justifiably claim to have advanced liberal reform on a broad front, the results of which have been expressed in a variety of ways in the changing face of the city. Space does not permit even a brief catalogue of these changes; but it is important to illustrate the way in which planning ideology can be translated into policies which have quite different effects on the fortunes of different neighbourhoods, and this is most readily apparent where evangelical zeal has been converted into strategic policies whose momentum has been sufficient to support the notion of 'bureaucratic offensives'.

One example is the practice of *zoning* parcels of land for specific uses, which stems directly from the strand of spatial determinism in the professional ideology. In essence, land-use planning, zoning and development control constitute police powers which have been designed to rationalize the urban system, maximizing efficiency and minimizing the incidence of public nuisances by separating each of the four major urban functions – commercial, industrial, residential and recreational. These powers have been acquired by planners in most countries and have been vigorously exercised by the 'getting things done' school of postwar planners. As a result, cities everywhere have become tidier: nonconforming land uses have been weeded out and order and stability imposed in their place. The benefits that this has brought, however, have been differentially distributed. Apart from the general reduction in the incidence of negative externalities arising from the juxtaposition of different land uses, the main benefits of land-use control have been enjoyed by the owners and developers of property. For the former, land-use regulations serve to secure and enhance the exchange value of property by reducing the uncertainty that new development nearby might be of the kind which would depress property values. For the latter, land-use regulations – especially the existence of an 'official map' of permissible land uses – serve to reduce the uncertainty involved in property investment.

On the other hand, the casualties of the planners' land-use 'offensive' have been the propertyless poor, the indigent, and inner-city residents in general. The excision of the traditional mixture of industry, warehousing and working-class residences in inner-city areas, for example, had hastened the decentralization of jobs, depriving inner-city neighbourhoods of their local employment base. The rigidity of land-use planning has also been criticized because of the consequent discouragement of imaginative development, the suppression of social interaction associated with uncontrolled 'organic' development, and the loss of the richness that is brought to urban living by the backstreet workshops, junk shops, embryo publishing firms, second-hand furniture shops, design studios and scrap metal merchants which are typical of inner-city neighbourhoods. The most regressive effects of land-use planning are associated with the American zoning system, in which qualitative standards as well as the broad category of land use may be stipulated. This has resulted in the use of zoning regulations as an instrument for reinforcing racial and class segregation (Danielson 1976; Mandelker 1971; Toll 1969). As we have seen (p. 186), many suburban municipalities stipulate large plot sizes or minimum floor space requirements to keep out low-income families as part of their strategy of fiscal mercantilism. But, while the motivation may be fiscal, the exclusionary effect is discriminatory in term of race and social class, serving to impact low-income families, the elderly, large families, welfare families (particularly those with a female head of household) and racial minorities in the inner city (Harvey 1972). Contrasting the fortunes of different groups in relation to land-use planning, Constance Perin suggests that zoning practices are a straight reflection of the social order: 'a shorthand of the unstated rules governing what are widely regarded as correct social categories and relationships – that is, not only how land uses should be arranged but how land users, as social categories, are to be related to one another' (Perin 1977: 3). She also goes on to point out that the adoption of complex zoning legislation by so many conservative city councils in the United States could never have come about if zoning were not so advantageous to powerful property interests – a significant point in relation to the competing theories outlined above.

Urban renewal can be reckoned to have been the focus of the biggest 'offensive' ever launched by the planning profession. It is not surprising, therefore, that the objectives of urban renewal conform very closely with several of the major strands of professional ideology. The dislike of the 'impure' associated with environmentalism has its expression in the first phase of urban renewal – slum clearance. It is the abhorrence of slum conditions and their effects on people's well-being that has given urgency to slum clearance programmes, thereby justifying a certain amount of evangelical aggression on the part of planners as they attempt to sweep the housing problem away in one fell plan, for the benefit of everyone. The second phase of urban renewal – redevelopment – serves to satisfy several more ideological urges. The removal of deteriorating housing from highly desirable inner-city locations allows the land to be given over to a 'higher and better use' (Rothenberg 1967), thus helping to fulfil the imperatives of spatial determinism. And the concern with aesthetics and futurism finds expression in the redevelopment

schemes themselves – architecturally adventurous, technologically advanced and visually and functionally integrated.

As with land-use planning, however, the benefits of urban renewal have been rather unevenly distributed. In excising the worst slums from city centres, urban renewal has undoubtedly contributed significantly to the 'common good' in terms of environmental quality and public health. But in rehousing the residents of clearance areas and replacing the built environment, planners have presided over some spectacular débâcles. The principal charge against them in this context is the dismantling of whole communities, scattering their members across the city in order to make room for luxury housing, office developments (including, in many instances, new accommodation for the urban bureaucracy), shopping areas, conference centres and libraries (Gans 1975). A secondary charge – urban blight – stems from the discrepancy between the ambitions of planners and what can actually be achieved within a reasonable future. During the intervening period, neighbourhoods scheduled for renewal are allowed to slide inexorably down a social and economic spiral. No landlord will repair a condemned house if he can help it; tenants who can afford it will move out; shopkeepers will close and drift away; and the city council, waiting for comprehensive redevelopment, will meanwhile defer any 'unnecessary' expenditure on maintenance. Schools, public buildings, roads and open space become rundown, matching the condition of the remaining population of the poor and the elderly (Dennis 1972; Wiener 1976). This dereliction has been extensive in many cities. Combined with the actual demolition of condemned property, the effect has been to empty large tracts of the inner city, turning its inhabitants into refugees. As Smith (1977) observes in relation to Liverpool, Lord Haw-Haw could never have envisaged, when making his dire predictions about the fate of the city in 1941, that the mantle of the Luftwaffe would be inherited by the city's own bureaucracy. Although this analogy is somewhat forced, it is not altogether misplaced. Large areas been laid waste and thousands of families have been displaced. Moreover, the problem has been compounded since, as the worst parts of cities' housing stock has been cleared, the bureaucratic offensive has gone on to condemn housing which is relatively sound, turning slum clearance from a beneficent if blunt instrument into a bureaucratic juggernaut. As Norman Dennis has described in his book on *People and Planning* (1970), the criteria for deciding which areas to include in second- and third-generation clearance schemes can be arbitrary, with the result that a substantial number of the houses scheduled for demolition are neither insanitary nor unsafe; and are consequently regarded by their inhabitants as providing a satisfactory environment.

These families have been the biggest losers in the crusade for urban renewal. By removing the structure of social and emotional support provided by the neighbourhood, and by forcing people to rebuild their lives separately amid strangers elsewhere, slum clearance has often imposed a serious psychological cost upon its supposed beneficiaries (Fried 1963). At the same time, relocatees typically face a steep increase in rents because of their forced move 'upmarket': the median rent of the families in Hartman's study (1964) of Boston's West End rose by over 70 per cent. In Britain, most slum clearance families are rehoused in the public sector, but this also brings disadvantages which may outweigh the attractions of more modern accommodation at subsidized rents. Slum clearance families must face the vicissitudes of a housing bureaucracy whose scale and split responsibilities tend to make it insensitive to their needs (English, Madigan and Norman 1976). Since they are 'slum dwellers', the new accommodation which is offered to them is likely to be in low-status estates. Even the offer of accommodation in new maisonettes or high-rise apartments may compare unfavourably with the tried-and-tested environment of old inner-city neighbourhoods. The open spaces, pedestrian pathways and community centres regarded as major advantages by planners may seem of minor importance to their users; while some such 'amenities' serve only as focal points of vandalism, souring the whole social atmosphere. Moreover, because much new residential planning has been guided by the objective of fostering 'community' feelings, problems of a different nature can be precipitated by the lack of privacy on new estates. Apartments and maisonettes tend to be worst in this respect, since common stairways, lifts and deck access mean that interaction with uncongenial neighbours is unavoidable (Dennis 1970). On the other hand, the planned and regulated environment of new estates has little of the richness of opportunity associated with older neighbourhoods. As Gladstone puts it (1976: 22), 'The death of pigeon fancying is spelt by the death of a place to keep the pigeons.' Finally, it is worth noting that not everyone from clearance areas ends up being relocated in sound accommodation, let alone satisfactory or desirable housing. Hartman's early study of rehousing in Boston, for example, found that over 25 per cent of families displaced from slum clearance areas were not properly rehoused. Furthermore, it transpires that renewal sometimes creates new slums (especially in North American cities where the public housing stock is so small) by pushing relocatees into areas and buildings which become overcrowded and therefore deteriorate

rapidly. This has principally been the case with black families who, for both economic and racial reasons, have been forced to double up in other ghettos (Hartman 1964; Anderson 1964).

The chief beneficiaries of urban renewal, apart from the planners themselves (who get the kind of city they want to see) are the dominant political and economic élites of the city. The former benefit from the existence of a much more lucrative tax base with which to finance public services, as well as the feelings of civic pride generated by redevelopment schemes and the symbolization of power they represent. One particularly well-documented example of this is Newcastle upon Tyne, where a unique Victorian townscape, as well as the less appealing housing of the terraced streets off the Scotswood Road, has been replaced by a city centre which earned the leader of the council the title of 'man of the year' from the *Architect's Journal* and led the city's politicians proudly to boast of the city as the 'Brasilia of the North' (Davies 1972). The dominant business élite, meanwhile, benefits in much more tangible ways. In his book on *The Rape and Plunder of the Shankhill*, for example, Wiener (1976) has shown how the redevelopment of Belfast city centre has served to benefit monopoly capital by wiping out small retailers, thus giving the big stores and large supermarkets the market they require. But it is the speculative developers of property whose interests have been best served by urban renewal (Hartman and Kessler 1978). Obtaining sites which have been cleared at public expense, they have been encouraged by planners to develop them for 'higher' uses – offices, hotels, conference centres and shopping precincts. The planners' 'Reconquest of Paris', for example, has resulted in the replacement of deteriorating housing (but not the worst housing, which did not happen to occupy prime sites), public facilities and public open space with large-scale commercial installations and office blocks (Castells 1977). Such developments have been highly lucrative, and it is therefore not surprising to find that, in many cities, developers have 'worked' the planning system in order to secure ever greater profits (Ambrose and Colenutt 1975; Sandercock 1976).

Planning and social welfare: area-based positive discrimination

In recent years a concern with social justice and social welfare has emerged as an additional strand of planning ideology in response to the changing climate of opinion within society in general and within the social sciences in particular (Eversley 1973; Diamond 1975; Healey and Underwood 1978). In terms of planning praxis, this concern has found expression in area-based policies of positive discrimination. Much of the impetus for this stems from the 'rediscovery' of poverty in the social sciences which was itself precipitated by the civil unrest of the 1960s (see p. 92). The existence of localized pockets of severe deprivation in large cities was recognized in a series of influential government reports in the latter part of the same decade. In the United States, these included the President's Committee on Juvenile Delinquency, the Report of the Advisory Commission on Civil Disorder, and the President's Committee on Urban Housing; and in Britain problems of urban deprivation were given prominence in publications such as the Plowden Report (on primary education), the Milner Holland Report (on housing in London), and the Seebohm Report (on social welfare services). Area-based programmes of positive discrimination, whose antecedents can be traced to Ford Foundation demonstration projects in the 1950s (Eyles 1979), were introduced on a large scale soon afterwards in order to complement existing welfare policies which, it was believed, were failing to reach the most deprived. There is now, as Donnison (1974) points out, a three-pronged anti-poverty strategy in most Western countries, aimed at: (i) *structural* effects (with policies designed to provide cheaper and better education, health service, housing, etc.); (ii) effects related to the *lifetime cycle of incomes* (with the provision of family allowances, old age pensions, etc.); and (iii) *area effects* whereby the spatial concentration of deprivation serves to compound and reinforce individual deprivations – the 'treatment' of which is undertaken through area-based positive discrimination. The latter is especially attractive to politicians and administrators, since it secures the major advantage of selective welfare systems (concentrating resources where they are most needed) whilst avoiding the major disadvantages (means testing and limited take-up). Furthermore, it also offers a means of staving off local unrest and discontent, combining maximum political effect with minimum public expenditure (Coates, Johnston and Knox 1977).

For these reasons, area-based policies of positive discrimination have become widely adopted. Following the Ford Foundation initiatives, the War on Poverty declared by the Kennedy administration gave rise to Community Action Programs (Kramer 1969); these were subsequently supplemented by other area-based programmes in the form of Project Headstart (an educational programme) and the Model Cities Program (involving localized demonstration projects encompassing renewal, rehabilitation, health and educational facilities, and job opportunities). The ideas involved in these schemes did not take long to diffuse across the Atlantic, albeit in slightly modified form

(Edwards and Batley 1978). In Britain, several important programmes had been established by the mid-1970s, including the Educational Priority Area scheme (Halsey 1974), the General Improvement Area scheme (Roberts 1976), the Housing Action Area scheme (Kirby 1977), the Urban Programme, and the Community Development Project scheme (Edwards and Batley 1978; CDP 1974). These programmes, and others like them organized on an *ad hoc* basis by individual city planning departments, represent an important new agent of socio-spatial change. As such, they merit attention in their own right. Indeed, it has been found that they operate to the advantage of certain groups and to the disadvantage of others even within their 'target' areas (Bassett and Hauser 1975; Duncan 1974; Kilroy 1972).

But, as the 'offensive' of positive discrimination gets under way, driven by planners' renewed concern over social welfare , doubts are being expressed in some quarters as to its real value in tackling urban deprivation. As we have seen (pp. 95– 100), there are important methodological difficulties associated with the social indicators commonly used to identify target areas. In particular, there is widespread disagreement and confusion about the concept of multiple deprivation itself (Edwards 1975). This confusion is critical, in that the model or theory of deprivation held by policy-makers determines the way in which deprivation is viewed, the causes thought to be operative, and the type of aid deemed most appropriate (Hamnett 1976). In fact, there are several explanations of deprivation, ranging from the concept of a 'culture of poverty' – which sees urban deprivation as pathological condition – to the theoretical formulations which interpret deprivation as a product of structural class conflict. Currently, there are five major themes within the social sciences; these are set out in Table 8.2.

The idea of a *culture of poverty* was first advanced by Oscar Lewis (1966) in the context of Mexico, but it has had a strong influence on the development of anti-poverty programmes in the more advanced economies on both sides of the Atlantic (Gittus 1976; Halsey 1974). Lewis himself described the culture of poverty as being both an adaption and a reaction of the poor to their marginal position in society, representing an effort to cope with the feelings of helplessness and despair which develop from the realization of the improbability of achieving success within a capitalist system. In short, it results in a vicious cycle of lack of opportunity and lack of aspiration. There is, however, considerable debate as to whether culture is more of an effect than a cause of poverty and, indeed, whether the values, aspirations and cultural attributes of the poor in Western cities really are significantly different from

Table 8.2 Differing explanations of urban deprivation

Theoretical Model	Explanation	Location of the problem
1. Culture of poverty	Problems arising from the internal pathology of deviant groups	Internal dynamics of deviant behaviour
2. Transmitted deprivation (cycle of deprivation)	Problems arising from individual psychological handicaps and inadequacies transmitted from one generation to the next	Relationships between individuals, families and groups
3. Institutional malfunctioning	Problems arising from failures of planning, management or administration	Relationship between the 'disadvantaged' and the bureaucracy
4. Maldistribution of resources and opportunities	Problems arising from an inequitable distribution of resources	Relationship between the underprivileged and the formal political machine
5. Structural class conflict	Problems arising from the divisions necessary to maintain an economic system based on private profit	Relationship between the working class and the political and economic structure

Source: *Community Development Project* 1975.

those of the rest of society (Gans 1972; Coates and Silburn 1970; Valentine 1972).

The idea of *transmitted deprivation* has also been influential in policy-making circles, having been adopted by Sir Keith Joseph when he was Britain's Secretary of State for Health and Social Security during 1972-3. It is really concerned with explaining why, despite long periods of full employment and the introduction of improved welfare services, problems of deprivation persist. According to this model, the answer lies in a cyclical process of transmission of social maladjustment from one generation to another. Thus, while it is acknowledged that low wages, poor housing and lack of opportunity are important factors, the emphasis is on the inadequacies of the home background and the upbringing of children (Bowlby 1965; Rutter and Madge 1976).

The three other models outlined in Table 8.2 all take a wider perspective, and each can be related to theoretical stances discussed earlier in this chapter. The idea of *institutional malfunctioning* shares some common ground with the managerialist school of thought, since the behaviour of bureaucrats is given a central role in explaining the persistence of deprivation. Here, however, it is not so much the 'gatekeeping' role of bureaucrats which is emphasized as the administrative structure within which they work. Thus, it is argued, the formulation of public policy in separate departments concerned with housing, education, welfare, planning and so on is inevitably ineffective in dealing with the interlocking problems of deprivation. Moreover, such organizational structures are vulnerable to inter-departmental rivalries and power struggles which can only reduce their overall effectiveness.

The idea of a *maldistribution of opportunities and resources* can be accommodated within pluralist political theory, with deprivation being seen as the result of failures of participation and representation of certain interests in the political process (Eyles 1978). Finally, the model based on *structural class conflict* clearly stems from Marxist theory, in which problems of deprivation are seen as an inevitable result of the overall economic order (Bor 1973; Miliband 1974).

While they are not mutually exclusive, these five models of deprivation do tend to point towards very different solutions. Those subscribing to the 'culture of poverty' model, for example, tend to regard expenditure on housing, slum clearance, income maintenance and so on as superfluous, advocating instead a concentration of resources on social education (Banfield 1974). Adherents to the idea of transmitted deprivation, although accepting the necessity for a broad range of anti-poverty programmes, emphasize the importance of the provision of facilities and services such as playgrounds and health visitors which help parents in the upbringing of children; while the solution to institutional malfunctioning is seen in terms of corporate management. Policies of positive discrimination are favoured mostly by those who see deprivation as the result of a maldistribution of resources and opportunities, whereas they make little sense at all in terms of the 'structural class conflict' model.

Interestingly, this last view came to be supported by those involved in the British Community Development Project initiative, which was established with the objective of tackling localized pockets of deprivation through 'action teams' and 'research teams' whose job was to co-ordinate personal social services in the field and mobilize self-help and mutual aid in the community. This kind of involvement, however, led the teams to conclude that

The problems of the 12 CDP areas are not reducible to problems of employment, housing, income and education. They are not isolated pockets suffering an unfortunate combination of circumstances. They are a central part of the dynamics of the urban system and as such represent those who have lost out in the competition for jobs, housing and educational opportunity... The problems in these areas are not going to be solved by marginal re-arrangements to take account of their special minority needs' (CDP 1974: 52).

This view, of course, made the original role of the project teams somewhat superfluous, and eventually the Home Office, embarrassed by the teams' activities, phased the whole programme out.

The CDP teams are not alone in doubting the utility of area-based programmes, however. There is a growing feeling amongst geographers (if not planners) that it is not possible to abstract the problems of particular areas from the wider societal context. Thus Anderson (1973), Lawless (1979), Lee (1976), Hamnett (1979a) and others have criticized the 'fetishism of space', whereby relations between social groups are viewed as relations between areas, and spatial causes are inferred from spatial manifestations. In addition, area-based projects have been criticized on the grounds that they neglect large numbers of the deprived who do not happen to live within deprived neighbourhoods (Glennerster and Hatch 1974; Berthoud 1976); that they are the product of a covert system of discretionary bureaucracy – with social indicators being used as 'vindicators' for planners' preferred policies (Brand 1975; Dennis 1978); and that they are merely cosmetic, serving only to 'gild the ghetto' and 'paper over the cracks' without touching the underlying causes of deprivation (Duncan 1974; Carney and Taylor 1974).

Planning, public participation and urban social movements

Given the generally regressive nature of much urban planning and the incidence of unforeseen and unfortunate side effects, it is not surprising to find one commentator observing that 'the contemporary city is cast from a split mould of which one side is avarice and the other systems analysis. Human values appear to have little or no influence...' (Smith 1977: 12). Nevertheless some attempts have been made to incorporate the values of the 'man in the street' within the planning process. Indeed, the idea of 'citizen participation' in planning can be traced back to the early 1960s: the Ford Foundation projects in the US laid considerable emphasis on the idea of local citizen involvement, and the idea of public participation was written into the Community Action Program section of the 1964 Economic Opportunity Act and the Model Cities Program section of the 1966 Demonstration Cities and Metropolitan Development Act (Kasperson and Breitbart 1974). In Britain, public participation was introduced on the recommendation of the Skeffington Report (1969), and planning authorities now have a statutory obligation to ascertain public reaction to major planning proposals before proceeding with them. In Scotland, an additional framework for public participation has been set up in the form of Community Councils – neighbourhood-based 'consumer panels' intended to ascertain, co-ordinate and express the views of residents to relevant public bodies (SDD 1974).

The official rationale for the introduction of public participation is that it is a mechanism for transferring power from government and the bureaucracy to the people. At the same time, it is suggested, the planning profession will benefit from an increased flow of information, thus making for more rational decision-making. It is also possible to argue, however, that the formal recognition of participation merely helps to legitimize the activity of planners, reinforcing the myth of a civic democracy whilst in reality providing the means by which the public can be 'managed' more effectively. Whatever the theoretical standpoint on this issue, it is now clear that public participation has not really been successful in accommodating the values and priorities of the public within the planning process. Although people seem keen on the idea of 'having a say', they do not seem so keen on getting up and saying it. Levels of turnout for the election of neighbourhood representatives for the Community Action Programs in the US for example, were desperately low: only 4.2 per cent in Boston, and 0.7 per cent in Los Angeles (Rubin 1967). In Britain also the 'silent majority' has remained silent even after having been assailed by expensive displays, broadsheets, newspapers (in 'popular' tabloid format), comic strips and door-to-door interviewing. A national survey of over 1,600 adults in 1974 found 70 per cent knew nothing about participation in planning. Only 7 per cent had been to public meetings, 9 per cent to exhibitions, 3 per cent had completed questionnaires and 1 per cent had been interviewed by planning officials (Jones and Eyles 1977). Moreover, the socio-economic composition of those who do become involved in participation exercises suggests that any influence that might be brought to bear on the decision-making process is likely to favour the interests of the propertied middle classes. Professionals, businessmen and owner-occupiers are nearly always over-represented, partly because they are better able to operate within the legal and administrative framework that exists for participation, and partly because working-class people are simply reluctant to join in this form of social activity (Cox 1976; Stringer and Taylor 1974). It has also been suggested that certain sections of the community lack the economic resources to sustain an effective contribution to participatory programmes; that some local political cultures are unreceptive to group activity of any kind; and that the effectiveness of middle-class amenity groups tends to deter the emergence of other groups with different social compositions. The net effect of all this, of course, is to 'accentuate existing disparities between the favoured environments of the powerful and wealthy and the degraded environments of the deprived' (Lowe 1977: 35).

For their part, planners have been less than wholehearted in their commitment to participation exercises. Although such exercises have now become a conventional part of the planning process, they are often regarded as a way of educationg the public into the planners' ways of thinking and not vice versa. As one British chief officer said in an interview, the objective is 'to tell the people what you are going to do . . . so as to carry them along with you' (Batley 1972: 107). The assumption, therefore, is that plans would be well advanced before being exposed to public comment. Verba (1961: 220) has described this concept of participation as referring 'not to a technique of decision but to a technique of persuasion'; and it is not difficult to find examples where the limits of debate are set by planners before 'participation' begins by the simple strategy of restricting consideration to clearcut alternatives. In this context, participation merely serves to legitimize the planners' own ideas. Thus Peter Hall, reviewing the West Central Scotland Plan, writes that it is 'an elitist plan, in which a perfunctory consultation exercise is used to support professional prejudice wherever convenient' (Hall 1975: 344). The reasons for planners' reluctance to enter into the spirit of participation are twofold. First, there exists within every bureaucracy an imperative not to waste resources of time, money and manpower, which results in a tendency to (i) consider a minimum number of alternatives, (ii) favour those strategies prepared in advance and 'ready to go', and (iii) restrict participation to as small a number of actors as possible (Downs 1964). Second, many planners believe that participation is an extravagance of democracy which undervalues their professional expertise. Eagland (1973), for example, suggests that basing planning decisions on public opinion would be like a blindfolded man 'picking his football pool selection with a pin'. Others, such as Powell (1973), argue that the preference of different

groups will cancel each other out or, at best, produce only a broad and indecisive picture which can only be resolved by the planner's expertise.

The complacent vanity of these sentiments fits well with Davies' (1972) image of the evangelistic bureaucrat, while the perfunctory nature of some participation exercises lends support to Scott Greer's description of planning as 'sympathetic magic and public ritual' (Greer 1971: 261). Moreover, the idea of participation itself has been criticized on a number of grounds. Apart from the bias towards middle-class interests which results from their over-representation and the bias towards planners' predilections ensured by the restriction of discussion, the main charge is that participation programmes simply serve to co-opt and disarm opposition to the ruling élite. In relation to citizen involvement in the United States Community Action Program, for example, it has been suggested that the result has been to skim off the local leadership of deprived communities, to divert 'troublemakers', and to encourage compromise and conciliation in return for minimal concessions (Coit 1978). Similarly, the role of the new Scottish community council system has been questioned on the grounds of its potential as a locus for a small community élite, as an intelligence system for more effective evangelism, bureaucratic aggression and obstruction, and as part of the planners' ideology of localism, in which the place-oriented organization of society helps to maintain an inegalitarian social structure. 'In this context, community councils would be seen as internal survival mechanisms of local government, helping an elite oligarchy to preserve power by internalizing opposing forces (such as action groups, squatters and tenants associations) which would otherwise exist outside orthodox political structures and therefore pose a volatile, less manageable and more dangerous threat to the *status quo*' (Knox 1978a: 391).

Advocacy planning, bureaucratic guerrillas and urban social movements

One of the intrinsic weaknesses of the idea of citizen involvement in the planning process is that the very groups who are most disadvantaged by the traditional system find themselves least able to communicate with people who insist on speaking the language of statistics, diagrams, maps and computers. An awareness of this situation, together with a recognition of the regressive effects of planning in general has prompted the introduction of *advocacy planning* : the use of experts by neighbourhood organizations and special interest groups to articulate their needs and make their case in the technical language of professional planners (Davidoff 1965; Peattie 1968). In practice, two kinds of advocacy planning have emerged. One is where experts are retained by individual groups to prepare plans for them and to argue for their adoption much as a lawyer pleads for his client. The other is where a 'clientless' professional activates a group because he or she feels that an important community issue is not being properly dealt with (Kasperson and Breitbart 1974). Both kinds rely on individuals whose ideology is very different from that of the mainstream, 'traditional' planners. In particular, they question the objectivity of many evaluative planning techniques, reject the idea that the existing political system can accommodate all the conflicting interest groups which exist in the city, and deny the planner's role as a neutral mediator.

A good deal of advocacy planning has focused on specific issues involving urban renewal schemes and plans for the construction of motorways through low-income neighbourhoods (Blecher 1971; Corey 1972), although there have also been attempts to broaden the scope of advocacy activities. These include the work of the Suburban Action Institute in New York (Davidoff, Davidoff and Gold 1970) and the Detroit Geographical Expedition. The latter, under the leadership of William Bunge in the late 1960s and early 1970s, attempted to train 'folk geographers' from local black and poor-white communities to control their own research and come up with their own planning proposals as part of a broad attempt to expand the power base of such communities (Bunge 1971; Colenutt 1971). In general, however, advocacy planning has achieved only limited success. While it has been reasonably effective in blocking the implementation of official plans it has not been particularly successful in winning acceptance for alternative proposals drawn from community groups. This has brought about a certain amount of disillusionment with advocacy. Goodman, for example, having been a supporter of advocacy as a means of ensuring that the inarticulate poor obtain their legal, welfare and planning rights, now feels that it simply promulgates the myth that only professional knowledge can solve the problems of the poor (Goodman 1972). Such feelings have led some to abandon the role of advocate in favour of that of the *bureaucratic guerrilla*, working covertly in the interests of deprived communities whilst in the employment of the city bureaucracy. One example of such activity given by Hartnett (1975) is of a local authority employee in London who was sympathetic to the aims of the Southwark Family Squatting Association, which had been protesting against the policy of Southwark Borough Council of acquiring property for redevelopment and keeping it vacant for periods of up to five years prior to demolition, all in the context of an acute local shortage of housing. The borough refused to negotiate with the Squatting Association and adopted

the policy of gutting most of its short-life housing, blocking drains and sewers and pulling up floorboards. In addition, public statements systematically understated the number of council-owned properties that were kept empty. The 'bureaucratic guerrilla', feeling that these policies were aggravating the housing crisis, supplied information to the squatters on the number and location of suitable empty properties acquired by the borough. After an unsuccessful witch-hunt the borough, finding its position undermined, signed an agreement with the Squatting Association whereby the Association would rehabilitate, with volunteer labour, properties the borough considered uneconomic to let.

As with advocacy planning, however, the achievements of bureaucratic guerrillas have been modest. Quite simply, it is difficult to work effectively within the system when the cause of the problem is often the system itself. Furthermore, critics of both advocacy planning and the idea of guerrilla tactics have stressed the limitations of their 'fire-fighting' role in reacting to issues raised by official policy. This, it is argued, has limited change to palliative adjustments within the existing social, economic and political system, at the same time serving to divert the poor from more effective forms of gaining power. A second general criticism concerns the lack of involvement of the disadvantaged themselves in deciding upon the strategies with which to counter the policies of the bureaucracy, thereby placing the advocate planner/guerrilla in a position of undue power and leaving powerless communities just as vulnerable to manipulation after their departure as they had been originally. This leads, in turn, to a third criticism: the danger of group opinion being moulded to fit the advocate's own conception of what the community's desires should be (Kasperson and Breitbart 1974; Marris and Rein 1973).

These criticisms inevitably raise the question of whether it is possible for disadvantaged groups to achieve greater power in the modern city and, if so, how. Piven and Cloward (1977), reviewing the activities of 'poor people's movements', observe that most attempts to achieve greater power are based on the conviction that formal organization is the key to success. This conviction, they suggest, is based on the assumption that formal organization facilitates the co-ordination of the economic and political resources of large numbers of people who separately have few such resources. Formal organization also permits the strategic use of these resources in political conflict and helps to ensure the continuity of lower-class mobilization over time. Their conclusion, however, is that this concern for organization serves only to blunt and curb the disruptive force which lower-class communities are sometimes able to mobilize, and that 'leaders and organizers of the lower classes act in the end to facilitate the efforts of the elites to channel the insurgent masses into normal politics, believing all the while that they are taking the long and arduous but certain road to power' (Piven and Cloward 1977: 12). In contrast, Castells (1977) regards organization as crucial to the success of urban social movements; although he does not regard it as sufficient in itself. According to his 'theory' of urban social movements, the vital rupture to the political *status quo* will result from crises in the provision of the means of collective consumption, whose effects will injure the middle as well as working classes. Thus, it is argued, the middle class needs hospitals, uses public transport (especially commuter rail links), sends its children to state schools, and so on just as the working class does; and conflict over the provision of such facilities provides the opportunity for a new kind of class struggle, with urban social movements being based on a broad alliance of anti-capitalistic classes rather than on the proletariat alone. The significance of such movements is therefore twofold: they open up new fronts in the class struggle as well as creating new alliances.

Supporters of this argument have found encouragement in a series of events during the 1970s in continental Europe. In Paris, lower-class groups have mobilized against evictions and the commercial redevelopment of their neighbourhoods (Olives 1976; Castells 1977); in Copenhagen, citizens have organized to force the city authorities to increase facilities and initiate improvements (Gamst-Nielsen 1974); and in the major industrial cities of Italy there has been widespread occupation of newly built public housing as well as the 'autoreduction' of public utility rates by users – that is, the refusal to pay more than a proportion of the price of public transport, telephones, rents, etc. (Coit 1978). Little empirical work is yet available on the emergence of urban social movements in Britain, North America or Australasia, although Castells's ideas have found a receptive audience in many quarters. Nevertheless, there are several reasons for doubting the relevance of his analysis to the situation within cities of the English-speaking world. The evidence to hand for these cities suggests that most urban struggles, including squatting movements, rent strikes and campaigns against disruptive planning proposals, are generally sporadic and isolated both from each other and the working-class movement. Indeed, the most successful struggles have usually been those of the middle class, which have resulted in a redistribution of resources away from more disadvantaged areas. On the continent, working-class radicalism is much stronger, and in several countries there exist well-organized communist parties capable of integrating sporadic urban protest movements into the broader political arena.

REFERENCES AND BIBLIOGRAPHY

Aaron, H.J. (1972) *Shelter and subsidies*, The Brookings Institution, Washington, DC.

Aase, A. (1978) Interregional and interurban variations in levels of living, paper delivered to the joint seminar of the Committee for Space Economy and Planning at Polska Akademia Nauk and the Norden Section of the Regional Science Association, Kazimierz, Poland.

Abler, R., Janelle, D., Philbrick, A. and **Sommer, J.** (eds) (1975) *Human Geography in a Shrinking World*, Duxbury Press, North Scituate, Mass.

Abrams, M. (1973) Subjective social indicators, *Social Trends*, **4**, 35–50.

Abrams, P. and **Wrigley, E.A.** (eds) (1978) *Towns in Societies*, Cambridge University Press, Cambridge.

Abrams, R.H. (1943) Residential propinquity as a factor in marriage selection, *American Sociological Review*, **8**, 288–94.

Abu-Lughod, J.L. (1969) Testing the theory of social area analysis: the ecology of Cairo, Egypt, *American Sociological Review*, **34**, 198–212.

Abu-Lughod, J.L. and **Foley, M.M.** (1960) Consumer strategies, pp. 387–447 in Foote, N., Abu-Lughod, J.L., Foley, M.M. and Winnick, L. (eds), *Housing Choices and Constraints*, McGraw-Hill, New York.

Adams, J.S. (1969) Directional bias in intra-urban migration, *Economic Geography*, **45**, 302–23.

Adams, J.S. (1970) Residential structure of Midwestern cities, *Annals, Association of American Geographers*, **60**, 37–62.

Adams, J.S. (1973) *New homes, vacancy chains and housing sub-markets in the Twin City Area*, Center for Urban and Regional Affairs, University of Minnesota, Minneapolis.

Adams, J.S. (ed.) (1976) *Urban Policymaking and Metropolitan Dynamics*, Ballinger, Cambridge, Mass.

Adams, J.S. and **Gilder, K.** (1976) Household location and intra-urban migration, pp. 159–93 in Herbert, D. and Johnston, R.J. (eds) *Social Areas in Cities*, Vol. 1, Spatial Processes and Form, Wiley, Chichester.

Aiken, M. and **Alford, R.R.** (1970) Community structure and innovation: the case of public housing, *American Political Science Review*, **64**, 843–64.

Alihan, M.M. (1938) *Social Ecology: A Critical Analysis*, Columbia University Press, New York.

Allan, C.M. (1965) The genesis of British urban redevelopment with special reference to Glasgow, *Economic History Review*, **18**, 598–613.

Almond, G.A. and **Verba, S.** (1965) *The Civic Culture*, Little, Brown, Boston.

Alonso, W. (1960) A theory of the urban land market, *Papers and Proceedings of the Regional Science Association*, **6**, 149–58.

Alonso, W. (1964) The historic and structural theories of urban form: their implications for urban renewal, *Land Economics*, **40**, 227–31.

Ambrose, P. (1976) *The Land Market and the Housing System*, Working Paper No. 3, Department of Urban and Regional Studies, University of Sussex, Brighton.

Ambrose, P. (1977a) Access and spatial inequality, pp. 91–123, in *Values Relevance and Policy*, Units 22–24, Course D204, Open University Press, Milton Keynes.

Ambrose, P. (1977b) The determinants of urban land use change, *Values, Relevance and Policy*, Section III, Unit 26, Open University Press, Milton Keynes.

Ambrose, P. and **Colenutt, R.** (1975) *The Property Machine*, Penguin, Harmondsworth.

American Institute of Public Opinion (1973) *Gallup Opinion Index*, American Institute of Public Opinion, Princeton, N.J.

Amos, F.J.C. (1972) The development of the planning process, *Journal of the Royal Town Planning Institute*, **58**, 341–3.

Anderson, J. (1973) Ideology in geography: an introduction, *Antipode*, **5**, 1–6.

Anderson, J. (1977) *Engels' Manchester: Industrialization, Workers' Housing and Urban Ideologies*, Architectural Association, Political Economy of Cities and Regions, No. 1.

Anderson, M. (1964) *The Federal Bulldozer*, M.I.T. Press, Cambridge, Mass.

Anderson, T.R. (1962) Social and economic factors affecting the location of residential neighbourhoods, *Papers and Proceedings of the Regional Science Association*, **9**, 161–70.

Anderson, T.R. and **Bean, L.L.** (1961) The Shevky-Bell social areas: confirmation of results and a reinterpretation, *Social Forces*, **40**, 119–24.

Anderson, T.R. and **Egeland, J.A.** (1961) spatial aspects of social area analysis, *American Sociological Review*, **36**, 392–9.

Antunes, G.E. and **Plumlee, J.P.** (1977) The distribution of an urban public service: ethnicity, socio-economic status and bureaucracy as determinants of the quality of neighbourhood streets, *Urban Affairs Quarterly*, **12**, 312–32.

Appleyard, D. (1970) Styles and methods of structuring a city, *Environment and Behaviour*, **2**, 100–117.

213

Arbuthnot, J. (1977) The roles of attitudinal and personality variables in the prediction of environmental behaviour and knowledge, *Environment and Behaviour*, **9**, 217–32.

Ardrey, R. (1966) *The Territorial Imperative*, Atheneum, New York.

Ardrey, R. (1970) *The Social Contract*, Delta, New York.

Arensberg, C.M. (1937) *The Irish Countryman*, Macmillan, London.

Arrow, K.J. (1951) *Social Choice and Individual Values*, Wiley, New York.

Ashworth, W. (1954) *The Genesis of Modern British Town Planning*, Routledge & Kegan Paul, London.

Babcock, R.F. and **Bosselman, F.P.** (1973) *Exclusionary Zoning*, Praeger, New York.

Bachrach, P. and **Baratz, M.** (1970) *Power and Poverty*, Oxford University Press, London.

Baldassare, M. and **Fischer, C.S.** (1975) Suburban life: powerlessness and need for affiliation, *Urban Affairs Quarterly*, (March), 314–26.

Baldassare, M. and **Fischer, C.S.** (1976) The relevance of crowding experiments to urban studies, pp. 85–99 in Stokols, D. (ed.), *Psychological Perspectives on Environment and Behaviour*, Plenum Press, New York.

Baldwin, J. (1975) Urban criminality and the problem estate, *Local Government Studies*, **1**, 12–20.

Baldwin, J., Bottoms, A.E. and **Walker, M.A.** (1976) *The Urban Criminal*, Tavistock, London.

Ball, M.J. (1973) Recent empirical work on the determination of relative house prices, *Urban Studies*, **10**, 213–23.

Ball, M.J. and **Kirwan, R.M.** (1977) Accessibility and supply constraints in the urban housing market, *Urban Studies*, **14**, 11–32.

Banfield, E.C. (1974) *The Unheavenly City Revisited*, Little, Brown, Boston.

Banfield, E.C. and **Wilson, J.Q.** (1963) *City Politics*, Harvard University Press and M.I.T. Press, Cambridge, Mass.

Banham, R. (1973) *Los Angeles: The Architecture of Four Ecologies*, Penguin, Harmondsworth.

Barbolet, R.H. (1969) *Housing classes and the socio-ecological system*, University Working Paper No. 4, Centre for Environmental Studies, London.

Barnes, J.A. (1954) Class and community in a Norwegian island parish, *Human Relations*, 7, 39–58.

Barnett, J.R. (1978) Race and physician location: trends in two New Zealand urban areas, *New Zealand Geographer*, **34**, 2–12.

Barnett, J.R. and **Sheerin, I.G.** (1977) Public policy and urban health: a review of selected programmes designed to influence the spatial distribution of physicians in New Zealand, *Proceedings, Ninth New Zealand Geography Conference*, Christchurch.

Barrett, F.A. (1973) *Residential Search Behaviour: A study of Intra-Urban Relocation in Toronto*, Geographical Monographs No. 1, York University, Atkinson College, Toronto.

Bassett, K. and **Hauser, D.** (1975) Public policy and spatial structure: housing improvement in Bristol, pp. 20–66 in Peel, R., Chisholm, M. and Haggett, P. (eds) *Processes in Physical and Human Geography*, Heinemann, London.

Bather, N.J. (1976) *The speculative residential developer and urban growth*, Geographical Paper No. 47, Department of Geography, University of Reading.

Batley, R. (1972) An explanation of non-participation in planning, *Policy and Politics*, **1**, 95–114.

Bauer, R.A. (ed.) (1966) *Social Indicators*, M.I.T. Press, Cambridge, Mass..

Baum, A. and **Epstein, Y.** (eds) (1979) *Human Response to Crowding*, Wiley, Chichester.

Beckmann, M.J. (1973) Equilibrium models of residential location, *Regional and Urban Economics*, **3**, 361–8.

Bederman, S. (1974) The stratification of 'Quality of Life' in the black community of Atlanta, Georgia, *Southeastern Geographer*, **14**, 26–37.

Bederman, S. and **Adams, J.S.** (1974) Job accessibility and underemployment, *Annals, Association of American Geographers*, **64**, 378–86.

Bell, C. and **Bell, R.** (1972) *City Fathers*, Penguin, Harmondsworth.

Bell, C.R. and **Newby, H.** (1971) *Community Studies*, Allen & Unwin, London.

Bell, C.R. and **Newby, H.** (1976) Community, Communion, Class and community action: the social sources of the new urban politics, pp. 189–208 in Herbert, D. and Johnston, R.J. (eds), *Social Areas in Cities*, Vol. 2, *Spatial Perspectives on Problems and Policies*, Wiley, Chichester.

Bell, W. (1955) Economic, family and ethnic status: an empirical test, *American Sociological Review*, **20**, 45–52.

Bell, W. (1958) Social choice, life styles and suburban residence, pp. 225–47 in Dobriner, W. (ed.), *The Suburban Community*, Putnam, New York.

Bell, W. (1968) The city, suburb and a theory of social choice, pp. 132–68 in Greer, S. *et al.* (eds), *The New Urbanization*, St. Martin's Press, New York.

Bell, W. and **Moskos, I.** (1964) A comment on Udry's increasing scale and spatial differentiation, *Social Forces*, **42**, 414–17.

Bengston, S.F. (1974) Housing and planning in Sweden, pp. 99–109 in Fuerst, J.S. (ed.), *Public Housing in Europe and America*, Croom Helm, London.

Berger, B. (1960) *Working Class Suburb*, University of California Press, Berkeley.

Berger, B.M. (1971) *Looking for America: Essays on Youth, Suburbia and Other American Obsessions*, Prentice-Hall, Englewood Cliffs, New Jersey.

Berger, P., Berger, B. and **Kelliner H.** (1973) *The Homeless Mind*, Vintage, New York.

Berkowitz, L. and **McCauly, B.** (1972) *Altruism and Helping Behaviour*, Academic Press, New York.

Bernstein, S.J. (1973) Mass transit and the urban ghetto, *Traffic Quarterly*, **27**, 431–49.

Berry, B.J.L. (1959) Ribbon developments in the urban business pattern, *Annals, Association of American Geographers*, **49**, 145–55.

Berry, B.J.L. (ed.) (1972) *City Classification Handbook: Methods and Applications*, Wiley, New York.

Berry, B.J.L. (1973) *The Human Consequences of Urbanization*, St. Martin's Press, New York.

Berry, B.J.L. and **Horton, F.E.** (eds), (1970) *Geographical Perspectives on Urban Systems*, Prentice-Hall, Englewood Cliffs, New Jersey.

Berry, B.J.L. and **Kasarda, J.D.** (1977) *Contemporary Urban Sociology*, Macmillan, New York.

Berry, B.J.L. and **Rees, P.H.** (1969) The factorial ecology of Calcutta, *American Journal of Sociology*, **74**, 455–91.

Berthoud, R. (1976) Where are London's poor? *Greater London Intelligence Quarterly*, **36**, 5–12.

Beshers, J.M. (1962) *Urban Social Structure*, Free Press, New York.

Best, G. (1968) The Scottish Victorian City, *Victorian Studies*, **11**, 329–58.

Bible, B.L. (1970) Physicians' views of medical practice in nonmetropolitan communities, *Public Health Reports*, **85**, 11–21.

Blecher, E. (1971) *Advocacy Planning for Urban Development*, Praeger, New York.

Bloch, P.B. (1974) *Equality of distribution of police services*, The Urban Institute, Washington, D.C.

Blowers, A. (1973) The neighbourhood: exploration of a concept, pp. 49–90 in *The City As A Social System*, Open University, Milton Keynes.

Boaden, N. (1971) *Urban Policy Making*, Cambridge University Press, Cambridge.

Boal, F.W. (1972) The urban residential sub-community: a conflict interpretation, *Area*, **4**, 164–8.

Boal, F.W. (1974) Territoriality in Belfast, pp. 191–212 in Bell, C. and Newby, H. (eds). *The Sociology of Community*, Cass, London.

Boal, F.W. (1976) Ethnic residential segregation, pp. 41–79 in D. Herbert and R. Johnston (eds), *Social Areas in Cities*, Vol. 1, Wiley, Chichester.

Boal, F.W. (1978) Territoriality on the Shankhill-Falls Divide, Belfast: the perspective from 1976, pp. 58–77 in Lanegran, D. and Palm, R. (eds), *An Invitation to Geography*, (2nd ed.), McGraw-Hill, New York.

Boal, F.W. (1979) *Ethnic Residential Segregation*, Arnold, London.

Boal, F.W., Doherty, P. and **Pringle D.G.** (1978) *Social Problems in the Belfast Urban Area: An Exploratory Analysis*, Occasional Paper No. 12, Department of Geography, Queen Mary College, London.

Boddy, M. (1976a) The structure of mortgage finance: building societies and the British social formation, *Transactions, Institute of British Geographers*, New Series, **1**, 58–71.

Boddy, N. (1976b) Political economy of housing: mortgage-financed owner-occupation in Britain, *Antipode*, **8**, 15–24.

Bogardus, E. (1926) Social distance in the city, pp. 48–54 in Burgess, E. (ed.), *The Urban Community*, University of Chicago Press, Chicago.

Boggs, S.L. (1965) Urban crime patterns, *American Sociological Review*, **30**, 899–908.

Boissevain, J. (1974) *Friends of Friends: Networks, Manipulators and Coalitions*, St. Martin's Press, New York.

Bollens, J.C. and **Schmandt, H.J.** (1975) *The Metropolis: Its People, Politics and Economic Life*, Harper & Row, New York.

Booth, A. (1976) *Human Crowding and Its Consequences*, Praeger, New York.

Booth, C. (1893) Life and labour of the people of London, *Journal of the Royal Statistical Society*, **55**, 557–91.

Booth, C. (1903) *Life and Labour of the People of London*, Macmillan, London.

Boots, A. *et al.* (1972) *Inequality in Local Government Services*, The Urban Institute, Washington, D.C.

Boots, B.N. (1979) Population density, crowding and human behaviour, *Progress in Human Geography*, **3**, 13–64.

Bor, W. (1973) Problems of inner city areas, with special reference to the Birmingham study, *Housing Review*, Sept./Oct., 156–63.

Borchert, J.R. (1967) American metropolitan evolution, *Geographical Review*, **57**, 301–32.

Bott, E. (1957) *Family and Social Networks*, Tavistock, London.

Bottomore, T. (1954) Social stratification in voluntary organisations, pp. 193–215 in Glass D.V. (ed.), *Social Mobility in Britain*, Routledge, London.

Boulding, K.E. (1956) *The Image*, University of Michigan Press, Ann Arbor.

Bourne, L.S. (1968) Market, location and site selection in apartment construction, *Canadian Geographer*, **12**, 211–26.

Bourne, L.S. (1969) Location factors in the redevelopment process: a model of residential change, *Land Economics*, **45**, 183–93.

Bourne, L.S. (1976) Housing supply and housing market behaviour in residential development, pp. 111–58 in Herbert, D.T. and Johnston, R.J. (eds), *Social Areas in Cities*, Vol. 1, *Spatial Processes and Form*, Wiley, Chichester.

Bowlby, J. (1965) *Child Care and the Growth of Love*, Penguin, Harmondsworth.

Bowley, M. (1945) *Housing and the State 1919–1944*, George Allen & Unwin, London.

Boyer, B.D. (1973) *Cities Destroyed for Cash: The FHA Scandal at HUD*, Follett, Chicago.

Bradley, J.E., Kirby, A.M. and **Taylor, P.J.** (1978) Distance decay and dental decay: a study of dental health among primary school children in Newcastle upon Tyne, *Regional Studies*, **12**, 529–40.

Brand, J. (1975) The politics of social indicators, *British Journal of Sociology*, **26**, 78–90.

Brantingham, P.L. and **Brantingham, J.** (1975) Residential burglary and urban form, *Urban Studies*, **12**, 273–84.

Breitbart, M. and **Peet, R.** (1974) A critique of advocacy planning, pp. 97–108, in Ley, D. (ed.), *Community Participation and the Spatial Order of the City*, Tantalus Research, Vancouver.

Brennan, T. (1948) *Midland City*, Dobson, London.

Briggs, A. (1968) *Victorian Cities*, Penguin, Harmondsworth.

Briggs, R. (1973) Urban cognitive distance, pp. 361–88 in Downs, R. and Stea, D. (eds), *Image and Environment*, Aldine, Chicago.

Brooks, E. (1977) Geography and public policy, pp. 1–40 in *Values, Relevance and Policy*, Open University Course D204, Unit 30, Open University Press, Milton Keynes.

Brown, L.A. and **Holmes, J.** (1971) Search behaviour in an intra-urban migration context: a spatial perspective, *Environment and Planning*, **3**, 307–26.

Brown, L.A. and **Longbrake, D.B.** (1970) Migration flows in intra-urban space: place utility considerations, *Annals, Association of American Geographers*, **60**, 368–87.

Brown, L.A. and **Moore, E.G.** (1970) The intra-urban

migration process: a perspective, *Geografiska Annaler*, **52B**, 1–13.

Brown, W.H., Jr. (1972) Access to housing: the role of the real estate industry, *Economic Geography*, **48**, 66–78.

Brunn, S.D. (1974) *Geography and Politics in America*, Harper & Row, New York.

Bryant, B. (1975) Citizen – official perceptions of metropolitan problems: a four-city study, pp. 5–24 in Wells, T.L. (ed.), *Urban Problems in a Metropolitan Setting*, Old Dominion University, Norfolk, Virginia.

Bunge, W. (1971) *Fitzgerald: Geography of a Revolution*, Schlenkman, Cambridge, Mass.

Bunge, W. (1975) Detroit humanly viewed: the American urban present, pp. 147–182 in Abler, R., Janelle, D., Philbrick, A. and Sommer, J. (eds) *Human Geography in a Shrinking World*, Duxbury Press, North Scituate, Mass.

Burgess, E.W. (1924) The Growth of the City: An introduction to a research project, *Publications, American Sociological Society*, **18**, 85–97.

Burgess, E.W. (1925) The growth of the city: an introduction to a research project, pp. 47–62 in Park, R.E., Burgess, E.W. and McKenzie, R.D. (eds), *The City*, University of Chicago Press, Chicago.

Burgess, E.W. (ed.) (1926) *The Urban Community*, University of Chicago Press, Chicago.

Burgess, E.W. (1964) Natural area, p. 458 in Gould, J. and Kolb, W.L. (eds) *A Dictionary of the Social Sciences*, Free Press, New York.

Burke, G. (1976) *Townscapes*, Penguin, Harmondsworth.

Burney, E. (1967) *Housing on Trial*, Oxford University Press, Oxford.

Burnley, I.H. (1972) European immigration and settlement patterns in metropolitan Sydney 1947–1966, *Australian Geographical Studies*, **10**, 61–78.

Burrell, F.A. (1865) *Report of the Council of Hygiene and Public Health upon the Sanitary Conditions of the City*, Citizens' Association of New York, New York.

Busteed, M.A. (1975) *Geography and Voting Behaviour*, Oxford University Press, Oxford.

Butler, E.W., Chapin, F.S., Hemmens, G.C., Kaiser, E.J., Stegman, M.A. and **Weiss, S.F.** (1969) *Moving Behaviour and Residential Choice: A National Survey*, National Co-operative Highway Research Program Report No. 81, Highway Research Board, Washington, D.C.

Buttimer, A. (1972) Social space and the planning of residential areas, *Environment and Behaviour*, **4**, 279–318.

Byrne, D.S. (1974) *'Problem Families': A Housing Lumpenproletariat*, Working Paper No. 5, Department of Sociology and Social Administration, University of Durham.

Cadwallader, M.T. (1979) Neighbourhood evaluation in residential mobility, *Environment and Planning*, **11A**, 393–401.

Calhoun, J.B. (1962) Population density and social pathology, *Scientific American*, **206**, 139–48.

Callow, A.B., Jr. (ed.) (1976) *The City Boss in America: An Interpretative Reader*, Oxford University Press, New York.

Campbell, R., Converse, P. and **Rodgers, W.L.** (1976) *The Quality of American Life: Perceptions, Evaluations and Satisfactions*, Russell Sage, New York.

Canter, D.V. (1975) Distance estimation in Greater London, SSRC Final Report, University of Surrey.

Canter, D.V. and **Tagg, S.K.** (1975) Distance estimation in cities, *Environment and Behaviour*, **7**, 59–80.

Carey, L. and **Mapes, R.** (1972) *The Sociology of Planning*, Batsford, London.

Carlstein, T., Parkes, D. and **Thrift, N.** (eds) (1978) *Human Activity and Time Geography*, Arnold, London.

Carney, J. and **Taylor, C.** (1974) Community development projects : review and comment, *Area*, **6**, 226–31.

Carp, F.M. (1975) Life-style and location within the city, *The Gerontologist*, **75**, 27–33.

Carp, F.M., Zawadski, R.T., and **Shokrkon, H.** (1976) Dimensions of urban environmental quality, *Environment and Behaviour*, **8**, 239–64.

Carstairs, G.M. (1969) Overcrowding and human aggression, pp. 751–64 in Graham, H.D. and Gurr, T.R. (eds) *Violence in America*, Bantam, New York.

Carter, A. (1977) D'you mean south? *New Society*, 28 July, 188–9.

Carter, H. (1975) *The Study of Urban Geography*, Arnold, London.

Carter, R.L. and **Hill, K.Q.** (1976) The criminal's image of the city and urban crime patterns, *Social Science Quarterly*, **57**, 597–607.

Cartwright, A. (1967) *Patients and their Doctors*, Routledge & Kegan Paul, London.

Cassel, J. (1972) Health consequences of population density and crowding, pp. 149–63, in Guttman, R. (ed.), *People and Buildings*, Basic Books, New York.

Castells, M. (1977) *The Urban Question*, Arnold, London.

Castells, M. (1978) *City, Class and Power*, Macmillan, London.

Castells, M., Cherki, E., Godard, F. and **Mehl, D.** (1977) *Crise du logement et mouvements sociaux. Enquête sur la région Parisienne*, Mouton, Paris.

Castle, I. and **Gittus, E.** (1957) The distribution of social defects in Liverpool, *Sociological Review*, **5**, 43–64.

Cater, J. and **Jones, T.** (1978) Asians in Bradford, *New Society*, **44**, 13 April, 81–2.

Cave, P.W. (1969) Occupancy duration and the analysis of residential change, *Urban Studies*, **6**, 58–69.

Central Housing Advisory Committee (1969) *Council Housing: Purposes, Procedures and Priorities*, Ninth Report of the Housing Management Subcommittee, H.M.S.O., London.

Chamberlain, S. (1972) *Aspects of developer behaviour in the land development process*, Research Paper No. 56, Centre for Urban and Community Studies, University of Toronto.

Chapin, F.S. and **Weiss S.F.** (1968) A probabilistic model for residential growth, *Transportation Research*, **2**, 375–90.

Chapman, S.D. (1971) *The History of Working Class Housing*, David & Charles, Newton Abbot.

Chapple, E.D. (1942) The measurement of interpersonal behaviour, *Transactions, New York Academy of Sciences*, **4**, 222–32.

Cherry, G.E. (1979) The town planning movement and

the late Victorian city, *Transactions, Institute of British Geographers*, **NS4**, 306– 19.

Choldin, H. (1978) Urban density and pathology, *Annual Review of Sociology*, **4**, 91– 115.

Clark, D. (1964) Immigrant enclaves in our cities, pp. 205– 218 in Elias, C.E., Jnr., Gillies, J. and Riemer, S. (eds), *Metropolis: Values in Conflict*, Wadsworth, Belmont, California.

Clark, W.A.V. (1970) Measurement and explanation in intra-urban residential mobility, *Tijdschrift voor Economische en Sociale Geografie*, **61**, 49– 57.

Clark, W.A.V. (1971) A test for directional bias in residential mobility, pp. 71– 83, in McConnell, H. and Yasheen, D.W. (eds) *Models of Spatial Variation*, Illinois University Press, Illinois.

Clark, W.A.V. (1976) Migration in Milwaukee, *Economic Geography*, **52**, 48– 60.

Clark, W.A.V. and **Cadwallader, M.T.** (1973) Residential preferences: an alternate view of intra-urban space, *Environment and Planning*, **5A**, 693– 703.

Clark, W.A.V. and **Moore, E.G.** (1978) *Population Mobility and Residential Change*, Northwestern University Studies in Geography, No. 25, Evanston, Illinois.

Clawson, M. (1971) *Suburban Land Conversion in the United States: An Economic and Governmental Process*, Johns Hopkins University Press, Baltimore.

Cleland, E.A., Stimpson, R.J., and **Goldsworthy, A.J.** (1977) *Suburban health care behaviour in Adelaide*, Centre for Applied Social and Survey Research Monograph Series No. 2, Flinders University, Adelaide.

Cliff, A.D. and **Ord, J.K.** (1973) *Spatial Autocorrelation*, Pion, London.

Coates, B., Johnston, R.J., and **Knox, P.L.** (1977) *Geography and Inequality*, Oxford University Press, London.

Coates, K. and **Silburn, R.** (1970) *Poverty: the Forgotten Englishmen*, Penguin, Harmondsworth.

Cockburn, C. (1977) *The Local State*, Pluto Press, London.

Cohen, A.K. (1955) *Delinquent Boys*, Free Press, Chicago.

Cohen, S. (1973) *Folk Devils and Moral Panics*, Paladin, London.

Coit, K. (1978) Local action, not citizen participation, pp. 297– 311 in Tabb, W. and Sawers, L. (eds) *Marxism and the Metropolis*, Oxford University Press, New York.

Colenutt, R. (1971) Postscript on the Detroit Geographical Expedition, *Antipode*, **3**, 85.

Collins, A.H. and **Pancoast, D.L.** (1976) *Natural Helping Networks: a strategy for prevention*, National Association of Social Workers, Washington, D.C.

Collinson, P. (1963) *The Cutteslowe Walls*, Faber & Faber, London.

Committee on the Management of Local Government (1967) *The Local Government Councillor*, H.M.S.O., London.

Community Development Project (1974) *Inter-Project Report*, C.D.P. Information and Intelligence Unit, H.M.S.O., London.

Community Development Project (1975) *Final Report, Part I: Coventry and Hillfields: Prosperity and the persistence of Inequality*, C.D.P. Information and Intelligence Unit, H.M.S.O., London.

Community Development Project (1976) *Whatever Happened to Council Housing?* CDP Information and Intelligence Unit, H.M.S.O., London.

Connell, J. (1973) Social networks in urban society, pp. 41– 52 in Clark, B. and Gleave, M. (eds) *Social Patterns in Cities*, Institute of British Geographers, London.

Conzen, M.R.G. (1960) Alnwick: a study in town plan analysis, *Transactions, Institute of British Geographers*, **27**, 1– 122.

Cooper, C. (1976) The house as symbol of the self, pp. 435– 48 in Proshansky, H., Ittelson, W. and Rivlin, L. (eds) *Environmental Psychology: People and their Physical Settings*, Holt, Rinehart & Winston, New York.

Coppock, J.T. and **Prince, H.C.** (1964) *The Geography of Greater London*, Faber, London.

Corey, K.E. (1966) *Urban house types: a methodological experiment in urban settlement geography*, Discussion Paper No. 3, Department of Geography, University of Cincinnati.

Corey, K. (1972) Advocacy in planning: a reflective analysis, *Antipode*, **4**, 46– 63.

Corina, L. (1976) *Housing Allocation Policy and its Effects*, Department of Social Administration, University of York.

Corsi, T.M. and **Harvey, M.E.** (1975) The socio-economic determinants of crime in the city of Cleveland, *Tijdschrift Voor Economische en Sociale Geografie*, **66**, 323– 36.

Costelloe, B.F.C. (1899) *The Housing Problem*, J. Heywood, Manchester.

Coulter, J. (1978) *Grid-square census data as a source for the study of deprivation in British conurbations*, Working Paper No. 13, Census Research Unit, Department of Geography, University of Durham.

Cowlard, K. (1979) The identification of social (class) areas and their place in nineteenth-century urban development, *Transactions, Institute of British Geographers*, **4**, 239– 57.

Cox, K. (1973) *Conflict, Power and Politics in the City: A Geographic View*, McGraw-Hill, New York.

Cox, K. (1977) Location and State in Market Societies, Discussion Paper No. 61, Department of Geography, Ohio State University, Columbus.

Cox, K. (ed.), (1978) *Urbanization and Conflict in Market Societies*, Methuen, London.

Cox, K. and **Agnew, J.** (1974) *The location of public housing: towards a comparative analysis*, Discussion Paper No. 45, Department of Geography, Ohio State University, Columbus.

Cox, K. and **Dear, M.J.** (1975) *Jurisdictional Organization and Urban Welfare*, Discussion Paper No. 47, Department of Geography, Ohio State University, Columbus.

Cox, K. and **Reynolds, D.R.** (1974) Locational approaches to power and conflict, pp. 19– 41 in Cox, K.R., Reynolds, D.R. and Rokkan, S. (eds), *Locational Approaches to Power and Conflict*, Halstead Press, New York.

Cox, W.H. (1976) *Cities: The Public Dimension*, Penguin, Harmondsworth.

Craig, J. and **Driver, A.** (1972) The identification and comparison of small areas of adverse social conditions, *Journal of the Royal Statistical Society*, Series C, **21**, 25–35.

Craven, E. (1975) Private residential expansion in Kent, pp. 124–44 in Pahl, R.E., *Whose City?*, Penguin, Harmondsworth.

Cripps, E.L. and Foot, D.H.S. (1969) A land-use model for sub-regional planning, *Regional Studies*, **3**, 243–68.

Cullingworth, J.B. (1979) *Essays on Housing Policy*, George Allen & Unwin, London.

Curl, J.S. (1970) *European Cities and Society*, Leonard Hill, London.

Curtis, J.E. and Petras, J.W. (1970) Community Power, Power Studies, and the Sociology of Knowledge, *Human Organization*, **29**, 204–18.

Curtis, J.H., Avesing, F. and Klosek, I. (1967) Urban Parishes as Social Areas, *The American Catholic Sociological Review*, **18**, 319–25.

Cybriwsky, R.A. (1978) Social aspects of neighbourhood change, *Annals, Association of American Geographers*, **68**, 17–33.

Dahl, R. (1961) *Who Governs?* Yale University Press, New Haven.

Dahl, R. (1967) *Pluralist Democracy in the United States*, Rand-McNally, Chicago.

Dahya, B. (1974) The nature of Pakistani ethnicity in industrial cities in Britain, pp. 77–118 in Cohen, A. (ed.) *Urban Ethnicity*, Tavistock, London.

Damer, S. (1974) Wine Alley: the sociology of a dreadful enclosure, *Sociological Review*, **22**, 221–48.

Damer, S. and Madigan, R. (1974) The housing investigator, *New Society*, **29**, 226–7.

Daniel, W.W. (1968) *Racial Discrimination in England*, Penguin, Harmondsworth.

Danielson, M.N. (1976) *The Politics of Exclusion*, Columbia University Press, New York.

Davidoff, P. (1965) Advocacy and pluralism in planning, *Journal of the American Institute of Planners*, **31**, 331–8.

Davidoff, P., Davidoff, L. and Gold, N. (1970) Suburban action: advocate planning for an open society, *Journal of the American Institute of Planners*, **36**, 12–21.

Davie, M.R. (1937) The pattern of urban growth, pp. 133–61 in Murdock, G. (ed.), Studies in the Science of Society, Yale University Press, New Haven.

Davies, B. (1968) *Social Needs and Resources in Local Services*, Michael Joseph, London.

Davies, B. (1976) Territorial injustice, *New Society*, **36**, 352–54.

Davies, J.G. (1972) *The Evangelistic Bureaucrat*, Tavistock, London.

Davies, J.L. (1965) *The Elevated System and the Growth of Northern Chicago*, Studies in Geography, **10**, Northwestern University Press, Evanston, Illinois.

Davies, S. and Albaum, H. (1973) The mobility problems of the poor in Indianapolis, pp. 106–25 in Albaum, M. (ed.), *Geography and Contemporary Issues*, Wiley, New York.

Davies, W. and Barrow, G. (1973) Factorial ecology of three prairie cities, *Canadian Geographer*, **17**, 327–53.

Deakin, N. (1970) Race and human rights in the city, pp. 107–29 in Cowan, P. (ed.), *Developing Patterns of Urbanization*, Oliver & Boyd, Edinburgh.

Dear, M.J. (1976) Abandoned housing, pp. 59–99 in Adams, J.S. (ed.), *Urban Policymaking and Metropolitan Dynamics*, Ballinger, Cambridge, Mass.

Dear, M.J. and Long, J. (1978) Community strategies in locational conflict, pp. 113–27 in Cox, K.R. (ed.), *Urbanization and Conflict in Market Societies*, Methuen, London.

Dench, G. (1975) *Maltese in London: A Case study in the Erosion of Ethnic Consciousness*, Routledge & Kegan Paul, London.

Dennis, N. (1970) *People and Planning*, Faber and Faber, London.

Dennis, N. (1972) *Public Participation and Planning Blight*, Faber and Faber, London.

Dennis, N. (1978) Housing policy areas: criteria and indicators in principle and practice, *Transactions, Institute of British Geographers*, N.S. **3**, 2–22.

Department of the Environment (1977) *Housing Policy: Technical Volume, Part III*, H.M.S.O., London.

Department of the Environment (1978) *Study of Intending Migrants*, Department of the Environment, London.

Diamond, D. (1975) Planning and the urban environment, *Geography*, **60**, 189–93.

Dickinson, J.C., Gray, R.J. and Smith, D.M. (1972) The quality of life in Gainesville, Florida: An application of territorial social indicators, *Southeastern Geographer*, **12**, 121–32.

Diseker, R.A., and Chappell, J.A. (1976) Relative importance of variables in determination of practice location: a pilot study, *Social Science and Medicine*, **10**, 559–64.

Dodgshon, W. and Butlin, R.A. (eds.) (1978) *An Historical Geography of England and Wales*, Academic Press, London.

Doherty, J. (1973) Race, class and residential segregation in Britain, *Antipode*, **3**, 45–51.

Doling, J.F. (1973) A two-stage model of tenure choice in the housing market, *Urban Studies*, **10**, 199–211.

Donald, O.D. (1978) *Access to Medical Care in Sydney*, Paper presented to the Regional Science Association, Australian and New Zealand Section, Third Annual Meeting, Monash University, Melbourne (mimeo).

Donaldson, S. (1969) *The Suburban Myth*, Columbia University Press, New York.

Donnison, D. (1974) Policies for priority areas, *Journal of Social Policy*, **3**, 127–35.

Douglas, J.W.B. (1964) *The Home and the School*, McGibbon, St Albans.

Downs, A. (1964) *Inside Bureaucracy*, Rand, Chicago.

Downs, A. (1973) *Federal Housing Subsidies: How are they working?* D.C. Heath, Lexington, Mass.

Downs, R. and Stea, D. (eds) (1973) *Image and Environment*, Aldine, Chicago.

Drake, S. and Cayton, H.R. (1962) *Black Metropolis: A Study of Negro life in a Northern City*, New York, Harper & Row.

Drewnowski, J. (1974) *On Measuring and Planning the Quality of Life*, Mouton, The Hague.

Duncan, O.D. and Duncan, B. (1955a) A methodological analysis of segregation indexes, *American Sociological Review*, **20**, 210–17.

Duncan, O.D. and Duncan, B. (1955b) Occupational

stratification and residential distribution, *American Journal of Sociology*, **50**, 493–503.

Duncan, O.D. and **Lieberson, S.** (1959) Ethnic segregation and assimilation, *American Journal of Sociology*, **64**, 364–74.

Duncan, O.D. and **Schnore, L.F.** (1959) Cultural, behavioural and ecological perspectives in the study of social organization, *American Journal of Sociology*, **65**, 132–46.

Duncan, S. (1977) Mental maps of New York, *New York Magazine*, December 19, pp. 51–72.

Duncan, S.S. (1974) Cosmetic planning or social engineering? Improvement grants and improvement areas in Huddersfield, *Area*, **6**, 259–71.

Duncan, S.S. (1976) Self-help: the allocation of mortgages and the formation of housing sub-markets, *Area*, **8**, 307–16.

Duncan, T.L.C. (1971) *Measuring Housing Quality*, Occasional Paper No. 20, Centre for Urban and Regional Studies, University of Birmingham.

Durant, R. (1959) *Watling: A Survey of Social Life on a New Housing Estate*, King, London.

Durkheim, E. (1893) *De La Division du Travail Social*, Alcan, Paris.

Dutton, D. (1978) Explaining the low use of health services by the poor: costs, attitudes or delivery systems? *American Sociological Review*, **43**, 348–68.

Dyos, H.J. (1968a) The speculative builders and developers of Victorian London, *Victorian Studies*, **11**, 641–90.

Dyos, H.J. (1968b) *The Study of Urban History*, Arnold, London.

Dyos, H.J. and **Wolff, M.** (eds.) (1973) *The Victorian City: Images and Realities*, Vol. 2, Routledge & Kegan Paul, London.

Dzus, R. and **Romsa, G.** (1977) Housing construction, vacancy chains and residential mobility in Windsor, *Canadian Geographer*, **21**, 223–36.

Eagland, R.M. (1973) Evaluation and practice, pp. 197–213 in *Urban and Regional Models*, PTRC Seminar Proceedings, Planning and Transport Research and Computation, London.

Earickson, R. (1970) *The spatial behaviour of hospital patients*, Research Paper No. 124, Department of Geography, University of Chicago.

Edney, J.J. (1976) The psychological role of property rights in human behaviour, *Environment and Planning*, **8A**, 811–22.

Edwards, J. (1975) Social indicators, urban deprivation and positive discrimination, *Journal of Social Policy*, **4**, 275–87.

Edwards, J. and **Batley, R.** (1978) *The Politics of Positive Discrimination*, Tavistock, London.

Elesh, D. and **Schollaert, P.T.** (1971) *Race and urban medicine: factors affecting the distribution of physicians in Chicago*, Institute for Research on Poverty, Madison, Wisconsin.

Elliot, B. and **McCrone, D.** (1975) Landlords in Edinburgh: some preliminary findings, *Sociological Review*, **23**, 539–62.

Engels, F. (1844) *The Condition of the Working Class in England*, Panther, London (reprint 1969).

English, J. (1976) Housing allocation and a deprived Scottish estate, *Urban Studies*, **13**, 319–23.

English, J. (1979) Access and deprivation in Local Authority housing, pp. 113–35 in Jones, C. (ed.), *Urban Deprivation and the Inner City*, Croom Helm, London.

English, J., **Madigan, R.** and **Norman, P.** (1976) *Slum Clearance*, Croom Helm, London.

Esser, A.H. (ed.), (1971) *Behaviour and Environment*, Plenum, New York.

Evans, A.W. (1973) *The Economics of Residential Location*, Macmillan, London.

Evans, D.J. (1973) A comparative study of urban social structures in South Wales, *Institute of British Geographers, Special Publication*, **5**, 87–102.

Everitt, B. (1974) *Cluster Analysis*, SSRC Reviews of Current Research, No. 11, Heinemann, London.

Everitt, J.C. (1976) Community and propinquity in a city, *Annals, Association of American Geographers*, **66**, 104–16.

Everitt, J.C. and **Cadwallader, M.T.** (1972) The home area concept in urban analysis: the use of cognitive mapping and computer procedures as methodological tools, pp. 1.2.1.–1.2.10 in Mitchell, W.J. (ed.), *Environmental Design: Research and Practice*, University of California Press, Los Angeles.

Everitt, J.C. and **Cadwallader, M.T.** (1977) Local area definition revisited, *Area*, **9**, 175–6.

Eversley, D. (1973) *The Planner in Society: The Changing Role of a Profession*, Faber & Faber, London.

Eversley, D. (1975) The landlords' slow farewell, *New Society*, **31**, 119–21.

Ewen, L.A. (1978) *Corporate Power and Urban Crisis in Detroit*, Princeton University Press, Princeton, N.J.

Eyles, J. (1968) *Inhabitants' images of Highgate Village (London)*, Discussion Paper 15, Graduate School of Geography, London School of Economics.

Eyles, J. (1973) Spatial opportunity and the concept of the reference group, *Professional Geographer*, **25**, 121–3.

Eyles, J. (1978) Social geography and the study of the capitalist city: a review, *Tijdschrift voor Economische en Sociale Geografie*, **69**, 296–305.

Eyles, J. (1979) Area-based policies for the inner city: context, problems and prospects, pp. 226–43 in D. Herbert and D.M. Smith (eds), *Social Problems and The City*, Oxford University Press, Oxford.

Falcocchio, J., **Pignataro, L.** and **Cantilli, E.** (1972) Modal choices and travel attributes of the inner-city poor, *Highway Research Record*, **403**, Highway Research Board, Washington, D.C.

Faris, R.E.L. and **Dunham, H.W.** (1939) *Mental Disorders in Urban Areas*, University of Chicago Press, Chicago.

Feiffer, J. (1968) *Little Murders*, Random House, New York.

Feldman, S.D. and **Thielbar, G.W.** (eds) (1975) *Life Styles: Diversity in American Society*, Little, Brown, Boston.

Festinger, L., **Schacter, S.** and **Back, K.** (1950) *Social Pressures in Informal Groups*, Harper, New York.

Fine, J., **Glenn, N.D.** and **Monts, J.J.** (1971) The residential segregation of occupational groups in central cities and suburbs, *Demography*, **8**, 91–102.

Firey, W. (1945) Sentiment and symbolism as ecological variables, *American Sociological Review*, **10**, 140–148.

Firey, W. (1947) *Land Use in Central Boston*, Harvard University Press, Cambridge, Mass.

Fischer, C.S. (1973) On urban alienation and anomie, *American Sociological Review*, **38**, 311–26.

Fischer, C.S. (1975) Toward a subcultural theory of urbanism, *American Journal of Sociology*, **80**, 1319–41.

Fischer, C.S. (1976) *The Urban Experience*, Harcourt, Brace Jovanovich, New York.

Fischer, C.S. and **Jackson, R.M.** (1976) Suburbs networks and attitudes, pp. 279–306 in Schwartz, B. (ed.), *The Changing Face of the Suburbs*, University of Chicago Press, Chicago.

Fischer, E.M. and **Winnick, L.** (1951) A reformulation of the filtering concept, *Journal of Social Issues*, **1**, 47–58.

Fischer, R.M. (ed.) (1955) *The Metropolis in Modern Life*, Doubleday, New York.

Flowerdew, R. (1976) Search strategies and stopping rules in residential mobility, *Transactions, Institute of British Geographers*, New Series, **1**, 47–57.

Foggin, P. and **Polese, M.** (1977) *The Social Geography of Montreal in 1971*, University of Toronto, Centre for Urban and Community Studies, Research Paper No. 88, Toronto.

Foley, D.L. (1973) Institutional and contextual factors affecting the housing choice of minority residents, pp. 85–147 in Hawley, A.H. and Rock, V.P. (eds) *Segregation in Residential Areas*, National Academy of Sciences, Washington, D.C.

Foley, D.L. (1975) Accessibility for residents in the metropolitan environment, pp. 157–200 in Hawley, A.H. and Rock, V.P. (eds), *Metropolitan America in Contemporary Perspective*, Halstead Press, New York.

Forbes, J. and **Robertson, I.M.L.** (1978) Intra-urban migration in Greater Glasgow, paper given to the Population Studies Group of the Institute of British Geographers, Glasgow, September 1978.

Ford, J.R. (1975) The role of the building society manager in the urban statification system: autonomy versus constraint, *Urban Studies*, **12**, 295–302.

Ford, L.R. (1973) Individual decisions in the creation of the American Downtown, *Geography*, **58**, 324–7.

Forman, R. (1971) *Black Ghettos, White Ghettos and Slums*, Prentice-Hall, Englewood Cliffs, New Jersey.

Foster, J. (1974) *Class Struggle and the Industrial Revolution*, Weidenfeld & Nicolson, London.

Francescato, D. and **Mebane, W.** (1973) How citizens view two great cities: Milan and Rome, pp. 131–47 in Downs, R. and Stea, D. (eds), *Image and Environment*, Aldine, Chicago.

Fraser, D. (1976) Urban Politics in Victorian England, Leicester University Press, Leicester.

Frazier, E.F. (1967) The Negro family in Chicago, pp. 224–38 in Burgess, E.W. and Bogue, D.J. (eds), *Urban Sociology*, University of Chicago Press, Chicago.

Freedman, J.L. (1975) *Crowding and Behaviour*, Freeman, San Francisco.

Freestone, R. (1975) On urban resource allocation: the distribution of medical practitioners in Sydney, *Geographical Bulletin*, New South Wales Geographical Society, **7**, 14–25.

Fried, J.P. (1971) *Housing Crisis U.S.A.*, Praeger, New York.

Fried, M. (1963) Grieving for a lost home, pp. 151–71 in Duhl, L.J. (ed.), *The Urban Condition*, Basic Books, New York.

Friedrichs, C.R. (1978) Capitalism, mobility and class formation in the Early Modern German city, pp. 187–214 in Abrams, P. and Wrigley, E.A. (eds) *Towns in Societies*, Cambridge University Press, Cambridge.

Frisch, M.H. (1969) The community elite and the emergence of urban politics: Springfield, Massachusetts, 1840–1880, pp. 277–96 in Thernstrom, S. and Sennett, R. (eds) *Nineteenth Century Cities*, Yale University Press, New Haven.

Fuerst, J.S. (ed.) (1974) *Public Housing in Europe and America*, Croom Helm, London.

Gad, G. (1973) Crowding and 'pathologies': some critical remarks, *Canadian Geographer*, **17**, 373–90.

Gagnon, G. (1960) Les zones sociales de l'Agglomeration de Quebec, *Recherches Sociographiques*, **1**, 255–67.

Gale, S. and **Moore, E.G.** (eds) (1975) *The Manipulated City*, Maaroufa Press, Chicago.

Gamst-Nielsen, K. (1974) Resistance from below – against exploitation of housing conditions, unpublished paper, University of Copenhagen.

Gans, H.J. (1961) Planning and social life: friendship and neighbour relations in suburban communities, *Journal of the American Institute of Planners*, **27**, 134–40.

Gans, H.J. (1962) *The Urban Villagers*, Free Press, New York.

Gans, H.J. (1967) *The Levittowners*, Allen Lane, London.

Gans, H.J. (1969) Planning for people, not buildings, *Environment and Planning*, **1A**, 33–46.

Gans, H.J. (1972) *People and Plans*, Penguin, Harmondsworth.

Gans, H.J. (1975) The failure of urban renewal: a critique and proposals, pp. 199–212 in Gale, S. and Moore, E.G. (eds), *The Manipulated City*, Maaroufa Press, Chicago.

Gardiner, J.A. and **Olson, D.J.** (eds) (1974) *Theft of the City: Readings on Corruption in Urban America*, Indiana University Press, Bloomington, Indiana.

Gauldie, E. (1974) *Cruel Habitations*, Allen & Unwin, London.

Geddes, P. (1915) *Cities in Evolution*, reprinted in 1947, J. Tyrwhitt, (ed.) Williams & Norgate, London.

Gelfant, B.H. (1954) *The American City Novel*, University of Oklahoma Press, Norman, Okla..

Gettys, W.E. (1940) Human ecology and social theory, *Social Forces*, **18**, 469–76.

Girt, J.L. (1972) Distance and patterns of revealed ill-health in a spatially dispersed population, paper presented to I.G.U. Commission on Medical Geography, Guelph, Ontario.

Gittus, E. (1964) The structure of urban areas, *Town Planning Review*, **35**, 5–20.

Gittus, E. (1976) Deprived areas and social planning, pp. 209–33 in Herbert D. and Johnston, R. (eds), *Social Areas in Cities*, Vol. 2, *Spatial Perspectives on Problems and Policies*, Wiley, London.

Gittus, E. and **Stephens, C.J.** (1973) Some problems in the use of canonical analysis, unpublished discussion paper, University of Newcastle upon Tyne.

Glaab, C.N. and **Brown, A.T.** (1967) *A History of Urban America*, Macmillan, New York.

Gladstone, F. (1976) *The Politics of Planning*, Temple Smith, London.

Glass, D.V. (ed.) (1954) *Social Mobility in Britain*, Routledge & Kegan Paul, London.

Glass, R. *et. al.* (1964) *London: Aspects of Change*, MacGibbon & Kee, London.

Glass, R. (1968) Urban sociology in Great Britain, pp. 21–46 in Pahl, R.E. (ed.), *Readings in Urban Sociology*, Pergamon, Oxford.

Glennerster, H., and Hatch, S. (1974) *Positive Discrimination and Inequality*, Fabian Research Series No. 314, Fabian Society, London.

Goffman, E. (1959) *The presentation of self in everyday life*, Doubleday, New York.

Goffman, E. (1971) *Relations in Public*, Basic Books, New York.

Goheen, P. (1970) *Victorian Toronto, 1850 to 1900*, Research Paper No. 127, Department of Geography, University of Chicago.

Gold, J.R. (1979) *An Introduction to Behavioural Geography*, Oxford University Press, London.

Goldstein, S. and Mayer, K.B. (1961) *Metropolitanization and Population Change in Rhode Island*, Rhode Island Development Council, Rhode Island.

Goldthorpe, J.H. *et al.* (1967) The affluent worker and the thesis of embourgoisement: some preliminary research findings, *Sociology*, 1, 11–31.

Goldthorpe, J.H., Lockwood, D., Bechhofer, F. and Platt, J. (1968) *The Affluent Worker*, Cambridge University Press, Cambridge.

Gollege, R.G., Briggs, R. and Demko, D. (1969) The configuration of distances in intra-urban space, *Proceedings, Association of American Geographers*, 1, 60–8.

Gollege, R.G. and Zannaras, G. (1970) The perception of urban structure: an experimental approach, pp. 56–67 in Archea, J. and Eastman, C. (eds), *EDRA 2, Proceedings of Second Annual Conference*, Carnegie Press, Pittsburgh.

Gollege, R.G. and Zannaras, G. (1973) Cognitive approaches to the analysis of human spatial behaviour, pp. 59–94 in Ittleson, W.H. (ed.) *Environmental Cognition*, Seminar Press, New York.

Goodchild, B. (1974) Class differences in environmental perception, *Urban Studies*, 11, 157–69.

Goodey, B., Duffet, A., Gold, J. and Spencer, D. (1971) *The City Scene: An Exploration into the Image of Central Birmingham as seen by Area Residents*, Research Memorandum No. 10, Centre for Urban and Regional Studies, University of Birmingham.

Goodman, R. (1972) *After the Planners*, Penguin, Harmondsworth.

Gordon, G. (1979) The status areas of early to mid-Victorian Edinburgh, *Transactions, Institute of British Geographers*, New Series, 4, 168–91.

Gordon, M.M. (1964) *Assimilation in American Life*, Oxford University Press, New York.

Gottman, J. (1961) *Megalopolis*, Twentieth Century Fund, New York.

Graham, H.D. and Gurr, T.R. (eds) (1969) *Violence in America*, Bantam, New York.

Granovetter, M.S. (1976) Network sampling: some first steps, *American Journal of Sociology*, 81, 1287–303.

Gray, F. (1976a) Selection and allocation in council housing, *Transactions, Institute of British Geographers*, New Series, 1, 34–46.

Gray, F. (1976b) The management of local authority housing, pp. 81–102, in *Housing and class in Britain*, Political Economy of Housing Workshop, Conference of Socialist Economists, London.

Greenwood, W. (1933) *Love on the Dole*, Jonathan Cape, London.

Greer, S. (1971) Policy and the urban future, pp. 256–68 in Bell, W. and Mau, J. (eds), *Sociology of the Future*, Russell Sage Foundation, New York.

Greer, S. *et. al.* (eds) (1968) *The New Urbanization*, St. Martin's Press, New York.

Greer, S. and Orleans, P. (1962) The mass society and the parapolitical structure, *American Sociological Review*, 27, 634–46.

Greer-Wootten, B. (1972) Changing social areas and the intra-urban migration process, *Review de Geographie de Montreal*, 26, 271–92.

Gregory, D. (1978) *Ideology, Science and Human Geography*, Hutchinson, London.

Grigsby, W.G. (1963) *Housing Markets and Public Policy*, University of Pennsylvania Press, Philadelphia.

Grigsby, W.G., Rosenburg, L., Stegman, M. and Taylor, J. (1970) *Housing and Poverty: An Abstract*, Institute for Environmental Studies, University of Pennsylvania, Philadelphia.

Gutman, R. (ed.) (1972) *People and Buildings*, Basic Books, New York.

Haar, C.M. (1963) The social control of urban space, pp. 175–229, in Wingo, L. Jr. (ed.) *Cities and Space*, Johns Hopkins University Press, Baltimore.

Haddon, R. (1970) A minority in a welfare state: Location of West Indians in the London housing market, *New Atlantis*, 2, 80–123.

Hagerstrand, T. (1970) What about people in regional science?, *Papers, Regional Science Association*, 24, 7–21.

Haggett, P. and Chorley, R.J. (1969) *Network Analysis in Geography*, Arnold, London.

Haig, R.M. (1926) Toward an understanding of the metropolis, *Quarterly Journal of Economics*, 40, 179–208, and 351–6.

Hall, P. (1974) *Urban and Regional Planning*, Penguin, Harmondsworth.

Hall, P. (1975) Book review, *Urban Studies*, 12, 343–4.

Hall, P., Thomas, R., Gracey, H. and Drewett, R. (1973) *The Containment of Urban England*, Allen & Unwin, London.

Halsey, A.H. (1974) Government against poverty in school and community, pp. 121–46 in Wedderburn, D. (ed.) *Poverty, Inequality and Class Structure*, Cambridge University Press, Cambridge.

Hamnett, C. (1973) Improvement grants as an indicator of gentrification in Inner London, *Area*, 5, 252–61.

Hamnett, C. (1976) Multiple deprivation and the inner city, Unit 15, Course D302, *Patterns of Inequality*, Open University Press, Milton Keynes.

Hamnett, C. (1979a) The flat break-up market in London: a case study of large-scale disinvestment – its causes and consequences, pp. 35–55 in Boddy, M. (ed.), *Land, Property and Finance*, Working Paper No. 2, School for Advanced Urban Studies, University of Bristol.

Hamnett, C. (1979b) Area-based explanations: a critical appraisal, pp. 244–60 in D. Herbert and D.M. Smith (eds) *Social Problems and the City*, Oxford University Press, Oxford.

Hampton, W. (1970) *Democracy and Community*, Oxford University Press, London.

Hannerz, U. (1974) Ethnicity and opportunity in urban America, pp. 37–76 in Cohen, A. (ed.), *Urban Ethnicity*, Tavistock, London.

Harloe, M. (ed.) (1977) *Captive Cities*, Wiley, London.

Harloe, M., Isacharoff, R. and **Minns, R.** (1974) *The Organization of Housing*, Heinemann, London.

Harries, K.D. (1974) *The Geography of Crime and Justice*, McGraw-Hill, New York.

Harrison, J. and **Howard, W.** (1972) The role of meaning in the urban image, *Environment and Behaviour*, **4**, 389–411.

Harrison, J.A. and **Sarre, P.** (1971) Personal construct theory in the measurement of environmental images: problems and methods, *Environment and Behaviour*, **3**, 351–74.

Harrison, M.L. (1972) Development control: the influence of political, legal and ideological factors, *Town Planning Review*, **43**, 254–74.

Harrison, M.L. (1975) British town planning ideology and the welfare state, *Journal of Social Policy*, **4**, 259–74.

Harrison, P. (1974) The life of cities, *New Society*, **30**, 5 December, 559–604.

Hart, J.F. (1960) The changing distribution of the American Negro, *Annals, Association of American Geographers*, **50**, 242–66.

Hart, J.T. (1971) The inverse care law, *Lancet*, **i**, 405–12.

Hartman, C. (1964) The housing of relocated families, *Journal of the American Institute of Planners*, **30**, 266–86.

Hartman, C. and **Kessler, R.** (1978) The illusion and reality of urban renewal: San Francisco's Yerba Buena Center, pp. 153–78 in Tabb, W. and Sawers, L. (eds), *Marxism and the Metropolis*, Oxford University Press, New York.

Hartnett, B. (1975) Advocacy planning and bureaucratic guerrillas, *Journal of the Royal Australian Planning Institute*, **13**, 46–9.

Harvey, D.W. (1972) *Society, The City and the Space-Economy of Urbanism*, Resource Paper No. 18, Commission on College Geography, Association of American Geographers, Washington, D.C..

Harvey, D.W. (1973) *Social Justice and the City*, Arnold, London.

Harvey, D.W. (1974) Class-monopoly rent, finance capital and the urban revolution, *Regional Studies*, **8**, 239–55.

Harvey, D.W. (1975) Class structure in a capitalist society and the theory of residential differentiation, pp. 354–69 in Peel, R., Chisholm, M. and Haggett, P. (eds) *Processes in Physical and Human Geography: Bristol Essays*, Heinemann, London.

Harvey, D.W. (1977) Government policies, financial institutions and neighbourhood change in U.S. cities, pp. 123–140 in Harloe, M. (ed.) *Captive Cities*, Wiley, London.

Harvey, D.W. and **Chatterjee, L.** (1974) Absolute rent and the structuring of space by governmental and financial institutions, *Antipode*, **6**, 22–36.

Harvey, R.O. and **Clark, W.A.V.** (1965) The nature and economics of urban sprawl, *Land Economics*, **41**, 1–9.

Hatch, S. (1973) Estate agents as urban gatekeepers, paper presented to British Sociological Association, Stirling.

Hatch, S. and **Sherrott, R.** (1973) Positive discrimination and the distribution of deprivations, *Policy and Politics*, **1**, 223–40.

Hatt, P. (1946) The concept of Natural Area, *American Sociological Review*, **11**, 423–7.

Hawley, A.H. (1950) *Human Ecology: A Theory of Community Structure*, Ronald Press, New York.

Hawley, A.H. and **Duncan, O.D.** (1957) Social area analysis: a critical appraisal, *Land Economics*, **33**, 227–45.

Hawley, A.H., and **Rock, V.P.** (eds) (1975) *Metropolitan America in Contemporary Perspective*, Halstead Press, New York.

Hay, A. (1979) Positivism in Human Geography: response to critics, pp. 1–26 in Herbert, D. and Johnston, R.J. (eds) *Geography and the Urban Environment*, Vol. 2, Wiley, Chichester.

Healey, P. and **Underwood, J.** (1978) Professional ideals and planning practice, *Progress in Planning*, **9**, 73–127.

Heclo, H.A. (1969) The Councillor's job, *Public Administration*, **43**, 185–202.

Helper, R. (1969) *Racial policies and practices of real estate brokers*, Minneapolis University Press, Minneapolis.

Hennock, E.P. (1973) *Fit and Proper Persons*, Arnold, London.

Herbert, D.T. (1967a) Social area analysis: a British study, *Urban Studies*, **4**, 41–60.

Herbert, D.T. (1967b) The use of diagnostic variables in the analysis of urban structure, *Tijdschrift voor Economische en Sociale Geografie*, **58**, 5–10.

Herbert, D.T. (1968) Principal components analysis and British studies of urban-social structure, *Professional Geographer*, **20**, 280–3.

Herbert, D.T. (1972) *Urban Geography: A Social Perspective*, David & Charles, Newton Abbot.

Herbert, D.T. (1973a) Residential mobility and preference: a study of Swansea, pp. 103–21 in Clark, B.D. and Gleave, M.B. (eds), *Social Patterns in Cities*, Institute of British Geographers, Special Publication No. 5, London.

Herbert, D.T. (1973b) The residential mobility process: some empirical observations, *Area*, **5**, 44–8.

Herbert, D.T. (1975) Urban deprivation: definition, measurement and spatial qualities, *Geographical Journal*, **141**, 362–72.

Herbert, D.T. (1976a) Social deviancy in the city: a spatial perspective, pp. 89–121 in Herbert D. and Johnston R.J. (eds), *Social Areas in Cities*, Vol. 2, Wiley, London.

Herbert, D.T. (1976b) The study of delinquency areas: a social geographical approach, *Transactions, Institute of British Geographers*, N.S. **1**, 472–492.

Herbert, D.T. (1976c) Urban education: problems and policies, pp. 123–58 in Herbert, D. and Johnston, R.J. (eds), *Social Areas in Cities*, Vol. 2, Wiley, London.

Herbert, D.T. (1977a) Crime, delinquency and the urban environment, *Progress in Human Geography*, **1**, 208–39.

Herbert, D.T. (1977b) An areal and ecological analysis

of delinquency residence: Cardiff 1966 and 1971, *Tijdschrift voor Economische en Sociale Geografie*, **68**, 83–99.

Herbert, D.T. (1979) Urban crime: a geographical perspective, pp. 117–38 in D. Herbert and D.M. Smith (eds), *Social Problems in the City*, Oxford University Press, Oxford.

Herbert, D.T. and Johnston, R.J. (1976a) *Social Areas in Cities*, Vol. 1, *Spatial Processes and Form*, Wiley, London.

Herbert, D.T. and Johnston, R.J. (1976b) *Social Areas in Cities*, Vol. 2, *Spatial Perspectives on Problems and Policies*, Wiley, London.

Herbert, D.T. and Johnston, R.J. (eds) (1978) *Geography and the Urban Environment: Progress in Research and Applications*, Vol. 1, Wiley, Chichester.

Hill, D. (1970) *Participating in Local Affairs*, Penguin, Harmondsworth.

Hill, R.C. (1978) Fiscal collapse and political struggle in decaying central cities in the United States, pp. 213–40 in Tabb, W. and Sawers, L. (eds); *Marxism and the Metropolis*, Oxford University Press, New York.

Hillery, G.A. (1955) Definition of Community: Areas of Agreement, *Rural Sociology*, **20**, 111–23.

Hiorns, F.R. (1956) *Town Building in History*, Arnold, London.

Hiro, D. (1973) *Black British, White British*, Penguin, Harmondsworth.

Hirschman, A.O. (1970) *Exit, Voice and Loyalty*, Harvard University Press, Cambridge, Mass.

Hofstadter, R. (1955) *The Age of Reform*, Knopf, New York.

Hoggart, R. (1958) *The Uses of Literacy*, Penguin, Harmondsworth.

Hoivik, T. (1973) *Norvege 1990, Analyse et Prévision*, *Etudes Futuribles*, O.E.C.D., Paris.

Holmes, J. (1976) Urban housing problems and public policy, pp. 400–20 in Yeates, M. and Garner, B. *The North American City*, (2nd ed.), Harper & Row, New York.

Homans, G.C. (1950) *The Human Group*, Harcourt Brace, New York.

Homans, G.C. (1961) *Social Behaviour: Its Elementary Forms*, Routledge & Kegan Paul, London.

Honey, R.D. (1976) Metropolitan governance, pp. 425–62 in Adams, J.S. (ed.), *Urban Policymaking and Metropolitan Dynamics*, Ballinger, Mass.

Hopkins, E.J., Pye, A.M., Soloman, M. and Soloman, S. (1968) The relation of patients' age, sex and distance from surgery to the demand on the family doctor, *Journal of the Royal College of General Practitioners*, **16**, 368–78.

Howard, E. (1902) *Garden cities of Tomorrow*, reprinted by Faber & Faber, London (1946).

Hoyt, H. (1939) *The Structure and Growth of Residential Neighbourhoods in American cities*, Federal Housing Administration, Washington, D.C.

Hunter, A.A. (1974) Community change: a stochastic analysis of Chicago's local communities, 1930–1960, *American Journal of Sociology*, **79** 923–47.

Hunter, F. (1953) *Community Power Structure: A Study of Decision Makers*, University of North Carolina Press, Chapel Hill.

Hurd, R.M. (1903) *Principles of city land values*, The Record and Guide, New York.

Hurst, M.E. (1975) *I Came to the City: Essays and Comments on the Urban Scene*, Houghton Mifflin, Boston.

Hyland, G. (1970) Social interaction and urban opportunity: the Appalachian in-migrant in the Cincinnati Central City, *Antipode*, **2**, 68–83.

Inglis, F. (1975) Roads, office blocks and the new misery, pp. 168–88 in Abbs, P. (ed.), *The Black Rainbow*, Heinemann, London.

Isard, W. (1942) A neglected cycle: the transport building cycle, *Review of Economic Statistics*, **24**, 149–58.

Irving, H. (1978) Space and environment in interpersonal relations, pp. 249–84 in Herbert, D. and Johnston, R.J. (eds), *Geography and the Urban Environment*, Vol. 1, Wiley, Chichester.

Isler, M. (1970) *Thinking About Housing*, Urban Institute, Washington.

Jackson, B. (1968) *Working Class Community*, Routledge & Kegan Paul, London.

Janelle, D.G. and Millward, H.A. (1976) Locational conflict patterns and urban ecological structure, *Tijdschrift voor Economische en Sociale Geografie*, **67**, 102–13.

Janson, C-G. (1971) A preliminary report on Swedish urban spatial structure, *Economic Geography*, **47**, 249–57.

Jacobs, J. (1961) *The Death and Life of Great American Cities*, Vintage, New York.

Jephcott, P. (1971) *Homes in High Flats*, Oliver & Boyd, Edinburgh.

Johnson, J. (ed.), (1974) *Suburban Growth*, Wiley, London.

Johnson, J.H., Salt, J. and Wood, P.A. (1974) *Housing and the migration of labour in England and Wales*, Saxon House, Farnborough.

Johnston, R.J. (1966) The location of high status residential areas, *Geografiska Annaler*, **48B**, 23–35.

Johnston, R.J. (1969a) Towards an analytical study of the townscape: the residential building fabric, *Geografiska Annaler*, **51B**, (1), 20–32.

Johnston, R.J. (1969b) Population movements and metropolitan expansion, *Transactions, Institute of British Geographers*, **46**, 69–91.

Johnston, R.J. (1969c) Some tests of a model of intra-urban population mobility: Melbourne, Australia, *Urban Studies*, **6**, 34–57.

Johnston, R.J. (1969d) Process of change in the high status residential districts of Christchurch, 1951–64, *New Zealand Geographer*, **25**, 1–15.

Johnston, R.J. (1970) On spatial patterns in the residential structure of cities, *Canadian Geographer*, **14**, 361–67.

Johnston, R.J. (1971) *Urban Residential Patterns: An Introductory Review*, Bell, London.

Johnston, R.J. (1973a) Social area change in Melbourne 1961–1966, *Australian Geographical Studies*, **11**, 79–98.

Johnston, R.J. (1973b) The factorial ecology of major New Zealand urban areas: a comparative study, *Institute of British Geographers, Special Publication*, **5**, 143–68.

Johnston, R.J. (ed.) (1973c) *Urbanization in New Zealand: Geographical Essays*, Reed, Wellington.

Johnston, R.J. (1973d) Spatial patterns in suburban evaluations, *Environment and Planning*, **5A**, 385–95.

Johnston, R.J. (1974) Local effects in voting at a local election, *Annals, Association of American Geographers*, **64**, 418–29.

Johnston, R.J. (1976a) Residential area characteristics: research methods for identifying urban sub-areas – social area analysis and factorial ecology, pp. 193–236 in Herbert, D. and Johnston R.J. (eds) *Social Areas in Cities*, Wiley, London.

Johnston, R.J. (1976b) *Classification in Geography*, Catmog 6, Institute of British Geographers, London.

Johnston, R.J. (1977) Urban geography: city structures, *Progress in Human Geography*, **1**, 118–23.

Johnston, R.J. (1978) *Multivariate Statistical Analysis in Geography*, Longman, London.

Johnston, R.J. (1979a) Urban geography: city structures, *Progress in Human Geography*, **3**, 133–8.

Johnston, R.J. (1979b) *Political, Electoral and Spatial Systems*, Oxford University Press. Oxford.

Johnston, R.J. and **Rimmer, P.J.** (1969) *Retailing in Melbourne*, Publication HG/3, Department of Human Geography, Australian National University, Canberra.

Jones, E. (1958) The delimitation of some urban landscape features in Belfast, *Scottish Geographical Magazine*, **74**, 150–62.

Jones, E. and **Eyles, J.** (1977) *An Introduction to Social Geography*, Oxford University Press, London.

Jones, F.L. (1969) *Dimensions of Urban Social Structure*, Australian National University Press, Canberra.

Jones, G.S. (1971) *Outcast London*, Oxford University Press, London.

Jones, G.S. (1981) *Urbanization and class consciousness*, Arnold, London.

Jones, G.W. (1969) *Borough Politics: A Study of the Wolverhampton Town Council 1888–1964*, Macmillan, London.

Jones, P.N. (1979) Ethnic areas in British cities, pp. 158–185 in D. Herbert and D.M. Smith (eds), *Social Problems and the City: Geographical Perspectives*, Oxford University Press, Oxford.

Jones, T.P. and **McEvoy D.** (1978) Race and space in cloud cuckoo land, *Area*, **10**, 162–6.

de Jonge, D. (1962) Images of urban areas: their structure and psychological foundations, *Journal of the American Institute of Planners*, **28**, 266–76.

Kain, J.F. (1962) The journey to work as a determinant of residential location, *Papers and Proceedings, Regional Science Association*, **9**, 137–60.

Kain, J.F. and **Quigley, J.M.** (1970) Measuring the quality of the residential environment, *Environment and Planning*, **2**, 23–32.

Kain, J.F. and **Quigley, J.M.** (1972) Housing market discrimination, homeownership, and savings behaviour, *American Economic Review*, **62**, 263–77.

Kaiser, E.J. and **Weiss, S.F.** (1970) Public policy and the residential development process, *Journal of the American Institute of Planners*, **36**, 30–7.

Kantrowitz, N. (1973) *Ethnic and Racial Segregation in the New York Metropolis*, Praeger, New York.

Kaplan, H. (1967) *Urban Political Systems*, Columbia University Press, New York.

Kaplan, S. and **Kaplan, R.** (eds) (1978) *Humanscape: The environments for people*, Duxbury/Wadsworth, Mass.

Karp, D.A., Stone, G.P. and **Yoels, W.C.** (1977) *Being Urban: A Social Psychological View of City Life*, Heath, Lexington, Mass.

Kasarda, J. (1972) The impact of suburban population growth on central city service functions, *American Journal of Sociology*, **77**, 1111–24.

Kasperson, R.E. and **Breitbart, M.** (1974) *Participation, Decentralization and Advocacy Planning*, Resource Paper No. 25, Commission on College Geography, Association of American Geographers, Washington, D.C.

Kearsley, G.W. and **Srivastava, S.R.** (1974) The spatial evolution of Glasgow's Asian community, *Scottish Geographical Magazine*, **90**, 110–24.

Kellett, J.R. (1969) *The Impact of Railways on Victorian cities*, Routledge & Kegan Paul, London.

Kennedy, R. (1943) Premarital residential propinquity, *American Journal of Sociology*, **48**, 580–4.

Kennedy, C.G. (1962) Commuter services in the Boston area 1835–1860, *Business History Review*, **26**, 277–87.

Kennedy, J.W. (1975) *Adapting to new environments: residential mobility from the mover's point of view*, University of Toronto, Centre for Urban and Community Studies, Major Report No. 3, Toronto.

Kennedy, M. (1970) *Portrait of Manchester*, Hale, Manchester.

Kilroy, B. (1972) Improvement grants threaten North Kensington, *Housing Review*, **21**, 79–80.

Kirby, A.M. (1976) Housing market studies: a critical review, *Transactions, Institute of British Geographers*, N.S., **1**, 2–9.

Kirby, A.M. (1977) *Housing Action Areas in Great Britain: 1975–1977*, Geographical Paper No. 60, Department of Geography, University of Reading.

Kirby, A.M. (1979a) *Towards an Understanding of the Local State*, Geographical Paper No. 70, Department of Geography, University of Reading.

Kirby, A.M. (1979b) *Education, Health and Housing*, Saxon House, Farnborough.

Kirby, D.A. (1979) *Slum Housing and Residential Renewal: The Case in Urban Britain*, Longman, London.

Kirk, W. (1963) Problems in Geography, *Geography*, **48**, 357–71.

Kirmeyer, S. (1978) Urban density and pathology: a review of research, *Environment and Behaviour*, **10**, 247–270.

Klein, H.J. (1967) The delimitation of the town centre in the image of its citizens, pp. 286–306 in Brill, E.J. (ed.) *Urban Core and Inner City*, University of Leiden.

Klein, J. (1965) *Samples from English Culture*, Routledge & Kegan Paul, London.

Knox, P.L. (1976) Fieldwork in urban geography: assessing environmental quality, *Scottish Geographical Magazine*, **92**, 101–7.

Knox, P.L. (1978a) Community councils, electoral districts and social geography, *Area*, **10**, 387–91.

Knox, P.L. (1978b) The intra-urban ecology of primary medical care: patterns of accessibility and their policy implications, *Environment and Planning*, **A10**, 415–35.

Knox, P.L. (1979a) Medical deprivation, area deprivation, and public policy, *Social Science and Medicine*, **13D**, 111–21.

Knox, P.L. (1979b) The accessibility of primary care to urban patients: a geographical analysis, *Journal of the Royal College of General Practitioners*, **29**, 160–8.

Knox, P.L. (1980a) Measures of accessibility as social indicators, *Social Indicators Research*, 7, 367–77.

Knox, P.L. (1980b) Urban deprivation and health care provision, *Medicine in Society*, 5, 54–9.

Knox, P.L. and **Pacione, M.** (1980) Locational behaviour, place preferences and the inverse care law in the distribution of primary medical care, *Geoforum*, 11, 43–55.

Knox, P.L. and **MacLaran, A.C.** (1978) Values and perceptions in descriptive approaches to urban social geography, pp. 197–247 in Herbert, D. and Johnston, R.J. (eds) *Geography and the Urban Environment*, Vol. 1, Wiley, Chichester.

Kohl, J.G. (1841) *Der Verkehr und die Ansiedlung der Menschen in ihrer Abhängigkeit von der Gestaltungder Erdoberfläche*, Arnoldische Buchhandlung, Leipzig.

Korte, C. and **Kerr, N.** (1975) Response to altruistic opportunities in urban and non-urban settings, *Journal of Social Psychology*, 95, 183–4.

Kramer, J.R. (1970) *The American Minority Community*, Crowell, New York.

Kramer, R.M. (1969) *Participation and the Poor*, Prentice-Hall, Englewood Cliffs, N.J.

Kristoff, F.S. (1970) Economic facets of New York City's housing problems, pp. 79–93 in Fitch, L. and Walsh, A. (eds) *Agenda for a City*, Institute for Public Administration, New York.

Kuper, L. (ed.) (1953) *Living in Towns*, Cresset, London.

Lambert, C. (1976) *Building Societies, Surveyors and the Older Areas of Birmingham*, Working Paper No. 38, Centre for Urban and Regional Studies, University of Birmingham.

Lambert, J., Paris, C., and **Blackaby, R.** (1978) *Housing Policy and the State*, Macmillan, London.

Lambert, J.R. (1970) *Crime, Police and Race Relations: A Study in Birmingham*, Oxfore University Press, London.

Land, K. (1969) Duration of residence and prospective migration: further evidence, *Demography*, 6, 133–40.

Lanegran, D.A. and **Palm, R.** (eds) (1978) *An Invitation to Geography*, McGraw-Hill, New York.

Lankford, P. (1971) The changing location of physicians, *Antipode*, 3, 68–72.

Lansing, J.B., Clifton, C.W. and **Morgan, J.N.** (1969) *New Homes and Poor People: A Study of Chains of Moves*, Institute for Social Research, University of Michigan, Ann Arbor.

Lasswell, H. (1979) *The Signature of Power*, Transaction Books, New Brunswick, N.J.

Latane, B. and **Darley, J.M.** (1969) By-stander apathy, *American Scientist*, 57, 244–68.

Laumann, E.O. (1966) *Prestige and Association in an Urban Community*, Bobbs Merrill, Indianapolis.

de Lauwe, P.H.C. (1952) *Paris et l'Agglomeration Parisienne*, Mouton, Paris.

Lave, L.B. (1970) Congestion and urban location, *Papers and Proceedings, Regional Science Association*, 25, 133–50.

Lavedan, P. (1926–52) *Historie de l'urbanisme* (4 vols) Laureus, Paris.

Lavedan, P. (1941) *Historie de l'urbanisme: Renaisance et temps modernes*, Laureus, Paris.

Lawton, R. (1959) Irish immigration into England and Wales in the mid-nineteenth century, *Irish Geography*, 4, 35–54.

Lawton, R. (1972) An age of great cities, *Town Planning Review*, 43, 199–224.

Lawless, P. (1979) *Urban Deprivation and Government Initiative*, Faber & Faber, London.

Lazarus, R.S. (1969) *Patterns of Adjustment and Human Effectiveness*, McGraw-Hill, New York.

Lee, J.M. (1963) *Social Leaders and Public Persons*, Oxford University Press, London.

Lee, R. (1976) Public finance and urban economy: some comments on spatial reformism, *Antipode*, 8, 44–50.

Lee, T. (1968) Urban neighbourhood as a socio-spatial schema, *Human Relations*, 21, 241–68.

Lee, T. (1970) Perceived distance as a function of direction in the city, *Environment and Behaviour*, 20, 40–51.

Lee, T. (1976) Cities in the mind, pp. 159–87 in Herbert, D.T. and Johnston, R.J. (eds), *Social Areas in Cities*, Vol. 2, Wiley, Chichester.

Lee, T.R. (1977) *Race and Residence*, Clarendon Press, Oxford.

Lees, A. and **Lees, N.** (1976) *The Urbanisation of European Society in the Nineteenth Century*, D.C. Heath, Lexington, Mass..

De Leeuw, F. (1972) *The Distribution of Housing Services*, Urban Institute, Washington.

Lewin, K. (1938) *The conceptual representation and the measurement of Psychological Forces*, Duke University Press, Durham, North Carolina.

Lewis, C.R. (1979) A Stage in the development of the industrial town: a case study of Cardiff, 1845–75, *Transactions, Institute of British Geographers*, New Series, 4, 129–52.

Lewis, J.P. (1965) *Building cycles and Britain's Growth*, Macmillan, London.

Lewis, N. (1976) Council housing allocation: problems of discretion and control, *Public Administration*, 54, 147–60.

Lewis, O. (1966) The culture of poverty, *Scientific American*, 215, 19–25.

Lewis, O. (1952) Urbanisation without breakdown, *Scientific Monthly*, 75, 31–41.

Ley, D. (1972) The Black inner city as frontier outpost: images and behaviour of a Philadelphia neighbourhood, unpublished Ph.D. dissertation, Pennsylvania State University.

Ley, D. and **Cybriwsky, R.** (1974) The spatial ecology of stripped cars, *Environment and Behaviour*, 6, 63–7.

Lieberson, S. (1958) Ethnic groups and the practice of medicine, *American Sociological Review*, 23, 542–49.

Liebow, E. (1967) *Tally's Corner*, Little, Brown, Boston.

Lindley, D.V. (1961) Dynamic programming and decision theory, *Applied Statistics*, 10, 39–51.

Lineberry, R.L. (1977) *Equality and Urban Policy*, Sage, Beverly Hills.

Linton, Mields and **Coston, Inc.** (1971) *A Study of the Problems of Abandoned Housing*, Report PB 212–198, National Technical Information Service, Springfield, Va.

Lojkine, J. (1974) *La politique urbaine dans la région Lyonnaise 1945–1972*, Mouton, Paris.

Lojkine, J. (1976) Contribution to a Marxist theory of capitalist urbanization, pp. 119–46, in Pickvance, C. (ed.) *Urban Sociology*, Tavistock, London.

London Borough of Southwark (1973) Preliminary Research, unpublished report, Planning Division, Southwark Development Department, London.

Lovrich, N.P. (1974) Differing priorities in an urban electorate: service preferences among Anglo, Black and Mexican American voters, *Social Sciences Quarterly*, **4**, 704–17.

Lowe, P.D. (1977) Amenity and equity: a review of local environmental pressure groups in Britain, *Environment and Planning*, **A9**, 35–58.

Lowenthal, D. (1961) Geography, experience and imagination: towards a geographic epistemology, *Annals, Association of American Geographers*, **51** 241–60.

Lowenthal, D. and **Prince, H.C.** (1964) The English landscape, *Geographical Review*, **54**, 309–46.

Lowery, R.A. (1973) A method for analysing distance concepts of urban residents, pp. 338–60 in Downs, R. and Stea, D. (eds), *Image and Environment*, Aldine, Chicago.

Lowry, L.S. (1960) Filtering and housing standards: a conceptual analysis, *Land Economics*, **36**, 362–70.

Lupton, J. and **Mitchell, G.D.** (1954) *Neighbourhood and Community*, Liverpool University Press, Liverpool.

Lynch, K. (1960) *The Image of the City*, M.I.T. Press, Cambridge, Mass.

Lynd, R.S. and **Lynd, H.M.** (1956) *Middletown*, Harcourt, Brace and World, New York.

Lyon, D. (1970) Capital spending and the neighbourhoods of Philadelphia, *Business Review* (May), 16–27.

Lyon, S. and **Wood, M.E.** (1977) Choosing a house, *Environment and Planning*, **9**, 1169–76.

McCann, L.D. and **Smith, P.J.** (1972) Residential morphology and urban social structure. Paper presented to section XI of the I.G.U. Conference, Montreal, Canada (mimeo).

McCarthy, D. and **Saegert, S.** (1978) Residential density, social overload and social withdrawal, *Human Ecology*, **6**, 253–272.

McCarthy, M.P. (1977) on bosses, reformers and urban growth: some suggestions for a political typology of American cities, *Journal of Urban History*, **4**, 29–38.

McDowell, L. (1978) University accommodation officers: welfare workers or estate agents? *Higher Education Review*, **10**, 55–62.

McElrath, D.C. (1962) The social areas of Rome: A comparative analysis, *American Sociological Review*, **27**, 376–91.

McElrath, D.C. (1968) Societal scale and social differentiation, pp. 33–52 in Greer, S. *et al.* (eds) *The New Urbanization*, St. Martin's Press, New York.

McGinnis, R. (1968) A stochastic model of social mobility, *American Sociological Review*, **33**, 712–21.

McGregor, A. (1977) Intra-urban variations in unemployment duration: a case study, *Urban Studies*, **14**, 315–26.

McKenzie, R. (1968) *On Human Ecology*, University fo Chicago Press, Chicago.

McLeod, H. (1974) *Class and Religion in Victorian Britain*, Croom Helm, London.

McLoughlin, J.B. (1969) *Urban and Regional Planning: A Systems approach*, Faber & Faber, London.

Malpass, P. (1975) Professionalism and the role of architects in local authority housing, *Journal, Royal Institute of British Architects*, **82**, 6–29.

Mandelker, D.R. (1971) *The Zoning Dilemma*, Bobbs-Merrill, New York.

Mann, P. (1965) *An Approach to Urban Sociology*, Routledge & Kegan Paul, London.

Maris, R.W. (1969) *Social Forces in Urban Suicide*, Dorsey Press, Illinois.

Marris, P. and **Rein, M.** (1973) *Dilemmas of Social Reform*, Aldine, Chicago.

Maslow, A.H. (1970) *Motivation and Personality*, Harper & Row, New York.

Massam, B. (1975) *Location and Space in Social Administration*, Arnold, London.

Mawby, R.I. (1977) Defensible space: a theoretical and empirical appraisal, *Urban Studies*, **14**, 169–79.

Mayhew, H. (1862) *London Labour and the London Poor*, Griffin, Bohn, London.

Mays, J.B. (1963) Delinquency areas: a re-assessment, *British Journal of Criminology*, **3**, 216–30.

Means, R. (1977) *Social Work and the 'Underserving' Poor*, Occasional Paper No. 37, Center for Urban and Regional Studies, University of Birmingham.

Mearns, A. (1883) *The Bitter Cry of Outcast London: An Inquiry into the Condition of the Abject Poor*, publisher unspecified, London.

Mechanic, D. (1968) *Medical Sociology: A Selective View*, Free Press, New York.

Megee, M. (1976) Restructuring the health care delivery system in the United States, pp. 293–330 in Adams, J.S. (ed.) *Urban Policymaking and Metropolitan Dynamics*, Ballinger, Cambridge, Mass.

Mellor, R. (1973) Planning for housing: market processes and constraints, *Planning Outlook*, **13**, 45–9.

Mercer, C. (1975) *Living in Cities: Psychology and the Urban Environment*, Penguin, Harmondsworth.

Mercer, J. and **Hultquist, J.** (1976) National progress toward housing and urban renewal goals, pp. 101–62 in Adams, J.S. (ed.), *Urban Policymaking and Metropolitan Dynamics*, Ballinger, Cambridge, Mass.

Merton, R. (1957) *Social Theory and Social Structure*, Free Press, Glencoe, Illinois.

Michelson, W. (1977) *Environmental Choice, Human Behaviour and Residential Satisfaction*, Oxford University Press, New York.

Milgram, S. (1970) The experience of living in cities, *Science*, **167**, 1461–8.

Milgram, S. and **Jodelet, D.** (1976) Psychological maps of Paris, pp. 104–24 in Proshansky, H., Rivlin, L. and Ittelson, W.H. (eds), *Environmental Psychology*, Holt, Rinehart and Winston, New York.

Miliband, R. (1969) *The state in capitalist society*, Weidenfeld & Nicolson, London.

Miliband, R. (1974) Politics and poverty, pp. 183–96 in Wedderburn, D. (ed.) *Poverty, Inequality and Class Structure*, Cambridge University Press, Cambridge.

Miliband, R. (1977) *Marxism and Politics*, Oxford University Press, London.

Mills, E.S. (1967) An aggregate model of resource allocation in a metropolitan area, *American Economic Review*, **57**, 197–211.

Mills, E.S. and **MacKinnon, J.** (1973) Notes on the new urban economics, *Bell Journal of Economics and Management Science*, **4**, 593–601.

Mintz, N.L. and **Schwarz, D.T.** (1964) Urban psychology and psychoses, *International Journal of Social Psychiatry*, **10**, 101–17.

Mitchell, J.C. (ed.), (1969) *Social Networks in Urban Situations*, Manchester University Press, Manchester.

Mogey, J.M. (1956) *Family and Neighbourhood*, Oxford University Press, London.

Molotch, H. (1972) *Managed Integration: Dilemmas of Doing Good in the City*, University of California Press, Berkeley.

Moore, E.G. (1969) The structure of intra-urban movement rates: an ecological model, *Urban Studies*, **6**, 17–33.

Moore, E.G. (1971) Comments on the use of ecological models in the study of residential mobility in the city, *Economic Geography*, **47**, 73–84.

Moore, E.G. (1972) *Residential Mobility in the City*, Association of Resource Paper, Commission on College Geography, American Geographers, No. 13, Washington, D.C.

Moore, G.T. and **Golledge, R.G.** (eds) (1976) *Environmental Knowing: Theories, Research and Methods*, Dowden, Hutchinson & Ross, Stroudsburg, Pa.

Morgan, B.S. (1971) The morphological region as a social unit, *Tijdschrift voor Economische en Sociale Geografie*, **72**, 226–33.

Morgan, B.S. (1973) Housing type and the social characteristics of residents: the case of Exeter, Devon, *Geografiska Annaler*, **55B**, 57–70.

Morgan, B.S. (1976) The bases of family status segregation: a case study in Exeter, *Transactions, Institute of British Geographers*, New Series, **1**, 83–107.

Morgan, B.S. (1979) Residential segregation, marriage and the evolution of the stratification system: a case study in Christchurch, New Zealand, *Environment and Planning*, **11A**, 209–17.

Morrill, R.L. (1965) The negro ghetto: problems and alternatives, *Geographical Review*, **55**, 339–61.

Morris, A.E.J. (1972) *History of Urban Form*, Godwin, London.

Morris, D. (1967) *The Naked Ape*, McGraw-Hill, New York.

Morris, J. (1976) Access to community health services in Melbourne, *Papers of the First Australia–New Zealand Regional Science Conference*, Australia–New Zealand Regional Science Association, Brisbane.

Mortimore, M.J. (1969) Landownership and urban growth in Bradford and its environs in the West Riding conurbation, *Transactions, Institute of British Geographers*, **46**, 99–113.

Morton, J. (1977) How we pay for housing, *New Society*, **41**, 7 July, 18–19.

Mowrer, E.R. (1958) The family in suburbia, pp. 186–201 in Dorbriner, W.M. (ed.) *The Suburban Community*, Putnam, London.

Muller, P.O. (1976a) *The Outer City*, Association of American Geographers, Resource Paper No. 22, Washington, D.C.

Muller, P.O. (1976b) Social transportation geography, *Progress in Geography*, **8**, 208–31.

Muller, T. (1975) *Growing and Declining Urban Areas: A Fiscal Comparison*, The Urban Institute, Washington, D.C.

Mumford, L. (1934) *Technics and Civilisation*, Routledge, London.

Mumford, L. (1940) *The Culture of Cities*, Secker & Warburg, London.

Mumford, L. (1961) *The City in History*, Secker & Warburg, London.

Murdie, R.A. (1969) *Factorial Ecology of Metropolitan Toronto 1951–1961*, Research Paper No. 116, Department of Geography, University of Chicago.

Murdie, R.A. (1976) Spatial form in the Residential Mosaic, pp. 237–72 in Herbert, D. and Johnston, R.J. (eds) *Social Areas in Cities*, Vol. 1, Wiley, Chichester.

Murdock, G.P. (ed.) (1937) *Studies in the Science of Society*, Yale University Press, New Haven.

Murie, A., Niner, P. and **Watson, C.** (1976) *Housing Policy and the Housing System*, Urban and Regional Studies No. 7, University of Birmingham, Allen & Unwin, London.

Muth, R.F. (1969) *Cities and Housing*, University of Chicago Press, Chicago.

National Urban League (1971) *National Survey of Housing Abandonment*, The Centre for Community Change, New York.

Neenan, W.B. (1972) *Political Economy of Urban Areas*, Markham, Chicago.

Nelson, H. and **Clark, W.A.V.** (1976) *Los Angeles: The Metropolitan Experience*, Ballinger, Cambridge, Mass.

Neutze, M. (1971) *People and Property in Randwick*, Urban Research Unit, Australian National University, Canberra.

Nevitt, A.A. (1978) Issues in housing, pp. 183–215 in Davies, R. and Hall, P. (eds), *Issues in Urban Society*, Penguin, Harmondsworth.

Newman, O. (1972) *Defensible Space*, Macmillan, New York.

Newson, J. and **Newson, E.** (1965) *Patterns of Infant Care in an Urban Community*, Penguin, Harmondsworth.

Newton, K. (1975) Social class, political structure and public goods in American urban politics, *Urban Affairs Quarterly*, **11**, 241–64.

Newton, K. (1976) *Second City Politics*, Oxford University Press, London.

Newton, K. (1978) Conflict avoidance and conflict supression: the case of urban politics in the United States, pp. 76–93 in Cox, K.R. (ed.) *Urbanization and Conflict in Market Societies*, Methuen, London.

Newton, P.W. and **Johnston, R.J.** (1976) Residential area characteristics and residential area homogeneity: further thoughts on extensions to the factorial ecology method, *Environment and Planning*, **A8**, 543–52.

Newton, R. (1968) Society and politics in Exeter 1837–1914, pp. 301–14 in Dyos, H.J. (ed.) *The Study of Urban History*, Arnold, London.

Niner, P. (1975) *Local authority housing policy and practice: a case study approach*, Occasional Paper No. 31, Centre for Urban and Regional Studies, University of Birmingham.

Niner, P. and **Watson, C.J.** (1978) Housing in British cities, pp. 319–51 in Herbert, D.T. and Johnston, R.J. (eds) *Geography and the Urban Environment*, Vol. 1, Wiley, Chichester.

Norborg, K. (ed.) (1962) *Proceedings of the I.G.U. Symposium in Urban Geography*, Lund Series B, No. 24., Lund, Sweden.

Nordstrand, E.A. (1973) Relationships between intra-urban migration and urban residential social structure, M.A. thesis, University of Minnesota, Minneapolis.

Norman, P. (1975) Managerialism: a review of recent work, pp. 62–86 in Harloe, M. (ed.), *Proceedings of the Conference on Urban Change and Conflict*, Centre for Environmental Studies, London.

O'Connor, J. (1973) *The fiscal crisis of the state*, St. Martin's Press, New York.

OECD (1977) *Measuring Social Well-Being*, OECD Social Indicator Development Programme Series, No. 3, Paris.

Offe, C. (1974) Structural problems of the capitalist state, pp. 79–93 in Beyme, K. (ed.) *German Political Studies*, Vol. 1, Sage, Beverly Hills.

Offe, C. (1976) Political authority and class structures, pp. 388–421 in Connerton, P. (ed.) *Critical Sociology*, Penguin, Harmondsworth.

Office of Population Censuses and Surveys (1976) *The General Household Survey: Introductory Report*, H.M.S.O., London.

Office of Population Censuses and Surveys (1978) *The General Household Survey 1976*, OPCS Social Survey Division, H.M.S.O., London.

Ogden, P. and **Winchester, S.** (1975) The residential segregation of provincial migrants in Paris in 1911, *Transactions, Institute of British Geographers*, 65, 29–44.

O'Loughlin, J. (1976) Malapportionment and gerrymandering in the ghetto, pp. 539–65 in Adams, J.S. (ed.), *Urban Policymaking and Metropolitan Dynamics*, Ballinger, Cambridge, Mass.

Olives, J. (1976) The struggle against urban renewal in the 'Cité d'Aliarte' (Paris), pp. 174–97 in Pickvance, C. (ed.) *Urban Sociology*, Tavistock, London.

Olsen, M.E. (1968) Two categories of political alienation, *Social Forces*, 47, 288–99.

Olson, E. (1969) A competitive theory of the housing market, *American Economic Review*, 59, 612–22.

Olson, M. (1971) *The Logic of Collective Action*, Shocken Books, New York.

Openshaw, S. (1969) *Canonical correlates of social structure and urban building fabric: an explanatory study*, Seminar Paper No. 11, Department of Geography, University of Newcastle upon Tyne, Newcastle upon Tyne.

Orleans, P. (1973) Differential cognition of urban residents: effects of social scale on mapping, pp. 115–30 in Downs, R. and Stea, D. (eds) *Image and Environment*, Chicago, Aldine.

Orr, D.M., Jr. (1969) The persistence of the gerrymander in North Carolina congressional redistricting, *Southeastern Geographer*, 9, 39–54.

Pahl, R.E. (1969) Urban social theory and research, *Environment and Planning*, A1, 143–53.

Pahl, R.E. (1970a) *Whose City?* Longman, London.

Pahl, R.E. (1970b) *Patterns of Urban Life*, Longman, London.

Pahl, R.E. (1975) *Whose City?* Penguin, Harmondsworth (2nd ed.).

Pahl, R.E. (1977) Managers, technical experts and the state: forms of mediation, manipulation and dominance in urban and regional development, pp. 49–60 in Harloe, M. (ed.) *Captive Cities*, Wiley, London.

Pahl, R.E. (1979) Socio-political factors in resource allocation, pp. 33–46 in D. Herbert and D.M. Smith (eds), *Social Problems and the City*, Oxford University Press, Oxford.

Palm, R. (1973) Factorial ecology and the community of outlook, *Annals, Association of American Geographers*, 63, 341–6.

Palm, R. (1976a) Real estate agents and geographical information, *Geographical Review*, 66, 226–80.

Palm, R. (1976b) The role of real estate agents as information mediators in two American cities, *Geografiska Annaler*, 58B, 28–41.

Palm, R. (1978) Spatial segmentation of the urban housing market, *Economic Geography*, 54, 210–21.

Palm, R. (1979) Financial and real estate institutions in the housing market: a study of recent house price changes in the San Francisco Bay area, pp. 83–123 in Herbert, D. and Johnston, R.J. (eds), *Geography and the Urban Environment*, Vol. 2, Wiley, Chichester.

Palm, R. and **Caruso, D.** (1972) Labelling in factorial ecology, *Annals, Association of American Geographers*, 62, 122–33.

Palmer, R. (1955) Realtors, as social gatekeepers, Ph.D. thesis, Yale University, New Haven.

Papageorgiou, G.J. (1976) On spatial consumer equilibrium, pp. 145–76 in Papageorgiou, G.J. (ed.), *Mathematical Land Use Theory*, Lexington Books, Lexington, Mass.

Park, R.E. (1916) The city: suggestions for the investigation of human behaviour in an urban environment, *American Journal of Sociology*, 20, 577–612.

Park, R.E. (1936) Human ecology, *American Journal of Sociology*, 42, 1.

Park, R.E., Burgess, E.W. and **McKenzie, R.D.** (1925) *The City*, University of Chicago Press, Chicago.

Parker, J. and **Dugmore, K.** (1976) *Colour and the Allocation of G.L.C. housing: The Report of the G.L.C. Lettings Survey 1974–5*, Greater London Council, London.

Parry, H.B. (ed.) (1974) *Population and its problems*, Clarendon, Oxford.

Parsons, T. (1951) *The Social System* Tavistock, London.

Paterson, J. (1976) The poet and the metropolis, pp. 93–108 in Watson, J. and O'Riordan, *The American Environment: Perceptions and Policies*, Wiley, London.

Patrick, J. (1973) *A Glasgow Gang Observed*, Eyre Methuen, London.

Peach, G.C.K. (1975) Immigrants in the inner city, *Geographical Journal*, 141, 372–9.

Pearson, P. and **Henney, A.** (1972) *Home Improvement: People or Profit?* Shelter, London.

Peattie, L. (1968) Reflections on advocacy planning, *Journal of the American Institute of Planners*, 34, 80–8.

Pedersen, P.O. (1967) *Modeller for Befolkningsstruktur og Befolkningsudvikling i Storby-morader Specielt med Henblik pa Storkobenhavn*, Copenhagen State Urban Planning Institute, Copenhagen.

Peel, N. *et al.* (1971) Racial Discrimination in Public Housing Site Selection, *Stanford Law Review*, 23, 63–147.

Peet, R. (1975) The geography of crime: a political critique, *Professional Geographer*, 27, 277–80.

Peet, R. (1976) Further comments on the geography of crime, *Professional Geographer*, **28**, 96–100.

Perin, C. (1977) *Everything in Its Place: Social Order and Land Use in America*, Princeton University Press, Princeton, N.J.

Peucker, T.K. (1968) Johaan Georg Kohl, a theoretical geographer of the nineteenth century, *Professional Geographer*, **20**, 247–50.

Philliber, W. (1977) Patterns of alienation in inner city ghettos, *Human Relations*, **30**, 303–10.

Phillips, D.R. (1979) Public attitudes to general practitioner services; a reflection of an inverse care law in intra-urban primary medical care? *Environment and Planning*, **All**, 315–24.

Phillips, M. (1977) Earls Court: Top of the Pox, *The Guardian*, 19 August, p. 11.

Phillips, M. (1978) Health gap in a class of its own, *The Guardian*, 20 October, p. 3.

Phillipson, M. (1971) *Sociological aspects of crime and delinquency*, Routledge & Kegan Paul, London.

Philpott, T.L. (1978) *The Slum and The Ghetto: Neighbourhood Deterioration and Middle-class Reform, Chicago, 1880–1930*, Oxford University Press, New York.

Pickup, L. (1976) *A space-time approach to womens' quality of life and employment opportunity*, Department of Geography, University of Reading.

Pickvance, C. (1976a) On the study of urban social movements, pp. 198–218 in Pickvance, C. (ed.) *Urban Sociology*, Tavistock, London.

Pickvance, C. (ed.) (1976b) *Urban Sociology*, Tavistock, London.

Pinch, S. (1979) Territorial justice in the city: a case study of the social services for the elderly in Greater London, pp. 201–23, in Herbert, D. and Smith, D. (eds), *Social Problems and the City: Geographical Perspectives*, Oxford University Press, Oxford.

Piven, F. and **Cloward, R.A.** (1977) *Poor People's Movements: Why they Succeed, How they Fail*, Pantheon Books, New York.

Pocock, D. (1970) Land ownership and urban growth in Scunthorpe, *East Midland Geographer*, **5**, 52–61.

Pocock, D. (1972) City of the mind: a review of mental maps of urban areas, *Scottish Geographical Magazine*, **88**, 115–24.

Pocock, D. (1975) *Durham: Images of a Cathedral City*, Occasional Publications, Department of Geography, University of Durham.

Pocock, D. (1976) Some characteristics of mental maps: an empirical study, *Transactions, Institute of British Geographers*, New Series, **1**, 493–512.

Pocock, D. and **Hudson, R.** (1978) *Images of the Urban Environment*, Macmillan, London.

Political and Economic Planning (1967) *Racial Discrimination*, Political and Economic Planning Research Services, London.

Pollins, H. (1964) Transport lines and social divisions, pp. 27–54 in Glass, R., *et al.* (eds) *London: Aspects of Change*, McGibbon & Kee, London.

Polk, K. (1957) Juvenile delinquency and social areas, *Social Problems*, **5**, 214–217.

Pons, V. (1978) Contemporary interpretations of Manchester in the 1830s and 1840s, *Stanford Journal of International Studies*, **13**, 51–76.

Poole, M.A. and **Boal, F.W.** (1973) Religious residential segregation in Belfast in 1969: a multi-level analysis, pp. 1–40 in Clark, B.D. and Gleave, M.B. (eds) *Social Patterns in Cities*, Institute of British Geographers, Special Publication No. 5, London.

Poulantzas, N. (1973) *Political power and social classes*, New Left Books, London.

Powell, A.C. (1973) Methodology in the strategy for the North West Region with special reference to evaluation, pp. 167–75 in *Urban and Regional Models*, PTRC, Seminar Proceedings, Planning and Transport Research and Computation, London.

Pred, A. (1973) Urbanization, domestic planning problems, and Swedish geographic research, *Progress in Geography*, **5**, 1–76.

Pred, A. and **Palm, R.** (1974) *A time-geographic perspective on problems of inequality for women*, Working Paper No. 236, Institute of Urban and Regional Development, University of California, Berkeley.

Pred, A. and **Palm, R.** (1978) The status of American women: a time-geographic view, pp. 99–109 in Lanegran, D.A., and Palm, R. (eds), *An Invitation to Geography* , (2nd ed.), McGraw-Hill, New York.

Preteceille, E. (1973) *La Production des Grands Ensembles*, Mouton, Paris.

Priest, R.F and **Sawyer, J.** (1967) Proximity and peership: bases of balance in interpersonal attraction, *American Journal of Sociology*, **72**, 633–49.

Proshansky, H.M., Ittelson, W.H. and **Rivlin, L.G.** (eds) (1976) *Environmental Psychology: People and Their Physical Settings*, Holt, Rinehart and Winston, New York.

Pyle, G.F. (ed.) (1974) *The Spatial Dynamics of Crime*, Research Paper No. 159, Department of Geography, University of Chicago.

Pyle, G.F (1976) Geographic perspectives on crime and the impact of anticrime legislation, pp. 257–292 in Adams, J. (ed.), *Urban Policymaking and Metropolitan Dynamics*, Ballinger, Cambridge.

Quinn, J.A. (1939) The nature of human ecology: re-examination and redefinition, *Social Forces*, **18**, 166–72.

Raban, J. (1975) *Soft City*, Fontana, London.

Rainwater, L. (1966) Fear and the house-as-haven in the lower class, *Journal of the American Institute of Planners*, **32**, 23–31.

Ramsøy, N.R. (1966) Assortative mating and the structure of cities, *American Sociological Review*, **31**, 773–86.

Rakove, M.L. (1975) *Don't Make No Waves, Don't Back No Losers*, Indiana University Press, Bloomington.

Rapoport, A. (1977) *Human Aspects of Urban Form*, Pergamon, Oxford.

Ratcliff, R.U. (1949) *Urban Land Economics*, McGraw-Hill, New York.

Raveau, F. (1970) The use of minorities in the social sciences, *The New Atlantis*, **2**, 159–72.

Raynor, J. *et al.* (1974) *The Urban Context*, Open University, Milton Keynes.

Rees, P. (1967) *Movement and distribution of physicians in Metropolitan Chicago*, Working Paper No. 1.12, Chicago Regional Hospital Study, Chicago.

Rees, P. (1970) Concepts of social space, pp. 306–94 in

Berry, B. and Horton, F.E. (eds), *Geographic Perspectives on Urban Systems*, Prentice-Hall, Englewood Cliffs, New Jersey.

Rees, P. (1971) Factorial ecology: an extended definition, survey and critique, *Economic Geography*, **47**, 220–33.

Rees, P. (1972) Problems of classifying subareas as within cities, pp. 265–330 in Berry, B. (ed.), *City Classification Handbook: Methods and Applications*, Wiley, New York.

Rees, P. (1979) *Residential Patterns in American cities: 1960*, Research Paper No. 189, Department of Geography, University of Chicago.

Reiser, R. (1973) The territorial illusion and the behavioural sink, *Antipode*, **5**, 52–7.

Reiss, A.J. Jr. (1955) An analysis of urban phenomena, pp. 41–51 in Fisher, R.M. (ed.), *The Metropolis and Mental Life*, Doubleday, New York.

Relph, E. (1976) *Place and Placelessness*, Pion, London.

Report of the Committee on Public Participation in Planning (1969) **People and Planning** (Skeffington Report) H.M.S.O., London.

Reps, J.W. (1965) *The Making of Urban America*, Princeton University Press, Princeton.

Rex, J. (1968) The sociology of the zone of transition, pp. 211–31 in Pahl, R.E. (ed.), *Readings in Urban Sociology*, Pergamon, Oxford.

Rex, J. and Moore, R. (1967) *Race, Community and Conflict*, Oxford University Press, London.

Reynolds, D.R. (1976) Progress toward achieving efficient and responsive spatial-political systems in urban America, pp. 463–537 in Adams, J.S. (ed.), *Urban Policymaking and Metropolitan Dynamics*, Ballinger, Mass..

Rich, R.C. (1979) Neglected issues in the study of urban service distributions: a research agenda, *Urban Studies*, **16**, 143–56.

Richardson, H.W. (1971) *Urban Economics*, Penguin, Harmondsworth.

Richardson, H.W. (1977) *The New Urban Economics: and its Alternatives*, Pion, London.

Riesman, I. (1950) *The Lonely Crowd*, Yale University Press, New Haven.

Roberts, J.T. (1976) *General Improvement Areas*, Saxon House, Farnborough.

Robson, B.T. (1969) *Urban Analysis*, Cambridge University Press, Cambridge.

Robson, B.T. (1975) *Urban Social Areas*, Oxford University Press, London.

Roistacher, R.C. (1974) A review of mathematical methods in sociometry, *Sociological Methods and Research*, **3**, 123–71.

Romanos, M.C. (1976) *Residential Spatial Structure*, Lexington Books, Lexington, Mass.

Rose, H.M. (1969) *Social Processes in the City: Race and Urban Residential Choice*, Resource Paper No. 6, Commission on College Geography, Association of American Geographers, Washington, D.C.

Rose, H.M. (1970) The development of an urban sub-system: the case of the negro ghetto, *Annals, Association of American Geographers*, **60**, 1–17.

Rose, H.M. (1971) *The Black Ghetto: A Spatial Behavioural Perspective*, McGraw-Hill, New York.

Rosen, G. (1973) Disease, debility and death, pp. 625–68 in Dyos, H.J. and Wolff, M. (eds), *The Victorian City: Images and Realities*, Routledge, London.

Rosenthal, E. (1961) Acculturation without assimilation? The Jewish community of Chicago, Illinois, *American Journal of Sociology*, **66**, 275–88.

Rosser, C. and Harris, C. (1965) *The Family and Social Change*, Routledge & Kegan Paul, London.

Rossi, P.H. (1955) *Why Families Move*, The Free Press, Glencoe, Illinois.

Rothenberg, J. (1967) *Economic Evaluation of Urban Renewal*, Brookings Institution, Washington, D.C.

Rowley, G. (1975) Landownership in the spatial growth of towns: a Sheffield example, East Midland Geographer, **6**, 200–13.

Royal Commission on Local Government in England (1969) *Research Studies 9*, Community Attitudes Survey, H.M.S.O., London.

Rubin, L. (1967) Maximum feasible participation, *Poverty and Human Resources Abstracts*, **2**, 5–18.

Rummel, R.J. (1967) Understanding factor analysis, *Journal of Conflict Resolution*, **40**, 440–80.

Rutter, M. and Madge, N. (1976) *Cycles of Disadvantage*, Heinemann, London.

Rykwert, J. (1976) *The idea of a town: the anthropology of urban form in Rome, Italy and the Ancient World*, Faber & Faber, London.

Salins, P.D. (1971) Household location patterns in American metropolitan areas, *Economic Geography*, **47**, 234–48.

Sandercock, L. (1976) *Cities for Sale: Property, Politics and Urban Planning in Australia*, Heinemann, London.

Sargent, C.S., Jr. (1976) Land speculation and urban morphology, pp. 21–58 in Adams, J.S. (ed.), *Urban Policymaking and Metropolitan Dynamics*, Ballinger, Cambridge, Mass.

Saunders, P. (1979) *Urban Politics: A Sociological Interpretation*, Hutchinson, London.

Schacht, R. (1971) *Alienation*, Doubleday: Anchor Press, New York.

Scherer, J. (1973) *Contemporary Community*, Tavistock, London.

Schmid, C.F. (1960) Urban crime areas, *American Sociological Review*, **25**, 527–42, and 655–78.

Schmid, C.F. and Schmid, S.E. (1972) *Crime in the State of Washington*, Law and Justice Planning Office, Washington State Planning and Community Affairs Agency, Olympia.

Schmid, C.F. and Tagashira, K. (1965) Ecological and demographic indices: a methodological analysis, *Demography*, **1**, 194–211.

Schmitt, R.C., Zane, L.Y.S., and Nishi, S. (1978) Density, health and social disorganization revisited, *Journal of the American Institute of Planners*, **44**, 201–12.

Schnore, L.F. (1965) *The Urban Scene*, Free Press, New York.

Schwartz, B. (ed.) (1976) *The Changing Face of the Suburbs*, University of Chicago Press, Chicago.

Schwind, P.J. (1971) *Migration and regional development in the U.S., 1950–1960*, Research Paper, No. 133, Department of Geography, University of Chicago.

Scobie, R.S. (1975) *Problem Tenants in Public Housing*, Praeger, New York.

Scott, P. (1972) The spatial analysis of crime and delinquency, *Australian Geographical Studies*, **10**, 1–18.

Scottish Development Department (1973) *Summary Report of an investigation to identify areas of multiple deprivation in Glasgow City*, C.P.R.U. Working Paper 7, Central Research Unit, Scottish Development Department, Edinburgh.

Scottish Development Department (1974) *Community Councils*, H.M.S.O., Edinburgh.

Seeman, M. (1971) Alienation studies, *Annual Review of Sociology*, **1**, 91–124.

Shannon, G.W. and **Dever, G.E.A.** (1974) *Health care delivery: spatial perspectives*, McGraw-Hill, New York.

Shannon, G.W., Spurlock, C.W., Gladin, S.T. and **Skinner, J.L.** (1975) A method for evaluating the geographic accessibility of health services, *Professional Geographer*, **27**, 30–6.

Sharrod, D.R. and **Downs, R.** (1974) Environmental determinants of altruism, *Journal of Experimental Social Psychology*, **10**, 468–79.

Shaw, C.R. and **McKay, H.D.** (1942) *Juvenile delinquency and urban areas*, University of Chicago Press, Chicago.

Shaw, C.R. *et al.* (1929) *Delinquency Areas*, University of Chicago Press, Chicago.

Shaw, M. (1979) Reconciling social and physical space: Wolverhampton, 1871, *Transactions, Institute of British Geographers*, **4**, 192–213.

Shevky, E. and **Bell, W.** (1955) *Social Area Analysis*, Stanford University Press, Stanford, California.

Shevky, E. and **Williams, M.** (1949) *The Social Areas of Los Angeles*, University of California Press, Los Angeles.

Short J.F. (1971) *The Social Fabric of the Metropolis*, University of Chicago Press, Chicago.

Short, J.R. (1978a) Residential mobility, *Progress in Human Geography*, **2**, 418–47.

Short, J.R. (1978b) Residential mobility in the private housing market of Bristol, *Transactions, Institute of British Geographers*, N.S., **3**, 533–47.

Short, J.R. (1979) Landlords and the private rented housing sector: a case study, pp. 56–75 in Boddy, M. (ed.), *Land, Property and Finance*, Working Paper No. 2, School for Advanced Urban Studies, University of Bristol.

Silk, J. (1971) *Search behaviour*, Geographical Paper No. 7, Department of Geography, University of Reading.

Simey, T. (ed.) (1954) *Neighbourhood and Community*, Liverpool University Press, Liverpool.

Simmel, G. (1905) The metropolis and mental life, pp. 47–60 in Sennett, P. (ed.) *Classic Essays on the Culture of Cities*, Appleton-Century-Crofts, New York, 1969.

Simmie, J.M. (1974) *Citizens in Conflict*, Hutchinson, London.

Simmons, J. (1973) The power of the railway, pp. 277–310 in Dyos, H.J. and Wolff, M. (eds), *The Victorian City: Images and Realities*, Routledge & Kegan Paul, London.

Simmons, J.W. (1968) Changing residence in the city: a review of intra-urban mobility, *Geographical Review*, **58**, 621–51.

Sjoberg, G. (1960) *The pre-industrial city, past and present*, Free Press, Glencoe, Illinois.

Smailes, A.E. (1955) Some reflections on the geographical description and analysis of townscapes, *Transactions, Institute of British Geographers*, **21**, 99–115.

Smailes, A.E. (1964) Urban Survey, pp. 206–21 in Coppock, J.T. and Prince, H.C. (eds.) *The Geography of Greater London*, Faber, London.

Smailes, A.E. (1966) *The Geography of Towns*, Hutchinson, London.

Smith, C.A. and **Smith, C.J.** (1978) Locating natural neighbours in the urban community, *Area*, **10**, 102–10.

Smith, C.J. (1978) Self-help and social networks in the urban community, *Ekistics*, **45**, 106–115.

Smith, D.M. (1973a) *An Introduction to Welfare Geography*, Occasional Paper No. 11, University of Witwatersrand, Johannesburg.

Smith, D.M. (1973b) *The Geography of Social Well-Being in the United States*, McGraw-Hill, New York.

Smith, D.M. (1974a) Who gets what *where*, and how: a welfare focus for human geography, *Geography*, **59**, 289–97.

Smith, D.M. (1974b) *Crime rates as Territorial Social Indicators*, Occasional Paper No. 1, Department of Geography, Queen Mary College, London.

Smith, D.M. (1977) *Human Geography: A Welfare Approach*, Arnold, London.

Smith, D.M. (1979a) *Where the Grass Grows Greener*, Croom Helm, London.

Smith, D.M. (1979b) The identification of problems in cities: applications of social indicators, pp. 13–32 in Herbert, D. and Smith, D.M. (eds) *Social Problems and The City: Geographical Perspectives*, Oxford University Press, Oxford.

Smith, P.F. (1977) *The Syntax of Cities*, Hutchinson, London.

Soja, E.W. (1971) *The Political Organization of Space*, Resource Paper No. 8, Commission on College Geography, Association of American Geographers, Washington, D.C.

Sopher, D.E. (1972) Place and location: notes on the spatial patterning of culture, *Social Science Quarterly*, **52**, 321–37.

Southworth, M. and **Southworth S.** (1973) Environmental quality in cities and regions, *Town Planning Review*, **44**, 231–53.

Speare, A., Goldstein, S. and **Frey, W.H.** (1975) *Residential Mobility, Migration and Metropolitan Change*, Ballinger, Cambridge, Mass.

Spencer, D. and **Lloyd, J.** (1974) *The Small Heath schools session: mental maps of routes from home to school*, Working Paper No. 24, Centre for Urban and Regional Studies, University of Birmingham.

Spring, D. (1951) The English landed estate in the age of coal and iron: 1830–1880, *Journal of Economic History*, **11**, 3–24.

Stacey, M. (1960) *Tradition and Change*, Oxford University Press, London.

Stacey, M. (1969) The myth of community studies, **British Journal of Sociology**, **20**, 134–46.

Stanislawski, D. (1946) The origin and spread of the grid pattern town, *Geographical Review*, **36**, 105–20.

Stedman, G. (1958) The townscape of Birmingham in 1956, *Transactions, Institute of British Geographers*, **24**, 225–38.

Stein, M. (1960) *The Eclipse of Community*, Harper & Row, New York.

Stimpson, R.J. (1970) Patterns of immigrant settlement in Melbourne, 1947–61, *Tijdschrift voor Economische en Sociale Geografie*, **61**, 114–26.

Stimpson, R.J. (1978) The spatial characteristics of health care services provision and utilisation in Australia, paper presented to the annual conference of the Institute of British Geographers, Kingston-upon-Hull.

Stokols, D. (ed.) (1976) *Psychological Perspectives on Environment and Behaviour*, Plenum Press, New York.

Stone, M.E. (1978) Housing, mortgage lending, and the contradictions of capitalism, pp. 179–207 in Tabb, W.K. and Sawers, L. (eds), *Marxism and the Metropolis*, Oxford University Press, New York.

Straszheim, M. (1975) *An Econometric Analysis of the Housing Market*, National Bureau of Economic Research, New York.

Stetzer, D.F. (1975) *Special districts in Cook County: toward a geography of local government*, Research Paper No. 169, Department of Geography, University of Chicago.

Strauss, A. (1961) *Images of the American City*, Free Press, New York.

Stringer, P. and **Taylor, M.** (1974) *Attitudes and Information in Public Participation: A case Study*, Working Paper No. 3, Centre for Environmental Studies, London.

Stutz, F.P. (1976) *Social aspects of Interaction and Transportation*, Resource Paper 76–2, Association of American Geographers, Washington, D.C.

Sumner, W.G. (1906) *Folkways*, Ginn, Boston.

Suttles, G.D. (1968) *The Social Order of The Slum: Ethnicity and Territory in the Inner City*, University of Chicago Press, Chicago.

Suttles, G.D. (1972) *The Social Construction of Communities*, University of Chicago Press, Chicago.

Suttles, G.D. (1975) Community design: the search for participation in an urban society, pp. 235–97 in Hawley, A.H. and Rock, V.P. (eds) *Metropolitan America in Contemporary Perspective*, Halstead Press, New York.

Sweetser, F.L. (1965a) Factorial ecology: Helsinki, *Demography*, **2**, 372–85.

Sweetser, F.L. (1965b) Factor structure as ecological structure in Helsinki and Boston, *Acta Sociologica*, **8**, 205–25.

Taafe, E.J. and **Gauthier, L.** (1973) *Geography of Transportation*, Prentice-Hall, Englewood Cliffs, New Jersey.

Tabb, W.K. (1978) The New York City fiscal crisis, pp. 241–66, in Tabb, W.K. and Sawers, L. (eds) *Marxism and the Metropolis*, Oxford University Press, New York.

Tabb, W.K. and **Sawers, L.** (eds) (1978) *Marxism and the Metropolis*, Oxford University Press, New York.

Taeuber, K.E. (1965) Residential segregation, *Scientific American*, **213**, 12–19.

Taeuber, K.E. and **Taeuber, A.F.** (1965) *Negroes in cities: Residential Segregation and Neighbourhood Change*, Aldine, Chicago.

Tallman, I. and **Morgner, R.** (1970) Life-style differences among urban and suburban blue collar families, *Social Forces*, **48**, 334–48.

Tarn, J.N. (1973) *Five Per Cent Philanthropy*, Cambridge University Press, London.

Tata, R.J., Hurn, S. and **Lee, D.** (1975) Defensible space in a housing project: a case study from south Florida, *Professional Geographer*, **27**, 297–303.

Taylor, I., Walton, P. and **Young, J.** (1973) *The New Criminology*, Routledge & Kegan Paul, London.

Taylor, P.J. (1978) 'Difficult to let', 'Difficult to live in', and sometimes 'Difficult to get out of': An essay on the provision of council housing with special reference to Killingworth, Discussion Paper No. 16, Centre for Urban and Regional Development Studies, University of Newcastle Upon Tyne.

Taylor, P.J. and **Gudgin, G.** (1976) The myth of non-partisan cartography: a study of electoral biases in the English Boundary Commission's Redistribution for 1955–1970, *Urban Studies*, **13**, 13–25.

Taylor, P.J. and **Johnston, R.J.** (1979) *Geography of Elections*, Penguin, Harmondsworth.

Theodorson, G.A. (ed.) (1961) *Studies in Human Ecology*, Harper & Row, New York.

Thernstrom, S. and **Sennett, R.** (eds) (1969) *Nineteenth-Century Cities*, Yale University Press, New Haven.

Thomas, C.J. (1968) Geographical aspects of the growth of the residential area of Greater Nottingham in the twentieth century, unpublished Ph.D. thesis, University of Nottingham.

Thompson, D.L. (1963) New concepts, subjective distance, *Journal of Retailing*, **39**, 1–6.

Thompson, E.P. (1967) Time, work discipline and industrial capitalism, *Past and Present*, **38**, 56–97.

Thompson, E.P. (1968) *The Making of the English Working Class*, Penguin, Harmondsworth.

Thornhill Neighbourhood Project (1978) *Health Care in Thornhill: A Case of Inner City Deprivation*, Thornhill Neighbourhood Project, London.

Thurston, H.S. (1953) The urban regions of St Albans, *Transactions, Institute of British Geographers*, **19**, 107–21.

Tiebout, C.M. (1956) A pure theory of local expenditures, *Journal of Political Economy*, **64**, 416–24.

Tilly, C. (1961) Occupational rank and grade of residence in a metropolis, *American Journal of Sociology*, **67**, 323–9.

Timms, D.W.G. (1965) The spatial distribution of social deviants in Luton, England, *Australian and New Zealand Journal of Sociology*, **1**, 38–52.

Timms, D.W.G. (1969) The dissimilarity between overseas-born and Australian-born in Queensland, *Sociology and Social Research*, **3**, 363–74.

Timms, D.W.G. (1971) *The Urban Mosaic: Towards a Theory of Residential Differentiation*, Cambridge University Press, Cambridge.

Timms, D.W.G. (1976) Social bases to social areas, pp. 19–40 in Herbert, D.T. and Johnston, R.J. (eds) *Social Areas in Cities*, Vol. 1, Wiley, Chichester.

Timms, D.W.G. (1977) Factorial ecologies in central Scotland, Final Report to SSRC.

De Tocqueville, A. (1946) *Democracy in America*, Knopf, New York.

Toffler, A. (1970) *Future Shock*, The Bodley Head, London.

Toll, S. (1969) *Zoned America*, Grossman Publishers, New York.

Tomeh, A.K. (1964) Informal group participation and

residential pattern, *American Journal of Sociology*, **70**, 28–35.

Tönnies, F. (1887) *Community and Society*, translated by C.P. Loomis, Harper, New York, 1963.

Tranter, P. and **Parkes, D.** (1979) Time and images in urban space, *Area* **11**, 115–20.

Tuan, Y.F. (1974) *Topophilia*, Prentice-Hall, Englewood Cliffs, New Jersey.

Tuan, Y.F. (1976) Geopiety: a theme in man's attachment to nature and to place, pp. 11–39 in Lowenthal, D. and Bowden, M.J. (eds), *Geographies of the Mind*, Oxford University Press, London.

Tuan, Y.F. (1978) The city: its distance from nature, *Geographical Review*, **68**, 1–12.

Udry, J.R. (1964) Increasing scale and spatial differentiation: new tests of two theories from Shevky and Bell, *Social Forces*, **42**, 404–13.

Unit for Manpower Studies (1976) *The Role of Immigrants in the Labour Market*, Department of Employment, London.

United States Department of Health, Education and Welfare (1969) *Toward a Social Report*, U.S.G.P.O., Washington, D.C.

United States National Committee on Urban Problems (1968) *Building the American City*, U.S. Government Printing Office, Washington, D.C.

Valentien, C. (1972) Models and muddles concerning culture and inequality, *Harvard Educational Review*, **42**, 97–108.

Van Arsdol, M.D., Camilleri, S.F. and **Schmid, C.F.** (1958) The generality of urban social area indexes, *American Sociological Review*, **23**, 277–84.

Van Arsdol, Jr. M.D., Sabagh, G., and **Butler, E.W.** (1968) Retrospective and subsequent metropolitan residential mobility, *Demography*, **5**, 249–57.

Vance, Jr. J.E. (1964) *Geography and Urban Evolution in the San Francisco Bay Area*, Institute of Governmental Studies, University of California Press, Berkeley.

Vance, Jr. J.E. (1971) Land assignment in pre-capitalist, capitalist and post-capitalist cities, *Economic Geography*, **47**, 101–20.

Vance, Jr. J.E. (1976) Institutional forces that shape the city, pp. 81–110 in Herbert, D.T. and Johnston, R.J. (eds) *Social Areas in Cities*, Vol. 1, *Spatial Processes and Form*, Wiley, Chichester.

Vance, Jr. J.E. (1977) *This scene of man: The role and structure of the city in the geography of Western civilization*, Harper & Row, New York.

Van Den Berghe, P. (1974) Bringing beasts back in: toward a biosocial theory of aggression, *American Sociological Review*, **39**, 777–88.

Van Valey, T.L., Roof, W.C. and **Wilcox, J.E.** (1977) Trends in residential segregation 1960–1970, *American Journal of Sociology*, **82**, 826–44.

Verba, S. (1961) *Small Groups and Political Behaviour*, Princeton University Press, New Jersey.

Verba, S. and **Nie, N.H.** (1972) *Participation in America: Political Democracy and Social Equality*, Harper & Row, New York.

de Vise, P. (1968) *Slum medicine: Chicago style: how the medical needs of the city's Negro poor are met*, Working Paper No. 3IV.7, Chicago Regional Hospital Study, Chicago.

de Vise, P. (1973) *Misused and Misplaced Hospitals and Doctors*, Resource Paper No. 22, Commission on College Geography, Association of American Geographers, Washington, D.C.

de Vise, P. (1976) The suburbanization of jobs and minority employment, Economic Geography, **52**, 348–62.

de Vise, P. and **Dewey, D.R.** (1972) *More money, more doctors, less care: Chicago's changing distribution of physicians, hospitals and population, 1950 to 1970*, Working Paper No. 1.19, Chicago Regional Hospital Study, Chicago.

Vitarello, J. (1975) The redlining route to urban decay, *Focus*, **3**, 4–5.

Walker, R.A. (1978) The transformation of urban structure in the nineteenth century and the beginnings of suburbanization, pp. 165–212 in Cox, K. (ed.) *Urbanization and Conflict in Market Societies*, Methuen, London.

Wallis, C.P. and **Maliphant, R.** (1967) Delinquent areas in the county of London: ecological factors, *British Journal of Criminology*, **7**, 250–84.

Ward, C. (1978) *The Child in The City*, Architectural Press, London.

Ward, D. (1962) The pre-urban cadaster and the urban pattern of Leeds, *Annals, Association of American Geographers*, **52**, 150–66.

Ward, D. (1964) A comparative historical geography of streetcar suburbs in Boston, Massachusetts and Leeds, England: 1850–1920, *Annals, Association of American Geographers*, **54**, 477–89.

Ward, D. (1971) *Cities and Immigrants*, Oxford University Press, New York.

Ward, D. (1975) Victorian cities: how modern? *Journal of Historial Geography*, **1**, 135–51.

Warner, Jr. S.B. (1962) *Streetcar Suburbs: The Process of Growth in Boston, 1870–1900*, Harvard University and the M.I.T. Press, Cambridge, Mass.

Warner, Jr. S.B. (1972) *The Urban Wilderness: A History of the American City*, Harper & Row, New York.

Warner, W.L. and **Lunt, P.S.** (1941) *The Social Life of a Modern Community*, Yale University Press, New Haven.

Warner, W.L. and **Lunt, P.S.** (1942) *Status system of a Modern Community*, Yale University Press, New Haven.

Warner, W.L. and **Srole, L.** (1945) *The Social System of American Ethnic Groups*, Yale University Press, New Haven.

Warnes, A.M. (1973) Residential patterns in an emerging indistrial town, pp. 169–89 in Clark, B.D. and Gleave, M.G. (eds), *Social Patterns in Cities*, Special Publication No. 5, Institute of British Geographers, London.

Warren, R.L. (1963) *The Community in America*, Rand McNally, Chicago.

Watson, C.J. (1971) *Social Housing Policy in Belgium*, Occasional Paper No. 19, Centre for Urban and Regional Studies, University of Birmingham.

Watson, C.J. (1974) Vacancy chains, filtering and the public sector, *Journal, Institute of American Planners*, **40**, 346–52.

Watson, J.W. (1972) Mental distance in geography: its identification and representation, paper presented to I.G.U. Symposium, Montreal.

Watson, J.W. and **O'Riordan, T.** (1976) *The American Environment: Perceptions and Policies*, Wiley, London.

Webber, M.M. (1963) Order diversity: community without propinquity, pp. 23–56 in Wingo, L. (ed.) *Cities and Space*, Johns Hopkins University Press, Baltimore.

Webber, M.M. (1964) The urban place and the nonplace urban realm, pp. 79–153 in Webber, M.M. *et al.* (eds), *Explorations Into Urban Structure*, University of Pennsylvania Press, Philadelphia.

Webber, R.J. (1975) *Liverpool Social Area Study 1971 Data: Final Report*, Planning Research Applications Group, Centre for Environmental Studies, London.

Weber, A.F. (1899) *The Growth of Cities in the Nineteenth Century: a study in statistics*, Cornell University Press, Ithaca, New York, (reprint 1967).

Weber, M. (1947) *The Theory of Social and Economic Organization*, Free Press, Glencoe, Illinois.

Weicher, J.C. (1971) The allocation of police protection by income class, *Urban Studies*, **8**, 207–20.

Weir, S. (1976) Red Line Districts, *Roof*, **1**, 109–14.

Weiss, S.F., **Smith, J.E.**, **Kaiser, E.J.** and **Kenney, K.B.** (1966) *Residential Developer Decisions*, Centre for Urban and Regional Studies, University of North Carolina, Chapel Hill, North Carolina.

Wellman, B. (1979) The community question, *American Journal of Sociology*, **84**, 1201–31.

Wellman, B. and **Crump, B.** (1978) *Networks, Neighbourhoods and Communities*, Research Paper No. 97, Centre for Urban and Community Studies, University of Toronto.

Welsh Consumer Council (1976) *Council Housing: A Survey of Allocation Policies in Wales*, Welsh Consumer Council, Cardiff.

West, D.J. (1967) *The Young Offender*, Duckworth, London.

Wheatley, P. (1975) The ancient Chinese city as a cosmological symbol, *Ekistics*, **39**, 147–58.

White, M. and **White, L.** (1962) *The Intellectual Versus the City*, Mentor, New York.

Whitehand, J.W.R. (1967) Fringe belts: a neglected aspect of urban geography, *Transactions, Institute of British Geographers*, **41**, 223–33.

Whitehand, J.W.R. (1972) Building cycles and the spatial pattern of urban growth, *Transactions, Institute of British Geographers*, **56**, 39–55.

Whitehand, J.W.R. (1974) The changing nature of the urban fringe, pp. 31–52 in Johnson, J.H. (ed.), *Suburban Growth: Geographical Processes at the Edge of the Western City*, Wiley, London.

Whitehand, J.W.R. (1975) Building activity and the intensity of development at the urban fringe: the case of a London suburb in the nineteenth century, *Journal of Historical Geography*, **1**, 211–24.

Whitehand, J.W.R. (1977) The basis for a historico geographical theory of urban form, *Transactions, Institute of British Geographers*, N.S., **2**, 400–16.

Whyte, W.H. (1956) *The Organization Man*, Doubleday, New York.

Wiener, R. (1976) *The Rape and Plunder of the Shankhill in Belfast*, Notaems Press, Belfast.

Wilkinson, H. *et al.* (1970) *Kingston-upon-Hull and Haltemprice – Social Area Analysis 1966: Part I – Atlas*, Miscellaneous Series No. 10, Department of Geography, University of Kingston-upon-Hull.

Williams, P. (1976a) The role of institutions in the inner London housing market: the case of Islington, *Transactions, Institute of British Geographers*, N.S., **1**, 72–82.

Williams, P. (1976b) *The Role of Financial Institutions and Estate Agents in the Private Housing Market: A General Introduction*, Working Paper No. 39, Centre for Urban and Regional Studies, University of Birmingham, Birmingham.

Williams, P. (1978) Urban managerialism: a concept of relevance? *Area*, **10**, 236–40.

Williams, R. (1973) *The Country and the City*, Chatto & Windus, London.

Williams-Ellis, C. (ed.) (1938) *Britain and the Beast*, Dent, London.

Willmott, P. and **Young, M.** (1960) *Family and Class in a London Suburb*, Routledge & Kegan Paul, London.

Wilson, A.G. (1970) *Entropy in Urban and Regional Modelling*, London.

Wilson, A.G. (1974) *Urban and Regional Models in Geography and Planning*, Wiley, London.

Winchester, S.W.C. (1974) Immigrant areas in Coventry in 1971, *New Community*, **4**, 97–104.

Wing, J.K. (1974) Housing environments and mental health, pp. 75–89 in Parry, H. (ed.) *Population and Its Problems*, Clarendon Press, Oxford.

Wingo, L. (1961) *Transportation and Urban Land*, Johns Hopkins University Press, Baltimore.

Wingo, L. (1963) *Cities and Space*, Johns Hopkins University Press, Baltimore.

Wirth, L. (1928) *The Ghetto*, University of Chicago Press, Chicago.

Wirth, L. (1938) Urbanism as a way of life, pp. 143–64 in Sennett, R. (ed.) *Classic Essays on the Culture of Cities*, Appleton-Century-Crofts, New York.

Wohl, A.S. (1977) *The Eternal Slum*, Arnold, London.

Wolf, E. and **Lebeaux, C.N.** (eds) (1969) *Change and Renewal in an Urban Community*, Praeger, New York.

Wolpert, J. (1966) Migration as an adjustment to environmental stress, *Journal of Social Issues*, **22**, 92–102.

Wolpert, J., **Mumphrey, A.** and **Seley, J.** (1972) *Metropolitan Neighbourhoods: Participation and Conflict over Change*, Resource Paper No. 16, Association of American Geographers, Washington, D.C.

Wood, C.M., **Lee, N.**, **Loker, J.A.** and **Saunders, P.J.W.** (1974) *The Geography of Pollution: A Study of Greater Manchester*, Manchester University Press, Manchester.

Woods, R.A. (ed.) (1898) *The City Wilderness*, Houghton Mifflin, Boston.

Woods, R.I. (1976) Aspects of the scale problem in the calculation of segregation indices: London and Birmingham 1961 and 1971, *Tijdschrift voor Economische en Sociale Geografie*, **69**, 169–74.

Yablonsky, L. (1970) *The Violent Gang*, Penguin, Baltimore.

Yancey, W.L. (1971) Architecture, interaction and social control, *Environment and Behaviour*, **3**, 3–21.

Yeates, M. and **Garner, B.** (1976) *The North American City*, Harper & Row, New York.

Young, K. and **Kramer, J.** (1977) Local exclusionary policies in Britain: the case of suburban defence in a metropolitan system, pp. 229–51 in Cox, K. (ed.)

Urbanization and Conflict in Market Societies,
Methuen, London.

Young, M. and **Willmott, P.** (1957) *Family and Kinship
in East London*, Routledge & Kegan Paul, London.

Young, M. and **Willmott, P.** (1962) *Family and Kinship
in East London*, Penguin, Harmondsworth.

Zelinsky, W. (1975) Personality and self-discovery: the
future social geography of the United States,
pp. 108–21 in Abler, R. *et al.* (eds) *Human Geography
in a Shrinking World*, Duxbury Press, North Scituate,
Mass.

Zorbaugh, H.W. (1929) *The Gold Coast and the Slum*,
University of Chicago Press, Chicago.

INDEX